# TIBET'S GREAT *YOGĪ*
# MILAREPA

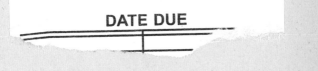

## DATE DUE

THE GREAT KARGYÜTPA *GURUS*

Described on pages xxiii–xxvi

# TIBET'S GREAT *YOGĪ*
# MILAREPA

## A BIOGRAPHY FROM THE TIBETAN

being the

### *JETSÜN-KAHBUM*

OR BIOGRAPHICAL HISTORY OF JETSÜN-
MILAREPA, ACCORDING TO THE LATE
LĀMA KAZI DAWA-SAMDUP'S ENGLISH
RENDERING

Edited with Introduction and Annotations

by

## W. Y. EVANS-WENTZ

M.A., D.LITT., B.SC.

Jesus College, Oxford ; Author of
*The Fairy-Faith in Celtic Countries*
*The Tibetan Book of the Dead*
*&c.*

SECOND EDITION

OXFORD UNIVERSITY PRESS
LONDON    OXFORD    NEW YORK

OXFORD UNIVERSITY PRESS
Oxford    London    Glasgow
New York    Toronto    Melbourne    Wellington
Nairobi    Dar es Salaam    Cape Town
Kuala Lumpur    Singapore    Jakarta    Hong Kong    Tokyo
Delhi    Bombay    Calcutta    Madras    Karachi

First published by Oxford University Press, London, 1928
Second edition, 1951
First issued as an Oxford University Press paperback, 1969

Printed in the United States of America

printing, last digit: 20  19  18

The Editor here gratefully acknowledges indebtedness to Mr. E. T. Sturdy, translator of The Nārada Sūtra, for having encouraged and supported the publication
of this, the second, edition of Tibet's Great Yogi Milarepa.

I DEDICATE THIS BIOGRAPHY OF MILAREPA
TO THOSE WHO CLING NOT TO BELIEF
BASED UPON BOOKS AND TRADITION
BUT WHO SEEK KNOWLEDGE
BY REALIZATION

# THE *YOGI'S* CAR OF VICTORY

'Whoso the Faith and Wisdom hath attained—
His state of mind, well-harnessed, leads him on ;
Conscience the pole, and Mind the yoke thereof,
And Heedfulness the watchful charioteer :
The furnishments of Righteousness, the Car ;
Rapture the axle, Energy the wheels ;
And Calm, yoke-fellow of the Balanced Mind ;
Desirelessness the drapery thereof.
Goodwill and Harmlessness his weapons are,
Together with Detachment of the mind.
Endurance is the armour of the Norm,
And to attain the Peace that Car rolls on.
'Tis built by self, by one's own self becometh—
This Chariot, incomparable, supreme ;
Seated therein the Sages leave the world,
And verily they win the Victory.'

The Buddha, from the *Saṃyutta Nikāya*, v, p. 6.

(F. L. Woodward's Translation.)

# PREFACE TO THE SECOND EDITION

## THE PATH TO SIMPLICITY AND FREEDOM

*'To have but few desires and satisfaction with simple things is the sign of a superior man.'—Precepts of the Gurus.*[1]

IT is the same oft-repeated and age-old call from the Supermen, throughout the millenniums, heard by Thoreau and Emerson and Whitman in America, to simple living and high endeavour, which this book transmits, from Tibet, the Land of the Snowy Ranges, to the peoples of the Occident, who have extolled and much preferred, but, of late, not without many disconcerting misgivings, their complex, industrialized way of life.

Whilst *The Tibetan Book of the Dead*, the first volume of our Oxford Tibetan Series, sets forth the art of knowing how rightly to die and to choose a womb wherefrom to be reborn, this, the second volume of the Series, sets forth the art of mastering life and directing it to the all-transcendent goal of liberation from conditioned existence.

Inasmuch as living and dying and being reborn are held to be inseparable parts of a universal life-process by the followers of the Buddha, and by the devotees of many other Faiths, the first volume of the Series is complementary to the second volume, although a separate and distinct *yogic* treatise in itself.

The first edition of this *Biography* of Milarepa, the illustrious Buddhist saint of Tibet, led to the writing of many letters of appreciation to the Editor, not only by laymen and members of the *Sangha*, of both Northern and Southern Buddhism, but also by Hindus and Christians, Catholic and Protestant alike. And now the Editor hereby thanks each of the writers of the letters for their words of appreciation and encouragement. Each of these correspondents recognized in Milarepa those universal characteristics of saintliness to which no religion

[1] Cf. W. Y. Evans-Wentz, *Tibetan Yoga and Secret Doctrines* (Oxford University Press, 1935), p. 80.

can, rightly, make exclusive claim, but which are common to the saints of all religions. Accordingly, Milarepa may be regarded as being one more light-bearer helping to disperse that darkness of Ignorance of which the Enlightened One spoke as enshrouding the world; and, as has been said of Abraham Lincoln, that he no longer belongs to his native land alone but to all lands, so it may be said of Jetsün Milarepa.

In Milarepa's *Biography* it is shown that the *yogic* path to Supramundaneness is transcendent over intellectually shaped formulas appertaining to salvation, and that it is ever open to all of human kind, irrespective of religious affiliation. In Milarepa's view, none of the world's methods of intellectual development are essential to the attainment of Wisdom; Right Knowledge was, for him, not to be won by study of books, nor by making professions of faith. Many of the most learned and cultured saints of Tibet and India have been illiterate, as will be seen by reference to the forthcoming and fourth volume of the Oxford Tibetan Series, to be entitled *The Tibetan Book of the Great Liberation*. Of these things Milarepa bore witness as follows:—

'Accustomed long to meditating on the Whispered Chosen Truths,
    I have forgot all that is said in written and in printed books.

'Accustomed long to application of each new experience to mine
        own growth spiritual,
    I have forgot all creeds and dogmas.

'Accustomed long to know the meaning of the Wordless,
    I have forgot the way to trace the roots of verbs, and source of
        words and phrases.'[1]

It is by self-disciplining of the mind, after the manner of disciplining a wild horse, and making the mind immune to the obsessing and *yogically* undesirable influences emanating from the illusory phantasmagoria of the world, that Milarepa would have us seek release from our present state of bondage to the world. And hereof he sings, in his song about the Horse of Mind, how the undisciplined mind is to be caught with the Lasso of Singleness of Purpose, tied to the Pole of Meditation, fed

---

[1] Cf. pages 246-7 of this volume.

with the *Guru's* Teachings, and watered from the Stream of Consciousness. The Horse of Mind is ridden by the Youth of Intellect, along the widespread Plain of Happiness, and carried on to Buddhahood.

As the chemist experiments with the elements of matter, Milarepa experimented with the elements of consciousness; and no other disciple has put to the test of practical application more efficiently than Milarepa did the precepts of his Great Teacher, the Buddha. Because of the successful outcome of Milarepa's practice of Buddhism, Milarepa is venerated not only by Buddhists of all Schools in his native Tibet and in countries of Asia adjacent to Tibet, who consider him to be a Fully Enlightened One, but, more especially since the publication of his *Biography* in the Occident, by an ever-increasing number of truth-seekers throughout all the continents.

Buddhists themselves, even of Milarepa's School, recognize, as we must, that Milarepa's path, being a short-cut to transcendence over the limitations of human existence, will be trodden only by the very exceptional devotee, whose evolutionary growth is adequate to the mighty effort to reach the goal far in advance of slowly evolving humanity as a whole. Though very few may have the spiritual fitness and physical hardihood, and the willingness, to emulate Milarepa, his discovery that the goal is not a mirage, but is attainable, is of paramount importance to the least of mankind; for, in the view of Milarepa's devotees, there will be found in Milarepa's *Biography* the necessary courage to prepare for the first steps upon the path, no matter how long and arduous the path may prove to be, nor how many lifetimes may be required to attain the goal, which Milarepa attained in one lifetime because of his superior preparedness.

However Milarepa, the Saint, be viewed, in this age of technology and utilitarianism, whether with veneration by the few, or with critical indifference by the many, it is anthropologically requisite to recognize, as our eminent Oxford historian, Professor Arnold J. Toynbee, does, that those of our human kind who have done the most to ameliorate the life of man on Earth have not been the scientists, with all their wonderful and laudable discoveries, nor the inventors or technicians, nor the leaders of industrialism, nor the captains and the kings and the statesmen, but the prophets and saints:—

' Now who are the individuals who are the greatest benefactors of the living generation of mankind? I should say: Confucius and Lao-tse; the Buddha; the Prophets of Israel and Judah; Zoroaster; Jesus, and Muhammad; and Socrates.' [1]

These were the rare fruitage of civilizations extending from the Pacific to the Mediterranean. In these very few individuals, the wisdom of all the known civilizations of the past culminates. In them is the crowning and glorious summation of the manifold evolutionary strivings of the innumerable generations of mankind who have lived upon our planet throughout the millenniums of the great cultures of China, of India, of Persia, of Syria and Egypt, of Arabia, and of Europe as represented by Greece. Truly it is that

' The works of artists and men of letters outlive the deeds of business men, soldiers and statesmen. The poets and philosophers outrange the historians; while the prophets and saints overtop and outlast them all.' [2]

Much more to the Occident than to the Orient (where simplicity, and the self-sufficiency of the village community still largely prevail), the *Biography* of Milarepa will reveal, perhaps rather startlingly, a method of living other than that of attachment to the things that pass away. To Milarepa, as to many other of the Sages of Asia, self-conquest is better than world-conquest, and renunciation of the world better than accumulation of all the riches of the world.

The worldly possessions which Mahātmā Gandhi left behind him are quite comparable in kind and intrinsic value to those left behind by Milarepa. They consisted chiefly of a wooden staff, two pair of sandals, an old-style watch, a small low writing-stand, used while one is sitting on the floor, with an inkpot, a pen and some writing paper thereon, a pair of old-fashioned spectacles, a mat to sit upon in prayer or meditation, a few religious books, including the *Bhagavad-Gītā*, two food-bowls,

[1] Cf. Arnold J. Toynbee, *Civilization on Trial* (Oxford University Press, New York, 1948), p. 156.
[2] Cf. *ibid.*, p. 5.

two spoons, and a few pieces of homespun cotton cloth, used to cover his nakedness. Milarepa's chief worldly goods were a bamboo staff, a robe and a mantle, also of homespun cotton cloth, a wooden bowl, a cup made of a human skull from a place of the dead, a flint and steel for producing fire, and a bone spoon.

Though frail physically, as a result of age and self-sacrifice, Gandhi, the Saint, moved, as no armies and armadas of the sea and air could have moved, the mighty and materially supreme world-encircling British Empire. In similar manner, when a delegation of high officials of government waited upon Milarepa to invite him to the presence of a Nepalese king, Milarepa, in refusing the royal summons, challenged the assumed supremacy of the monarch, and boldly asserted that he himself was a mighty king, abounding in riches, and unsurpassed in greatness and power in all the kingdoms of the world.

When Gandhi had audience with the King-Emperor, in Buckingham Palace, it was not in the formal dress, decreed, as Milarepa teaches, by 'ignorant conventionalities', but in the simple homespun loin-cloth garb of white cotton, such as is worn by the Hindu peasant, that Gandhi presented himself before his Sovereign in the resplendent palace. When Gandhi was asked if his scanty attire had proved to be sufficient for the occasion, he replied: 'The King had enough on for both of us.'

To one endowed with *yogic* powers such as those attained by Milarepa, which included the *yogic* power of bodily flight through the air, no need is there of motor-cars or aeroplanes or any other of the mechanical means of human transportation; and, correlatively, no need would there be for an industrialized society which fetters men to toil in coal-mines and iron-foundries and mass-production factories. Gandhi, too, struggled against industrialization, although more or less unsuccessfully, in his own India, and considered industrialization to be an avoidable and unnecessary evil, not because, as Milarepa's life suggests, that by means of *yoga* industrialism can be made obsolete, but because industrialism destroys the arts and crafts normally afflorescent in the simple and comparatively happy life of a peasant village community, and, thereby, impedes the manifestation of the Beautiful, which is innate in each one of mankind. For Gandhi, the peasant village communities, which in India, as in China, have been, during thousands of years, the centres of indigenous culture, flourishing independently of mass-production methods, represent the most satisfactory and economically stable form of human society. And this naturally simple and materially efficient form of social organization, being contributory and conducive to the Higher Culture, is more in keeping with Milarepa's teachings than is industrialism.

Milarepa was enabled to sustain life, although not without suffering, to which he was *yogically* indifferent, amidst the arctic-like climate of the high Himalayas, on simple and meagre food, in virtue of indomitable control of his physical body, and, not infrequently, with no other bodily sustenance than that derived, by an osmosis-like process, from air and water and sunshine, similar to the process whereby a plant produces chlorophyll. In his cave there was no central or other heating save that born of the *yogic* practice of *Tummo* within his own fleshly dwelling-house. The many and incessantly increasing products of a technological industrialism, which occidental man believes to be unquestionably necessary, and for which he willingly barters his bodily energy, and, commonly, his health and length of days, and the greater part of his brief time on Earth, would be, for Milarepa, as for the Buddha, merely so many impediments to Right Living. For the purpose of life in a human body is, as Milarepa teaches, not to wallow in the mire of ease and comfortableness, which create attachment to the world, but to evolve beyond worldly existence, however luxurious and comfortable and mundanely happy worldly existence may be made by the discoveries of Western science.

In his own day, Milarepa looked forth from his Himalayan cave with pity and compassion upon the manner of living of men enamoured of the luxuries and comforts which, in full measure, the world can give. And he saw, as in the song about the Five Comforts he teaches, that when desire for comfort, common to man and beast, has been transcended, and Freedom has been won, 'Nought is there uncomfortable; everything is comfortable'. And he requests that those uninspired by the ascetic life spare him their misplaced pity. Of comfortableness in monasteries, he sang:—

'Accustomed long to regard my fleshly body as my hermitage,
I have forgot the ease and comfort of retreats in monasteries.' [1]

With still greater pity and compassion would Milarepa behold the manner in which mankind now live amidst the multitudinous contrivances which in Europe and the Americas are considered to be indispensable, even by many monks who teach of the good life. For him, it is not exploitation and physical conquest of the world by science which really matters, but the conquest of the self and the breaking of every fetter that binds men to the treadmill of incarnate existence. To Milarepa, as to all saints of every religion, in all civilizations and epochs of human history, wantlessness and complete renunciation of the worldly way of living rather than all-consuming desire for, and acquisition of, the perishable things of the world, lead to the attainment of a standard of living which is the highest realizable on this planet.

Milarepa perceived early in life, as most men do when too late, that

'All worldly pursuits have but the one unavoidable and inevitable end, which is sorrow: acquisitions end in dispersion; buildings, in destruction; meetings, in separation; births, in death. Knowing this, one should, from the very first, renounce acquisition and heaping-up, and building, and meeting; and, faithful to the commands of an eminent *guru*, set about realizing the Truth [which hath no birth or death]. That alone is the best science.' [2]

And, when approaching his *Nirvāṇa*, Milarepa further counselled his disciples, thus:—

'Life is short, and the time of death is uncertain; so apply yourselves to meditation, Avoid doing evil, and acquire merit, to the best of your ability, even at the cost of life itself. In short, the whole purport may be stated thus: Act so that ye have no cause to be ashamed of yourselves; and hold fast to this rule. If ye do thus, ye can be sure of never disobeying the commands of the Supreme

[1,2] Cf. pages 247 and 259 of this volume.

Buddhas, notwithstanding any conflicting rules which may be found set down in writing.'[1]

Milarepa's rules for Right Living are, therefore, in essentials, the same as those enunciated by saints of all epochs, in ancient China, or India, or Babylonia, or Egypt, or Rome, or in our own epoch. It is only those very few individuals in any age or nation who, in virtue of having had the evolutionary fitness, and the willingness, to apply the rules and become in at-one-ness with the Brotherhood of Compassion and Peace, have aided in the transmission of the Torch of Wisdom from one generation to another.

So may it come to pass, in accordance with the words which Rechung, the faithful disciple of Milarepa, inscribed in the colophon of the original Tibetan version of Milarepa's *Biography*, that by the mere hearing, or thinking, or touching of Milarepa's *Biography* the devotee shall be spiritually aided, and that

'Through one's study and practice of this *Biography*, the Dynasty of Gurus will be fully satisfied.'[2]

The Tibetan *Guru* Phadampa Sangay, who seems to have flourished contemporaneously with Milarepa, and whose testamentary teachings will be published in the forthcoming fourth volume of this Series, *The Tibetan Book of the Great Liberation*, admonished his disciples and the people of the village of Tingri, Tibet, in the following words, which, being personally applicable by each reader of this volume, are here presented as a fitting ending of this Preface:—

'Like the sunshine from a clear space twixt the clouds the *Dharma* is:

Know that now there is such sunshine; wisely use it, Tingri folk.'

[1,2] Cf. pages 262 and 309 of this volume.

W. Y. E.-W.

San Diego, California
*All Saints Day*, 1950

# PREFACE TO THE FIRST EDITION

In my Introduction and Annotations to the present work, as in those to *The Tibetan Book of the Dead*, I am attempting to convey to the Western World, and so place on record, certain aspects of Higher or Transcendental Mahāyānic Teachings, which have been handed on to me for that purpose by the Translator, the late Lāma Kazi Dawa-Samdup, my Tibetan *Guru*. For such defects as critics may discover in my transmission—and I cannot hope to have escaped all error—I alone assume full responsibility.

Apart from the greater debt which I as the pupil owe to him who was my preceptor, I acknowledge indebtedness to those Himalayan and Indian *Yogīs* (who prefer that their names be left unmentioned) from whom I had the good fortune, during my wanderings as a research student in India, to gather, at first hand, authoritative information concerning the same ancient ideals of Asceticism and World Renunciation which Milarepa, faithful to his Chief *Guru*, Gautama the Buddha, has so eloquently expounded in this his Biography. These, happily, still find numerous adherents among Hindus, Buddhists, Jains, Taoists, Islamic Sufis, and even native Christians throughout Asia.

Among my teachers in the Occident, I am also greatly indebted to Dr. R. R. Marett, Reader in Social Anthropology in the University of Oxford, and Fellow of Exeter College, particularly for the inspiring encouragement with which he has favoured me in my rather unusual field of anthropological research, ever since I first came up to Oxford in the year 1907.

To Major W. L. Campbell, C.I.E., I.A. (retired), late Political Officer representing the British Government in Tibet,

Bhutan, and Sikkim, who assisted the Translator in perfecting
the translation of the *Biography*, all readers of this book, as
well as the Editor, are much indebted.  To Monsieur Jacques
Bacot I am under a special obligation for assistance with
the transliterations and renderings of Tibetan proper names
contained herein, and for the guidance afforded by his
interesting and well-illustrated French translation of the
*Jetsün-Kahbum*, entitled *Le Poète Tibétain Milarépa* (Paris,
1925).   I am also his debtor for information contained in two
lengthy letters from him, concerning versions and variants
of the text.

To Dr. F. W. Thomas, Boden Professor of Sanskrit in the
University of Oxford, I am indebted for some suggestions as
to spellings and transliterations of Oriental words ; and to
Mr. E. T. Sturdy, translator of the *Nārada Sūtra*, who read
the final proofs of the *Biography*, I acknowledge a like debt.

To my friend in Oxford, Mr. E. S. Bouchier, M.A. (Oxon.),
F.R.Hist.S., author of *Syria as a Roman Province, A Short
History of Antioch*, &c., I am exceedingly grateful for aid
which he has rendered in reading through and criticizing
my version of the translation both when in manuscript and in
proof, and for thus facilitating its publication at a time when I
found it necessary to leave England and return to my duties
in India.

I am, likewise, indebted to Sj. Atal Bihari Ghosh, of Calcutta, Joint Honorary Secretary with Sir John Woodroffe of
the *Āgamānusandhāna Samiti*, for having critically examined
the book in the light of Indian thought, especially Brāhmanism
and Tantricism, as also to Mr. Sri Nissanka, of Colombo,
Ceylon, for similar assistance, chiefly with respect to Southern
Buddhism ; and for the annotations which each has added.

It is the Editor's ardent hope that this book, too, will serve
in its own small way to help the peoples of Europe and

America to realize that the peoples of the Orient are moved by impulses common to all humanity, and hold fast to religious ideals, in essence, the same as their own ; that, anthropologically, the human race is One Family, that external differences due to hereditary racial characteristics, pigmentation, and physical environment are, in fact, purely superficial. Too long has the old barrier-wall, set up in Dark Ages, and built of prejudice and misunderstanding arising from lack of scientific knowledge, been allowed to stand. When, at last, Science shall have demolished it, then will the hour come for the leaders of the races and nations to work not merely for the Federation of the World, but for the Federation of the Truth that exists in all Religions.

I can end this Preface in no more fitting manner than by quoting the Translator's own words :

'That this translation of the life-history of Milarepa might contribute a little to help to make him as well known and esteemed in other lands as he is already in his own was the one wish which impelled me as I worked at my task, and remains my ardent prayer as I lay down my pen.'

W. Y. E.-W.

Jesus College, Oxford,
*June* 21, 1928.

# MILAREPA

'I am Milarepa, great in fame,
The direct offspring of Memory and Wisdom;
Yet an old man am I, forlorn and naked.
From my lips springeth forth a little song,
For all Nature, at which I look,
Serveth me for a book.
The iron staff, that my hands hold,
Guideth me over the Ocean of Changing Life.
Master am I of Mind and Light;
And, in showing feats and miracles,
Depend not on earthly deities.'

Milarepa, from the *Gur-Bum*
(after G. Sandberg's Translation).

# TABLE OF CONTENTS

## PART I

## THE PATH OF DARKNESS

# PART II

# THE PATH OF LIGHT

## KARMA

'The Buddhas and the *Arhants* alone have discovered my true nature, in its very essence, and have triumphed over me. All other beings but live under my despotic rule: I put them to death and I make them to live; I am the deity who giveth them the prosperity they enjoy, and I bring about the doing of good deeds and of evil deeds among mankind. Gods, emperors, kings, rich and poor, strong and weak, noble and ignoble, brute creatures, and the happy and the unhappy spirits existing in this world and in the upper and in the lower worlds—all these I elevate or cast down to their respective states. I humble the high and I exalt the low, according to their several works. Therefore am I, indeed, the God who ruleth this [phenomenal] Universe.'

From *Karma's Proclamation of His Omnipotence.*[1]
(Lāma Kazi Dawa-Samdup's Translation.)

'On what we practise now dependeth our future;
As the shadow followeth the body, *Karma* followeth us.
Each hath perforce to taste what he himself hath done.'

From *The Golden Rosary of the History of Padma*
[*Sambhava*],[2] Chapter ix.
(Lāma Kazi Dawa-Samdup's Translation.)

[1] The Editor found among the late Lāma Kazi Dawa-Samdup's papers an English translation consisting of three pages bearing this title (but without the Tibetan title of the original text) from which the quotation has been taken. At the end of the translation there is the following note: 'Translated by Dawa-Samdup in accordance with explanations given by the Rev. Prajñā Sathi. 28. 5. 1917.'

[2] Tib. *Padma-Thangyig-Serteng.*

# DESCRIPTION OF ILLUSTRATIONS

## I. FRONTISPIECE: THE GREAT KARGYÜTPA *GURUS*
*facing title-page.*

A photographic reproduction (about one-half of the original size) of a water-colour, painted by the late Lāma Kazi Dawa-Samdup, in Gangtok, Sikkim, during the year 1920, in strict accord with the traditions of Tibetan monastic art, showing the Chief *Gurus*, or Great Teachers, of the Kargyütpa (Tib. *Bkah-rgyud-pa*) School of Northern Buddhism. It was a parting gift from the Lāma to the Editor.

The uppermost figure represents the Divine *Guru*, the Celestial Buddha Dorje-Chang (Skt. *Vajra-Dhara*), the ' Holder of the *Dorje*' (the Spiritual Thunderbolt or Sceptre of the Gods), in Whom the Esoteric Lore of the Kargyütpas has its origin. The Established Church not only regards Him as an Emanation of the Buddha Shākya Muni, but venerates Him, as the Kargyütpas do, as the Chief of the Celestial Buddhas, analogous to the Ādi, or Primordial, Buddha of the Old School of Padma Sambhava. He is robed in the rich princely robes traditionally ascribed to the Dhyānī Buddhas (or Buddhas of Meditation) of the *Sambhoga-Kāya* Order to which He belongs. His being robed as a Prince indicates that He has direct dominion over sentient beings and their moral feelings. He shows a passive mien, and has a beautiful countenance, because He is naturally of a passive (or unimpulsive) nature, and the Source of Goodness, Truth, and Justice. He sits in the Buddha Posture (Skt. *Vajra-Āsana*), because His mind is ever in the unperturbed (or quiescent) state of *Samādhi*. The bell which he holds in His left hand symbolizes the Voidness (Skt. *Shūnyatā*) as Intellect; the *dorje* in His right hand symbolizes Divine Method and Spiritual Power. He is enthroned on a lion-throne, to indicate that He is beyond all fear of Change, the two lions at the base of the throne symbolizing Fearlessness. His blue colour symbolizes His immutability and the eternity of His existence, for it is like the blue of the eternal heavenly sky. Being the prototype of the *Heruka* Hierarchy of *Bodhic* Deities,[1] He wears a necklace of bone-beads, symbolic of

---

[1] As shown by certain of the deities of the *Bardo Thödol* (see *The Tibetan Book of the Dead*), the *Heruka* Buddha, often depicted as being male-female (Tib. *yab-yum*), either in peaceful (Tib. *Z'i-wa*) or wrathful (Tib. *T'o-wo*) aspect, is, esoterically, a Tantric personification of the Saving Power which alone makes possible the attainment of Enlightenment or Buddhahood. Herein this Power is expressed through the Divine Person of Dorje-Chang and thence through His Initiates incarnate on Earth, more especially those of them who are Great *Yogīs*; for these, having renounced the world, are, in an esoteric sense, the *Herukapas*,

renunciation and conquest of the *Sangsāra* (the Round of Death and Birth). Thus He combines in Himself the *yogic* qualities both of the *Heruka* and Dhyānī Buddha.

On the right of the Divine *Guru* is shown the first of the human *Gurus*, the Indian *Yogī* (or Saint) Tilopa, who received from the Divine *Guru* direct guidance and teaching. The golden fish which Tilopa holds aloft in his right hand symbolizes sentient beings immersed in the Ocean of *Sangsāric* (or Worldly) Existence, and indicates Tilopa's power to emancipate and save them.[1]  The blood-filled skull which Tilopa holds in his left hand symbolizes his ability to confer *lokic siddhi* (occult powers pertaining to the world) in his character as a *Heruka*, his *Heruka* nature being indicated by the tiara of human skulls and the bone ornaments adorning him. The lotus-throne upon which he sits shows that he belongs to the Lotus Order of *Gurus*. The red colour of the lotus petals is symbolical of Sukhāvatī (the Western Paradise) wherein reigns the Buddha Amitābha, He of Boundless Light, the Illuminator or Enlightener, whose symbol is the red, all-consuming and purifying and mystical Element Fire; for Tilopa is believed to have been an incarnation of Amitābha. The green of Tilopa's aura, and of other auras in the painting, represents *yogic* equal-mindedness, or harmony, and spiritual power.

Opposite Tilopa, on a similar lotus-throne, is shown the second of the human *Gurus*, the Indian *Yogī* (or Saint) Naropa, blowing a trumpet made of a ram's horn,[2] proclaiming the glory of his Order

'The Unclad,' being 'naked' as regards all things of the *Sangsāra* of which they have divested themselves.

[1] The fish-symbol adopted by the early Christians, especially in the catacomb period, very probably from Oriental sources, bore a similar significance with reference to the *Christos* as the Saviour of Mankind.

[2] Upon the outbreak of a serious cattle epidemic in India, whence Naropa originated, it is not unusual for the chief priest or astrologer of a village to take a trumpet made of a ram's horn and circumambulate the cattle and the village, blowing the trumpet in order to ward off or else to exorcize the epidemic. Similarly, seven Jewish priests each blowing a ram's-horn trumpet, followed by the ark of the covenant, circumambulated Jericho daily for six successive days and then on the seventh day made a sevenfold circumambulation, whereupon, after a long blast had been blown on the seven rams'-horn trumpets and the people had shouted with a great shout, as commanded by the Lord, the walls of the city fell down flat and the city was taken (*Joshua* vi. 4-20).

Thus among the ancient Jews, as among modern Hindus, the sound emitted by the ram's-horn trumpet is employed magically, as *mantric* sound is in *Mantra Yoga* (cf. *The Tibetan Book of the Dead*, section on 'Mantras, or Words of Power', p. 220). But among initiates into Tantricism there is an esoteric significance. This seems to be that the ram's-horn trumpet symbolizes, as it does in the hands of Naropa, the exorcizing of the Demons of Worldliness, Egoism, and Ignorance (Skt. *Avidyā*), so that the Illusion (Skt. *Māyā*) of *Sangsāric* Existence is dissipated and the *Nirvāṇic* Way to the Full Deliverance called Buddhahood is revealed.

and in honour of his *Guru* Tilopa. Naropa's, like Tilopa's, tiara of human skulls and bone ornaments worn on the body, in addition to indicating the *Heruka* estate of their wearer, esoterically symbolize the fundamental principle or foundation of the Universe, the *Dharma-Kāya* (or ' Body of Truth '), which is the Norm of Being, the Uncreated, Beyond-Nature *Nirvāṇa*, because they signify the Victory over Birth and Death—over all Becoming or Change. The *yogic* ornaments, such as Tilopa and Naropa wear, are commonly classified as being six in number: (1) the skull-tiara, (2) the armlets, (3) the bracelets, (4) the anklets, shown only on Naropa, (5) the bone-bead apron and waist-band combined, which are not visible in our painting, and (6) the double line of bone-beads extending over the shoulders to the breast, where they hold in place the breast-plate Mirror of *Karma*, wherein, as described in *The Tibetan Book of the Dead* (pp. xxi, 36, 166), are reflected every good and bad action. These six ornaments (usually of human bone) denote the Six *Pāramitā* ('Boundless Virtues'), which are: (1) *Dāna-Pāramitā* ('Boundless Charity'), (2) *Shīla-Pāramitā* ('Boundless Morality'), (3) *Kshānti-Pāramitā* ('Boundless Patience'), (4) *Vīrya-Pāramitā* ('Boundless Industry'), (5) *Dhyāna-Pāramitā* ('Boundless Meditation'), and (6) *Prajñā-Pāramitā* ('Boundless Wisdom'). To attain to Buddhahood, and as a Bodhisattva to assist in the salvation of all living creatures, the Six *Pāramitā* must be assiduously practised. Naropa, like the two preceding *Gurus*, is seated in one of the numerous *yogic* postures (or *āsanas*). His throne, too, is a red lotus, but less red than that of Tilopa; it, also, is symbolical of Sukhavātī, and of Naropa's membership in the Lotus Order of *Gurus*.

The *Guru* Marpa, popularly known as Marpa the Translator, on account of the many works, chiefly on Tantric *Yoga*, which he collected in manuscript form in India, whither he made a number of journeys from Tibet, and translated into Tibetan, is represented by the central figure at the bottom of the painting. He is dressed in the semi-lay dress (i. e. a dress partly *lāmaic* and partly laic) of a native Tibetan of good family; for he, although a very famous *Guru* of the Line, never renounced, as the other *Gurus* of the Line did, family life. He, too, holds a human skull filled with blood (represented in *lāmaic* ritual by holy-water coloured red) to show that he, also, has obtained the right and power to confer *lokic siddhi*. He is seated on a white lotus-throne, symbolical of his membership of the *Vajra* (Tib. *Dorje*) Order, otherwise known as the Order of the East, white being the colour assigned to the eastern quarter of the heavens.

Milarepa, more commonly called in Tibetan Jetsün Milarepa, is shown on the right of Marpa, who was his *Guru*, sitting in a cave on an antelope-skin such as *yogīs* place under them when practising *Yoga*. He is clad in a single cotton cloth, the dress of the Kargyütpa ascetic, which indicates that without any other covering for his body he can withstand intense cold, equal to that of the Arctic regions, such as prevails in the high snow-clad regions of Tibet. Like Tilopa and Marpa, Milarepa holds a blood-filled skull, in sign of his own power to confer *lokic siddhi*. He is singing a hymn ; and, therefore, holds his right hand to his ear. The red band across his breast, comparable to a Brāhmanical sacred-thread, is a *yogic* meditation-band such as Tibetan *yogīs* employ to keep their legs in the posture (or *āsana*) of deep meditation when in the trance-state of *Samādhi* (cf. p. 201[1]). Similar meditation-bands are worn by Tilopa and Naropa. The lion symbol over the entrance to his cave signifies that the cave is in a high, isolated Himalayan wilderness such as the solitude-loving mountain-lion frequents ; and Milarepa is himself ' The Fearless Lion of the *Dharma* (or Truth) '—cf. p. 35[3]—and the cave " The Den of the Lion '.

Gampopa, to the left of Marpa, is represented in the garb of a *lāma* of the Kargyütpa Brotherhood, sitting on a richly embroidered cushion in a preaching-booth. He is proclaiming, with the aid of the Tibetan Sacred Book which he holds, the Doctrine of the Enlightened One— the Ending of Sorrow and the Way to Final Deliverance. Gampopa is the fifth of the Great *Gurus* who took upon themselves the human form for the good of the many, and the sixth in the Succession which begins with the Celestial *Guru* Dorje-Chang, Who, so the modern Kargyütpas believe, still confers upon the Brotherhood on Earth spiritual benediction, telepathically transmitted in ' waves of grace ', direct from the Heaven-World wherein He reigns. From Gampopa, who was Milarepa's most spiritually-gifted disciple, onwards to our own day the Kargyütpa Dynasty of Teachers has continued without break.

## II. MILAREPA THE TIBETAN *YOGĪ* (Tib. *Nal-jor-pa*) or Saint
*facing* p. 31

Herein Milarepa (the central figure round about whom are a number of devotees, human and celestial, making offerings and obeisance to him) is pictured after the popular tradition, his right hand held to his ear to indicate that he is singing a hymn, surrounded by numerous miniature pictures interwoven together, each illustrating some episode described in the *Biography* (or *Jetsün-Kahbum*), of which our English text is a faithful rendering. In the central foreground, for example, just below Milarepa and extending to the bottom border of the picture, there are shown the buildings of various shapes which Milarepa constructed when undergoing severe penance under his *Guru* Marpa (cf. pp. 96 ff., 134) ; and to the right of Milarepa, at the edge of the picture, we see the four columns surmounted by the different symbolic animals, and the great mountain around which they are placed, as described in Milarepa's dream concerning the Kargyütpa Hierarchy (cf. pp. 149-51). As in the painting described above, Milarepa is seated in a *yogic* posture on an antelope-skin and clad in a single cotton cloth (which is here richly embroidered) with the meditation-band across his breast.

This illustration is a photographic copy of a picture to be met with in the homes of the laity throughout Tibet, as popular among Tibetan Buddhists as pictures of Christian Saints are among Christians. As such it suggests the veneration and respect which all classes of Tibetans continue to pay to Milarepa nearly nine centuries after the era in which he flourished.

With the kind permission given by Dr. L. A. Waddell to the Editor, this illustration has been reproduced from the plate facing p. 64 in Dr. Waddell's well-known work (of which we have made much use), *The Buddhism of Tibet, or Lāmaism* (London, 1895).

## III. THE DHYĀNĪ BUDDHA AKṢHOBHYA .   . *facing* p. 42

As described in our text and annotation on p. 42, Akṣhobhya (the 'Unagitated' or 'Unshakable') is one of the Five Dhyānī Buddhas peculiar to Northern Buddhism. He is second in the Order, Vairo-chana being first, Ratna-Sambhava third, Amitābha fourth, and Amogha-Siddhi fifth ; see *The Tibetan Book of the Dead*, pp. 105-18, for detailed description of each.

Akṣhobhya is herein shown seated with legs locked and soles of the feet uppermost, this being the *yogic* posture commonly assigned to all Buddhas of Meditation and their reflexes. His left hand lies on his lap in the *mudrā* of meditation. His right hand touches the Earth with the tips of the outstretched fingers, the palm turned inwards; it is in the *bhūmisparsha* or 'witness' *mudrā*, which the Gandhāra School of Buddhism assigned to the Buddha Gautama when representing His invoking the Earth to bear witness that He had resisted the temptation of Mārā, the Evil One. The third eye (Skt. *ūrṇā*) on the forehead of Akṣhobhya, near the junction of the eyebrows, indicates His spiritual insight and foreknowledge; and the *Bodhic* protuberance (Skt. *uṣhṇīṣha*) on the crown of His head indicates His Buddhahood.

This and the illustration number IV, following, are facsimile repro-ductions of photographs of bronze images as shown in *The Gods of Northern Buddhism* (Plate II, *b* and *d*), by Miss Alice Getty, to whom the Editor is indebted for permission to use them.

## IV. THE SUPREME *GURU*: THE ĀDI-BUDDHA VAJRA-DHARA . . . . . . . . *facing* p. 138

Herein, as in the Frontispiece, Vajra-Dhara is shown in the *yogic* posture of meditation, like a Dhyānī Buddha. His arms are crossed on his breast in the posture of the Supreme and Eternal Buddha (Skt. *vajra-hūṃ-kāra-mudrā*). His right hand holds the *vajra*, also symbolical of the Mystic Truth (which like the *vajra*, the thunderbolt of the gods, cannot be destroyed), or the Divine Wisdom that annihilates all passions and thus leads to dominion over *sangsāric* (or worldly) existence. His left hand holds the bell with the *vajra* handle, known in Sanskrit as the *ghaṇṭā*. Like Akṣhobhya, He possesses the *ūrnā* and the *uṣḥṇīṣha*, symbols of His Enlightenment.

## V. MILAREPA MANIFESTING OCCULT POWERS

*facing p. 268*

Herein Milarepa, transfigured and enhaloed, is seen in the midst of his chief disciples, seated in *yogic* posture, in the Cave of Brilche, in Chūbar, just before his *Pari-Nirvāṇa* (cf. pp. 268-9, 275, 281). He is manifesting the signs and symbols of his mastership of the Occult Sciences, as he bestows upon these disciples his final benediction. A glorified figurative *maṇḍala* is above him, and in the small adjoining cave are shown the symbolic Wheel of the Law (as depicted on the back of this volume and described below) and Flames of Wisdom, all magically produced. (Cf. Marpa's similar manifestations, p. 163.)

This illustration is a photographic copy of a reproduction of a Tibetan painting ('The Chief Disciples at Chūbar Asking for Benediction'), from p. 165 of *Le Poète Tibétain Milarépa* (Paris, 1925) by M. Jacques Bacot, who kindly allowed the Editor to reproduce the picture here.

# DESCRIPTION OF EMBLEMS

# INTRODUCTION

'Even as one desirous of reaching a longed-for city requireth the eyes for seeing [the way] and the feet for traversing the distance, so, also, whosoever desireth to reach the City of *Nirvāṇa* requireth the Eyes of Wisdom and the Feet of Method.'—*Prajñā-Pāramitā*.

## I. THE IMPORTANCE OF THE *JETSÜN-KAHBUM*

THIS *Biography* of one of the Great Religious Geniuses of our human race presents to us a vivid record of the social conditions which prevailed in the Tibet of the eleventh and twelfth century of the Christian Era. We of the West are too apt to forget that India, like China, was highly civilized at a time when Europe was still in an age of comparative barbarism; and that Tibet, from the seventh century onwards, favoured by the influx of culture from China on the east and India on the south, was, at the time Milarepa flourished, not inferior in its medieval limitations and was probably superior in its remarkable philosophical and religious development to the Western World at the same epoch. In Europe, the glory of Athens and of Alexandria had long been extinguished by the darkness of the Dark Ages; scientific and philosophical speculations were, by ecclesiastical authority, limited to the narrow confines of a pedantic Scholasticism; the Arab philosophers of Cordova and of Bagdad guarded the Learning of the Ancients until Europe should be re-born to a New Day at the Renaissance; but throughout the Orient the Promethean Fire was never allowed to die out. Even till now, China and India have preserved unbroken a culture whose origin is lost in the past.[1] The civilizations of Babylonia, Egypt, Greece, Rome, have all bloomed and faded, but those of China and India, despite social disturbances arising from contact with the utili-

---

[1] 'The East, even in the days of her material prosperity, never forgot the supremacy of things spiritual. Kings renounced their kingdoms to end their days in meditation, in jungle or mountain solitudes. "To die in harness" was then, as it still is, an evil to be avoided. Herein lies the secret of the imperishable vitality of the Orient.'—Sj. Atal Bihari Ghosh.

tarianism of the West, have lived on; and, if they continue
to retain their marvellous spiritual virility, may well survive
the materialistic civilization of the Occident, and continue to
lead humanity nearer that Higher Ideal of world-conquest by
the might of the divine in man rather than by his animal might
expended in the savagery of warfare. At least this is the ideal
upon which the teachings of Milarepa as applied to the problems of society on Earth are founded; and, in this way, they
are in agreement with the teachings of the Buddha, of the
Christ, and of all the Great Leaders of Asia, who by Love and
Compassion have done immeasurably more to raise the status
of mankind than have the innumerable hosts of armed troops
and their captains throughout the ages.

At the time when Milarepa was meditating amid the snowy
fastnesses of the Tibetan Himalayas, the culture of Islam was
flowing in over every part of Hindustan. It is owing to him, as
well as to his teacher Marpa, who made a number of journeys
to India to collect manuscripts of Indian and Buddhistic lore,
that much of India's spiritual inheritance, which was then
threatened with destruction, has been applied to the needs of
Tibetan society and preserved until to-day. And, at the same
epoch, England was experiencing the effects of the Norman
Conquest. Thus, to the student of religion, as to the historian,
the *Jetsün-Kahbum*,[1] or *Biographical History of Jetsün-Milarepa*, should be of more than ordinary importance.

## II. HISTORICAL VALUE OF THE NARRATIVE

On the whole, the biographical narrative, as it has come
down to us, may be accepted as a faithful account of the sayings
and doings of Jetsün, with due allowance for a certain amount of
folk-lore and popular mythology which has been incorporated in
it. As a Gospel of the Kargyütpa Sect, it is one of the many
Sacred Books of the East; and, as such, perhaps as historically
accurate as parts of the *New Testament*, if not more so.

To Oriental students interested in the complex problem of
the evolution of Tibetan and Mongolian religions it should be

---

[1] *Kah-bum* = '100,000 Words'; *Nam-thar*, the usual Tibetan term for
Biography, literally meaning 'The Full Deliverance', is more commonly applied
to this work.

of rare interest. To all who appreciate Buddhistic Philosophy, more especially in its Mahāyānic form, this book should bring fresh insight. To mystics the world over it should prove to be, as Rechung, its author, would call it, a most precious jewel, a treasure-house which can never be exhausted by the human mentality, and a nosegay of precepts which can be understood only by putting them to the test of practice.

In the first part of the *Biography*, we see Jetsün dominated in his youth, like many a great saint of other Faiths, by the lower nature. Urged on, as he was, by his vengeful mother, he became, for a time, a professional doer of evil, a black magician, treading the Path of Darkness. Then, in the second part, he repents, and is converted to the White Faith, which is Buddhism. Thenceforth, after having undergone very severe trials and penances imposed by his *Guru* Marpa, he enters upon The Path of Light ; and eventually reaches, in the words of the narrative, ' the greatest of all great successes that can ever fall to the lot of mortal man '.

Perhaps, to some readers, much of the matter contained in the last chapter may appear to be redundant. Account must, however, be taken of the fact that it is through this chapter alone that Rechung speaks to us as an eye-witness of events ; in all the previous chapters he is merely telling us what the Teacher has narrated, for Rechung did not become a disciple until Jetsün was an old man nearing the end of his days. For the Kargyütpas, this last chapter, concerning the passing away of their Master, is, no doubt, almost the most important of all. Contained in it there is not only the account of the marvellous phenomena attendant upon the cremation, and of how Jetsün reanimated his corpse in order to give answer to the fervent prayer of Rechung (who, having been far away at the time of Jetsün's *Nirvāṇa*, was late in arriving at the place of the funeral ceremonies) ; but there is also the quintessence of the Teacher's precepts, which are enjoined upon all the *shishyas* (or disciples) by the living *guru* (or spiritual preceptor). Moreover, it is a summary of the most essential teachings of Northern Buddhism, as therein chanted by the *Dākinīs* (or Angels) ; and is replete with interest for the lover of the marvellous.

To Jetsün's followers, these strange events, centring round their *Guru's* passing away and his funeral pyre, are no more incredible than is the story of the Transfiguration and Ascension of Jesus to Christians. As to what historical value is to be attached to them, each reader must decide for himself, after having made due allowance for accretions derived from tradition and popular belief.

### III.  TIBETAN SCHOOLS OF BUDDHIST PHILOSOPHY[1]

Throughout Tibet, and extending into Nepal, Bhutan, Sikkim, Kashmir, and parts of Mongolia, there are three chief Schools of Buddhist Philosophy: (1) the Mādhyamika, or 'Middle Way', known to Tibetans as the *Ūma-pa* (*Dbus-ma-pa*), which originated in India under Nāgārjuna during the second century A.D.; (2) the Mahāmudrā, or 'Great Symbol' (Tib. *Phyag-Ch'en*); and (3) the Ādi-Yoga, otherwise known as the 'Great Perfection' (Tib. *Dzogs-Ch'en*).

The adherents of the first are the Ge-lug-pas, the 'Followers of the Virtuous Order', popularly known as the Yellow Caps. This School, founded in Tibet at the beginning of the fifteenth century A.D., by the Reformer Tsong-khapa ('Native of the Onion Country'), of the Province of Amdo, North-East Tibet, on the frontiers of China, who was born in A.D. 1358 and died in 1417, grew out of the Sect of the Kah-dam-pas ('Those Bound by the Ordinances'), and is now the Established Church of Northern Buddhism, wielding through its spiritual Head, the Dalai-Lāma, the God-King of Tibet, both temporal and spiritual power.

The adherents of the Mahāmudrā School are the Kargyüt-pas, the 'Followers of the Apostolic Succession' (or 'Followers of the Successive Orders'), of which Milarepa is the greatest of the Tibetan Apostles. The history of this sect is contained in the account given below of the Apostolic Succession.

The followers of the 'Great Perfection', or Ādi-Yoga School, are the Ñing-ma-pas, the 'Old-style Ones', popularly known as the Red Caps, the adherents of the Unreformed Church, founded by the Indian philosopher, Padma Sambhava, in the

---

[1] As a general reference, and for more details, the student is here referred to L. A. Waddell, *The Buddhism of Tibet* (London, 1895), pp. 54-75.

year 749 A. D.[1]   He, better known to the Tibetans as *Guru*
Rinpoch'e (' The Precious *Guru*'), or as Padma Jungne (Skt.
*Padma-Janma*, ' The Lotus-Born'), was a very famous pro-
fessor of the Occult Sciences in the great Buddhist University
of Nālanda, then the Oxford of India.   The King of Tibet,
Ti-song De-tsen, hearing of the *Guru's* fame, invited him to
Tibet.   The *Guru* accepted the King's call ; and arriving in the
year 747, at Sam-yé, about fifty miles south-east of Lhasa,[2]

[1] Sj. Atal Bihari Ghosh comments as follows : ' Mādhavāchārya, in the *Sarva-
darshana-Samgraha*, mentions four schools of Buddhistic thought, namely, the
Mādhyamika, the Yogāchāra, the Sautrāntika, and the Vaibhāshika.   The
Mādhyamika School teaches that everything is void or unreal (Skt. *Sarva-
Shūnyatva*) ; the Yogāchāra, that the outer or material universe is unreal (Skt.
*Vāhya-Shūnyatva*) ; the Sautrāntika, that the outer or material universe is a
matter of inference (Skt. *Vahyānumeyatva*) ; and the Vaibhāshika, that the
outer or material universe is real so far as it can be experienced or be the
object of the senses (Skt. *Vāhyārtha-Pratyakshatva*).   As to the Tibetan Buddhists, they, as a whole, follow the Mādhyamika doctrine of the *Shūnya* (or
Void), which is like the monistic conception of the Brāhman in its *Nishkala* (or
attributeless) aspect.

' The three chief Tibetan Schools, to my mind, mark three stages on the Path
of Illumination or spiritual progress.   In the first, the *sādhaka* (or devotee) is
subject to injunctions and prohibitions (Skt. *Vidhi* and *Nishedha*), i. e. "bound by
the ordinances".   In the second, he adheres to traditional ways (Skt. *Pāramparya-Krama*), wherein the ordinary restrictions are to a certain extent relaxed,
although the *sādhaka* is not yet altogether free.   In the third, the Ādi-Yoga,
when through *yoga* practices the Light is seen, there are no longer any restrictions ; for the state of the Buddha or *Siddha* has been attained.   These three
stages correspond, roughly speaking, with what the *Tantras* mean by *Pashu-
bhāva* (State of the Animal-Man), *Vīrabhāva* (State of the Hero), and *Divyabhāva*
(State of the Divine or Enlightened).

' Padma Sambhava's teachings are "old" in the sense that the truth contained
in them preceded all things, has ever existed, and was conveyed in the "old-
style" manner.   So his School was the Ādi (or " First"), also known as the
Sanātana.   Teachers who succeeded Padma Sambhava did not " reform " the substance of his teachings ; they merely adapted the "form " of their own instruction
to the limited capacity of their disciples and trained them to acquire the ability
(Skt. *Adhikāra*) to understand the Ādi-Yoga doctrines.   The *Pashu* (Animal-
Man) becomes a *Vīra* (Hero) and then a *Divya* (Divine or Enlightened Being) ;
this is ever the process.'

The Editor adds : Nowadays the Yellow Caps oppose the old unreformed
Red Cap School and its illustrious *Guru* and Founder, Padma Sambhava, very
much as Protestant Christians oppose Roman Catholicism and the Papacy.
The Kargyütpas, however, being a semi-reformed body, wisely avoid either
extreme ; and, in this respect, are among Northern Buddhists like moderate
Anglicans among Christians.

[2] Cf. Sir Charles Bell, *Tibet Past and Present* (Oxford, 1924), p. 26.

where he subsequently founded a monastery, introduced among the Tibetans the Tantric and Mantrayānic aspects of Mahāyānic Buddhism.

A fourth School, the Sa-kya-pa (derived from *Sa-skya*, meaning 'Tawny Earth', with reference to the colour of the soil at the site of its first monastery in Western Tibet), beginning as a reformed sect, was originally of considerable importance; but nowadays it differs but little from the old-style Red Cap Sect.

In addition to these three chief Schools, and a number of sects detached from them, there are surviving monastic orders of the primitive pre-Buddhistic religion of Tibet called Bön, (or Pön), which, with its doctrine of rebirth, furnished a favourable soil for the sowing of the seed of Buddhism. The *Biography* records that Milarepa once performed a Bön rite (cf. p. 243), thus indicating his familiarity with the older Faith. On another occasion he made his Magic prevail over the Magic of a famous Bön sorcerer (cf. p. 240). The followers of the Bön, in contradistinction to the Yellow Caps and the Red Caps, are called the Black Caps, each of the three bodies wearing caps and dress of these respective colours.

### IV. THE KARGYÜTPA APOSTOLIC SUCCESSION [1]

A century before the time of *Guru* Padma Sambhava, during the reign of the first Buddhist King of Tibet, King Song-tsen Gam-po (who died about A. D. 650),[2] the mystical Vajra-Yāna ('Thunderbolt' or 'Adamantine [i. e. Immutable] Path') form of Buddhism, which the Kargyütpas afterward adopted, entered Tibet from two sources: (1) from Nepal, the native land of the Buddha, through the Tibetan King's marriage in the year 639 with Bhṛikuṭī, a Nepalese royal princess; and (2) from China, through the King's marriage with Wencheng, a daughter of the Chinese Royal House, in 641. Thereafter, the King, having been converted to Buddhism by his two wives, sent Sam-bhota to India to collect Buddhist books. Sam-bhota, like Marpa

---

[1] Cf. L. A. Waddell, op. cit., pp. 18 ff., 63–7.

[2] Song-tsen Gam-po was the Ashoka of Tibet. Under him Tibet was at the zenith of its power. Turkestan and Nepal seem to have been subject to him; and his conquests were so extensive in Western China that the Chinese Government was obliged to pay tribute to him to retain its own sovereignty. Cf. Sir Charles Bell, op. cit., p. 28.

four centuries later, returned to Tibet with a rich library, and so saved for the world much of the learning of India which afterwards was lost in the land of its origin. Tibet is also indebted to Sam-bhota for its alphabet, which he formulated on the model of the Sanskrit alphabet then prevalent in Kashmir and North India. Furthermore, he gave to Tibet its first systematic and written grammar.

It was not, however, until the time of Padma Sambhava, under King Ti-song De-tsen, that Buddhism took firm root in Tibet, for the Bönpas had until then successfully opposed it, in order to maintain their own religious authority. But Padma Sambhava, like St. Patrick in Ireland when opposed by the Druids, caused the New Magic to prevail over the Old Magic.

Then, in A.D. 1038, Atīsha, the first of the Reformers of Lāmaism, arrived in Tibet from India, and introduced celibacy and a higher morality among the priesthood. He, too, like Padma Sambhava, was a Professor of Philosophy, having been attached to the Vikramashīla Monastery in Magadha; and was born of the royal family of Gaur, Bengal, in the year 980. The cave wherein Atīsha lived, sixteen miles east of Lhasa, is still reverently preserved, embowered in wild rose and creepers.[1]

Marpa, Jetsün's own *Guru*, who, because of his scholarship and translations, came to be called the Translator, as he is throughout the *Biography*, is said to have studied under no less than ten famous *Gurus*. Part of Marpa's life is contemporaneous with that of Atīsha, who was one of his Teachers; but his chief work came a few years after the time of Atīsha's reformation. Thus Atīsha is not only the Chief Human *Guru* for the Gelugpas, whose origin lay in the Kahdampa Sect which Atīsha founded, but he is, in a not unimportant way, one of the *Gurus* of the rival Kargyütpa Sect which Marpa founded. Atīsha is not, however, recognized as of the Kargyütpa Apostolic Succession.

Most of Marpa's Teachers were of the ancient Indian Sect of Kusulipas, or those who seek to gain Enlightenment by meditation, in contradistinction to those called Paṇḍitas, who aim at the attainment of the Supreme Truth, as contained in the

[1] Cf. Sir Charles Bell, op. cit., p. 31.

Doctrine of the *Shūnyatā*, or Voidness, by intellectual means alone.[1] Atīsha not having emphasized the practical applications of Buddhism by means of the *yogic* ideal which the Kusulipas insisted upon, it fell to the lot of one of their Great *Gurus*, named Tilopa (or Telo), to become the first of the Apostles of the Kargyütpa Hierarchy.

According to tradition, Tilopa, who flourished about the middle of the tenth century, had the Mahāmudrā Philosophy, upon which the Kargyütpa School is chiefly based, imparted to him by the Celestial Buddha Dorje-Chang (Tib. *Rdo-rje-Hch'ang* : Skt. *Vajra-Dhara*). Tilopa, in turn, handed it down orally, as an esoteric doctrine—as it still is in its practical application—to his disciple Naropa ; Naropa transmitted it to Marpa, and Marpa to Milarepa.

As being their Divine *Guru*, the Kargyütpas have come to regard Dorje-Chang (Vajra-Dhara) as equal to the Ādi, or Primordial, Buddha, so that for them He is the Manifester of the Grace of the Ādi-Buddha and inseparable from Him.

Thus the second in the Succession on Earth is Naropa ; the third, Marpa ; and the fourth, Milarepa. Milarepa's successor in the Line was not Rechung, the author of this *Biography*, but the first of Milarepa's disciples, Dvag-po-Lharje, a native of Eastern Tibet, otherwise known as Je-Gampo-pa. This second name, meaning ' the Lord Gampopa ', was given to him because he was believed to have been the reincarnation of King Songtsen Gam-po, the first Buddhist ruler of Tibet, who had died five centuries previously. Je-Gampo-pa himself died in the year 1152, two years after he had founded the Monastery of Ts'ur-lka, the chief seat of the Kargyütpas, and ever since then the Kargyütpa Line of *Gurus* has remained unbroken.

## V. THE MODERN SUCCESSORS OF MILAREPA

At this very moment there are hundreds of the Kargyütpa ascetics living in the bleak solitudes of the Tibetan Himalayas, some of them in caves at the base and on the sides of Mount

[1] 'This is illustrated in various ways in the Brāhmanik *Tantras*, which teach that knowledge of the Brāhman is derived either through knowing words or through inner realization. The first method, being merely intellectual, cannot dispel the darkness within ; the second method alone leads to true wisdom.

Everest, wherein are still to be found, as places of special sanctity and pilgrimage, the hermitages of Jetsün. There nature remains as it has been since Earth's early ages, and the Kargyütpa hermits dwell undisturbed by the restlessness of the world beyond, wherein the ancient ideals which they uphold no longer govern men, but where there rules, instead, the opinion that success means the acquisition of worldly riches, fame, and power.

Their system of mystical insight, called in Tibetan *Ta-wa*, as taught by the various treatises on the Mahāmudrā Doctrine and practised in grottoes in mountain or jungle solitudes, distinguishes the Kargyütpas from all other Tibetan Sects. And in virtue of their vows of unqualified asceticism and renunciation of the worldly life and their actual application of them, they are not surpassed, in the soundness of their Buddhism, by any other body of followers of the Great *Yogī*, Gautama the Enlightened One.

Each little community of these Himalayan mystics has its own *Guru*, subordinate to the Apostolic *Guru*, the Head of the Sect, who, in turn, is subject to the Celestial Line of *Gurus*, and these, in order of hierarchical rank, are subject to the Supreme *Guru*, the Buddha Dorje-Chang (Vajra-Dhara).[1] As electricity may be passed on from one receiving station to another, so, the Kargyütpas maintain, is the Divine Grace, vouchsafed by the Buddhas, transmitted through the Buddha Dorje-Chang (Vajra-Dhara) to the Line of Celestial *Gurus* and thence to the Apostolic *Guru* on Earth, and, from him, to each of the subordinate *gurus*, and, by them, through the Mystic Initiation, to each of the neophytes.

As will be observed in Milarepa's hymns, the Apostolic *Guru* on Earth is frequently addressed as being the very em-

Again, it is said that *Jñāna* (Knowledge) is of two kinds : (1) that which arises from the study of the *Āgamas* (Tantric Scriptures), and (2) that which is born of *Viveka* (Inner Discrimination). It is likewise taught that by argumentation one cannot reach realization, certain truths being beyond the scope of discussion : "Apply not argument to what is beyond thought." '—Sj. Atal Bihari Ghosh.

[1] ' Brāhmanik *Tantras* refer to three Lines (Skt. *Ogha*, *Pangkti* ) of *Gurus* : (1) *Divya* (Celestial), (2) *Siddha* (Adept), and (3) *Mānava* (Human). Cf. the *Tantra-rāja*, ch. i, in *Tantrik Texts*, vol. viii, ed. by A. Avalon.'—Sj. Atal Bihari Ghosh.

bodiment of the Buddha Dorje-Chang (Vajra-Dhara) Himself;
for each living Apostle of the Succession is the Holder of
Mystic Power, or, literally, the Holder of the *Vajra* (the Spiritual Thunderbolt of the Gods, symbolized by the *lāmaic*
sceptre depicted on the cover of this book)—the meaning of
the name Dorje-Chang (Vajra-Dhara). By this appellation we
are to understand that the *Guru*, so addressed, is the Grand
Master of the Esoteric Ceremonies ; and, as the Great Initiator
on Earth, is the Conferrer of Spiritual Power, which Pro-
metheus-like he brings from the Divine Realms of the Spiritual
Thunderbolt to the Race of Men.

## VI. KARGYÜTPAS COMPARED WITH CHRISTIAN GNOSTICS

As basis for comparative explanation of this Kargyütpa
system of mystical insight, we may take, for instance, that of
the Christian Gnostics ('The Knowing Ones'), probably the
most similar to it among systems known to European thought,
wherein we meet with many remarkable parallels.

Thus, each of the numerous Gnostic communities—although
these were not welded into an organic whole like the Kargyütpa
communities—appears to have had its own Chief *Guru* (such
as Valentinus, Marcion, and Basilides) and its subordinate *gurus*
and Apostolic Succession on Earth, and its Supreme Spiritual
Head, in the *Christos*, from Whom, through the Saints and the
Aeons of Super-Human Intelligences, was transmitted to His
human followers the Divine Grace of the Father. Saturninus
of Antioch, another of the great Christian Gnostic *Gurus* (who
flourished about A. D. 120), taught that abstention from flesh-
food, and observance of strict asceticism—such as the Kargyütpas practise—lead to the Supreme through the Son, the
*Christos* Aeon (or Emanation of the Father). According to
some of the many Gnostic Schools, God the Father was
mystically the Primordial Man, the *Anthropos* (or 'Aδάμας [1]),
comparable to the *Ādi* (or 'First') Buddha of the Kargyütpas
and other Sects of Northern Buddhism.

---

[1] Cf. the Aeon Iaō (or Jeū) of the *Pistis Sophia*, one of the chief Gnostic
Christian Gospels of the Valentinians. See G. R. S. Mead's translation (London,
1921), and his *Fragments of a Faith Forgotten* (London, 1900), pp. 535-7.

In accord with Buddhists generally, the Christian Gnostics know no doctrine of Vicarious Atonement such as the Church Councils elaborated and made a dogma ; for, to both Faiths alike, Deliverance depends entirely upon one's own efforts, the Buddha and the Christ being regarded as Guides and not Saviours. There is, too, similarity between the ceremony of Initiation of Christian Gnostics and that among Mahāyānists, and in the use of *Mantras* by both. The Gnostic *Sophia* ('Wisdom') and the *Prajñā* ('Wisdom') of the *Prajñā-Pāramitā* are equally personified as the Female Principle of Nature, or *Shakti* (Tib. *Yum*). The Un-Created, Non-Being, or Body of All-Intelligence, the Impersonal Deity of Christian Gnosticism, may be compared with the Voidness of the Mahāyānic Schools. And the Supreme Pleroma of Light Ineffable, of the *Pistis Sophia*, is not unlike the Beyond-Nature *Nirvāṇa*.

In drawing all such parallels, it is necessary to differentiate the Gnostic Christian ideal of asceticism and renunciation from that of the non-Gnostic Christian hermits who dwelt in the deserts of Egypt and elsewhere in the Near East [1] and of their successors in the different monastic orders of the Christian Church as now organized.

The Gnostic Christian, like the Buddhist, but unlike the later Church-Council Christian, held as fundamental the doctrine of rebirth ; [2] so that his highest ideal was to acquire such degree of positive and direct spiritual insight while on Earth as, after many pious lifetimes, would ultimately produce in him the Enlightenment of Christhood. And the Gnostic Christian prayed that upon his own attainment of Christhood he might be empowered to assist all mankind to reach the same Goal. On the other hand, the Church-Council Christian, being forbidden, by the Second Council of Constantinople of A.D. 553, to believe in the doctrine of rebirth,[3] was unable to hold

---

[1] Cf. *The Paradise of the Holy Fathers*, as translated out of the Syriac by E. A. Wallis-Budge (London, 1907).

[2] Cf. G. R. S. Mead, *The Pistis Sophia* (London, 1921), p. xlv ; and *Fragments of a Faith Forgotten* (London, 1900).

[3] The decree is as follows : ' Whosoever shall support the mythical doctrine of the pre-existence of the soul, and the consequent wonderful opinion of its return, let him be anathema.' Thus not until A.D. 553 did the rebirth doctrine

the altruistic ideal of his Gnostic brother, and so came to adopt the lesser ideal of salvation for self alone, by faith in the infallibility of the Church's decrees and teachings. The effect on human society of the Gnostic hermit's altruistic ideal is positive, and creative, and unlimited, while that of the Church-Council Christian hermit's is, by contrast, negative, non-creative, and selfish.

The Christian Gnostic seeks Realization; and, like the Kargyütpas, and the *Yogīs* among the Hindus, and the *Sufīs* among the Moslems, rejects that peculiar form of Occidental intellectualism favoured by Church Councils which leads to the formulation of creeds beginning with ' I believe' and of decrees of anathema for not believing, and holds fast only to Realized or Realizable Knowledge.

From this point of view, the followers of Milarepa are the Gnostics (' Knowing Ones ') among Buddhists, as the followers of Valentinus and Marcion were among Christians; and, like all the Christian Gnostics, they are the 'heretical' opponents of every dogma or creed intellectually based wholly upon Scriptures and Traditions, as Milarepa's teachings contained herein show unmistakably.

## VII. DISSENTING SECTS

Marpa the Translator, a native-born Tibetan, is, as has been seen, the Apostle of the period of transition in the Kargyütpa history. Preceding him are the two Indian Apostles, Tilopa and Naropa, and after him Milarepa. In other words, Marpa was the scholar-transmitter, Milarepa the book-renouncing Gnostic-Buddhist saint, in whom the Kargyütpa Teachings were put to the test of scientific experimentation, so that their gold was extracted from their base metal. Whereas Tsongkhapa's reform was chiefly external and ecclesiastical, and led to the alliance of Buddhism and temporal power centred in a highly organized Church, Milarepa's reform was internal and far more conducive to a purification of the Faith.

become to official Christianity a ' heresy'. Before that date it was, presumably, tolerated among Church-Council Christians, especially among those of them who were friendly to the Gnostic form of Christianity.

The austerity of Milarepa's rules was, as was but to be expected, unpopular with those of Marpa's followers who loved the household life, which Marpa himself never renounced, and perhaps also loved the pomp of ecclesiasticism. Others, more given to Black than to White Magic, seceded from Milarepa. Hence there arose four chief dissenting sub-sects of the Kargyütpas : (1) The Karma-pa, named after its founder, Karma-pa Rangchung-Dorje, a pupil of Dvag-po-Lharje, Milarepa's chief disciple and apostolic successor, is the most important. Since its rise, in the latter half of the twelfth century, it has lived on in Tibet and in Sikkim. (2) The Dug-pa (from *Dug*, ' Thunder Dragon', and so referring to those who are of the Thunder-Dragon School), is second in importance. It consists of three branches: the Lower Dug-pa; the Middle and Southern Dug-pa (now the Established Church of Bhutan); and the Upper Dug-pa. (3) The Dī-Kung-pa, named after the Dī-kung Monastery, and (4) the Ta-lung-pa, named after the Ta-lung Monastery, are the other two of the surviving dissenting bodies. These dissenting sects differ from one another ' merely in having adopted a different revelation from the Ñingma Sect as a code of demoniacal worship, and so relaxing the purity of the former Kargyütpa practice '.[1]

As Dr. Waddell has very wisely emphasized, ' much confusion has been caused in European books by misusing the name Dug-pa, employing it as a synonym for the Red Cap Sect, which properly is the Ñingma '.[2] Furthermore, to assume, as certain non-Tibetan critics of Padma Sambhava seem to assume, that all Red Caps are Dug-pas, is equally erroneous. There appears, too, to be need to emphasize that despite the traditional antagonism existing between the ' Reformed' Yellow Cap Sects and the ' Old-Style' Red Cap Sects of Padma Sambhava, ' the Lāmas who belong to the Yellow Cap Sects acknowledge the superiority of their brethren in the various Red Cap Sects in all questions more or less connected with magic and occult sciences '.[3]

[1, 2] L. A. Waddell, *The Buddhism of Tibet* (London, 1895), pp. 67–9.
[3] A. David-Neel, *My Journey to Lhasa* (London, 1927), p. 181.

The following genealogical tree of *Lāmaist* Sects (based on
that published by Dr. Waddell in his *Buddhism of Tibet*,
p. 55) will help to correct such errors.  In addition, it indicates
very concisely the origin and interdependence of all the chief
sects of Tibetan Buddhism and the important place which the
Kargyütpa Sect occupies amongst them.

VIII.   GENEALOGICAL TREE OF *LĀMAIST* SECTS

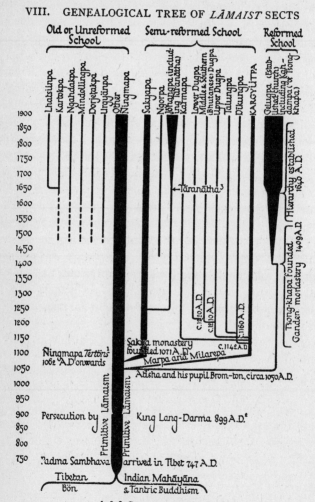

¹, ², ³ See page opposite.

## IX. THE DEFENCE OF THE HERMIT IDEAL

To the ordinary European and American, accustomed, perhaps too much, to modern comforts and luxuries, the life lived by the Kargyütpa hermits, and by others like them, amid the climatic rigours of the snowy Himalayas, clad only in a thin cotton garment, subsisting on a daily handful of parched barley, supplemented by roots and herbs, and now and then a little yak's milk brought by pious laymen, and freed from all worldly possessions and untroubled by worldly quests, may, possibly, seem an outcome of unreasoning religious zeal.

It should not be forgotten, however, that the hermit, in his turn, views with deep compassion his brethren immersed in the world ; and, while they struggle for the world's baubles, he is offering up prayer for them, that their Ignorance (*Avidyā*) may be dissipated and their feet set upon the Path of the Great Deliverance.   Full of pity, he looks out over the human race with eyes of spiritual insight, as the Buddha Gautama did, and beholds mankind fettered like chained slaves by their own conventionalities—many of which are, in fact, indefensible. He sees his fellow-men being held by their *karma*, the results of their previous actions, to the tread-mill of the Twelve *Nidānas*, the mutually interdependent causes of *sangsāric* existence,[1] and being reborn interminably, but to fall, each time, victims to sorrow, old age, illness, and death. And he contemplates the coming of the time when he shall be empowered to go forth and lead them to Freedom.

[1] The Twelve *Nidānas* are described on p. 138[2], following.

---

[1] The *Tertöns*, i.e. 'Takers-out of *Terma* (Hidden Revelations)', play an important part in the development of Lāmaism. The *Bardo Thödol* is itself such a *Terma;* see *The Tibetan Book of the Dead*, pp. 73-7.

[2] Lang-Dar-ma, having become an apostate from Lāmaism, appears to have instigated the murder of his brother Ti-song De-tsen, the famous Buddhist King, in A.D. 899. Thus gaining the throne, he persecuted Lāmaism for about three years, his reign ending with his assassination by Lāma Pal-dorje (Cf. L.A. Waddell, op. cit., p. 34).

[3] Tāranātha is one of the great personalities of Tibetan history. Born in Tsang, Tibet, in A.D. 1573, he died in Mongolia, where he had founded several monasteries under the auspices of the Chinese Emperor and was canonized, his reincarnated successors becoming the Grand Lāmas of Urgya (in the Khalka province of Mongolia, east of Lob-Nor). (Cf. L.A. Waddell, op. cit., pp. 70-71.)

Thus, to the *yogī*, human life is a Net of *Māyā* (Illusion), in which, like trapped creatures, human beings struggle ; desirable only when directed to the one aim, of reaching, by right use of it, the Beyond-Nature, freed from all conditioned states of transitory and phenomenal being, as by a boat one crosses an ocean to the farther shore.

As one of the Hindu *yogīs* once asked the writer, when, on pilgrimage to Badrinath, the latter met him at his hermitage near the wild frontiers of Garhwal and Tibet, 'Can aircraft and wireless telegraphy and all your modern comforts bring true happiness to the Race? Or can blind faith in the infallibility of Holy Books bring Emancipation without Knowledge won by practice of religion?'

We, too, ought seriously to consider whether the ideal which Milarepa offers to us is not, after all, more truly cultural than the ideal of the financier in Wall Street or that of the pleasure-seeker in Paris.

Apart from their comparative value to society, the *yogī* teaches that all states of human activity, being *karmic*, are in themselves justified ; for to him the world is a vast School of many gradations, some pupils being in the kindergarten, the majority in the middle forms, and a few ready to pass on to the University, wherein matriculation comes by successful world-renunciation. Those who have evolved beyond the desires of the worldly life are to him of greater value to society than those who are still enamoured of the world.

In Milarepa's *Gur-Bum*, or 'One Hundred Thousand Songs', it is recorded that when the King of Khokhom and Yerang, in Nepal, invited Milarepa to the royal presence and he refused to leave the hermitage, the one who delivered the invitation asked, 'When a *yogī*, who is a mere man, is summoned by a mighty king is it not seemly that he should set out and go to do homage at the king's feet?' Milarepa replied, 'I am likewise a mighty king, of the Wheel that Revolveth ; and a king who aboundeth in riches is in no wise happier or mightier than I.' Then when the spokesman asked where Milarepa's kingdom was, Milarepa answered: 'Ye circle of officials of the Kingdoms of the World, if ye but served such a Kingdom as is mine, ye would be transformed into the mightiest of monarchs ; and the power and wealth of all things would spring forth [for you].'[1]

Human beings immersed in the Illusion sprung from Ignorance, that Platonic Cave of Shadows, and not striving to know themselves, have been compared by the *yogī* to fish in a pond, which, satisfied with the pond and the fish existence, have no desire to quit the water-world and live in the air ; or to deer in a forest who prefer to continue to be deer though there be offered to them the chance of becoming human.

It must equally be kept in mind, in judging the *yogī*, that he claims to have proved, at least to himself, by methods as careful and scientific in their own realm as those known in the laboratories of the West in the realm of physical science, that the ideals of the worldly are merely the ideals of an immature social order, of races still in the lower and middle grades of the World-School. Whether he be believed or not does not affect his conviction. When, as he may point out, five centuries ago Europeans believed the world to be flat it was really spherical ; and now, likewise, the acceptance or rejection of his view of human life cannot possibly change whatever is.

It has been said, although usually not accepted, that the saints of Europe were in the past a lightning conductor to draw away from the West the wrath of God. This, in a manner, is not unlike the belief, current among Hindus and Buddhists, that the Great *Rishis* have been and are the Guardians of the Human Race. Even to-day, in Ceylon, the Buddhist prays that his next birth may be among the Gods on the Himalayas. A Bengali hermit who had renounced a vast worldly estate in Calcutta at the age of twenty-five and who, since then, had been practising *yoga* for seventy-five years, in the high Himalayas where I met him, pointed out to me some of the snowy ranges, in the direction of Mount Kailāsa, whence the Gods keep watch over and direct the spiritual growth of our Race. Though invisible to the eyes of normal men, these Beings are, he added, visible to Seers and can be communicated with by the pure in heart ; and, as Silent Sentinels, They look out with divine com-

[1] Cf. G. Sandberg, *Tibet and the Tibetans* (London, 1906), pp. 262-3.

passion from the Himalayan Ramparts of the Earth, till the Kali-Yuga Night shall have run its still long course and the Day of Awakening dawns over all the nations.

Milarepa, too, as one who had won admission into the Society of the Enlightened Ones, tells us in one of his hymns (see page 216) how he—Great *Yogī* that he was—shoots out, like arrows over the world, good thoughts, bearing grace and spiritual power, and how these, upon striking those who are receptive, implant his blessings in the hearts of men.

As from mighty broadcasting stations, dynamically charged with thought-forces, the Great Ones broadcast over the Earth that Vital Spirituality which alone makes human evolution possible; as the Sun sustains the physical man, They sustain the psychic man, and make possible mankind's escape from the Net of *Sangsāric* Existence. Linked, as They are, in the Chain of Being, with Humanity on Earth and the Enlightened Ones beyond Nature, they fulfil a function far more important than that of all the Kings and Rulers among men. This, in short, is the conviction to which the developed *yogī* eventually attains. The Translator himself supported it; for he, when a young man in Bhutan, renounced the worldly life and went into hermitage with his *Guru*, the late Hermit *Guru* Norbu, near Buxuadar, and would never have returned to the world had not his father, then an old man needing his support, called him home and requested him to marry and continue the family.

The worldly, in their foolish wisdom, regard the Great *Yogī*, sitting in silent meditation and *Samādhi* on the Himalayan Heights, as a useless member of society, as one who has deserted his duties in the world in order to win for himself a selfish salvation. If this were, perhaps, a criticism applicable to some of the hermits of the Egyptian deserts, it is not applicable to the Kargyütpa hermits, nor to such sincere Indian *yogīs* as the writer has met.

Nowhere, in the course of his researches among the living saints of the Himalayas and of Hindustan, has the writer encountered a genuine *yogī* whose ideal was not unselfish preparation for service to the Race. One of them, although by birth a Brāhmana, had left behind him all distinctions of caste and creed and, regarding all mankind as his brethren, was looking forward—though it may be that many incarnations were yet to be his lot—to the time when he would be able to return to the world and proclaim Truth Realizable. For him, Renunciation must precede Conquest of Life, as Jesus, too, proclaimed to the rich young man of the world who asked Him the way to Salvation ; and Truth Realized must precede the task of teaching and guiding an unenlightened humanity. If the Teacher has not himself seen the Light how can he proclaim it to others ?

Thus it is that the highest aim of every sincere *yogī*, be he Hindu, Buddhist, Jain, Taoist, Sufī, or Gnostic Christian, is first to fit himself to become a World-Teacher and then to return to human society and carry out his Vow.[1] To him, one lifetime is but as a day ; and though many thousand lifetimes in the fleshly form should be necessary to reach Enlightenment, all the while, through the centuries, he must unwaveringly hold fast to the life which he has voluntarily chosen. And he has so chosen, because, in past lives, he has lived the worldly life, marrying and giving in marriage, tasting pleasure, filled with insatiable ambitions ; and, learning the lessons taught by such lives, has risen to a place among the higher species of his race.[2]

---

[1] The Vow to attain the state of the Bodhisattva, or Great Teacher, leading to the treading of the Higher Path, as in the Mahāyāna School, is fourfold : (1) to bring about the salvation of all sentient beings, (2) to bring about the destruction of all *sangsāric* passions in oneself, (3) to realize and then to teach others the Truth, and (4) to set others on the Path leading to Buddhahood. The Vow implies that *Nirvāṇa* will not be entered into, by the one taking the Vow, until all creatures, from the lowest in sub-human kingdoms on this and every other planet to the highest of unenlightened gods in the heaven-worlds and the most fallen of dwellers in hell-worlds, are guided safely across the Ocean of the *Sangsāra* to the Other Shore of Eternal Deliverance. The doctrine of Never-Ending Damnation finds no place in this universal altruism, being held to be— as Origen, the great Christian, also maintained—incompatible with the All-Embracing Love of the Good Law.  (See p. 151[2].)

The Vow to attain the state of the Pratyeka (or Non-Teaching) Buddha belongs to the Lesser Path, the Hīnayāna. But even on this Path direct benefit to humanity is conferred in other ways, as, for instance, by silent and invisible broadcasting of spiritual influences over all the nations, thereby invigorating and helping to maintain in activity the higher nature of man, as the sun's rays do the physical man.

[2] This, however, does not imply that the *yogī's* asceticism precludes his

Having realized that the worldly life is not the highest state on Earth, he has relinquished it ; and, like one come out of a cave into the light of day, no longer has he any desire to return to the Shadows. The Path he has chosen leads to the Higher Evolution, to the Beyond-Nature ; its Goal is the deliverance from the limited personality in the All-Enlightenment, the transmutation, by the alchemy of Right Knowledge, of the mundane into the Supra-Mundane—the Uncognizable, the Unknowable, the Unborn, Unmade, *Nirvāṇa*.

## X. THE *ARHANT* PROBLEM

All of this leads us to a problem which has, of late, been discussed even among European thinkers. 'Are there', is a question which has been addressed to the writer, 'members of the human race who have reached, as Milarepa is believed to have done, the height of such spiritual and physical evolution as this planet admits ; and who being, as it were, a species apart from other human beings, are possessed of mastery over natural forces as yet undiscovered, but probably suspected, by Western Science ?' This, it seems to us, is the most important anthropological question which Milarepa's *Biography* raises.

That men so highly developed now exist, and that there have been others of the same species in every age, is the claim of all the Great *Rishis* who have made India illustrious. The Buddhists hold that the Buddha Gautama, Himself One of the Great *Rishis*, is but One of many Buddhas, the beginning of Whose Dynasty is lost in remote antiquity. The Hindus make the same claim concerning their Hindu *Rishis* ; and the modern followers of the Great *Rishis*, who are the *yogīs*, some of one Faith, some of another, a few Indian Christians being numbered among them, hold firmly to it.

The *Arhant* Problem obviously being of very great impor-

helping to continue the ordinary human species ; for one part of the ideal of asceticism in the Orient is indomitable control and right use of the whole of the physical organism rather than that common misuse of it which results in licentiousness. Many Great *Yogīs*. as was the case with Gautama the Buddha, have first entered the married state, and then, having passed out of it, have altruistically dedicated the larger portion of their life to working for social betterment. To work only for family or nation is for them selfish, there being but the One Family and the One Nation, Humanity.

tance in itself, and in relation to Milarepa, some consideration
of it may fittingly be included in this Introduction.

An *Arhant* being defined as a Perfected Saint on Earth,[1]
One who has reached the Goal of Enlightenment, it will, at the
outset, be seen that a saintly hermit, Kargyütpa or other, is not
necessarily an *Arhant*, and may, in fact, be no nearer Arhantship than an ordinary householder.[2] The following postulates
may, however, be made : (1) That hermits exist in Tibet and
in the adjacent Himalayan States, as in India, can easily be
proved. (2) That most of them are practising Buddhist ascetics
and Hindu *yogīs*, making serious efforts to tread the path to
Arhantship, is equally true. (3) That reliable evidence suggests
that among so many aspirants there are, as might perhaps
reasonably be expected, a few, exceedingly few, probably not
one per ten thousand, in advanced stages of sainthood, who do
reach or at least nearly reach the Goal, as Milarepa is represented
as doing.

The Tibetans, on their part, maintain that it is quite as
feasible to traverse the path to Arhantship to its very end in
this age as it has been in any past age ; and, in justification,
assert that there are men now living among them who have
done so, as Milarepa, their National Saint, did during the
eleventh century A. D.[3] Although the assertion may not be
demonstrable to a person who is not an *Arhant*, or who dis-
believes in *Arhants*, and therefore needs to be accepted, if at

---

[1] Following the Mahāyāna School, an *Arhant* (or *Arhat*) is one who has
attained to the first stage of Bodhisattvic perfections. Following the Tantric
School (as apart from the Mahāyāna, with which in Milarepa's *yogic* practices
it is amalgamated), an *Arhant* is one who has attained to such a high degree of
spiritual development as to have won initiation into the fourth order of Tantric
Initiates.

[2] 'An *Arhant* being one who, having eradicated Lust, Anger, and Ignorance,
is freed from the thraldom of the Twelve *Nidānas* and from every *sangsāric*
fetter, the state of the *bhikṣhu*, or ascetic who has renounced the worldly life,
affords the most natural approach to Arhantship. It is said that if a householder
attains to Arhantship he either renounces the world within seven days thereafter and becomes a monk, or else enters into his *Pari-Nirvāṇa*.'—Sri Nissanka.

[3] 'Although many of our scholars in the Southern School may not accept this
view of the Northern School, they are, however, unable to find anywhere in
the Pali Canon teachings of the Buddha to the contrary. The *Satipaṭṭhāna Sutta*
is emphatic on the possibility of the attainment of Arhantship.'—Sri Nissanka.

all, on faith, it may be literally true. How many of us know by personal realization that the sun is 93,000,000 miles or so distant, or that any other generally accepted fact of natural science is true? We believe such facts by force of our social psychology and of recently acquired mental predisposition. To have faith about *Arhants* appears to be, though it ought not to be, much more difficult. Perhaps this is due to our having unconsciously become so dominated by scientific faith, i. e. faith in physical facts, that we have become unfitted to retain our old ancestral faith in facts which are super-physical.

Nevertheless, the more the writer has examined the Tibetan's claim to *Arhants*, the more convinced he has become that it ought not to be lightly set aside as it is apt to be by Christians, and even by Southern Buddhists, who, probably seeing no evidence of actual *Arhants* among themselves, are inclined to conclude that there can be no *Arhants* anywhere else, more especially among 'heretical' Northern Buddhists and Hindus.

If the application of the Sermon on the Mount, or the treading of the Noble Eightfold Path, were no longer practicable, then there would be—so our *yogī* friends contend—sound reason to sustain this sceptical attitude of the European or of the Southern Buddhist.

The writer, in venturing herein to put on record some results of his Tibetan and Indian researches, extending over more than five years, can, of course, only speak for himself and let his conclusions be taken for what they are worth. He, as a result of his inquiries, has good reason to think that among the Himalayan hermits (a few of whom he has conversed with in their own environments) there are possibly some—if perchance there be but two or three—who, having gone forth into homelessness, as did the Great *Arhant*, the Truly Enlightened One, have reached the Goal. In other words, the path to Arhantship appears still to be open.

These Awakened Ones have reached Deliverance from Ignorance, from Craving for *Sangsāric* Existence, from further *karmic* need of birth and death. Of Milarepa, after he had reached Enlightenment, it is written, in Rechung's Introduction, '[He was] one who, having had the advantage of holy and sacred teachers, stored up the life-giving elixir that fell from their lips, and tasted it for himself in the delightful solitude of mountain retreats, thereby obtaining emancipation from the toils of Ignorance, [so that] the seeds of Experience and Inspiration sprouted up in him and attained to full growth. . . . [He was] one who reached Those dwelling in the City of the Great Emancipation, wherein every one existeth in indescribable bliss. . . .'

To the mystic of the Orient, an *Arhant* is one who reaches perfection on Earth only after many lives dedicated to the greatest of all great adventures; he is the quintessence of all human enlightenment and progress throughout the ages, the rare efflorescence of society, the link uniting mankind to the Higher Culture.

Given the beliefs of the Oriental mystic, it is not unreasonable, and certainly not unscientific, to believe that the ordinary man is far from the top of the ladder of spiritual achievement; and, therefore, it is not only probable, but necessary, that there should be, as there are said to have been, and as it is believed there will be in the future, from among this world's millions of human beings at least a few in every generation who keep open, as Plato would say, the Sacred Way from the Plains of Earth to the Heights of Olympus. If there be no such Guardians of the Sacred Way of the Greater Evolution, then, indeed, would the path to Arhantship be impassable and the Goal unrealizable for mankind; all escape from the *Sangsāra* would be cut off.

If this view of the Indian Seers be right, then all of the Supreme World-Teachers—Who were *Arhants*, and more than *Arhants*—become understandable to us who yet dwell in the *Sangsāra* through which They passed to Freedom; and we see Them as truly our own Brethren, as Guides Who have explored and marked out and still guard for us the Way, and bid us follow Them.

As the followers of Milarepa contend, in Truth-seeking, Truth can be found only through Realization of Truth, in the Gnostic sense, and not by intellectual speculation; so, in deciding whether or not there are *Arhants* now, in Tibet or elsewhere in the world, the only valid and scientific procedure is to explore for oneself the path leading to Arhantship, as Milarepa herein bids us do.

Even the sceptic need only have faith enough to believe in the possibility of such a path in order to find and examine it. If this faith be lacking, then, inevitably, the quest would be utterly hopeless and the sceptic would continue to be as Milarepa's School teaches that he is—the slave of Time and Change. Without faith that a certain experiment may lead to a certain result, no chemist or physicist could possibly discover fresh scientific truths ; and no man can ever expect to discover that New World, of which Milarepa sings in his ecstatic joy of triumph, unless he first sets up a postulate that there is a New World awaiting his discovery.

Among human beings, fortunately, a vast majority still do possess such faith, because they believe that Evolution does not come to an end in man, who is, biologically considered, merely the highest of the animal beings. The Hindu and the Jain, the Taoist and the Christian, and the Moslem Sufī, no less than the Buddhists of all Schools, have their own *Gurus* to point out the Way.

## XI. THE TEXT AND ITS TRANSLATION

The late Lāma Kazi Dawa-Samdup, of whom the Editor has given a brief biographical account in the Introduction to *The Tibetan Book of the Dead*, began the English translation of the *Jetsün-Kahbum*, upon which our version is based, on the twenty-second day of June, 1902 ; and, working on it periodically when he could spare time—he being the sole support of an aged father and mother and a wife and three children—completed it on the twenty-ninth day of January, 1917.

Then, during the year 1920, whilst he was Headmaster of the Maharaja's Bhutia Boarding School, near Gangtok, Sikkim (formerly a part of Tibet), he began preparing the translation for publication, aided by Major W. L. Campbell, who was then the Political Officer representing the British Government in Tibet, Bhutan, and Sikkim, and himself a Tibetan scholar. The Editor, too, was then in Gangtok, working with the Lāma on the translation of *The Tibetan Book of the Dead* and other Tibetan religious treatises, and saw something of the progress made with the *Jetsün-Kahbum*. Upon the premature death of the Lāma, in March 1922, shortly after his appointment to the Tibetan Professorship in the University of Calcutta, the work in preparation for the publishing of Jetsün's *Biography* was left unfinished.

Thereafter, the Editor, while on a visit to the late Lāma's home at Kalimpong, beyond Darjeeling, in the year 1924, secured from the late Lāma's surviving son the original manuscript translation; and in the autumn of the following year at Oxford began the adaptation of the translation which is here presented.

It had always been the hope of the Translator to supervise the publication of the translation; and had he lived to do so, all errors which may possibly have crept into our version would, no doubt, have been eliminated. But rather than postpone publication indefinitely, the Editor has thought it wiser to offer to the world the translation in the form which now has been given to it, while faithfully following the Translator's manuscript.

In his English rendering, the Translator kept as close to the literal sense of the Tibetan text as the idioms of the two languages permit, or as is compatible with literary English, except in a comparatively few instances, where, as he said, it was preferable to bring out, in a somewhat freer manner, the real meaning intended rather than translate literally abstruse metaphysical terms and phrases which—even if they could be Englished—would fail to convey the meaning an initiated *lāma* would gather from them in the original.

Extracts and parts, both from the *Biography* and from the *Songs* (or *Hymns*), have, of late, now and then appeared in translation in various European languages. The Government of India, for example, published in the year 1914 the late Lāma Kazi Dawa-Samdup's first English rendering of the chapter of the *Biography* recording Jetsün's Meditation in Solitude, which, according to our editing, is Chapter X, for use in connexion with the high proficiency examination in Tibetan.

During the summer of 1925 there appeared an abridged translation of the *Biography*, in French, by M. Jacques Bacot. There is a Mongolian version of the *Biography* and probably another in Chinese. Our English version is the first complete translation to be published in an Occidental tongue.[1]

As M. Bacot in his letters to me has stated, there seems to be one generally accepted and more or less standardized Tibetan text; but in different editions, according to the monastery in which the printing is done, there are minor differences in orthography. The Colophons, too, may differ according to the scribe who prepared the text for publication. M. Bacot adds that in the last two chapters of the late Lāma Dawa-Samdup's English rendering, copies of which were lent to him by Major W. L. Campbell, the folio numbers given of the corresponding Tibetan text do not agree with those from which he made his French translation. Evidently, then, our version and his are based upon different Tibetan editions.

The Appendix of our edition (see page 306) records that Gampopa also wrote a Biography of Jetsün. Of this, however, we have no knowledge. Nor can we determine whether or not there is more than one version attributed to Rechung. In his own valuable Introduction, M. Bacot has discussed these and kindred technical problems; and to his *Milarepa* the student is referred for further information.

The Editor's interest being anthropological rather than philological, he has not aimed at the production of a standardized version; nor would he have been fitted to produce one had all the necessary data and material been available. This important task remains for scholars of the future, who, it is hoped, will

---

[1] Apart from our own and M. Bacot's version of the *Biography*, the chief matter so far published in Europe and America concerning Milarepa is, in order of publication, as follows: H. A. Jäschke, *Proben aus dem tibetischen Legendenbuche; die hundert-tausend Gesänge des Milaraspa*, in the *Zeitschrift der Deutschen Morgenländischen Gesellschaft* (Leipzig, 1869), xxiii, 543–58; W. W. Rockhill, *The Tibetan Hundred Thousand Songs' of Milaraspa*, in the *Journal of the American Oriental Society* (New Haven, 1884), xi, Proc. 207-11; L. A. Waddell, *The Buddhism of Tibet* (London, 1895), pp. 64-7; Berthold Laufer, *Zwei Legenden des Milaraspa* (Wien, 1901), *Aus den Geschichten und Liedern des Milaraspa* (Wien, 1902); G. Sandberg, *Tibet and the Tibetans* (London, 1906), ch. xiii; Berthold Laufer, *Milaraspa* (1922).

eventually produce a scientifically accurate Tibetan text and so facilitate the eliminating from our own English version of any inaccuracies which may have crept into it.

### XII. THE PLACE OF THE *JETSÜN-KAHBUM* IN THE LITERATURE OF TIBET

In Tibet itself, the *Jetsün-Kahbum* possesses the rare distinction of being prized by the literary and learned classes as by the common unlearned folk. Of it the Translator has left behind him this scholarly judgement, which he recorded in manuscript to serve as part of an Introduction such as ours :—

'Although written more than eight hundred years ago, it is from beginning to end set down in such a plain and simple style of language that any ordinary Tibetan of to-day who can read at all can read it with ease and enjoyment. When we add to this that it tells the life-story of one who is looked up to and admired by all Tibetans, of every sect and school, as the Ideal Ascetic, or *Yogī*, and that he is no less esteemed as a poet and song-writer, whose songs are in everybody's mouth among the common people, somewhat like the songs of Burns in Scotland, we see how it is that this life of Milarepa is one of the most famous and favourite books of Tibet. For it is well admired by those who know how to write books as by those who only know how to read them when written.

'But in modern Tibetan works, the authors seem to be aiming more at dazzling and also puzzling the reader by their display of skill in framing cryptic, yet at the same time impeccably correct and grammatical sentences, with a view to arousing the reader's awe and admiration at their learning, than in setting down a plain tale in plain words that shall reach the reader's mind in the simplest and most direct manner.

'Notwithstanding the *Biography*'s simplicity and perfect freedom from needlessly complicated language, it possesses many beauties due to the way in which it is written, which can be appreciated, and are appreciated, by those who understand such things, even though they themselves do not feel inclined to imitate its simplicity and directness. What the author says in his versified note at the end of his work is no vain boast, but the simple truth :

> " This *Biography* [or *History*] hath been made beautiful at the beginning and end with ornate language ;
> May it thus be a feast of delight to all scholars and lovers of literature."

And such a feast of delight it truly is, in the original.

'Being thus both simple and yet studded with literary beauties, it is, in the original, about the best possible book that a foreign student of Tibetan can take up with a view to improving and extending his knowledge of the language. Alexander Csoma-de-Körös, the great Hungarian Tibetan scholar who made the first Tibetan Dictionary and Grammar, and Jäschke, and Sarat Chandra Das, have all taken this book as one of the standard works on Tibetan in compiling their Dictionaries. Yet, at the same time, such a student will also find, to his pleasure, that he is doing himself a benefit of another and as excellent a kind ; for he will discover that he is making the acquaintance of one who is numbered among the Great Saints of Tibet, as Sri Krishna is among those of India, or as Saint Francis is among those of Europe. And, perhaps, as he goes on with his reading and study, he may learn to love and admire Milarepa. Perhaps, too, as he follows the life of the Saint, he may come to pass a kindlier judgement upon Tibetan life and religion and custom than his reading of books by foreigners about our country may have led him to form.

'At any rate, something of this kind is what I (the present Translator) had in view in making this translation. I wished to show to cultured Western eyes one of our Great Teachers, as he actually lived, in a biography of him, much of which is couched in the words of his own mouth, and the remainder in the words of his disciple Rechung, who knew him in the flesh.'

### XIII.  MILAREPA AS ONE OF HUMANITY'S HEROES

Despite the many sectarian differences between the numerous sects of Tibetan Buddhism, all Tibetans alike unite in holding Jetsün Milarepa in the highest reverence and esteem ; and they consider him the very prototype of everything that a Great Saint should be. In this way, then, Milarepa may be said to belong to no one Sect or School.

Milarepa, the Socrates of Asia, counted the world's intellectualisms, its prizes, and it pleasures as naught; his supreme quest was for that personal discovery of Truth, which, as he teaches us, can be won only by introspection and self-analysis, through weighing life's values in the scale of the *Bodhi*-Illuminated mind. In him, the teachings of all the Great *Yogīs* of India, including the Greatest of them known to history, Gautama the Buddha, when put to the test of scientific experimentation, failed not. How many parallels, too, may be drawn between Jetsün's precepts recorded in this *Biography* and those of another Great Master of Life, will be seen by making comparison with the Sermon on the Mount.

As a member of the Mongolian Race, Milarepa, like Confucius, is but one more instance of the fact that genius recognizes no barriers in racial stock, or nationality, or creed, being as universally human as humanity itself.

May this Book help to spread understanding of this natural law of Universal Brotherhood. May it be one more humble memorial to its Great Hero. And may it go down to the generations yet unborn as a legacy from him who made possible its transmission to the European Races, its learned Translator, the late Lāma Kazi Dawa-Samdup.

## THE TRANQUIL

'Tranquil in body, speech, and mind, O mendicants,
Whoso in every way is well restrained,
Who all this world's desires hath thrown aside,
    He is "the tranquil" called.

'That mendicant, with utter joy and gladness filled,
Firm in the teaching of the Awakened One,
Reacheth the bliss where all conditions cease,
    Reacheth the State of Peace.'

The Buddha, from the *Dhammapada*, vv. 377, 380.
(F. L. Woodward's Translation.)

THE BANNER OF VICTORY

Described on pages 33[4], 87-8, 261

MILAREPA THE TIBETAN *YOGĪ*

Described on pages xxvi–xxvii

# INTRODUCTION

(from the Tibetan)

by

RECHUNG, DISCIPLE OF MILAREPA

Obeisance to the *Guru*!

[HEREIN] I wish to narrate the history of a Great *Yogī*, who lived in this high snow-clad table-land of Tibet. [He was] one who had been profoundly impressed from his early youth by the transient and impermanent nature of all conditions of worldly existence, and by the sufferings and wretchedness in which he saw all beings immersed. To him existence seemed like some huge furnace wherein all living creatures were roasting. With such piercing sorrow did this fill his heart that he was unable to feel any envy even of the celestial felicity enjoyed by Brahmā and Indra in their Heavens, much less of the earthly joys and delights afforded by a life of worldly greatness.

On the other hand, he was so captivated by the Vision of Immaculate Purity, by the Chaste Beauty found in the description of the State of Perfect Freedom and Omniscience associated with the attainment of *Nirvāṇa*, that he cared not even though he should lose his very life in the search on which he had set out, endowed as he was with faith, firm and full, a keen intellect, and a heart overflowing with all-pervading love and sympathy.

[He was] one who, having had the advantage of holy and sacred teachers, stored up the life-giving elixir that fell from their lips, and tasted it for himself in the delightful solitude of mountain retreats, thereby obtaining emancipation from the toils of Ignorance, [so that] the seeds of Experience and Inspiration sprouted up in him and attained to full growth.

[He was] one who, having thrown aside all concern for

worldly prospects, ease, name, and fame, resolutely devoted
himself to the single object of raising the banner of spiritual
development to such a height that it might serve as a guide
for future followers on the Path, as a signal sufficient to save
them from worldliness and dilatoriness, and to urge them on-
ward on the Upward Way.[1]

[He was] one who, having been favoured by gods and
angels, triumphed over the difficulties of the Path, obtaining
transcendent pre-eminence in spiritual truths and such depth
of knowledge and experience therein that religious devotion
became second nature to him.

[He was] one who, by his profound reverence for and sincere
belief in the Lineal *Gurus*,[2] obtained their grace and spiritual
support, and nomination as their adopted spiritual successor in
the promulgation of the Spiritual Truths, thereby manifesting
super-normal powers and signs of an incomparable nature and
unmistakable significance.

[He was] one who, by the power of the greatness of his
fervent, sincere, and altruistic love and compassion, was endowed with the power and gift of inspiring even unrighteous,
worldly, sin-hardened, sceptical scoffers and unbelievers with
involuntary emotion of soul-stirring faith, causing each hair on
their body to stand on end in thrilling ecstasy, and making the
tears to flow copiously from their eyes, thereby sowing in them
the seed of future redemption and enlightenment, and causing
it to sprout up in their heart by the mere hearing of his history
and name. Thus was he enabled to reclaim, redeem, and
protect them from the pains and terror of this low, worldly
existence.

[He was] one who, having mastered the mystic and occult

[1] The Upward Way is the Path of Renunciation (Skt. *Nivritti-Mārga*) leading
to *Nirvāṇa*, the Noble Eightfold Path, the *Via Sacra* of the Buddhas; whereas
attachment to worldliness is the Path of Enjoyment (Skt. *Pravritti-Mārga*).

[2] The Lineal *Gurus* are those of any School who are in apostolic succession,
Milarepa himself being the fourth in the Kargyütpa Line, as explained in our
Introduction. The importance of the spiritual succession is likewise recognized
in Brāhmanism with its three lines of *Gurus*, the *Divya*, *Siddha*, and *Mānava*,
the essential esoteric teachings being handed down not in books, but from *guru*
(teacher) to *shishya* (disciple). This process of transmission is known in Sanskrit
as *Pāramparya-krama*.

sciences, had communicated to him by the *Ḍākinīs*[1] con-
tinuously the four blissful states of ecstatic communion,[2] thus
furthering his spiritual growth.

[He was] one who eventually rid himself of the Twofold
Shadow [of Illusion and *Karma*[3]] and soared into Spiritual
Space, till he attained the Goal wherein all doctrines merge in
at-one-ment.

[He was] one who, having attained to omniscience, all-pervading goodwill, and glowing love, together with the acquisition of transcendental powers and virtues, became a self-de-
veloped Buddha, who towered above all conflicting opinions
and arguments of the various sects and creeds, like the topmost
gem that adorns the Banner of Victory.[4]

[He was] one who, having adopted the peerless *Vajra* Path,[5]
gave himself to assiduous endeavour, and attained the utmost
height of spiritual experience and knowledge.

[1] The *Ḍākinī*[s] (Tib. *Mkah-'gro-ma*—pron. *Kah-'gro-ma*) are fairy-like goddesses of various orders, possessed of peculiar occult powers. Many of them are
the chief deities invoked in the rituals of Tantricism, both Hindu and Buddhist.
In other contexts herein, *Ḍākinīs* has been translated as 'angels'.

[2] These, the four stages of *Dhyāna* (Tib. *Bsam-gtan*), have been given by the
Translator as follows : (1) Analysis (Skt. *Vitarka*) ; (2) Reflection (Skt. *Vichāra*) ;
(3) Fondness (Skt. *Prīti*) ; and (4) Bliss (Skt. *Sukha*). These are the four progressive mental states leading to the complete concentration of mind producing
ecstatic Illumination.

[3] Illusion (Skt. *Māyā* : Tib. *Sgyūma*—pron. *Gyūma*), or the universally human
animistic belief that phenomena in worlds, hells, and heavens are real, and that
the ego (itself a *karmic* conglomerate of characteristics acquired during in-
calculable aeons through experiences in the *Sangsāra* of phenomena) is real,
is the Twofold Shadow hiding Reality, which, being non-*sangsāric*, cannot
be realized either while one is immersed in existence on Earth or in any
after-death paradise—not even in the Heaven of the Semitic Faiths (Judaism,
Christianity, Islam), which is within the realm of phenomena, of appearances,
of personality, of sensation, of things. *Nirvāṇa* is beyond Nature, beyond
phenomena. It is the 'Unbecome, Unborn, Unmade, Unformed'—the One
Reality.

[4] This is one of the eight symbols of Northern Buddhism, called the Eight
Glorious Emblems, which are : (1) the Golden Fish, (2) the Royal Umbrella,
(3) the Conch-shell Trumpet of Victory, (4) the Lucky Diagram, (5) the
Banner of Victory, (6) the Vase, (7) the Lotus, and (8) the Wheel of the Law.
The Banner of Victory (Tib. *Rgyal-mts'an* : Skt. *Dhvaja*) symbolizes Victory
over the *Sangsāra*, or the attainment of Perfect Enlightenment—*Nirvāṇa*.

[5] The *Vajra* (or 'Immutable') Path (Skt. *Vajra-yāna*) is the Path of Mysticism
as known to the Kargyütpa Sect, in which Milarepa is one of the Great Dynasty,
or Line, of *Gurus*.

[He was] one whose fame of surpassing merit, being hymned by gods and angels, hath filled all the ten divisions of the universe[1] with the waving of the Banner of Fame, and with the reverberating tones of the Melody of Praise.

[He was] one whose physical body was pervaded by the descending bliss down to his very toes, and by the ascending bliss up to the crown of his head, where both merge in the moon-fluid bliss, thence rebounding and coursing down the three principal nerves, uncoiling the coils of the nerve-centres, and then finally enlarging the minutest nerves and changing them all into so many actual median-nerves.[2]

[He was] one who thus was able to expound fluently the meanings and ideas contained in the twelve collections of *Sūtras* and the Four Scriptures, and to render them into metrical stanzas to be sung in the rites and ritual of the *Vajra* Path.

[1] These are the four cardinal points, the four mid-way points, and the nadir and zenith.

[2] This paragraph refers to the *yogic* process, as in *Kuṇḍalinī Yoga*, of developing the psychic nerves (Skt. *nāḍī*) and psychic nerve-centres (Skt. *chakra*) of the human body. The psychic nerve situated in the hollow of the spinal column (Skt. *Brahma-daṇḍa*) is the chief, or median nerve (Skt. *suṣhumṇā-nāḍī*), and interconnected by it are the psychic nerve-centres, wherein are stored, like electricity in dynamos, the vital force (Skt. *prāṇa*), upon which all psycho-physical processes ultimately depend. Once the psychic nerve-centres have been awakened or uncoiled, beginning with the first, known as the Root-Support (Skt. *Mūlādhāra*) of the median-nerve, situated in the perineum, wherein the mighty occult power personified as the Goddess Kuṇḍalinī lies coiled like a serpent asleep, the *yogī* experiences Illumination. The Kuṇḍalinī, or Serpent, Power, having risen through the median-nerve and uncoiled the Root-Support, continues its upward course, penetrating and setting into psychic activity the second nerve-centre, called in Sanskrit the *Svādiṣhṭhāna*, which is the centre of the sex-organs, then the third, or navel nerve-centre, the *Maṇipūra-chakra*, then the fourth, or heart nerve-centre, the *Anāhata-chakra*, then the fifth, or throat nerve-centre, the *Vishuddha-chakra*, then the sixth, the *Ājñā-chakra*, situated between the eyebrows like a third eye, until, like mercury in a magic tube, it reaches the brain psychic nerve-centre, called the Thousand-Petalled Lotus (Skt. *Sahasrāra-Padma*), which is the Supreme, or Seventh, of the centres. Therein a subtle transformation is effected, in which the moon-fluid, or transmuted sex forces, are psycho-physically all-powerful. The divine bliss, arising from the Illumination, descends as heavenly ambrosia to feed all parts of the psychic body, even to the very toes. All the psychic nerve-centres are uncoiled, or set into functioning activity, and the smallest of the psychic nerves, compared to their undeveloped condition, are like median-nerves in the ecstatic condition of body such as Milarepa commonly enjoyed.

[He was] one who, having all his ideas and concepts merged with the Primal Cause, had eliminated the Illusion of Duality.[1]

[He was] one who, being well versed in the science of mind and intellect, read external phenomena like a book.

[He was] a being boundlessly endowed with grace, omni-science, and power, and able to develop and emancipate even dumb beasts by preaching to them.

[He was] a being who had passed beyond the need of ob-serving worldly rules, artificial conventions, and flattery, re-verently worshipped by all rational beings [gods and men] with profound obeisance, while he remained tranquil, dignified, and attentive.

[He was] a being most diligent and persevering in medita-tion upon the Rare Path, not excelled by, but rather excelling all other Great *Yogīs* and Bodhisattvas [2] of his own day who were similarly blest, becoming an object of worship even to them.

With the deep, thundering roar of a lion [3] he proclaimed the Truth of the realizable fact of the illusoriness of the Ego,[4] in the full assurance of its realization, awing and subduing beings and creatures of evil and selfish disposition, and revelled in freedom in the limitless and centreless sphere of the heavens, like an unbridled lion roaming free among the mountain ranges.

Having acquired full power over the mental states and faculties within, he overcame all dangers from the elements without, and directed them to his own profit and use.

Having obtained transcendental knowledge in the control

---

[1] The Primal Cause is Primordial Mind, the One Unity. All pairs of opposites being but concepts of the mundane mind, even the ultimate pair of opposites—*Sangsāra* and *Nirvāṇa*—when viewed by the supra-mundaneness of Enlightenment merge in at-one-ment, and Duality is realized to be Illusion.

[2] A Great *Yogī* (or Saint) is one who has attained mastery of the Occult Sciences; a *Bodhisattva* is one who, having progressed far on the *Bodhi* Path leading to Buddhahood, is destined to become a Buddha, or 'Enlightened One', and to teach the Way of Enlightenment to beings who are unenlightened.

[3] The proclamation of the Truth by one who has attained to *Bodhic* Enlighten-ment is figuratively known among Buddhists as the 'Lion's Roar' (Skt. *Singha-Nāda*).

[4] See p. 38[1], following.

of the ethereal and spiritual nature of the mind, he was enabled to furnish demonstration thereof by flying through the sky, by walking, resting, and sleeping [upheld by levitation] in the air.

Likewise he was able to produce flames of fire and springs of water from his body, and to transform his body at will into any object desired, thereby convincing unbelievers and turning them towards religious pursuits.

[He was] a being perfect in the practice of the four stages of meditation,[1] and thus able to project his subtle body so as to be present as the Presiding *Yogī* in all the Twenty-Four Holy Places where gods and angels assemble, like clouds, for spiritual communion.[2]

Being fearless in the knowledge of the indestructible nature of mind,[3] he was able to dominate gods and elementals of the eight different kinds, and make them carry out his commands instantaneously, in the fulfilment of the four classes of duties.[4]

[He was] a master architect, well versed in the exposition of the Science of the Clear Void of Mind,[5] wherein all forms and substances have their cause and origin.

---

[1] These are the four stages of *Dhyāna*, already given above, on page 33[2].

[2] These are the Twenty-Four Places of Pilgrimage (cf. p. 164), known also to Hinduism. With them are sometimes included the Eight Great Places of Cremation in India, where, if the cremation takes place, there results a more spiritual liberation and a consequent better rebirth than from cremation elsewhere. Taken together, they constitute the Thirty-Two Places of Pilgrimage (cf. p. 133), whence there are believed to emanate magnetic-like forces which aid psychic development and make devotion more meritorious and communion, of a telepathic sort, with such spiritual beings as naturally assemble there, very real. To Great *Yogīs*—as was the case with Milarepa—is commonly attributed the power of visiting these Sacred Centres of the Earth (comparable to the Psychic Nerve-Centres of the human organism) with an invisible or subtle body, in order to preside over, or take part in, the divine conclaves.

[3] This refers to the Mahāyāna doctrine that the state of mind as realized in the ecstatic illumination of Buddhahood is the only Reality. It is beyond the state of mundane and illusory or impermanent mind, which man, immersed in the *māyā* of *sangsāric* phenomena, alone knows. Being supra-mundane, it is beyond Nature (which is the Child of *Māyā*), beyond the *Sangsāra* (the phenomenal Universe) ; and so, subject neither to modification nor destruction, it is the Immutable, the Indestructible.

[4] These are : Love (Skt. *Maitreya*), Compassion (Skt. *Karuṇā*), Rejoicing (Skt. *Muditā*), and Almsgiving (Skt. *Upekṣhā*)—the four duties of a Bodhisattva.

[5] Here Mind is viewed as the Void (Tib. *Tong-pa-nyid* : Skt. *Shūnyatā*), which, however, is not the void of nothingness, but the primordial Uncreated.

[He was] a deeply skilled physician, well practised in the art of curing the chronic diseases of the [unenlightened] mind by applying the medicine of the Five Divine Wisdoms.[1]

[He was] an accomplished interpreter of the good or evil significations of the sounds inherent in all external and internal elements, while knowing each of them to be Audible Space.[2]

Unformed, incapable of being described in terms of phenomenal or *sangsāric* experience. In so far as it is the Uncreated, no attributes known to the finite world or mind can be given to it. As the *Dharma-Dhātu*, or 'Seed of Truth', it is the Source of the *Sangsāra*, or universe of phenomena. As the *Dharma-Kāya*, or 'Body of Truth', it is the Qualityless. It is the Thatness, the Norm of being, the Cause and Origin of all that constitutes finiteness.

[1] The Five Divine Wisdoms are: (1) the All-Pervading Wisdom of the *Dharma-Dhātu*; or the Wisdom born of the Voidness, which is all-pervading, symbolized in the first of the Five Dhyānī Buddhas, Vairochana, the Manifester, ' He who in Shapes Makes Visible' [the universe of matter]; (2) the Mirror-like Wisdom, symbolized by Akṣhobhya, the 'Unagitated One', or by his reflex Vajra-Sattva, the 'Triumphant One of Divine Heroic Mind', the second of the Dhyānī Buddhas; (3) the Wisdom of Equality, symbolized by the third of the Dhyānī Buddhas, Ratna-Sambhava, the 'Gem-born One', the Beautifier; (4) the Discriminating Wisdom, which enables the devotee to know each thing separately, yet all things as one, personified in the fourth Dhyānī Buddha, Amitābha, 'He of Boundless Light', the Illuminator or Enlightener; and (5) the All-Performing Wisdom, which gives perseverance and unerring action in things spiritual, symbolized in the fifth Dhyānī Buddha, Amogha-Siddhi, the ' Almighty Conqueror', the Giver of Divine Power. Through the Five Dhyānī Buddhas lies the Path leading to at-one-ment in the *Dharma-Kāya*, to the Perfect Enlightenment of Buddahood, to *Nirvāṇa*—which is spiritual emancipation from the round of births and deaths through the annihilation of the Flame of Desire.

[2] This paragraph refers to Milarepa's mastery of the occult science of *Mantras*, or Words of Power, based upon the physics of the law of vibration. According to the Mantrayāna ('Path of the Mantra') School, there is associated with each object and element of nature and with each organic creature, sub-human, human, and super-human, including the highest orders of deities—since all alike, being *sangsāric*, are subject to natural law—a particular rate of vibration. If this be known and formulated as sound in a *Mantra* and used expertly by a perfected *Yogī*, such as Milarepa was, it is held to be capable of disintegrating the object or element of which it is the key-note, or in vibratory accord; or, in the case of spiritual beings, of impelling the lesser deities and elementals to appear, and the superior deities to emit telepathically their divine influence in rays of grace. In *The Tibetan Book of the Dead* (p. 149) there occurs the following passage, referring to the six syllabic sounds—*Om Ma-ṇi Pad-me Hūṃ* (pron. *Ōm Mā-ṇi Pāy-mē Hüng*)—of the *Mantra* of Chenrazee (Skt. *Avalokiteshvara*), the National Divine Protector of Tibet, by means of which he is supplicated :—

' When the natural sound of Reality is reverberating [like] a thousand thunders,
      May they be transmuted into the sounds of the Six Syllables.'

[He was] a well-grounded mathematician who had attuned his own mental state to the unchanging level of Non-Ego,[1] while most clearly knowing all the inmost secrets and the deepest recesses of the minds of others.

[He was] a most learned professor in the Science of the Mind, having proved the Mind to be, beyond dispute, the Beginning and End of all visible phenomena, both material and spiritual, the Rays whereof, being allowed to shine unobstructedly, develop themselves, as he knew, into the three-fold manifestation of the Universal Divine Being through their own free, inherent power.[2]

[He was] a perfected adept in super-normal knowledge and powers, able to traverse and visit all the innumerable sacred Paradises and Heavens of the Buddhas, where, by the virtue of his all-absolving acts [of unsurpassed devotion], the Buddhas and Bodhisattvas presiding therein favoured him with dis-

---

[1] In the Buddhist view, the theory that there is a permanent, unchanging, eternal personal self, or ego, is erroneous. Reality implies supra-mundane consciousness undifferentiated, incompatible with individualized ego-consciousness. The supra-mundane consciousness is the All-Consciousness, to which, in comparison, the limited consciousness such as the soul hypothesis inculcates is incalculably and obviously inferior. Herein lies the fundamental difference between animistic Church-Council Christianity and metaphysical Buddhism.

[2] Supra-mundane Mind, being the One Reality, is the Source of Nature (or the *Sangsāra*), which, being wholly phenomenal, is in itself non-real. If the Rays, or the Inner Light, are allowed to dominate man, the mundane mind becomes transmuted into the Supra-mundane Mind, which has three aspects or manifestations : (1) *Dharma-Kāya*, ' Divine Body of Truth,' the Body of Complete Enlightenment ; (2) *Sambhoga-Kāya*, ' Divine Body of Perfect Endowment,' the primary reflex of the *Dharma-Kāya* ; and (3) *Nirmāṇa-Kāya*, ' Divine Body of Incarnation,' the secondary reflex of the *Dharma-Kāya*. The first is the Body of all Buddhas in *Nirvāṇa* ; the second, of all Bodhisattvas in Heaven-Worlds ; the third, of all Great Teachers on Earth.

In this context, ' Universal Divine Being' is not to be regarded as like the Personal Supreme God of the Semitic Faiths, but rather as a figurative personification of all supra-mundane forces, powers, or influences, that emanate from the Void, the Qualityless, the Unmade, Unformed, and make escape from the *Sangsāra*, from Nature, possible for mankind. Within It are contained, in indescribable unity, all the Great Ones of All the Ages, the Fully Enlightened Ones, the Buddhas, the Saviours of Mankind. No concepts of the limited human mind can be applied to It, only through Realization of It can It be understood. This is the teaching of the School of Milarepa, and of all the Esoteric Buddhism of the Higher Lāmaism, of which the uninitiated European knows very little, but about which he dogmatizes very much.

courses on the *Dharma*, and listened to his in return, so that he sanctified the Heaven-Worlds themselves by his visits and sojourns there.

Appearing to the creatures of the Six *Lokas*[1] in suitable and specially adapted forms and guises, on various occasions, in accordance with their *karmic* deserts, he taught them spiritual truths in a manner suited to the intellectual capacity and mood of his hearers, wrapping these truths in parables and metaphors which were in perfect accord with the Wisdom of the Victorious Ones,[2] thus by his Teachings procuring their emancipation.

In short, [he was] a being who within the space of one life-time obtained the Fourfold Personality,[3] and the Fivefold Perfections[4] which constitute the Omnipresent State of the Great Vajra-Dhara.[5]

[He was] one whose ceaseless grace and mercy were bestowed on the immeasurably countless multitude of sentient beings, for whose sake he continued setting the peerless Wheel of the Truth in motion, thereby redeeming them from the un-utterable anguish and woe of the *Sangsāra*.[6]

[He was] one who reached Those dwelling in the City of the Great Emancipation,[7] where every one existeth in indescribable

---

[1] The Six *Loka[s]* (or ' Planes ') of *Sangsāric* Existence are: (1) the World of the Gods (or *Devas*); (2) the World of the Titans (or *Asuras*); (3) the World of Mankind; (4) the World of Brutes; (5) the World of Unhappy Ghosts (or *Pretas*); and (6) the various Hells.

[2] That is, the Buddhas, Who are victorious over the *Sangsāra*, or the round of death and birth.

[3] The fourfold personality (or principle) consists of (1) Inhibiting evil thoughts, (2) Cutting off (or Annihilating) evil thoughts, (3) Encouraging good thoughts, and (4) Developing (or Perfecting) good thoughts.

[4] The fivefold perfections are those which flow from the Five Divine Wisdoms of the Dhyānī Buddhas. as outlined above on page 37[1].

[5] Tib. *Rdo-rje-ch'ang* (pron. *Dorje-Chang*): Skt. *Vajra-Dhara*, meaning ' The Indestructible (or Steadfast) Holder [of Mystic Power]', is one of the two Bodhisat reflexes of the Dhyānī Buddha Akshobhya, the other being Vajra-Sattva (' The Indestructible-minded One', or ' The Adamantine '). Both are esoteric deities. Vajra-Dhara is also the name of the Ādi (or Primordial) Buddha of the Gelugpa, the Established Church of Tibetan Buddhism; for the Ñingmapa, the ' Old-Style ' Church, Samanta-Bhadra is the name of the Ādi-Buddha.

[6] *Sangsāra*, or the round of death and birth, as known to mankind bound to the Wheel of Nature.

[7] That is, *Nirvāṇa*, known in Tibetan as ' The Sorrowless State.' (*Mya-ñan-med*).

bliss, at the same time obtaining and developing the Fourfold Principle of Immortality.

Such was the Great Being who shone the brightest among all Great Beings, called Glorious Jetsün-Mila-Zhadpa-Dorje,[1] the lustre of whose deeds and the effulgence of whose name shone like the sun and moon themselves.

Albeit the intrinsic value of the super-normal services he rendered to those whom he met can neither be described nor limited, yet I have attempted to set forth a brief eulogy of his various deeds. The *History* [or *Biography*] will be divided into two parts: first, that dealing with his worldly career, and second, that dealing with his religious career from its beginning right to the time when he attained *Nirvāṇa*.

At the outset, I shall proceed to relate some particulars regarding his surname Mila and its origin, his ancestors, and the circumstances of his birth. Then I shall tell of the loss of his father during his childhood, which turned his relatives into enemies who robbed the orphans and the widow of their whole patrimony and plunged them into great sorrow, which served to impress the truth of the existence of Sorrow indelibly upon Milarepa's heart. Then I shall tell of his studying the Black Art, so that he might be able to kill his enemies in compliance with his mother's command.

Of these three things, I shall now set forth, somewhat at length, the first, namely a few details concerning his birth and lineage.

---

[1] This is a shortened combination of Jetsün-Milarepa, the ordinary name, and of Pal-Zhadpa-Dorje, the initiatory name (as given on p. 133, following).

# PART I: THE PATH OF DARKNESS[1]

## CHAPTER I

## THE LINEAGE AND BIRTH

*Telling of Rechung's Dreams, which led to the Writing of this*
Biography; *and of Milarepa's Ancestry and Birth.*

AT one time, so I have heard, the Great *Yogī*, that Gem of
*Yogīs*—of the *Anuttara Vajra-Yāna School*[2]—Jetsün-Mila-
Zhadpa-Dorje, lived for a space in the Stomach-like Cave of
Nyanam,[3] which is now a most sacred place of pilgrimage. In
that place were to be found the illustrious Great Ones, Re-
chung-Dorje-Tagpa, Shiwa-Wöd-Repa, Ngan-Dzong-Repa,
Seban-Repa, Khyira-Repa, Bri-Gom-Repa, Lan-Gom-Repa,
Sangyay-Kyap-Repa, Shan-Gom-Repa, Dampa-Gya-Phūpa,
and Tönpa-Shākya-Guna.[4] These were his disciples of the

---

[1] All headings throughout the *Biography*, of Parts and Chapters, and the
Synopsis at the head of each chapter, have been added by the Editor, for the
purpose of securing greater clearness, the Tibetan of the text itself not containing,
but suggesting them.

[2] Or 'School of the Immutable (or *Vajra*) Path of the *Anuttara* [*Tantra*]'.
This is one of the distinctly Esoteric Schools of Mahāyāna Buddhism, based
chiefly upon that one of the two Higher *Tantras* called the *Anuttara Tantra*.
The other of the Higher *Tantras* is the *Yoga Tantra*. Of both these *Tantras*,
Milarepa was a practical master. (See p. 292 n.)

[3] Nyanam is a town, still existing, on the Tibetan frontier of Nepal, some
fifty miles north-east of Nepal's capital Katmandu, and about the same distance
south-east of Jetsün's birthplace, Kyanga-Tsa, near the modern Kirong (cf.
p. 52[4]). It was in the Stomach-like Cave of Nyanam that Jetsün narrated the
chief subject-matter of our text which follows (cf. p. 242).

[4] In their order as given, these names may be translated as follows: (1) Short-
Mantle Like a *Ḍorje* (the *lāmaic* sceptre, symbolizing the Thunderbolt of the
Gods, and Immutability), (2) Repa the Light of Peace, (3) Repa of Ngan-Dzong,
(4) Repa of Seban, (5) Repa the Hunter, (6) Repa the Hermit of Bri, (7) Repa
the Hermit of Lan, (8) Repa the Buddha-Protected, (9) Repa the Hermit of
Shan, (10) Saint of Mighty Breath, (11) Master Shākya-Guna. (Cf. J. Bacot,
*Le Poète Tibétain Milarépa*, Paris, 1925, p. 34.) The Tibetan term *Repa (Ras-pa* :
'cotton-clad one') given to eight of these disciples, as to Mila-Repa himself,
indicates that they are his followers, dressed, as he was, in a robe of white
cotton cloth. In virtue of the 'Vital Warmth', generated through a peculiar
*yogic* control of the respiration, they were proof against extremes of cold and

highest order, all deeply practised in *Yoga*, and possessed
of tranquillity of mind.   There also were Lesay-Būm and Shendormo, female novices, in addition to a large number of believing laity of both sexes.   And there also were the Five Immortal Goddesses of the higher order of fairies who subsequently were evolved into angels, besides several highly-gifted
*yogīs* and *yoginīs*, some human, some super-human beings, possessed of superior attainments.[1]   In the midst of this congregation, Jetsün set in motion the Wheel of Mahāyānic Buddhism.

One night, while Rechung sat meditating in his cell, he had
a dream which he described as follows :

' I was walking through a land which was said to be the
Western Land of Urgyan, inhabited by angels of both sexes.
The country was exquisitely beautiful and delightful, and the
houses and palaces were built of gold, silver, and precious
stones.   I was passing through the capital of this country and
noticed that its inhabitants were clad in silks and adorned with
garlands of jewels and precious metals and ornaments of bone,
and that every one of them was most beautiful to behold.   All
were regarding me with smiling faces and glances of approval,
though none ventured to speak to me.

' Among them, I encountered an old acquaintance whom I
had known in Nepal as a female disciple under Tiphupa, one
of my *Gurus*.   She, garbed in red, was presiding over the
congregation, and accosted me with words of welcome, saying,
" Nephew, I am most pleased that thou hast come."   She
forthwith led me into a palatial mansion filled with treasures,
where I was most sumptuously feasted.   She then said, " The
Buddha Akṣhobhya [2] is at present preaching the Doctrine in
this Land of Urgyan.   If thou, my nephew, wouldst like to
hear his preaching, I will go and obtain his permission."   I was

heat, and so needed to wear no other garment, even in the arctic winter of the
high Himalayan altitudes of Tibet.

[1] In the Appendix (pp. 305–7) a more complete list of names of the various
disciples is given.

[2] Tib. *Mi-bskyod-pa* (pron. *Mi-kyöd-pa*) : Skt. *Akṣhobhya* (meaning ' The
Unshakable [One]'), the Dhyānī Buddha of the Eastern Direction.   The other
four of the Five Dhyānī Buddhas are : Vairochana, of the Centre ; Ratna-
Sambhava, of the South ; Amitābha, of the West ; and Amogha-Siddhi, of the
North.

THE DHYĀNĪ BUDDHA AKṢHOBHYA

Described on pages xxvii, 42-3

extremely desirous of hearing him, and replied, " It is very kind of thee."

' Accompanying her, I came to the middle of the city, where I saw an immense throne made of precious metals and gems, and upon it, seated, the Buddha Akṣhobhya, of a beauty and majesty far surpassing in splendour the figure of my imagination on which I had been wont to meditate. He was preaching the *Dharma* to a huge congregation, seemingly as vast as the ocean. Upon seeing all this, I was filled with such ecstatic delight and bliss that I almost swooned. " Stay thou here, nephew, whilst I go and obtain the Buddha's permission," said the lady. Instantly obtaining it, she returned to conduct me into the Sacred Presence, whither going, I did obeisance to the Buddha, and received His blessing. I then sat down to listen to the religious discourse, and for a while the Holy One regarded me with smiling, benignant countenance and a look of infinite love.

' The subject on which He was preaching was the lineage, birth, deeds, and incidents connected with the various Buddhas and Bodhisattvas of the past. The narrative inspired me with profound belief. Finally He related the histories of Tilopa, Naropa, and Marpa,[1] at much greater length than I had been used to hear them told by Jetsün, so as to impart to each person present the deepest admiration and faith. In concluding His discourse, He said that He would narrate the story of Jetsün-Milarepa, which would surpass in wonder that of any of the aforementioned beings, and invited us all to come and hear it.

' Some present said that there could be nothing more wonderful than what we had already heard, but, if anything else did surpass this, it would have to be something very wonderful indeed. Others said : " The life stories we have just heard are of persons who had annihilated their evil deeds and acquired merit during several previous lifetimes, but Milarepa was one who acquired merit and attained enlightenment not inferior to that of any of these, all in one lifetime." Others again said :

---

[1] Concerning these three Great *Yogīs*, whence the Kargyütpa Sect arose, see pp. 7-8, and xvi–xvii.

" Oh, if this history be so interesting, it would really be a sin
on our part, as disciples, were we to miss hearing it, through
desisting from praying that it might be related for the benefit
of all beings. We ought by all means to try to get it told."
One asked : " Where is Milarepa now ? " Another replied :
" He is either in *'Og-min* [1] or in *Ngön-gah*." [2] I (Rechung)
thought : " Why, Milarepa is now living in Tibet, but these
people seem to be hinting that I should ask Milarepa himself
to tell the story of his life ; and that I will surely do." Thereupon, the lady laid hold of my hand, and shaking it gladly,
said, " Nephew, hast thou understood ? "

' Then I (Rechung) woke, and found that it was early dawn ;
and that morning, my mind felt very clear and my devotions
were hearty and sincere. Recalling the dream and reflecting
upon it, I thought that it was very auspicious to have dreamt
of being in the Urgyan Land, and of listening to the preaching
of the Buddha Akshobhya, and that I had good reason to con-
gratulate myself upon having met with Jetsün-Milarepa in real
life. My present privilege of listening to the preaching of the
Buddha, albeit only in dream, was likewise due, I considered,
to the grace of Jetsün. I reproached myself with lack of true
faith and spiritual insight when I recollected the thoughts I had
had as I listened to the people saying that Jetsün might either
be in *'Og-min* or in *Ngön-gah*. It was, I realized, irreverent
feelings of familiarity with my *Guru* that had caused me to
look upon him as merely a human being [3] when I thought of
him as being in Tibet. What a dull, stupid person I was !
Ought I not to have known that Jetsün had obtained perfect
enlightenment, in fact was a Buddha, and as such was able to

---

[1] *'Og-min* (Skt. *Akanishṭha*), the Heaven of the Ādi-Buddha, whence *Nirvāṇa*
may be attained without return to incarnation on Earth, as the meaning of
*'Og-min* (' No-Down ' or ' Without [Returning] Downward ') implies.

[2] *Ngön-gah* (Skt. *Amarāvatī* ), the Heaven of Indra, in the East, equivalent
to the Heaven of Akshobhya, the Dhyānī Buddha of the Eastern Direction.
*Ngön-gah* (*Mngon-dgah*), means ' Happy [to] know ', i. e. the Realm the very
thought of which fills one with bliss.

[3] ' This parallels the Tantric saying, " *Gurung na martyang budhyeta*," i. e.
"Never think of the *Guru* as a mortal." Brāhmanism teaches that the human
form is merely the vehicle through which the *Guru* manifests himself.'—Sj. Atal
Bihari Ghosh.

reproduce his form in inconceivably countless numbers![1]
Moreover, wheresoever Jetsün might be dwelling, did not that
place thereby become sacred and holy, yea, become equal to
'Og-min or Ngön-gah? I took my dream about the lady and
the others listening to the preaching to be a divine injunction
to write a biography of Jetsün, and firmly resolved to get Jetsün
himself to tell me all that had happened to him. In this frame
of mind I was filled with a feeling of deep and exalted true
faith in my Guru, to which I gave expression in fervent prayers.
Then I allowed my mind to rest tranquil awhile.

'Again I fell into a deep slumber and dreamed another dream,
though this was not so vivid as the first. Now it was five
beautiful young maidens, respectively white, blue, yellow, red,
and green,[2] said to be from the Urgyan Land, who came into
my presence together, one of them speaking, and saying, "To-
morrow the story of the life of Milarepa is to be told ; let us
·go and hear it!" whereupon another inquired : "Who is going
to ask him to relate it ?" To this a third replied, "Jetsün's chief
disciples are going to ask him." Meanwhile all were casting
sidelong glances at me and smiling. One spoke and said,
"This will be such an excellent sermon as all will be delighted
to hear. Should we not add our prayers as well, that it may
be delivered?" One answered, "It behoveth the disciples to
pray for the boon, and it shall be our duty and pleasure to
spread and protect the Faith." Upon this all disappeared, as
disappeareth a rainbow. Waking, I found that the sun was
already high, and I recognized that my dream was a sign
from the Five Immortal Sisters.'[3]

Having partaken of his morning meal in that happy state of
mind, Rechung sought the presence of his Guru [Jetsün], and
found that the company [of disciples and followers] had already

---

[1] This yogic power, with which Jetsün is credited, of assuming multifold
personalities and bodies, is illustrated in Chap. XII, wherein Jetsün exhibits it
when he is about to pass to another world. (See pp. 268-9.)

[2] These maidens are Tantric goddesses, otherwise known as Ḍākinīs; and
the colour of each has esoteric significance.

[3] These Ḍākinīs of the five colours are the Five Incarnations of the Goddess
Durgā who have their abode in the Tibetan Himalayas, some traditions say in
the Mt. Kailāsa region, other traditions say on Mt. Everest, sacred to Milarepa
as a place of his meditation. (Cf. p. 306.)

seated themselves. Rechung then prostrated himself in worship before Jetsün, and inquiring how he fared, with right knee on the ground and the palms of his hands joined, addressed him thus: ‘May it please our gracious Lord and Teacher to favour us with a recital of the events of his life for the benefit of the present gathering, and to serve as an example to future disciples and followers. The Buddhas of the past, too, have left behind them histories of Their Twelve Great Deeds,[1] and other records for the benefit of beings on Earth, which have contributed to the diffusion and general prosperity of the Buddhist Faith. Tilopa, Naropa, Marpa, and many other great saints, in leaving autobiographies behind, have done much to help the development of their fortune-favoured followers.

‘In like manner, O Lord Jetsün, thy biography also would greatly conduce to the development of many a being, to which end we pray our Lord that he may be pleased to favour us with an account of his eventful life.’

Entreated thus, Jetsün smiled and said, ‘ O Rechung, thou art already well acquainted with my life and history, but, as thou makest this request for the benefit of others, there is no harm in my complying with it. I am of the Josays (Descendants of Noblemen) Sept of the Khyungpo (Eagle) Clan, and my own personal name is Mila-Repa.[2] In my youth I committed some black deeds, in my maturity some white deeds; but now I have done away with all distinctions of black or white.[3] Having accomplished the chief task, I now am one

---

[1] These, the twelve great deeds (or rules of life) of a Buddha incarnate on Earth (Skt. *Dvādasha-avadhūta-guṇah*) are as follows : (1) wearing of cast-off (or torn) garments ; (2) wearing of only three sorts of garments, namely, the outer robe as a travelling cloak, and the inner robe and skirt for daily use ; (3) using a blanket in cold countries ; (4) begging of food (or living on alms) ; (5) partaking of but one meal per day—before or at noon ; (6) abstaining from liquid refreshments after midday; (7) meditation in the forest ; (8) sitting (or dwelling) under trees—and not in a house ; (9) dwelling in the open air—where there are no trees ; (10) dwelling in graveyards (or places of cremation)—for purposes of meditation on the impermanence of life ; (11) sleeping in a sitting posture, without reclining ; and (12) practising all the above rules voluntarily (or through liking them)—and not by compulsion.

[2] Meaning ‘ Mila the Cotton-Robed ’. (See pp. 201, 303[1].)

[3] In virtue of the Supreme Enlightenment of Buddhahood, Jetsün had come to realize the state of non-duality, wherein all opposites, even good and evil, are seen as unity, or as having a single source, which is Mind.

who needeth not strive any more in future.[1] Were I pressed
to describe at length the events of my life, the narration of
some of them would cause tears to flow while others would excite mirth; but there being little profit in such things, I prefer
that thou shouldst allow this old man to remain in peace.'

Again Rechung arose, and bowing down, entreated the
Teacher in these words : ' Gracious Lord, the narrative of the
manner in which thou didst first obtain the Transcendental
Truths, and of the great trouble and sacrifices it cost thee to
find them, and of how thou didst meditate upon them unceasingly until thou hadst mastered the real nature of Eternal
Truth and so attained to the Highest Goal of all spiritual
knowledge, and of the way in which thou hast been able to
soar beyond the network of *karmic* forces and prevent the
arising of future *karma*,[2] will be most interesting and profitable to all who cherish the like hopes and aspirations. Thy
clan being that of the Khyungpo (Eagle) and thy sept that of
the Josays (Descendants of Noblemen), how camest thou to be
called by the surname of Mila? Again, how didst thou come
to commit black deeds in thy youth and what led to thy committing white deeds, during which period thou sayest that there
were several incidents to excite laughter and some so painful
as to move to tears? To know of all these things would be of
inestimable value to future generations. So, out of compassion
for me and these my fellow-disciples, be pleased, O Lord,
kindly to set aside thy disinclination, and condescend to tell
us all in detail. I solicit my friends and brethren in the Faith
to join in this mine appeal.'

Hereupon, all present rose up, and prostrating themselves
several times, said : ' We also add our prayers to those of the
Reverend Rechung, and entreat thee, Lord, to set the Wheel
of the *Dharma* in motion.'

---

[1] The goal having been won, all striving, even death and birth, are at an end.

[2] If, as the *Bhagavad-Gītā* also teaches, the Master of Life performs actions in
this world wholly disinterestedly, and for the good of sentient beings, no future
*karma* such as leads to rebirth in this or any other realm of the *Sangsāra* arises,
and death and birth are normally at an end. Then the Conqueror returns, if at
all, to reincarnation voluntarily, as a Divine Incarnation, or *Avatāra*—a Buddha,
a Kṛishṇa, or a Christ.

Then Jetsün said, 'Well, if ye all so much wish it, I will gratify you, since there is nothing in my life that need be concealed.

'Regarding my clan and sept, I may add that in the northern part of the country called Urū there was a large tribe of nomads who owned cattle and sheep. Of their number there was one, belonging to the Eagle Clan, who having devoted himself to religious study, became a *lāma* of the Ñingmapa Sect, to which also his father had belonged. That father had been a Josay (nobleman's son). This young man came from Urū on pilgrimage along with some other pilgrims. He had developed certain super-normal powers, having become adept in the invocation of certain tutelary deities, and attained skill in magic. On his arrival in the Province of Tsang, at a place called Chūngwachī, his magical powers of curing illness and exorcizing persons obsessed by demons came to be very much in demand, so that his fame waxed great.

'In that place, in which he passed several years, he was known by the name of Khyungpo-Josay (Noble Son of the Eagle Clan), and whenever any one there was ill or troubled by an evil spirit he used to be sent for at once. But there was one family in the place who did not believe in him. On one occasion it happened that this family was tormented by a terribly evil spirit, which had never dared to approach Khyungpo-Josay, but could not be exorcized by any one else. For although the afflicted family called in other *lāmas* and had them try their exorcisms, the demon only made ironical retorts at the attempts to drive him out; and, making a mock of the family, tortured them and tyrannized over them the more, till they ceased from efforts which all alike proved wholly ineffectual.

'At last some relatives of that unbelieving family advised them to call in Khyungpo-Josay, quoting the proverb, "Apply even the fat of a dog if it cureth the sore." The head of the family said "Yes; by all means invite him to come." Accordingly, Josay was invited to come, and, approaching the demon, said three times in fierce tones, " I, Khyungpo-Josay, am coming to eat the flesh and drink the blood of all ye demons. Wait! Wait!" at the same time rushing forward

quickly.   The poor demon was filled with terror even before
Khyungpo-Josay had come near him, and cried out "*Apa!
Ama! Mila! Mila!* (O man, thou art my father, O man,
thou art my mother!)"[1] When Josay had come near to him,
the demon said : "*Mila!* I would never have come where
thou art ; spare my life!" Then Josay, having made the demon
take an oath that in future he would afflict no one, allowed him
to depart. Thereupon the demon went to a family who were
accustomed to worship him, and said to them, "*Mila! Mila!*
I never before suffered as I did this time." Upon their inquiring of him who had caused his suffering, he replied that
Khyungpo-Josay had come and inflicted upon him such excruciating pain as had nearly killed him, and at last had wrung
an oath from him. From that day Josay was called *Mila*, by
way of extolling his wonderful magical powers, and thus his
descendants came to be called by the surname *Mila*.[2] And
now, when every one saw that the demon afflicted no other
person, all concluded that the demon had been killed, or rather,
that it had transmigrated into another form of existence.

'Khyungpo Josay now married a wife, and had a son, who
had two sons, the eldest of whom was called Mila-Dotun-Sengé
(Mila the Lion who teacheth the *Sūtras*), his eldest son in
turn being called Mila-Dorje-Sengé (Mila the Immutable Lion).
Thenceforth that family came to be noted for having only one
male heir in each generation.

'This Mila-Dorje-Sengé was an expert and passionate gambler,
and used to win considerable wagers. Now it happened that
there was a man in that part of the country who was a still
greater expert in gaming, one who had many relatives and connexions on the father's side. This man came to Mila-Dorje-
Sengé with intent to test his skill, and challenged him to a few
games for small stakes, and playing with him soon obtained

---

[1] *Apa* literally meaning 'father'; *Ama*, 'mother'; and *Mila!* 'O man!'

[2] In his·French version (p. 40[2]), M. Bacot very plausibly takes '*Mila!*' to be
an ancient and more or less local interjection denoting fright or fear. The late
Lāma Dawa-Samdup has rendered 'Mila!' as 'O man!'. As an appellation
popularly given to a person, it would, in the former sense, suggest that its
bearer—as is clearly the case with Eagle Josay—has power to frighten and so
exorcize evil spirits.

a fair idea of the strength of his play. That day the man played as if fortune herself were watching over him, and won quite a number of wagers from Mila-Dorje-Sengé. This was unbearable to the latter, and he accordingly asked his opponent to give him his revenge the next day, to which the other consented. Next day the stakes were increased, and the wily man, to lure Dorje on, lost to him thrice. Then he in his turn asked for satisfaction, and Dorje agreed, after settling the stakes to be played for. These were to consist of the entire property possessed by each, lands, houses, money, and household effects, and they drew up a signed compact to this effect, so that neither might be able to evade his obligation by prayer or entreaty. They then played, with the result, which might have been foreseen, that Mila's opponent won the game. The man's male relatives thereupon took possession of the whole of the landed and movable property of Mila-Dorje-Sengé, and the two Milas, father and son, Dotun-Sengé and Dorje-Sengé, had to leave everything behind them and, wandering forth in the direction of the province of Gungthang [in Tibet on the frontier of Nepal], and arriving at a place called Kyanga-Tsa, settled down there.

'The father, Dotun-Sengé, used to spend his days in reading the Scriptures. He also performed exorcism ceremonies for the prevention of hail-storms ;[1] he prepared charms for the protection of children ;[2] and did many other things of a like nature. Thus he became quite popular as a *lāma*-performer of ceremonies. Meanwhile, his son Dorje-Sengé took to trading, dealing mostly in wool in the south during the winter, and

[1] In the high valleys of Tibet, where hail-storms are apt to be very frequent and destructive to crops, especially to the barley, the chief cereal produced, there are nowadays, as in the time of Milarepa, many *lāmas* whose duty is to ward off the hail. On the mountain-sides or hills, overlooking all the high, cultivated valleys there are small watch-towers in which these hail-exorcizing *lāmas* dwell during the growing season and until the harvest is gathered in. As soon as any dark cloud presaging hail is seen rising over the mountain peaks and coming towards the fields, the *lāmas*, on guard, at once launch powerful exorcisms, accompanied by handfuls of magic clay-pellets to drive the hail away. A further account of this is given later, on pp. 77–9, 117–19.

[2] M. Bacot renders this phrase thus : 'to protect children threatened by vampires' (p. 42).

going to the northern cattle-pastures in summer. He also went to and fro between Mang-Yül and Gungthang on shorter trips. In this way, these two, father and son, amassed much wealth.

'About this time, Dorje-Sengé happened to meet the favourite daughter of one of the families of the place. They fell in love; and, on their being united in marriage, a son was born to them, who received the name of Mila-Sherab-Gyaltsen (Mila the Trophy of Wisdom). While the boy was being brought up, his grandfather died, and the funeral ceremonies were performed with great pomp.

' Mila-Dorje-Sengé, still following his trading profession, acquired more wealth than ever. Paying a good price in gold and merchandise of the north and south, he bought a fertile field, triangular in shape, which lay near Kyanga-Tsa, from a man named Worma, and called it " Worma Tosoom (Worma Triangle) ".[1] Bordering this field there was an old house-site belonging to a neighbour, and this also he bought and upon it built a large house. It was just in the twentieth year of his age that Mila-Sherab-Gyaltsen was married to a girl belonging to a good family among the people of Tsa,[2] of the royal race of Nyang, called Karmo-Kyen (White Garland). She was a most lovely young lady, clear-headed and energetic, who understood how to treat friends and enemies according to their several dues, with love or with hatred; and so received the name of White Garland of the Nyang. Then, adding to the aforementioned house, Mila-Dorje-Sengé constructed a three-storied building with outhouses and kitchens, the whole resting upon four columns and eight pillars. It was one of the best houses in Kyanga-Tsa, and became known as " The Four Columns and Eight Pillars ". In this house they [he and his wife and father] lived in great affluence.

' Meanwhile, Mila-Dotun-Sengé's old relations who lived in Chūngwachī heard that he and his son were prospering at Tsa. So a cousin of Mila-Dorje-Sengé, named Yungdung-

---

[1] M. Bacot notes that the field was so named in accord with the Tibetan custom of giving to purchased fields, houses, horses, and mules the name of their former owner (p. 42[2]).

[2] A shortened form of Kyanga-Tsa.

Gyaltsen (Svastika-Banner of Victory) together with his family and a sister named Khyung-tsa-Palden (Demonstrator of the Nobility of the Descendants of the Eagles) removed from that place and came to Kyanga-Tsa. Dorje, being fond of his relatives, welcomed them upon their arrival with unfeigned pleasure and delight. He gave them all the assistance in his power in teaching them how to trade, and they also came to amass much wealth.

'About this time White Garland of the Nyáng found herself great with child, at a season when Mila-Sherab-Gyaltsen was away on a trading journey, in the North Taktsi Mountains, with a variety of southern merchandise, in the course of which he was considerably delayed.

'It was in the Male Water-Dragon year [1] [A. D. 1052], in the first autumn month [2] and on the twenty-fifth day,[3] under a propitious star, that I was born ; [4] and no sooner was my mother

[1] The Tibetan system of chronology, derived from China and India, is based upon the twelve-year and sixty-year cycles of the planet Jupiter. In the twelve-year cycle, employed for measuring short periods of time, each year bears the name of one of the twelve cyclic animals, which are : (1) Mouse, (2) Ox, (3) Tiger, (4) Hare, (5) Dragon, (6) Serpent, (7) Horse, (8) Sheep, (9) Monkey, (10) Bird, (11) Dog, and (12) Hog. In the sixty-year cycle the names of these animals are combined with the names of five elements—Wood, Fire, Earth, Iron, and Water—and each of these elements is allotted a pair of animals, the first animal being considered male and the second female. For example, A. D. 1900 was Iron-Mouse year and the thirty-fourth of the cycle of sixty years ; and A. D. 1867, the Fire-Hare year, having been the first of the last sixty-year cycle, the current year, A. D. 1928, is the second of a new sixty-year cycle. The Male Water-Dragon year, in which Milarepa was born, is the twenty-sixth year of the sixty-year cycle.

The Tibetan year being lunar, nominally of 360 days, the difference from the solar year is made good by adding seven intercalary months each nineteen years. The year begins with the rise of the new moon in February. The Tibetan week, following the Aryan system, is of seven days, named after the Sun, Moon, Mars, Mercury, Jupiter, Venus, and Saturn. (Cf. L. A. Waddell, *The Buddhism of Tibet, or Lāmaism*, London, 1895, pp. 451-5.)

[2] Or, according to the Tibetan year, which begins with February, the seventh month, i. e. August.

[3] The Tibetan month being lunar, this is the twenty-fifth day of the moon.

[4] M. Bacot and the Translator agree in their calculation that Milarepa was born in the year A. D. 1052, but according to Dr. Waddell's reckoning the year was A. D. 1038. (Cf. L. A. Waddell, op. cit., p. 65[5].) The place of Milarepa's birth, Kyanga-Tsa, in the Province of Gungthang, is on the Tibetan frontier of Nepal, a few miles east of the modern Kirong, about fifty miles due north of Katmandu, the capital of Nepal.

delivered of me than a messenger was dispatched with a letter to my father which said, " The work of the autumn is approaching, and I have been delivered of a son. Come with all the speed thou canst, to name the child and perform the naming ceremony." The messenger who carried the letter also conveyed to him the news verbally. My father was highly delighted and said, " O, well done ! My son hath already received his name. My race produceth but one male heir, and I am delighted to get the news that the child is a son. Call him Thö-pa-ga (Delightful-to-hear). As my trading business is all finished, I can return home at once." So saying, he returned homewards, and my name was fixed as Thö-pa-ga, the naming ceremony being carried out with great pomp and display. During my childhood I was tended with great care. In course of time I became endowed with a beautiful voice, which so delighted every one who heard it that people used to say I had been very appropriately named " Delightful-to-hear ".

' When I was about four years old, my mother gave birth to a daughter who was named Gön-ma-kyit (Fortunate Protectress), but she was also called, by way of a pet name, Peta, whence she came to be spoken of as Peta-Gönkyit. I remember even now that we two [Peta and I] used to have our hair plaited with gold and turquoises. We were very influential, being connected by marriage with the highest families in the place ; and the poor people, all coming under our influence, we were in a position to regard almost as our tenants or subjects ; so that the natives of the place used to say of us quietly among themselves, " Never could there be adventurous settlers from other parts more industrious and wealthy than these folk. Look at the house outside ! Look at the furnishing and wealth inside ! And the ornaments for both sexes ! They are worthy of regard from every point of view."

' At the time when we were thus the envy of all, my father, Mila-Sherab-Gyaltsen, died ; and the ceremonies in connexion with his funeral were performed on a magnificent scale.'

This is the first part of the story, and telleth of the manner of Jetsün's birth.

CHAPTER II

## THE TASTING OF SORROW

*Telling of the Death and Last Will of Milarepa's Father;
the Misappropriation of the Estate by the Paternal Uncle and
Aunt; and the Resulting Sorrows which Milarepa and his
Mother and Sister endured.*

AGAIN Rechung spoke, and said : ' O Teacher, be pleased to
relate the details of thy sufferings, and of the troubles that
followed the death of thy father.'

Jetsün then continued : 'When I had about reached the age
of seven, my father, Mila-Sherab-Gyaltsen, was seized with
a very serious illness. Physicians and *lāmas* attendant upon
him alike offered no hope of his recovery, but announced his
approaching end. All his relatives were also aware that he
was dying, and even the patient himself despaired of living and
resigned himself to death. Mine uncle and aunt, other kinsfolk
and friends, and all the neighbours gathered together, and, in
the presence of all, my father made known his last wishes,
entrusting the care of his widow and orphans to mine uncle and
aunt, as also the management of his entire estate. Finally, he
had a written testament made out, and had it read, signed,
and sealed in the presence of all assembled.

' Then he spoke as follows: " I well perceive that I shall
not survive this illness. My son being at present of tender
years, I confide him to the care of all my relatives, especially
his uncle and aunt. All my possessions, including my herds
of cattle, sheep, and ponies on the pastures high up in the
hills ; my fields, including ' Worma Triangle ', and several
smaller fields ; my cows, goats, and donkeys here below the
house ; my household utensils of gold, silver, copper, and iron ;
my personal ornaments and wardrobe ; my turquoises, silks,
and garments ; my granaries, and, in short, all those my possessions, regarding which I need not bear envy towards others,
I leave behind me. Out of these let a portion be spent upon
my funeral ceremonies. As regardeth the remainder, I entrust
the care of them to all of you [who are here gathered together],

until such time as my son is of age to look after everything for himself. But chiefly I entrust this property to the care of my child's uncle and aunt. When my son cometh to be of age, Zesay having been betrothed to him in infancy, let the pair be married ; and when the bride hath been received into the house, let the twain be put in charge of the entire property, and let them manage the household by themselves, following in the footsteps of their parents. But until my son attaineth mature age I entrust everything to you, all my relatives, but chiefly to you two, my children's uncle and aunt. See that they come to no harm ! Be sure that I will watch you from the realm of the dead ! " Saying this, my father expired.

' When my father's funeral ceremonies had been completed, all the relatives said, " Let White Garland of the Nyang herself be given the charge of the whole property, and let each of us from time to time render her such help and assistance as she may stand in need of, to the best of our ability."

' But mine uncle and aunt said, " Ye can all say what ye please, but we are the nearest relatives, and we will see to it ourselves that the widow and the orphans do not suffer. As for the property, we will take care of it." And despite all that my maternal uncle and the father of Zesay might say, my father's personal property was then divided between mine uncle and aunt thus : mine uncle took all the men's ornaments and raiment, while mine aunt took all the female appurtenances ; the remainder of the property was divided equally between them, and we were bidden to go and live with each of them by turn. And thus we were deprived of all rights over our property, and not only that, but compelled in summer to work as field-labourers for mine uncle, and in winter as spinners and carders of wool for mine aunt. The food given us was so coarse that it was fit only for dogs. Our clothing was miserable rags tied to our bodies with a rope for girdle. Compelled to work without respite, our hands and feet became cracked and blistered. The insufficiency and coarseness of our food made us miserably emaciated and haggard. Our hair, once adorned with gold and turquoises, now became hard and stiff, and infested with lice.

' Tender-hearted folk who had known us in the days of our

prosperity could not withhold their tears at the sight of us. Whispered talk about the villainous conduct of mine uncle and aunt ran through the whole neighbourhood, but they paid no attention to it. My mother, my sister, and myself were reduced to such a state of misery that my mother used to say of my aunt, "She is not Khyung-tsa-Palden (Demonstrator of the Nobility of the Descendants of the Eagles), but a *Dumo-Takden* (a Demoness who showeth the nature of the tigress)," and thenceforth mine aunt was known by the nickname of "Tiger-Demon". My mother also used to say that the proverb, "Entrust the ownership to others and have thyself turned into the dog that guardeth the door", had been proved true in our case. "For see," she said, "while thy father Mila-Sherab-Gyaltsen was alive, every one used to watch our faces to see if we smiled or frowned. But now, they who own the wealth becoming as it were the kings, all now regard the smiles and frowns of our uncle and aunt." My mother also came in for a share of the compliments whispered about, and people said "'Rich husband, able wife! Soft wool, fine blanket!' How true this saying is in this instance. See what happeneth when a clever man is no longer to the fore. Formerly, when her husband was living, White Garland of the Nyang used to be called the model housewife because of her energy and ability; her hand used to be called nourishing. But now her energy and ability have been put to the test, and her weakness is exposed." Thus the more we suffered, the more unpleasant were the things said about us, and the common folk, our former inferiors, missed no opportunity of decrying us behind our back.

'Zesay's parents used to provide me with a piece of cloth or a pair of shoes from time to time. They also used to say to me, "As long as men themselves are not turned into property, property is not stable; it is like the dew on the blades of the grass. So thou needest not mourn too much the loss of thy wealth. Thy parents and ancestors acquired wealth by their own exertions and industry. They were not always wealthy, but only acquired wealth latterly. And a time will come when thou also wilt earn wealth thyself." In this way they often consoled me.

'About my fifteenth year, my mother possessed a small field of her own called "Tepe-Tenchung (Little Famine Carpet)" which, though bearing a not very auspicious name, yielded a very fair crop of grain. This field was cultivated by my maternal uncle, and its yield stored away. With part of it he bought stores of meat, while the brown barley was brewed into *chhang*[1] and the white ground into flour.

'Now the news was spread abroad that White Garland of the Nyang and her children were going to give a feast with a view to recovering their patrimony. Many carpets were borrowed from all sides, and spread on the floor of our large house. To the feast were invited all our neighbours, more especially those who had been present at my father's decease and knew about his will, and all our relatives headed by our uncle and aunt. One whole sheep each was given to mine uncle and aunt, and the other guests were treated to quarters, legs, chops, and ribs, according to their position and the degree of their relationship to us. *Chhang* was served in brimming cups, and the feast began.

'Then my mother stood up in the midst of the assembly and spoke as follows: "I beg the honourable company here assembled to give me leave to explain why they have been invited to be present on this occasion, for, as the saying goeth, 'The birth of a son maketh necessary a naming ceremony; and the offer of *chhang*, a talk.' So I have a few words to say touching the last wishes of my deceased husband, Mila-Sherab-Gyaltsen, the father of these children,—a matter known to all of you, the elders of the place, headed by their uncle and aunt. So please listen to the will which I am now going to have read." Thereupon my maternal uncle proceeded to read the will aloud to the company. When he had finished, my mother again spoke, saying, "All here present are aware of the oral

---

[1] *Chhang*, a beer of very small alcoholic content, is made in the higher parts of Tibet chiefly of home-grown barley; in Sikkim and other lower-lying countries tributary or formerly, as Sikkim was, a part of Tibet, *chhang* is commonly made by pouring boiling water over fermented millet. Either Chinese tea, in which butter has been melted at the time of the brewing, or else *chhang*, is the ceremonial beverage offered to guests by all Tibetans; and no hospitality shown to travellers or pilgrims would be complete without one or the other.

testament uttered in their presence by my late husband, so I shall not weary them with a repetition of it. To come to the point, we [mother and children] are deeply grateful for all that we owe to our uncle and aunt, and for all their care in looking after us up to the present moment. But now that my son is able to manage a house for himself, I request that the property be restored to our care. I also ask you all to see that he be married to Zesay, and that she be duly installed in their joint home, in accordance with the wishes of my late husband."

' Upon my mother saying this, mine uncle and aunt, although at variance on all other matters, here united forces, since they had jointly misappropriated my patrimony to their own use. Moreover, I was an only son, while mine uncle had several sons. Mine uncle and aunt, thus in agreement in a scheme to defraud us, replied : " Where is this property ye are talking about ? When Mila-Sherab-Gyaltsen was alive, he borrowed these houses, fields, cattle, ponies, gold, and silver. They all were ours, he restoring them to us only when at the point of death. This was only the restoration of the property to its rightful owners. Where did ye ever have a particle of wealth, a measure of barley, a roll of butter, a piece of cloth, or even a living head of cattle of your own ? We never saw any. And now ye have the audacity to say a thing like this ! Who wrote that will of yours ? Ye ought to be thankful we did not leave miserable creatures like you to perish of starvation. Indeed the saying, ' Rather try to measure a running stream with a quart measure, than to oblige wicked people ', would seem to apply to you."

' Sneering at us, they rose abruptly from their seats, shook their garments, and, stamping the heels of their shoes on the floor, said, " If it really cometh to that, this very house we are in is ours. Out with you, ye ungrateful orphans, out with you ! " With that, they slapped my mother, my sister, and myself in the face with the ends of their long sleeves.[1] And all my mother could say, was, " O Mila-Sherab-Gyaltsen ! look at the treatment we have to endure, thou who didst say, ' I will watch over you from the realm of the dead ! ' Now, if thou canst,

---

[1] That is, the long loose sleeves of the national Tibetan dress, which when hanging free cover the hands and so protect them from the cold.

surely is the time to do so." And falling down in a fit of hysterical weeping she swooned away. I and my sister could render no aid other than weeping.

'My maternal uncle, seeing that mine other uncle had many sons, did not dare to fight him. The other neighbours who were kindly disposed towards us added their tears to my mother's, saying, "Poor widow! Poor orphans!" Many were sobbing, and few there were who did not shed tears.

'Mine uncle and aunt continued : "Ye are asking for wealth from us, but ye seem to have quite a lot yourselves, since ye have been able to invite all your neighbours and friends to such a grand feast. Ye need not ask for anything from us, for we have not got any of your wealth, say what ye like. And even if we have, we are not going to restore it. Do your worst, ye wretched orphans! If ye feel yourselves strong enough in numbers, fight us! If ye think yourselves too few, curse us!"

'Having said this, they went out. Those who sided with them followed next, mother still weeping, until our maternal uncle and Zesay's folk, with a few others who sided with us, alone remained behind to console my mother. These continued drinking what was left of the *chhang*, saying, "Oh, do not weep! It is of no avail." They proposed that a subscription be raised from all who had been at the dinner, offering themselves to give their share, and that our paternal uncle and aunt should again be appealed to with the confident expectation of their making at least a decent contribution. With the sum so raised it was proposed that I should be sent away to be educated. My maternal uncle said to my mother : "Yes, yes, let us do that, and send the boy away to learn something. As for thyself and thy daughter, ye may come and live with me while ye cultivate your fields by your own labour. We must do our best to put to shame that uncle and aunt."

'But my mother said, "Since we are not to get back our own property, I do not consider it possible to bring up my children by means of wealth obtained in charity from others. Besides, there is not the least probability of their uncle and aunt ever restoring to us even a portion of our property. As for my son, he must, of course, be educated. After this refusal

of the uncle and aunt to restore to us our own, they will do
their utmost to expose us to shame should we again submit
ourselves to them.   They will ill-treat us worse than ever; and
we should be like a drum on its stand or smoke in flight.[1]   We
shall remain here and work our field."

' Accordingly, I was sent to a place in Tsa, called Mithong-
gat-kha (The Invisible Knoll), and there put under the tuition
of a *lāma* of the Red Sect called Lu-gyat-khan (Eight Serpents), a very popular teacher of the place.

' During this period, our relatives seem to have contributed
some pecuniary aid towards our support.   Zesay's parents, especially, were very kind; from time to time they sent us flour
and butter, and even fuel; and often let Zesay herself come to
the place where I was studying, to console me.   My maternal
uncle supplied my mother and sister with food so that they
were not forced to beg nor to serve others, and he used to
have the wool for spinning and weaving brought to his house
to save my mother going from door to door to ask for it.
Thus he greatly assisted us to make a living and earn a little
money.   My sister, on her part, doing such tasks as others
gave her, by dint of hard work managed somehow to take care
of herself [so far as having money to spend was concerned].
But, in spite of everything, we got only coarse food, and had
to content ourselves with ragged clothes.   All this caused me
much grief; at that time, not the least joy whatsoever did I
ever know.'

As the narrative ceased, all those listening were, without ex-
ception, deeply moved with sorrow and distress.   Tears trickled
down their cheeks, and for a while all were silent.


This is the account of that part of his life in which Jetsün
had actual experience of the existence of sorrow.

---

[1] That is, made to run when the drum-call sounds or wafted about like smoke
by the wind—an idiomatic expression similar to 'at their beck and call from
early till late'.

## CHAPTER III

# THE PRACTISING OF THE BLACK ART

*Telling of Jetsün's Guru and Mastery of the Black Art; and of how Jetsün Destroyed Thirty-Five of his Enemies and the Rich Barley Harvest of the Others, by Magic.*

AGAIN Rechung addressed Jetsün, saying, 'O Jetsün, thou hast said that thou didst first commit some black deeds. What were those black deeds, and how were they committed?'

Jetsün made answer, 'By black magic, and by bringing on hail-storms, I heaped up piles of demerit.'

Rechung then asked, 'How didst thou happen to have recourse to such a thing? What led thee to do so?'

And Jetsün replied, 'Once I accompanied my preceptor to a feast held in the lower village of Tsa, at which feast he was the most important personage present, and seated at the head of the entire company. He was plied with drink by the guests and by several others also, and thus partaking too freely of the liquor provided was in a state of considerable excitement. At this stage, I was sent home in advance of my preceptor with the presents which he had received.[1] Being somewhat tipsy myself, and having seen several persons at the feast singing, I was seized with an irresistible desire to sing, being moved thereto by a desire to show off my fine voice, of which I was very proud.

'I came singing all along the way. The road to "The Invisible Knoll" passed right in front of our own house; and I still went on singing, even when I was nearing the house. My mother, who was roasting some barley inside the house, hearing my voice, could scarcely believe her ears, albeit my voice on account of its unusual sweetness could hardly be mistaken. Still, she thought, it could not be possible that I

---

[1] Here reference is made to the custom of making gifts to preceptors, in this instance of food, to be taken home. At this time, Milarepa's preceptor is an ordinary *lāma*, probably the village schoolmaster. Had he been a *lāma-guru*, highly developed spiritually, Milarepa would have been safeguarded from the deplorable evil of drunkenness, which, according to Buddhist teachings, is as reprehensible as it is productive of bad *karma*.

should be singing at a time when our circumstances were such that it could be said of us that we were about the most unhappy creatures alive. But looking out and seeing that it really was myself, she was utterly dumbfounded.

' She dropped her tongs to the right and her roasting-whisk to the left, and, leaving the barley to burn in the pan, came out with a rod in her right hand and a handful of ashes in her left. Sliding down the longer steps and jumping down the shorter steps, she came and threw the ashes in my face, and striking me several times on the head with the rod exclaimed, " O, Mila-Sherab-Gyaltsen, see what a son hath been born to thee ! Surely it cannot be thy blood that floweth in the veins of this vagabond ! O, look what we have come to !" Thereupon she fell fainting to the ground.

' At that moment my sister came out, and saying, " O brother, what art thou thinking of ? See to our mother !" she burst out weeping. This brought me to my senses ; and feeling the justice of the rebuke I also wept. Then, for a time, we two continued tugging at our mother's hands, calling to her in our anguish.

' After a while she revived, and regarding me with a fixed, displeased look on her tear-stained faced, said, " Son, dost thou really feel merry enough to sing ? As for me, I think we are the most unhappy of all the unhappy beings existing in all the world ; and the only thing I can do is to weep for very sorrow and grief." And all three of us again wept loudly.

' Then I said, " Mother, thou art right ; but do not take it so much to heart. I solemnly promise to do for thee whatever thou mayst desire of me. What is thy will, my mother ? "

' My mother said, " What I should like is to see thee dressed in a coat of mail and mounted on a steed, dragging thy stirrups over the necks of these our enemies ; but that would be a difficult thing to bring to pass, and attended, too, by much risk. However, what I wish is that thou shouldst learn the Black Art thoroughly, so that thou mayst be able to kill these enemies of ours, chiefly thine uncle and aunt who have caused us so much grief and misery, and cut off the root of their posterity down to the ninth generation. See if thou canst do that for me."

' I faithfully promised to do my best to fulfil her wish, if she would provide the fees for the *Gurus*[1] of the Black Art, as also mine expenses on the road and for the time that I should be engaged in study.

' My mother then sold half of the field called " Little Famine Carpet" in return for a splendid turquoise called " Radiant Star ", and a white pony called " Unbridled Lion ", well known in the place. She also managed to get together two loads of madder for dyeing, and two loads of raw sugar. The sugar I disposed of to meet my present needs ; and, setting out, duly arrived at Gungthang. In this place there was an inn called " Self-perfected Inn ", and there I stayed some days looking out for companions—fellow-travellers who might be going the same way as myself. Thither soon arrived five favourite sons of good families, of Ngari-Döl, bound for Ü and Tsang,[2] to learn something of religion as well as of black magic. I told them that I was out on the same errand as themselves, and asked if I might be allowed to accompany them. To this they agreed. Then I took them down to the lower part of Gung-thang and there treated them to the best food and refreshments procurable.

' Meanwhile, my mother had taken them aside and entreated them thus : " Young gentlemen, my son is not of a very studious disposition, neither doth he possess much perseverance. So I beg you to urge him to study, and to make himself proficient. And when ye return, I shall know how to show you my gratitude, and repay you for your kindness to him."

' When the two loads of dye-stuff had been set upon the

---

[1] The title *Guru* (Spiritual Preceptor, or Teacher) is applied to one who follows the Left-hand Path, of Black Magic, as well as to one who follows the Right-hand Path, of White Magic. Up to a certain point the process of developing the *shiṣhya* psychically is much the same for either Path. Afterwards, the vast gulf separating Black and White Magic is due entirely to the intention of the *shiṣhya* or *Guru* and the use to which the psychic powers are put ; in Black Magic the aim and practice is purely selfish and evil, in White Magic altruistic and productive of benefit to all sentient beings.

[2] The Provinces of Ü and Tsang, frequently mentioned throughout this *Biography*, are known to Tibetans as Pöd, i. e. Tibet proper. Their respective capitals, Lhāsa and Tashi-lhünpo, are Tibet's chief cities. The former is the seat of the Dalai Lāma ; the latter, the seat of the Tashi Lāma.

pony, and I had secured the turquoise about my person, we set forth. My mother accompanied us a considerable way, every now and then, at each halt, serving out *chhang*; and while we were walking and also during halts she appealed again and again to my companions to look after me. I was her only son, and she could hardly bear to part from me; she clung to my hand and shed many tears. At length, taking me aside, she gave me the following parting admonition, in a low voice broken with sobs: " My dear son, consider what a state of wretchedness we are in, and carry out the object that lieth before thee. Thou must show thy power here in this place, by working some destruction. Thy study of magic is not the same as that of these young men; theirs is a matter of acquiring fame, but ours is a matter of desperate necessity. Shouldst thou return without being able to give some visible manifestation of thy power here, I swear to thee that I will kill myself in thy very presence."

' Having thus admonished me, she left us; but I could hardly bear the parting, my heart was attached to her so fondly. Again and again I looked back at her, and could not withhold the tears which flowed unbidden down my cheeks despite all that I could do to keep them back. My mother, too, suffered no less. I being her only son, she keenly felt the anguish of parting. I could see her gazing back at me as long as we were within sight of one another; and a well-nigh irresistible desire came over me to turn back and see her once more, but, by an almost superhuman effort, I conquered it. Later events caused me to see that this was a premonition of what was to occur—a feeling foreshadowing that I was never to see my mother alive again. When we were completely out of sight of one another, my mother went back weeping to the village. And a few days later it was rumoured far and wide that the son of White Garland of the Nyang had gone away to learn black magic in order to be able to avenge his wrongs.

' I and my companions now proceeded along the Ü-Tsang road till we came to a place called Yakde, in Tsang-rong. Here I sold my pony and my dye-stuffs to a rich man, and receiving payment in gold secured it about my person. Crossing the

Tsangpo (Purifier) River, we struck towards the Province of Ü, arriving duly at a place called Thön-luk-rakha (Sheep-Pen of Thön), where we met several *lāmas* from Ü. On inquiring of them as to who was the most noted adept in the Black Art for producing death, and destruction of property by hail-storms, one of them replied that there was a famous sorcerer named Lāma Yungtun-Trogyal (Wrathful and Victorious Teacher of Evil), of Nyak, in a village called Yarlung-Kyorpo, who was well known for his accomplishments in the art of producing death and destruction by means of black magic, of which Lāma he himself was a pupil. So we all turned our steps towards Lāma Yungtun-Trogyal.

'On arriving at Yarlung-Kyorpo, and meeting the Black Magician, I saw that my companions made a present to him of part of their money only ; but, as for me, I presented to him everything I had—all my pieces of gold, and the turquoise, and, in addition, even my very self, body and life, begging only that he would teach me black magic in such wise that I might be able to demonstrate mine attainments in unmistakable fashion by working some havoc on those who had robbed me of my patrimony. A further request I made was that he would provide me with food and clothing until I had acquired proficiency in the Art. The Lāma smiled and said, "I will consider thy request."

'And so we all began our studies, which, however, were not of a really effectual kind. We were taught some branches of black magic bearing high-sounding titles, such as that which was said to bestow the power of joining heaven and earth ; also a method of dealing death ; and, in addition, a few others of a beneficial kind.

'At this sort of study we were kept for nearly a year, about which time my companions began to think of returning home. As a parting gift, our Teacher presented each of us with a coat made of the fine woollen cloth that is woven in the Province of Ü. But I was far from feeling satisfied. I thought that such magical lore as we had mastered up till then was hardly enough for the production of any real effect in my village. And I knew that if I were not able to do something striking my mother would certainly kill herself in my presence. So I could not think of returning home. Observing my reluctance, my companions asked me if I did not want to go home. I replied that I had not yet learned anything. To this they rejoined, " What we have received is quite sufficient ; all now dependeth upon our own application and perseverance. We had best follow these methods. Our Teacher telleth us that he hath nothing better to impart to us ; and we know that to be true. However, if thou wish to stay on, by all means do so, and see if thou can learn a little more." Thereupon, they prostrated themselves before the Teacher, and, offering him such gifts as they thought fit, started homeward.

' Putting on the coat given me by the Teacher, I accompanied them the distance of a morning's walk, by way of seeing them off ; and then, bidding them farewell, retraced my steps towards my Teacher's house. On the way up, I collected in the lap of my robe quite a quantity of manure which I found lying on the road. My Teacher having a nice piece of garden land, I dug a hole in it and buried the manure there. From the roof of his house, the Teacher, having seen what I had done, is said to have spoken to the pupils at that moment round about him thus :—" Among all the pupils I ever have had, I never had nor ever shall have one more affectionate and industrious than that boy. It seemeth that the reason why he did not come to bid me farewell this morning was because he was returning to me. I recollect that on his first coming here he spoke of some neighbours having ill-treated him, and that he wished me to teach him magic so that he might be able to give demonstration of his acquirements in his native place, at the same time offering himself to me body and life. What a simple fellow he is ! If what he sayeth be true, it would be a shame, nay, downright cruelty, to refuse to teach him the Art." I was told of this afterward by one of the young pupils ; and I was filled with joy at the prospect of being favoured with really effective instruction.

' Upon my going into the presence of my Teacher, he addressed me thus : " Well, Thöpaga, how is it that thou hast not gone home ? " I had folded up the dress which he had presented to me, and now offered it to him as a fresh gift.

Then, bowing in reverence before him, and touching his feet with my forehead, I said, "O Venerable *Guru*, I am an orphan, with a widowed mother and a sister. We have been deprived of our patrimony by our neighbours, headed by our paternal uncle and aunt, and ill-treated beyond endurance. As we had no power to obtain our rights or avenge ourselves, my mother hath sent me away to learn the Black Art; and if I return without being able to wreak vengeance upon those who have wronged us, my mother will kill herself in my presence. So I did not dare to go home; and I now entreat thee to teach me the Art in a manner that will be really effective." The *Guru* then asked me to tell him the whole story of our ill-treatment, and of how we had been defrauded. I related to him all that had happened from the time of my father's death, and of how we had been wronged and ill-treated by our uncle and aunt, my narrative being broken by my sobs, while the tears streamed from mine eyes.

' On hearing the whole story, my Teacher, too, was unable to restrain his tears, which I could see coursing down his cheeks. Then he said, " If what thou sayest be true, thou hast indeed been treated most cruelly and unjustly. I could myself wreak vengeance by mine Art, but must not do so without due cause, after full inquiry. Many an appeal hath been made to me by various people that I might teach them this peerless Art of mine. Unlimited quantities of gold and turquoises from the Ngari-Province, silks and brick-tea from Kham and Amdo, grain, butter, and woollen fabrics in loads upon loads from the Provinces of U and Tsang, cattle and ponies by the thousands from Dzayul, Tagpo, and the Kongpo Provinces, have come pouring in upon me, as offerings in exchange for this Art. But none yet hath said as thou hast, that he offered himself to me, body and life. So I will make inquiry into thy case."

' My Teacher had a disciple who was fleeter than a horse and stronger than an elephant. This disciple was sent to my native place with instructions to make inquiry into the facts of my case; and in a few days he came back with a report that all my statements were perfectly true, and that it seemed only an act of justice to bestow on me the Art.

'Thereupon my *Guru* said to me, " I withheld the Art from thee in the beginning, because I feared that thou mightst use it stupidly, without having sufficient cause for its exercise.[1] But now that I am satisfied as to thy truthfulness, I shall teach thee the whole Art.  Only, thou must go to another place to learn it.  Formerly I had a most destructive piece of black magic called the Zadong-Marnak (Purple Basilisk), potent to paralyse and to kill, which I taught to Khulung-Yöntön-Gyatso (Ocean of Virtue of Khulung), of Nub-Khulung, in the valley of the Tsangpo.  He was a physician and also a Tantric.[2]  He possessed a knowledge of the art of launching hail-storms and of guiding them with the tips of his fingers, which art he taught to me.  We then swore friendship to each other, and arranged that whoever went to him to learn the art of launching hail-storms should be sent to me, while those who came to me to learn the art of producing death should be sent to him with my recommendations.  It will, therefore, be necessary for thee to go to him to learn the art thou desirest, and thither I now shall send thee."

'Thereupon he provided me and his eldest son named Darma-Wangchuk (Powerful Young Man) with a yak-load of eatables and with presents, consisting of fine woollen cloth, and, also having received from him a letter of recommendation bound with a scarf,[3] we set out upon our journey and in due time arrived at Nub-Khulung, in the valley of the Tsangpo. There we each made a gift of a piece of fine woollen cloth, and presented our letter ; and, relating all the circumstances again, I prayed that I might be favoured with instruction in the Art.

'Khulung-Yöntön-Gyatso said, " My friend is constant in friendship and keepeth his promises.  Assuredly I will give

---

[1] It is an inviolable rule observed to the present day that no *guru* of any school, either of black or white magic, communicates to the disciple the essential teachings until satisfied that they will not be abused.

[2] That is, one versed in the ritual and occult lore of the Tantric School.

[3] No introduction or ceremonial presentation is complete in Tibet and neighbouring countries, as far as Mongolia, without the accompaniment of a scarf ; this applies to both the highest and lowest personages, from the peasant to the Dalai Lāma, Europeans themselves conforming to it.  The scarf is usually white, except in Mongolia, where it is said to be blue. (Cf. The Earl of Ronaldshay, *Lands of the Thunderbolt*, London, 1923, pp. 120-2.)

thee the instruction thou desirest. Build thyself a strong cell which cannot easily be pulled down with the hands, at the end of that spur down there," pointing out the intended site to me. "Let it have three stories all underground; while one story more, on top of these three, must be built with strong beams, closely joined together. At the outer angles let it be covered with stones large as the body of a yak. Let it be so constructed that none will be able to find the entrance to it, or force their way into it." He then gave me the necessary instructions [in magical practice].

' After I had applied the instructions during seven days, my Teacher came and said, "Usually seven days are enough in which to achieve results, and they ought also to be sufficient in the present case." But, since it was a far-off part of the country in which I wished to operate, I prayed that I might be allowed another seven days; and this prayer was granted.

' On the night of the fourteenth day, my Teacher again came to see me, and said, "To-night, at the end of thine altar, [or circle of offerings], thou wilt see the sign of thy success, and the accomplishment of thy wishes." And, sure enough, that very night the Tutelary Deities made their appearance, bringing with them the bleeding heads and hearts of thirty-five persons, and laying down the trophies in a heap said, "Were not these the objects of thy wishes, in calling upon us over and over again these last few days?"

' Next morning, my Teacher came again, and said that there were two more persons who ought to be sacrificed, asking me whether I wanted them killed or not. I prayed that they might be spared alive as objects over which to gloat, and cite as examples of my power in the future. Thus it was that my two worst enemies, mine uncle and aunt, were omitted from the general destruction. I next offered thanks to the *Karmic* and Tutelary Deities, and left my cell-retreat. The site of that cell can be seen to the present day in Khulung.

' To come now to the practical phase of the accomplishment of my vengeance by means of the Black Art; if ye would like to know how it appeared to others, it took place thus: The eldest son of my paternal uncle was going to be married, and all who had taken my paternal uncle's side were invited to the wedding feast. There were assembled in the house the other sons of that uncle, the bride, and those particular persons who had ill-treated us most, thirty-five persons in all. Some of the invited guests, of whom most were among those who inclined to our side, were on their way to the feast, talking and whispering to one another, saying, " These people are acting exactly according to the proverb : ' Trust others with possession of thy house, and be turned out of doors.' Even if Thöpaga's efforts at vengeance by means of black magic do not take effect, it is high time that the effect of *karma* should overtake them."

' Thus, walking along and talking at their ease, they had just come in sight of the house, but had not had time to enter, when a maidservant, formerly ours, but now our uncle's, came out of the house to fetch some water. As she passed the fenced-in yard where a large number of ponies had been enclosed, she could not see anything of them ; but, instead, the whole place seemed to be filled with scorpions, spiders, snakes, frogs, and lizards; and, in the midst of them all, one monstrous scorpion [1] was driving its claws into the principal pillar of the house, tugging at it and pulling it outwards. She was terrified at the sight, and barely had time to get away when several colts and mares, which had been tethered together below the house, became excited and raised a great commotion. Some of the colts, getting loose, rushed upon the mares. The whole lot were flung into the utmost confusion, the colts neighing and the mares kicking, until one of them knocked against the main pillar with such terrific force that it broke and fell, and the whole house came down with a tremendous crash.

' In all, there perished thirty-five persons, among them the bride, and all mine uncle's sons. Clouds of smoke and dust obscured the sky. Dead bodies of men, women and children, and ponies choked the ruins.

' A heart-rending wail arose from those outside, which was heard by my sister, who, when she saw what had happened,

---

[1] M. Bacot's version reads : ' a scorpion as big as a yak ' (p. 64)—the yak being the great shaggy buffalo used as a beast of burden in Tibet.

rushed to her mother, crying out, " O mother, come and look!
Our uncle's house hath fallen down, and a lot of people have
been killed."

' My mother got up and came to see what had happened,
all the while very much doubting if it really could be so. But
seeing the fallen house covered with clouds of dust, and hearing the piteous cries and wailing which filled the air, she was
filled with astonishment, as also with cruel joy. Putting some
rags on the end of a long pole, and raising it aloft like a banner, she cried aloud, " All glory to the Teachers and to the
Gods! All ye neighbours, look now and see if Mila-Sherab-
Gyaltsen hath begotten a worthy son or not, and if I have
avenged myself or not. Though I had to eat coarse food and
wear rags for a dress, see if this is not well worth our sacrifices.
Look and tell whether or not that paternal uncle's challenge
hath been answered,—he who said, ' Fight if strong, and curse
if weak!' Now the curse of the weak and the few hath done
more than the might of the many could ever have done.
Look, just look at the human beings above and the animals
below! See the treasures and provisions ruined! O what a
cheering sight hath my son brought before mine eyes to bless
mine old age! Delighted am I to have lived to enjoy such a
scene! Could any other moment of my life be the equal of
this in perfect triumphant joy! "

' With exclamations such as these, my mother gloated over
the cruel spectacle, being heard by all the neighbours. Some
of them said that she was right; others said that she was
going too far,—that it was quite enough to have been avenged
and that she ought not to give vent to such an excess of ill
will.

' News of my mother's joy came to the ears of the people
who had lost relatives in the catastrophe, and they began to
say, " Not only hath she been the cause of the mischief, but
she giveth vent to her malignant triumph in language which is
unbearable. Let us put her to the torture and wring out her
wicked heart." The older and more prudent said, " What advantage will it be to kill her, since her son will only do the
same thing over again, and kill us all. Rather let us hunt out

the cub first, and kill him on the spot; then we can do what
we like with the dam." To this all agreed.

'My paternal uncle, coming to hear of their plan, said, "Ha!
I have no more sons or daughters to lose; death will be welcome!" and rushed forth intending to kill my mother forthwith.
But the neighbours caught hold of him and said, "Listen! It
was through our siding with thee that we have brought this
calamity upon our heads. Thou art its main cause, and now
again thou art about to do something of the same sort. If thou
do not abide by the plan of action on which we have decided,
of seeking out the son first and then dispatching the mother,
we will fall out; for we are resolved to oppose thee in this
matter." Mine uncle, accordingly, had no choice but to submit
to them.

'Meanwhile, they concocted a plot against my life, and were
considering how best to send some persons to seek and kill me,
when news of their plot came to the ears of my maternal
uncle, who, going to my mother, upbraided her roundly with
her rashness. "Thy recklessness", he said, "is likely to imperil
thine own life and that of thy son. The neighbours are conspiring against thee. What benefit was it to vent thy malignant joy in that fashion? Was it not enough to have wrought
such havoc upon them?" Thus he scolded her at great length.

'My mother only wept and said, "O my dear brother and
uncle of my children, I feel the justice and the sound sense of
thy rebuke, but put thyself in my place, and think of what
I have endured! The property, vast and extensive as it was,
taken from me by fraud, and myself subjected to such indignities and ill treatment! Could any mortal help feeling as
I did?"

'My uncle replied, "Thou hast some reason on thy side, but
I fear for thee. Look to the doors—fasten them well—murderers may come." As soon as he had gone, my mother
fastened the doors securely, and sat down to ponder what she
should do next.

'The maidservant who had escaped the catastrophe, getting
an inkling of the plot against us, and unable to bear the thought
of the orphans of her dear old mistress and her late master

being massacred, sent a private message informing my mother
of the conspiracy, and exhorting her to send me warning of
the danger.

'My mother, perceiving that for some time at least her life
was safe, made up her mind how to act.  She sold the remaining
half of her field, "Little Famine Carpet", getting seven pieces
of gold for it.  But seeing no one in the place whom she felt
she could trust to take them to me, and being unable to find
a reliable messenger elsewhere, she thought of coming herself to
bring me the gold, as well as to warn me of the impending danger.

'However, as luck would have it, a pilgrim from Ü, who
had been on pilgrimage to the sacred places in Nepal [1] and
was on his way home again, came to the door to beg alms.
She asked him to come in; and, artfully putting a number of
questions regarding his home and so forth, discovered that he
would be a suitable person to whom to entrust a message for
me.  She next invited him to stay in her house for a few days,
telling him that she had a son in Ü or Tsang to whom she
wished to send a message.  During the time that he stayed she
treated him to the best of everything she had and made him
very comfortable.

'Trimming a lamp and addressing a prayer to the Deities
invoked and worshipped by me, she begged them to give her
a sign whether her message would be safely delivered or not,
and whether her wishes would be accomplished.  If she were to
have success, so she prayed, then the lamp was to continue
burning for a long time; but if failure were to attend her, then
the lamp was to go out speedily.  It so happened that the
lamp continued burning for a whole day and night.  Thus
assured that her message would not miscarry, she gave the
pilgrim some pieces of cured hide to serve as soles for his
leather boots, and told him to get them put on, as he would
find them needful.

'The pilgrim had an old blanket-cloak, and my mother,
offering to mend it for him wherever it had rents or holes, took
it and put a somewhat large patch on the back; and, unknown
to its owner, hid the seven pieces of gold within the patch.

---

[1] Nepal, like India, is still a place of many pilgrimages for Tibetan Buddhists.

She sewed over it another patch, black in colour and square in shape, and ornamented it with a star prominently worked in thick white thread-work. In doing this, she fastened the seven pieces of gold by putting in stitches all around each, so as to make the pattern look like a group of six stars, one in each angle of the large enclosing star, and one in its centre,[1] but showing less prominently than the large star itself. She then handed the pilgrim a sealed letter which he was to deliver to me, and, giving him a handsome present, charged him to convey the letter to me in safety.

' When the pilgrim-devotee had departed, my mother, wishing to instil fear in the minds of the neighbours, instructed my sister Peta to tell some of the folk that the pilgrim had brought a letter from me. The letter which, of course, was a sham one, ran thus: " I hope that my mother and sister are quite well, and that they have seen the results of my magical powers. Doth any one dare to bear enmity towards you or to intimidate and ill-treat you? If so, ye have only to let me know that one's name and family, together with the causes of his or her behaviour, and so forth, and I will simply annihilate that one. It is easily done. Indeed it is easier for me to kill a person than to say grace before meat. I will not only kill one, two, or three persons, but I will root out entire generations, even down to the ninth generation. If it be the whole community that beareth you ill will, just come here, and I will simply sweep the whole countryside with destruction, leaving not a trace of any one behind. Here I am living in ease and comfort. Ye need not have any anxiety about me. I am spending my days in the study of the Art."

' This letter was signed and sealed in a way to make it appear as if it had come from me, and was shown to those round about whom we knew to be on our side ; and, finally, it was handed over to our maternal uncle, that it might be shown to all in the place. This stratagem had the intended effect of causing the enraged people to abandon their design of having recourse to desperate measures. They consulted together, and induced my

---

[1] Or, 'the pattern was made to represent the constellation of seven stars known as the Pleiades'.

paternal uncle to restore our field called "Worma Triangle", my patrimony, to my mother.

'Meanwhile, the pilgrim-messenger went on from place to place inquiring for my whereabouts; and learning that I was at Nub-Khulung, came thither; and, finding me and giving me all the news concerning the welfare of my mother and sister, handed me my mother's letter, part of which ran thus: "My dear son Thöpaga, I hope thou art enjoying sound health. I am well satisfied with thee; thou hast proved thyself worthy of the name of thy father, the noble Mila-Sherab-Gyaltsen, and my desires have been accomplished. The manifestations of thy knowledge of black magic have been seen here in most impressive fashion. Thirty-five persons have been killed in a house which fell down on them. But the occurrence hath embittered the people against us; they hate us and mean us no good. I now request thee to launch a terrible hail-storm. I have heard that there are nine different kinds of hail-storms. Launch one of them. That will complete the satisfaction of thine old mother. These people here are conspiring against our lives. They speak of sending some men to kill thee and, after thee, myself. So, for both our sakes, take good care of thyself. Shouldst thou be short of means, search for a valley facing north, overshadowed by a black cloud, and lit by the stars called Mindook (the Pleiades). There thou wilt find seven of our relatives. Ask of them, and thou wilt obtain whatever thou desirest in the way of provisions. Shouldst thou fail to find the valley, know that the pilgrim-devotee who beareth this liveth in that valley. Do not inquire about it from any one else."

'Now here was a riddle indeed. I was quite unable to make out what the letter meant. My desire to return home and see my mother was very great. I had run short of money and needed it sorely, but I knew not where these relatives lived. I knew nothing of the valley. My cheeks ran with floods of tears. I inquired of the pilgrim concerning the relatives, whom, so the letter said, he knew. I asked him who they were, and where they lived; I also asked him where he himself lived. He replied that he belonged to Ngari-Gungthang. On my questioning him further as to the whereabouts of my relatives spoken of in the letter, as also about himself and his movements, he said that he had been to several places, but knew of none where any relatives of mine lived nor anything of such relatives themselves. He himself was a native of U. So I asked him to wait a little until I came back. I then went and showed the letter to my *Guru*, at the same time telling him the news that I had got by word of mouth from the messenger.

'My *Guru* glanced once at the letter and said, "Thöpaga, thou seemest to have a very vindictive mother. So many persons dead, and yet she commandeth thee to launch hail-storms! What relatives hast thou in the North?" "I never before heard that I had any," I replied, "and the letter is very obscurely worded. I have asked the pilgrim, but he knoweth nothing about them."

'My *Guru's* wife was a lady endowed with supernatural intelligence, being the incarnation of a *ḍākinī*. She read through the letter once, and then ordered me to call the pilgrim, which I did. She then had a nice big fire made, and *chhang* served, and caused the pilgrim to take off the cloak he was wearing. Then, assuming a playful air, she put it on her own back, and strutting up and down the room said, "Happy indeed those persons must be who can go everywhere with no other clothing but this on their back!" Thereupon she danced about a little and moved out of the room with the cloak on her back. Going to the roof of the house, she cut open the patch, took out the gold pieces, replaced the patch as it had been before, and, coming back into the room, restored the cloak to the pilgrim. Thereafter she gave him some dinner and sent him off to another apartment.

'Having seen the pilgrim safely lodged, the lady called to me, saying, "Thöpaga, thy Teacher requesteth thee to come here into his presence." Going thither, she presented me with the seven pieces of gold. On asking her where she had found the gold, she replied that it had been in the pilgrim's cloak, and continued, "Thöpaga must have a very shrewd mother. The valley facing north was the pilgrim's cloak; for, as the sun doth not shine into a valley facing north, so also the pilgrim's cloak was one through which no sun-rays could pierce.

The black cloud referred to the square black patch. The constellation referred to the thread-work on the patch, and the seven relatives referred to the seven pieces of gold. Her ambiguous remark about not inquiring of any one else save the pilgrim himself referred to the fact that the pilgrim was clad in the cloak ; and the remark itself was intended to direct thine attention to his own person, which thou wert to search." At this my Teacher was highly pleased, and said, "Ye women are proverbially sharp-witted and keen-sighted, and this is only another proof of it."

' Out of the sum which thus came into my hands, I gave the pilgrim a tenth of one piece, at which he was delighted. I also offered the lady seven tenths ; and to my Teacher gave three pieces, entreating him to teach me the art of launching hail-storms which my mother desired me to learn. For a knowledge of the Hail-Charm, he, in his turn, referred me back to my former *Guru*, Lāma Yungtun-Trogyal. Furnished with the necessary letter and a scarf, recommending that my request should be granted, I returned to Yarlung-Kyorpo.

' Meeting my former *Guru*, I presented to him the letter and the scarf sent by Khulung-Yöntön-Gyatso, and made offering to him of the three pieces of gold that still remained to me. He inquired as to my success in my former studies. I told him that I had been successful ; that thirty-five people had been killed ; and that I had received a letter asking for a plague of hail, and now prayed him to grant my request. "Very good," said he, and at once imparted to me the Charm, ordering me to complete the ceremonial connected therewith in an old secluded cell [of a hermitage].

' At the end of seven days I saw clouds gathering in the cell and lightning flashing, and heard the growling of thunder. I now thought I might direct the course of a hail-storm with my finger, and my Teacher agreed, saying, " Now thou art able to launch hail-storms," at the same time asking me how tall the barley would be at that time.

' So I told him at about what time the seed was usually sown, when the young shoots commonly appeared, when it was high enough to hide pigeons, and finally at about what time the season for weeding arrived. My Teacher listened to me, and said that it was still too early. Later on, he again asked me about the seasons of the barley. I told him when the ears would appear, and when they would be full. He then said that it was time for me to go and launch my hail-storm; and with me he sent the strong, fleet pupil already mentioned.

'We disguised ourselves as pilgrims; and, coming to my village, saw that the harvest that year was so abundant that even the oldest folk of the place could not remember anything like it. On this account, a regulation was made for that year to the effect that nobody should reap at his or her own pleasure; a few days more, and all would begin to reap at one and the same time.[1]

'Then I erected the apparatus required for the working of my spell, on the heights above the valley, and began to chant the Charm; but not even a cloud as big as a sparrow gathered. I then called upon the names of the deities; and reciting the tale of our wrongs and the cruelty of our neighbours I struck the earth with my folded robe and wept bitterly.

'Almost immediately a huge, heavy, black cloud gathered in the sky; and when it had settled down there burst from it a violent hail-storm, which destroyed every single ear of grain in the fields. Three falls of hail followed in succession and cut deep gorges in the hill-sides. The country folk, thus deprived of their harvest, set up one great wail of distress and grief.

'The hail was followed by a heavy downpour of rain and a strong wind, which made the two of us feel very cold. So we sought a rocky cave facing north, and, having made a fire of stunted shrubs, were busy warming ourselves when we heard the voices of some people of the place who had come out hunting for game, with which to celebrate the usual harvest

---

[1] In Tibet, as in other lands with primitive manners, the peasantry are accustomed to cultivate and harvest their fields in common.

The exact dates for sowing and reaping crops are fixed by the village astrologer, who, after examining the relative positions of the planets and constellations, utters predictions as to the possibility of rain, while the older and more experienced peasants tell when the rains will start by examining the condition of the soil. Such predictions are no less accurate than those of our modern meteorological bureaus.

thanksgiving. They were saying among themselves, "Oh, this Thöpaga hath plagued the countryside more than any one ever hath done. See how many people he hath killed! And now this rich harvest, the like of which was never before seen, is all destroyed! If he fell into our hands at this moment, chopping him up piecemeal and dividing his flesh by morsels and his blood by drops would hardly suffice to satisfy our vengeance."

'As they thus spoke, they were passing right in front of our cave, and one of the older persons said, "Keep quiet; talk low! I see smoke in the cave over yonder. We do not know who it may be." One of the younger men said, "It must surely be Thöpaga. He cannot have seen us. Let us hurry down to the village and bring up men, surround him, and kill him, else he will certainly work more mischief on the village."

'So saying, they turned back to the village; whereupon my companion said to me, "Get thyself away first and I will impersonate thee and mock them." We made an agreement to meet again on the fourth night at the Inn of Tingri. Knowing how fleet and strong he was, I had no misgivings in leaving him behind; and, much as I then yearned to see my mother, I had to forgo my wish. Because of mine enemies, I had to get away as quickly as possible and go round by the Nyanam Pass. On the way I was bitten by a dog, which caused me some delay and prevented mine arrival at the Inn within the appointed time.

'Meanwhile, my friend had been surrounded, but had burst right through the line of those seeking his life; and, eluding them by running swiftly when they neared him and walking slowly again when they were far behind, he lured them on. When they began to shoot arrows and throw missiles at him he retaliated by hurling a big stone amongst them, saying at the same time, "Beware, ye rascals! I will surely destroy by magical means whoever of you singles himself out as my most prominent foe. Have I not cause to feel delight at having killed so many of you before? How comforting to my heart! More than that, I have destroyed the whole of this year's rich harvest so completely that not a single grain of corn is left for any of you to pick up. Is not that splendid too? For the future, if ye do not behave properly to my mother and my sister, I will put a curse upon your hill-tops and a blight upon your valleys, and make what is left of you barren and accurst down to the ninth generation. I will turn this country into a desolate wilderness! See if I do not." And as he went on speaking thus, his pursuers became frightened and began to say each to the other, "It was thou who brought on this," and so forth and so on, upon which they all turned back.

'Thus it was that my friend, having reached Tingri before me, asked the inn-keeper there if a pilgrim answering to my description had come to the Inn. The inn-keeper replied, "No"; and added, "Ye pilgrims have no objection to drinking when ye get the chance. Now if thou go over there thou wilt find a marriage-feast going on, where thou wilt be welcome. If thou have no bowl of thine own, I will lend thee mine, and thou canst have a proper time of it. Wilt thou go?"

'Of course my friend said "Yes", and took the bowl, which was as big as the head of Shinje,[1] deep and capacious, shapeless and unpolished. Armed therewith, he proceeded to the house of feasting, where I already was, seated in one of the back rows. My friend approached me and asked, "How is it that thou didst not reach the appointed place earlier?" I replied, "As I was going out begging one morning, a dog bit me on the leg and that delayed me." My friend said, "Never mind!" And from that place we proceeded on our way together.

'On our arrival at Yarlung-Kyorpo, our *Guru* said, "Ye two have been attended by success and good fortune." As there was no one who could have reached him before us and informed him we were astonished, and asked, "Who hath told thee? No one went ahead of us to inform thee." He replied that the deities had appeared to him with countenances beam-

---

[1] Tib. *Gshin-rje* (pron. *Shin-je*), the King and Judge of the Dead, otherwise known by his Sanskrit names as *Yama-Rāja* ('King of the Dead') and *Dharma-Rāja* ('King of Truth'). He is called Yama-Rāja because he rules or judges with restraint (Skt. *Sangyama*), and Dharma-Rāja because he judges and metes out punishment in strict accordance with the *karmic* deserts of each of the dead, or in accordance with Truth (Skt. *Dharma*).

ing with light like the full moon ; and that he had already performed the due thanksgiving ceremonies. On the whole, he seemed highly pleased.

'In this wise it was that I committed black deeds, avenging the wrongs done to me by mine enemies, waging war to the death with them.'

This is the first act [done by Jetsün]—the worldly act of destroying his enemies.

# LIFE ON THE PATH

'I heeded all He said and left the world
And all its cares behind, and gave myself
To follow where He taught, and realize
Life on the Path to great good fortune bound.
Now all my sorrows are hewn down, cast out,
Uprooted, brought to utter end,
In that I now can grasp and understand
The base on which my miseries were built.'

Vāsiṭṭhī, a Bhikkhunī.
*Psalms of the Early Buddhists*, I. li.

(Mrs. Rhys Davids' Translation.)

# PART II: THE PATH OF LIGHT

## INTRODUCTION

NEXT come the acts of his attaining the Perfect State of Buddhahood, which are as follows:

First: The act of his repentance and sincere search for a gifted and accomplished *Guru* [to guide him towards *Nirvāṇa*].

Second: The act of his unwavering obedience in fulfilling every command of his *Guru* when once found, despite the pain and anguish and despondency to which he was subjected that his sins might be expiated.

Third: The act of his obtaining the Truths which procured for him spiritual development and Final Emancipation.

Fourth: The act of his meditation under the personal guidance of his *Guru*, whence the shoots of experience and knowledge began to grow.

Fifth: As the Truths began to take their own course of development, the act of his obtaining the final ear-whispered occult truths, when led by an injunction given in a dream, after which he departed from his *Guru*.

Sixth: The act of his impulsion to take the vow of devoting his life wholly to the attainment of the Highest Goal, having been impressed by some unfortunate occurrence with the triviality of worldly pursuits.

Seventh: The act of his carrying out the commands of his *Guru*, by an undistracted application to ascetic devotion in an entirely secluded place, high on a hill, far removed from the haunts of men, putting away all thoughts of worldly fame, with boundless energy and untiring perseverance.

Eighth: The act of his acquiring Transcendental Knowledge and Experience as the result of such devotion, whereby he was able to confer great benefit upon all sentient beings.

Ninth: His final act, that of the dissolution of his mortal body into Cosmic Space, with intent to impart by example his last teaching of all, so that every sentient being might find in it an impulsion to live the religious life.

CHAPTER IV

# THE SEEKING OF THE HOLY *DHARMA*

*Telling of how Jetsün departed from his Guru of the Black Art; and of how Jetsün found his Guru of the True Doctrine, Marpa the Translator.*

AGAIN Rechung spoke and said, 'O Teacher, thou didst mention some white deeds done by thee which, of course, must mean devotion to the Holy *Dharma*. How and by what chance wert thou brought to seek religion, and how didst thou come to encounter it?'

Jetsün said, ' I deeply repented the destruction and mischief I had wrought by sorcery, in the killing of so many of mine enemies and in producing hail-storms. I longed so for religion that I forgot to eat. In the day-time I wished to be sitting down when I was going about, and to be going about when I was sitting down. At night I was unable to sleep. I was thus full of remorse and repentance, and yet I could not bring myself to ask my Teacher to allow me to adopt a religious life. Thus I continued serving my Teacher, all the while earnestly desirous of an opportunity to ask him to let me go and learn the Holy Doctrine.

' About this time, a wealthy and devout lay supporter of my Teacher fell seriously ill, and my Teacher was immediately invited to attend upon the sick man. Three days later my Teacher returned with a sad and downcast mien. I asked the reason of his looks, and he replied, " How transitory are all states of existence! Last night that excellent layman passed away, and I cannot but mourn his loss deeply. I realize the misery of all worldly existence. Moreover, from my youth up I have spent my whole time in the practice of sorcery, dealing in the Black Art of producing death and in bringing about hail-storms. And thou, too, my son, from thy youth hast taken to this sinful Art, and already hast gathered a heap of evil *karma*, all of which will lay a heavy load on me, since I am responsible for what thou hast done." [1]

[1] The *Guru*, whether of the Left-hand Path or of the Right-hand Path, be-

'I asked him if it were not true that all sentient beings killed by means of sorcery were in some manner saved and sent to higher states of existence. He replied, "I understand that all sentient beings possess a ray of the Eternal, and that we must work for their salvation and development. I also know the rituals to be used for the purpose ; but everything dependeth upon a true understanding of the purport of the ritual, as also of the meaning of the words used. I do not, however, feel confident that this superficial knowledge would stand the test of real danger. I therefore wish now to devote myself to such sound doctrine as will stand firm and solid in the face of everything that may threaten. Do thou remain here and act as guardian to my children and disciples, and I will go and work for thy salvation along with mine own. Or else, go thou thyself, learn and practise the Holy *Dharma* on my behalf as well as thine own, so as to save me and procure me a birth in my next existence which will further my progress on the Path of Emancipation. I will supply thee with all material support."

'This was exactly what I wished, and it filled me with great joy. I immediately prayed to be permitted to take to the religious life. My Teacher at once gave his consent, saying, "Certainly. Thou art young, and richly endowed with energy, abundant perseverance, and faith. Thou wilt make a very sincere devotee. Go, and live a life of pure religious study."

'He presented me with a yak-load of fine Yarlung woollen cloth, with the yak itself—a cow yak—and directed me to a place in the Tsang Valley called Nar, where lived a famous Lāma of the old mystic sect named Rongtön-Lhaga. This Lāma was said to have acquired supernormal faculties in the doctrine called " The Great Perfection ", of the Ñingma Sect.

comes spiritually responsible for whatever he directs his disciples to do—reaping evil *karma* from evil deeds thus done, and good *karma* from good deeds.

Sj. Atal Bihari Ghosh has here added the following : 'The Sanskrit terms *Vāma* (Left) and *Dakṣiṇa* (Right) have also a higher significance, the first being the Path of Renunciation (Skt. *Nivṛitti-Mārga*), the second the Path of Worldly Acquisition and Enjoyment (Skt. *Pravṛitti-Mārga*). This is the primary distinction as understood by the learned in India.'

My Teacher asked me to go and learn the doctrine from this *Guru*, and to practise it well. In accordance with his wish I went to Nar, in the Tsang Valley, and sought the Lāma.

'There I found the Lāma's wife and some of the Lāma's disciples, who told me that the place was the seat of the chief monastery, but that the Lāma himself was not at home at the time, that he had a branch monastery at Rinang, in the upper Nyang Valley, where he would be found. Thereupon, I told them that I had been sent by Lāma Yungtun Trogyal, and that I was willing to reward any one who would take me to the Lāma. The lady accordingly sent one of the disciples with me as a guide.

'At Rinang I found the Lāma, and offered him the cow yak and the bale of woollen cloth as a present, saying that I was a great sinner who had come from the West Highlands in search of a doctrine which would lead to deliverance from all *sangsāric* existence in one lifetime, and prayed him that he would impart it to me.

'The Lāma said, " My doctrine, called ' The Great Perfection ', is perfection indeed. It is excellent alike in its root, in its trunk, and in its branches,[1]—profitable to him from whom it hath been obtained, to him who hath obtained it, and in its fruit, which is the knowledge of *Yoga*. He who meditateth upon it in the day is delivered in the course of that day; and the like happeneth to him who meditateth upon it in the night. To the gifted, to those whose *karma* favoureth, the mere hearing of the doctrine is sufficient to procure them Deliverance; they do not need to meditate upon it. This is a doctrine for those intellects that are most highly developed. I will impart it to thee." He initiated me there on the spot and gave me the necessary instruction.

'At this the thought arose within me that formerly, while I was engaged in learning sorcery for killing purposes, it had taken me fourteen days to attain my desire, and in the case of launching hail-storms I had required seven days, whereas now I had met a doctrine which would emancipate me at any

---

[1] This parallels the Buddha's saying that His doctrine is 'perfect in the beginning, perfect in the middle, and perfect in the end '.

time, by day or by night, whenever I chose to meditate upon it; while to the gifted and specially favoured by their good *karma* the mere hearing thereof was sufficient to deliver them. I said to myself, "Why, I myself may be one of these favoured and gifted persons!" Thus was I so puffed up with pride that I would not meditate, but instead went to sleep over my task, and so failed to put the doctrine to the test of practice.

' After a few days, the Lāma came to me and said, " Thou didst call thyself a great sinner, hailing from the Highlands, and in that thou wert quite correct. On my part, however, I have been rather too lavish in my praises of my doctrine. At all events, I see quite well that I shall not be able to convert thee. Now there is a monastery called Dowo-Lung (Wheat Valley), in Lhobrak, wherein liveth at present a faithful disciple of Naropa, the great Indian Saint. He is the worthiest among the worthiest of men, a very prince among translators, —one who hath obtained supernormal knowledge in the new Tantric Doctrines, unequalled in all the three worlds; he is called Marpa the Translator. Between thee and him there is a *karmic* connexion, which cometh from past lives. To him thou must go."

' On hearing the name Marpa the Translator, my mind was filled with an inexpressible feeling of delight, and a thrill went through my whole body, setting in motion every hair, while tears started from mine eyes, so strong was the feeling of faith aroused within me. I therefore set out with the single purpose of finding this *Guru*, carrying only a few books and some provisions for the journey. All along the way I was possessed by but one idea : " When shall I set eyes upon my *Guru*? When shall I behold his face?"

' The night before mine arrival at Wheat Valley, Marpa had a dream to the effect that his *Guru*, the great Saint Naropa, came to him and performed the Initiation Ceremony and gave him a *dorje* made of lapis lazuli, five-pointed and slightly tarnished, and along with it a golden pot for holding holy water, filled with elixir; and ordered him to wash the dirt off the *dorje* with the elixir in the pot and to raise up the *dorje* upon a Banner of Victory. He added that this would please the Victorious Ones of the past, and be welcome to all sentient beings, thus fulfilling the aims both of ourselves and of others. Having said this, the Saint reascended into the Heaven-World.

'Then in his dream Marpa saw that he carried out the instructions of his *Guru*, washing the *dorje* with the holy elixir, as directed, and elevating it upon a Banner of Victory. Thence the *dorje* shed abroad such a brilliant radiance as filled all the worlds with its light, and falling upon the sentient beings existing in the Six *Lokas* dispelled all their griefs and sadness, filling them instead with bliss unalloyed with sorrow, so that in their delight they all looked upon Marpa and his Banner of Victory with overflowing faith and reverence, some worshipping, some singing praises, and some making offerings. He further saw in his dream that the Victorious Ones pronounced benedictions upon the Banner and performed the consecration ceremony, and that he himself was somewhat elated and proud. He then awoke feeling very happy.

'When his wife came in to serve breakfast, she said, "O Master, I dreamt last night that two women who said they were from the Urgyen Land of the West came carrying in their hands a crystal reliquary,[1] which was a little dirty, and asked me to tell thee that thy *Guru* Naropa enjoined thee to consecrate the reliquary with all the due ceremonial of a proper consecration, and to place it on the top of a hill. And thou wert saying that already it had been blessed by the great Saint Naropa, but that whatever he commanded must be obeyed, and thereupon didst wash it with holy water from the urns, perform the consecration ceremony over it, and place it on the top of a hill. Thence it emitted a light bright as the sun and the moon, and in addition reproduced several other reliquaries similar to itself, which settled down on the tops of neighbouring hills, two female forms acting as guardians. What doth this mean?"

'Albeit inwardly pleased at the coincidence in the purport of these two dreams, outwardly Marpa only said, "I do not

---

[1] This is a reliquary in the shape of a miniature *stūpa*. Compare with it the crystal reliquary borne by the *Ḍākinīs* at the time of Milarepa's translation, pp. 291-2.

know the meaning of dreams which have no cause. I am going down along the road there to plough the field to-day. Make ready." His wife said, "But thou hast ever so many labourers to work for thee. What will people say if thou, a great Lāma, go and work in the fields like a common labourer? It will create quite a scandal. Please stay at home; do not go!" But despite all her pleading Marpa went to the field, merely saying, "Bring me a good supply of *chhang*!" Upon his wife taking a jarful down to him, he said, "This may perhaps do for myself; bring some more for visitors." Another jar was brought, which he placed on the ground, covering it with his hat; and, sitting down beside the jar, he sipped the *chhang*, and rested himself after his ploughing.

'Meanwhile, I was approaching by the road, asking every one I met, "Where doth the Great *Yogī*, Marpa the Translator, live?" But none could give me the information I sought. I asked one person more, and he said that there was a man called Marpa who lived thereabouts, but that there was nobody there who bore such a grand title as Great *Yogī*, Marpa the Translator. I then asked him where Wheat Valley lay. He pointed it out, saying, "There it is." I then asked who lived there, and he answered that the person he had called Marpa lived there. "Was he not called anything else?" I next inquired. To this he replied that some called him Lāma Marpa also. That settled my doubts, and I knew that this must be the abode of the Marpa I sought. So I next inquired the name of the ridge on which I stood, and was told that it was called *Chhö-la-gang* (Ridge of the *Dharma*). I thought to myself that it was a very auspicious omen to have obtained my first view of my *Guru's* dwelling from this ridge.

'Nevertheless, as I went along the road, I still kept on inquiring for Marpa. I met some cowherds and put my question to them, too. The elder ones replied that they did not know. But a bright-looking young lad, well dressed and adorned with ornaments, with oiled and well-combed hair, said, "Thou must be meaning my Lord and father who used to sell off everything in our house, purchase gold, and then take it away to India and come back with ever so many rolls of paper. If it be he thou meanest, he is ploughing his field to-day—a thing he never did before." I considered it likely that this might be the person I sought, but I very much doubted whether a great translator would be found ploughing.

'Thus thinking, I was walking along the road, when I came upon a heavily built Lāma, rather inclined to corpulence, with full eyes, but very dignified in appearance. He was ploughing. The moment my eyes fell upon him, I was thrilled by a feeling of inexpressibly ecstatic bliss, in which I lost all consciousness of my surroundings. When I recovered, I said, "O Reverend Sir, where in this place doth the faithful disciple of the famous Saint Naropa, called Marpa the Translator, live?"

'For a while, the Lāma scanned me attentively from head to foot, and then asked, "Whence comest thou? What dost thou do?" I replied that I was a great sinner from the Highlands of Tsang, and that hearing of the fame for knowledge and learning of Marpa the Translator I had come to him to learn the True Doctrine by means of which I might obtain Deliverance.

'To this the Lāma replied, "Very good; I will procure thee an introduction to him if thou wilt finish this bit of ploughing for me," at the same time bringing out the *chhang* from under his hat and offering it me to drink, on accepting which I was very much refreshed. He charged me to plough the field well, and went off. I finished the *chhang*, and then ploughed the field with a will.

'After a short time, the lad I had seen among the cowherds who had given me the information I wanted came to call me in, at which I was highly pleased, and said to him, "The Lāma hath been successful in procuring the introduction for me, so I will finish this bit of ploughing for him." And I set to work and completed the portion that still remained to do. This field having aided me to an introduction to my *Guru*, it was afterwards called "Aid Field". In summer, a path runneth round the border of the field, and straight through it in winter.

'Going now with the lad, I found the Lāma seated on two thicknesses of cushions with a carpet over them, thus making a triple seat. I saw that he had been at some pains to wipe himself clean, but that his brow and the corners of his nose still bore some traces of dust. There he sat with his fat paunch protruding prominently in front of him. Although I thought that this was the same gentleman that had parted from me lately, to make sure, I looked about to see if another Lāma might be seated somewhere else.

'Thereupon the occupant of the cushion seat said, "Of course, thou didst not know me. I am Marpa himself, so thou mayst salute me."[1] I at once bowed down, touched his feet with my forehead, and placed them on the crown of my head. Having performed this ceremonial, I said, "I, O Precious *Guru*, am a great sinner from the West Highlands, and I have come here to offer body, speech, and mind to thee. I pray thee to provide me with food, clothing, and spiritual instruction, and enable me to obtain Liberation in this very lifetime."

'The Lāma replied, "Thy being a great sinner hath nothing to do with me. I did not send thee to commit sins on my behalf. But what sins hast thou committed?" On relating in full the circumstances of my case, the Lāma said, "Very well; I like thine offer to devote body, speech, and mind to me, but I cannot give thee food, clothing, and instruction, all three. I will either provide thee with food and clothing, thou seeking spiritual instruction elsewhere, or thou wilt have to find food and clothing elsewhere, while I give thee the spiritual instruction thou desirest. Choose whichever thou preferrest. If I impart to thee the Truth, it will entirely depend upon thine own perseverance and energy whether thou attainest Liberation in one lifetime or not."

'I replied, "I have come to thee, my Lāma, for the Truth. I will find my food and clothing elsewhere," and at once proceeded to accommodate myself there, bestowing the few books I had with me upon the altar shelf. But this the Lāma immediately forbade me to do, saying, "Out with thine old books; they will infect my holy reliques and sacred volumes and give them a cold!"[2]

[1] It is necessary that the *shishya* do reverence to the *Guru*.

[2] It is, as Milarepa's surmise in the following paragraph suggests, believed by Tibetan masters of the Occult Sciences that books, as well as persons, emanate definite auric influences; hence Marpa refused to have the works on Black Magic placed near works on White Magic or in contact with holy reliques.

' I immediately thought within myself that he knew there were some books of black magic among them, and on that account objected to their being put along with his books and images and other things. So for some days I kept them in the quarters assigned to me. My *Guru's* wife gave me nice food and other necessities.

' This is that part of my history which telleth of the manner of my coming to find my *Guru*, the same constituting the First of my Meritorious Acts.'

## CHAPTER V

## THE PROBATION AND PENANCE

*Telling of how Jetsün Obeyed the Commands of his* Guru
*Marpa, thereby Suffering Strange Trials and Great Tribula-
tions; and of how, in Despondency, he Thrice Deserted Marpa
and Sought another* Guru, *and then returned to Marpa.*

' I NOW went forth in search of alms up and down the whole
Lhobrak Valley, whereby I obtained four hundred and twenty
measures of barley.[1] With two hundred and eighty of them
I purchased a big copper vessel, free from speck or flaw inside
and outside, and having four handles, one on each of the four
sides. With twenty measures I procured meat and *chhang*.
The remaining hundred and twenty measures I put into a big
sack, and putting the copper vessel on top of it I carried the
whole home to my *Guru's* dwelling.

' Arriving there somewhat fatigued, I happened to throw
down my load a bit heavily, so that it made the house tremble
a little. This seemed to make my *Guru* angry, for he jumped
to his feet, saying, " Ha, thou appearest to be a particularly
strong little devotee. Dost thou wish to kill all of us, too,
shaking the house down by mere physical strength ? Out with
thy sack ! " And he kicked the sack out of the house, so that
I was obliged to place it outside. At the time, I thought that
my *Guru* was simply a little short-tempered, and that I must
be careful to behave properly in his presence ; I was not the
least shaken in my faith in him.[2] Then, after emptying the

---

[1] M. Bacot's version (p. 94) gives the number of measures as twenty-one,
each of these apparently being equal to twenty of the smaller measures mentioned in our rendering, and correspondingly for the measures mentioned in
the next sentence.

[2] As will be seen later on in the *Biography*, the various moods—anger, ill-will,
cruelty, and others—which Marpa apparently exhibits in his relationship as
*Guru* to his *Shishya*, Milarepa, are wholly feigned. No true *Guru* would ever
allow such unworthy passions in their real form to dominate or in any degree
control him ; and the feigned display of them, when seen all together, has a twofold purpose, namely, to test Milarepa and to make him do penance for the evils
which he had wrought through practising the Black Art. Before being accepted
as a *Shishya*, the aspirant is always subjected to certain severe tests respecting

copper vessel, I again took it into the house, and, bowing down, offered it to the Lāma.   He accepted it by laying his hand on it ; and then, without removing his hand from it, he remained for a while with his eyes closed in prayer.   His invocation ended, I could see tears trickling down his face, as he said, " It is auspicious; I offer it to my *Guru* Naropa " ; and simultaneously he made with his hands the motion of offering something.   He next took hold of the handle-rings and shook them violently, and struck the vessel with a rod, making as loud a noise thereby as he possibly could.   Finally, he took the vessel over to the end of the altar and laid it there, filling it with clarified butter for burning in the altar lamps.

' Being much concerned about my Liberation, I repeatedly entreated him to bestow upon me some instruction, whereupon he said, "I have a number of devoted disciples and lay-followers in the Ü and Tsang Provinces who would much like to come here, but they have been repeatedly robbed on the way by the nomad shepherds of Yamdak and Talūng, as well as by the Lingpas.   Thus frequently plundered, they are prevented from coming here with any provisions or presents.   Go thou and launch a plague of hail upon the robbers.   That itself is a religious duty ; afterwards I will then give thee instruction in the Truth."

' Accordingly, I went and launched a terrific hail-storm on each of the places mentioned, and, returning, asked for the instruction promised.   But the Lāma replied, "What! Thou presumest to ask for the Most Sacred *Dharma*, which I procured at such cost and self-sacrifice from India, in return for two or three paltry hail-stones!   Now, Sir, if thou art really in earnest about the Truth, thou wilt go and by means of sorcery, in which thou claimest to be an adept, destroy a number of the Lhobrak hill-men, for these, also, have often robbed disciples of mine who have been on their way here from Nyal-Lo-ro, and frequently offered indignities to myself too.   If thou can work some signal piece of havoc in proof of thy magical power, I will undertake to impart to thee the Mystic

his or her competency (*adhikāra*).   Only after such tests does the *Guru* decide for what training, if for any, the aspirant is fitted.

Truths, handed down to me by my reverend *Guru*, the great Paṇḍit Naropa—Truths whereby one can gain Liberation in a single lifetime and attain to Buddhahood."

' Again I did as I was bidden; and my magical curse taking effect among the Lhobrak hill-men a feud broke out among them ; and in the fighting many of them were killed. The sight of the bloodshed, however, affected me with the deepest remorse and anguish. My *Guru*, perceiving that among the killed were several of those who had offended him, said to me, " It is quite true that thou art an adept in sorcery." And he gave me the title of *Thüchhen* (Great Sorcerer).

' Upon my asking him again for the saving Truths, he said, " Ha, ha ! Must I give thee the most sacred Truths, which I brought from India with such great pains, expending all my worldly goods in gold for them—Truths which still emit the holy breath of the Angelic Beings who gave them, and all in return for thy having done evil deeds ? Why, Sir, that would be such a great jest as would make everybody laugh. Were it any one else save myself, he would have killed thee for such presumption. Now, Sir, thou shalt go and make good all the mischief and damage which thou hast caused to the crops of the shepherd-folk, and restore to life the killed among the Lhobrak men. If thou can do that, well and good; I will let thee have the Truths. If thou can not, thou hadst better not enter my presence again." Thus he scolded me as if about to beat me. As for myself, I was plunged into the depths of despair and wept bitterly, the Lāma's wife, the while, seeking to comfort me.

' Next morning the Lāma was kind enough to come to me himself and say, " I fear I was a little too hard on thee yester-day evening, but do not take it too much to heart. Have patience and wait, and thou shalt have the Teachings. But thou seemest to me to be a handy person. I should therefore like thee to build a house for my son, Darma-Doday (The Youth, the Bouquet of *Sūtras*). When thou hast completed it, not only will I impart the Truths to thee, but I will also supply thee with all needful food and clothing for the period of thy study." " But ", I urged, " what will happen to me if in the interval I happen to die undelivered ? " He answered, " I promise thee that thou shalt not die undelivered in the interval. Mine is not a doctrine empty of all definite promise. So, as thou appearest to possess a considerable stock of energy and perseverance, thou canst please thyself, with none to hinder, whether thou obtainest the Deliverance in one lifetime or not. My Sect is not quite the same as other sects. In it are to be found more emanation of Divine Grace-Waves and a more direct Spiritual Revelation than in any other sect.[1] Consoled and rejoiced by these comforting promises, I at once asked the Lāma for a plan of the proposed house.

'Now, in asking me to do this work for him, the Lāma, as I subsequently perceived, had three objects in view. Firstly, not having been included in an oath-taking party held by his male relatives on a certain place [of strategic importance, whereby it was agreed that no stronghold should be erected thereon[2]], he wished to build a house there, for the site was very desirable, being safe and not easily reached and closed forever to those who had taken the oath. Secondly, he wished me to expiate mine evil deeds. And thirdly and lastly, he wished to mislead the aforementioned parties into allowing him to proceed unopposed with the building of his house on the site he desired.

' He had recourse to the following stratagem. He took me to a mountain ridge having an eastern aspect, and, pointing out a particular place, described a circular structure and ordered me to begin building it there; and this I at once did. When I had finished about half of it, he came along and said that, when giving me my orders at the outset, he had not well considered the matter, and that I must stop work on the

[1] This refers to the *lāmaic* belief, much like the Christian, that divine grace may be received by human beings on earth in the form of waves radiated by spiritual beings. Marpa held the superhuman *Gurus* of his Sect to be more capable of helping the devotee than those of any less spiritually-endowed sect, because of the direct guidance thus telepathically given by them.

[2] As M. Bacot notes (p. 97), in Milarepa's time there was no centralized government in Tibet, the power of the Tibetan kings having disappeared and the authority of China not yet having been established; hence the local feudal lords, being jealous of one another, had apparently agreed not to fortify the site referred to in our text.

building and demolish it, and carry back to the place whence I had taken them the earth and stones I had used.

'When I had carried out this order, the Lāma, appearing to me to be intoxicated,[1] took me to a ridge having a western aspect and, ordering me to build another house there, after describing a crescent-shaped ground-plan, went away. When I had built this house up to about half the height required, the Lāma again came to me while I was working and said that even this house would not do, and that I must restore the clay and the stones to the places whence I had taken them. Again I obeyed his commands.

'Once more the Lāma took me away, this time to a ridge with a northern aspect, and there addressed me thus : " My Great Sorcerer, I seem to have been tipsy when I last told thee to build a house, and so gave thee a mistaken order. Apparently it was a thorough mistake all through. But now thou shalt build me a really nice house on this site." I ventured to observe that it was a useless expense to himself, and a great trouble to me, to be over and over again building up and pulling down houses. I entreated him to consider matters well, and then to give me his orders. He said, " I am not tipsy to-day, and I have thought well over the matter. A Tantric mystic's dwelling ought to be triangular, so build me one of that shape. This one shall not be demolished."

'So I proceeded to build a triangular-shaped house. When I had finished about a third of it, the Lāma one day came down and said, " Who gaveth thee the order to build a house like this?" I answered, " Why, it is the house for Thy Reverence's son, and was ordered by thyself." " I have no recollection of having given thee any such order," said he. " But if it be as thou sayest, then it must have been at a time when I was not in full possession of my senses, or I must have been mad outright." " But," I urged, " fearing that something of this kind might happen, I ventured to impress upon Thy Reverence the necessity of careful consideration ; and then thou wert pleased to assure me that thou hadst carefully con-

---

[1] This, too, was feigned by Marpa, in order that his plans for imposing penances of a very severe nature on Milarepa should succeed.

sidered everything, and that this building should not be demolished. And Thy Reverence at the time appeared to be in
a perfectly normal state of mind." The Lāma replied, "What
witness hast thou for this? What! Wert thou seeking to destroy me and mine by means of sorcery, or what, by thrusting
us into this triangular building of thine, which looketh like a
magical triangle? Why, man, I have not robbed thee of thy
patrimony! Besides, if thou art really anxious for religious
instruction—why, the very shape of this house is enough to
set all the Local Deities against thee! See, then, that thou
demolish it at once and take all the stones and clay back
where thou didst find them. Thereupon, I will give thee the
instruction thou desirest, or else, thou canst go away!" And the
Lāma went off, apparently very angry. I was very much grieved
at this, but there was no help for it. I stood in need of the
Truth, and so had no other choice but to demolish the triangular
house like the others, and to do as bidden with the materials.

'By this time I had a big sore on my back, between my
shoulder and my spine, but I did not dare to show it to the
Lāma, who, I feared, would be displeased if I did so. Neither
did I venture to show it to his wife, lest she should think I
wanted her to notice how hard I was working for them. So
I kept my misery to myself, and only solicited her aid in praying the Lāma to give me the promised instruction.

'The motherly lady kindly went in to her husband, and said,
"My Lord, thine useless building undertakings are only wearing out the poor youth's life. Pray take pity on him now and
give him some instruction." The Lāma answered, "Get a nice
dinner ready, and bring him in to me." The lady, accordingly,
prepared some food, and led me in. The Lāma then said to
me, "Great Sorcerer, do not falsely accuse me, as thou didst
yesterday, of things which I have not done. As for instruction,
I now give it thee." And he imparted to me the four formulas
of the Refuges,[1] with the prayers and the injunctions and vows;

---

[1] The Refuges are the *Buddha*, the *Dharma* (or Rules of Right Conduct as
contained in the Buddhist Scriptures), and the *Saṅgha* (or Buddhist Community
of which the Priesthood is the most important part). Amongst Northern Buddhists,
the Refuges are made the basis of various formulas, similar to professions of
faith.

and added, " These are called Temporal Religious Instructions. But if thou seek the Non-Temporal Religious Instructions, or Mystic Truths, thou must do such and such things in order to merit them." And he proceeded to recite a brief story from the life of his *Guru* Naropa, and ended by saying, " But thou wilt hardly be able to attain to such ideal height as this ; that will be too difficult for thee I fear." Hearing this, I was so moved to the very depths of my heart with faith that I was unable to repress my tears ; and I inwardly resolved to do whatsoever the Lāma commanded me.

' A few days after this, the Lāma invited me to go for a walk with him, and I did so. In the course of our stroll, we came to the spot already mentioned, whereon the uncles and cousins of the Lāma had agreed not to build, and which was now guarded by them. Here the Lāma came to a halt, and said, " Thou art now to build on this spot an ordinary quadrangular house, nine stories high, with an ornamental upper part forming a tenth story. This house shall not be demolished ; and upon its completion I will bestow on thee the Truths for which thou art pining and maintain thee while thou art in retreat performing *Sādhanā* (Meditation), providing thee with all needed food and clothing." Here I ventured to suggest that he should allow me to ask his wife—whom I was used to call Reverend Mother—to come and be witness to his words. He granted my request ; so I went and called the Reverend Mother, while the Lāma occupied himself in marking out the ground-plan. Then, in the presence of both, I said, " Up to the present I have built three houses and again demolished each of them. In the case of the first, the Lāma said that he had not given due consideration to the matter; in the case of the second, that he had been tipsy when he gave the order for it ; and, in the case of the third, that he had either been out of his senses or quite mad at the time, and did not remember having ever given me the order to build it. Upon my reminding him of the circumstances in connexion with the third house I built, he asked me to produce a witness to his words, and seemed highly displeased. Now once more he is giving me the order to begin building another house, so I pray that thou, my

Reverend Mother, mayst be pleased to act as witness to this present order."

'The lady replied, "Of course I can stand as witness; but thy *Guru* [the Reverend Father] is so imperious that he will not pay any attention to us. Moreover, the Reverend Father is doing a perfectly useless thing; there is no necessity for all these building projects. It is altogether needless trouble to cause thee to build houses so often, only to pull them down as often again. Besides, this site is not ours by right, but closed and guarded by all thy *Guru's* relatives, it being the site on which a joint vow hath been taken by them. But the Reverend Father will pay no heed to such a weak voice as mine. I shall only incur risk of contention." Addressing his wife, the Lāma said, "Merely do what thou art asked to do, namely, stand witness, and then get away home, and leave me to see to the performance of my part in the business! Thou needest not raise questions no one asketh thee to raise."

'So I set about laying the foundation of the quadrangular building ordered, and then proceeded with its erection. But now Ngogdun-Chudor, of Zhung, Tsurtön-Wang-gay, of Döl, and Metön-Tsönpo, of Tsang-rong—all advanced disciples of my *Guru*—happened in sport to bring to that spot a big boulder. As it was a good-sized stone, I set it in, as a corner stone, just above the foundation, near to the doorway, and had got up to about the second story from the ground when Marpa came on a visit to the scene of my toil. After inspecting the building all round very carefully, he pointed to the stone that had been brought by the three advanced disciples of his, and said, "Great Sorcerer, whence didst thou procure that stone?" I replied, "Reverend Sir, it was brought in sport by Thy Reverence's three chief disciples." "Oh, was it?" he said. "Well, thou hast no business to use for thy building purposes a stone brought by them. See that it is taken out and returned to the place from which it was taken." I reminded him of his promise not to have this building pulled down. He only replied, "But I did not promise to let thee employ, as thy workmen, my chief disciples who have been initiated into the Mystic Truths of twice-born beings. Besides, I am not ordering thee to pull down the entire edifice, but only to take out that stone brought by my chief disciples, and to restore it to its original place."

'Thus once more I had to pull down, from top to bottom, a wall which I had erected. Taking out the stone, I put it back whence it had come. As soon as the Lāma saw that I had accomplished this, he came and said, "Now thou mayst go and bring back that same stone thyself, and set it in the same place." Putting forth the strength of the three men, I managed to get it up and put it into the same place as before. This stone was ever after called my "Giant Stone", in token of the unusual physical strength I displayed in connexion with it.

'While I was thus engaged in laying the foundation of this edifice on the prohibited site, some of those who saw me said, "It seemeth as though Marpa really meaneth to build on this spur. Had we not better object to it?" But others said, "Marpa is beside himself. He hath got hold of a strong young novice from the Highlands, and, being possessed with a mania for building, he keepeth the poor young man busy all the time building houses of unapproved patterns on every ridge, spur, and knoll round about. Then, when the building is half finished, he getteth the same young man to pull it all down again and carry the materials back to where they came from. He will surely do the same in this case, too. But if he should not, there will be ample time to stop him. Let us wait and see."

'However, they soon saw that this house was not to be pulled down, but continued. Then, when it had reached the seventh story—and another sore had come on my body near the waist—Marpa's relatives said to one another, "He is not going to pull down this building. The pulling down of the others was only a feint designed to mislead us, and prevent our objecting, at the outset, to the building of this one. Let us pull it down now!" And with this intent, they collected in a body. But the Lāma produced by magical power a vast body of armed troops who crowded the house both outside and inside. The would-be attackers were all filled with fear. Each looked on the other and asked, "From where hath Marpa the Translator managed to call up such a number of troops?" They did not dare to fight with them. Instead, each one privily paid his respects to Marpa, and subsequently all became his followers.

'At about this time, Metön-Tsönpo, of Tsang-rong, came to receive the Grand Initiation into the *Dēmchog Maṇḍala*.[1] My Reverend Mother [my *Guru's* consort] thereupon spoke to me, saying, "Now is the time for thee also to try to get initiated. Let us make the attempt." I also thought that since I had succeeded in erecting such an edifice entirely single-handed, without receiving so much as a piece of stone the size of a goat's head, a basketful of earth, a jugful of water, or a spadeful of clay in the way of help from any one else, I surely must deserve some consideration ; and I felt quite sure that the Initiation would now be bestowed on me. So, bowing down, I took my seat among the candidates for initiation.

'Seeing me there, the Lāma asked, "Great Sorcerer, what hast thou as the offering ? " I replied, " Thy Reverence promised me that when I had completed the building of the house for Thy Reverence's son, I should be favoured with initiation and instruction. So I hope Thy Reverence will now be pleased to grant me the Initiation." Upon this, the Lāma exclaimed, "What presumption ! What impertinence ! Just because thou hast put together a few cubits of mud-wall, I, forsooth, must impart to thee the sacred lore which I obtained from India only at much personal sacrifice and cost. If thou can pay the initiation fees, well and good ; pay them ! If thou can not, out thou walkest from this Mystic Circle." And he struck me, and, dragging me by the hair, flung me out. Thereupon I wished that I were dead, or that I might die there and then, upon the spot. I wept the whole of that night through.

'Then the Lāma's lady came to me, and said, " The Lāma is beyond all comprehension. He sayeth that he hath brought the Sacred Doctrine from India into this land for the benefit of all sentient beings ; and, as a rule, he will teach, and preach to, even a dog that may happen to come into his presence, and

---

[1] That is, Initiation into the practical application of such mystic doctrines as are contained in the *Dēmchog* (Bde-mch'og : Skt. *Shamvara*) *Tantra*, which is a part of the very voluminous *Kah-gyur* or canon of Northern Buddhism.

wind up by praying for its welfare. Still, do not lose faith in him." Thus the good woman tried to cheer me.

'Next morning, the Lāma himself came to me, and said, "Great Sorcerer, thou hadst better cease work on this house thou hast under construction, and begin on another dwelling-house of twelve pillars, having a hall-chamber and a chapel, to serve as an annexe to the main edifice. When thou hast finished this, I will surely give thee the Instructions."

'Once more I laid the foundations of a building. All the while the Lāma's lady continued to supply me with excellent food and condiments daily, together with a little *chhang*; and she consoled me and gave me good advice.

'As the annexe was approaching completion, Tsurtön-Wang-gay, of Döl, came to receive the Great Initiation into the *Mandala* of The Esoteric.[1] Thereupon, the Lāma's lady said to me, "This time, at any rate, my son, we shall manage to get thee initiated." She provided me with a roll of butter, a piece of blanket-cloth, and a small copper vessel, and told me to go and take my seat among the *shishyas* who were about to go and receive initiation. The Lāma, noticing me, said, "Great Sorcerer, what hast thou as thine initiation fees that thou takest thy seat in the ranks of the novices?" I produced my roll of butter, blanket-cloth, and copper vessel, and said that these should be mine offerings. To this the Lāma replied that these things already belonged to him, since they had been brought as initiation fees by others; that they would not do, and that I must bring something belonging to myself or else get out of the mystic circle of those to be initiated. And, at this, he arose, seemingly in a furious temper, and drove me out with blows from his foot, so that I wished I could sink into the earth.

---

[1] Text: *Sang-dü*, here refers to a very abstruse and esoteric part of the instruction given to candidates for Initiation into the Occult Sciences of the Kargyütpa School. In other contexts, as on pp. 169, 287–8, 300, Sang-dü (Gsang-'düs) is the Tibetan name of a Tantric deity known in Sanskrit as Guhya-kāla. Literally, *Sang-dü* means 'Esoteric' (or 'Hidden'), with reference to mystic insight conferred by the super-normal power of *Siddhi* (lit. 'Accomplishment'). The other classes of such insight as a *Siddha* enjoys are known as *Ch'ir-Dü*, meaning 'Exoteric' (or 'External'), and *Nang-Dü*, 'Internal'.

'Then the thought came to me, "Seeing that I have caused the death of so many people by means of sorcery, and destroyed such a number of crops with storms of hail, all that I now am suffering is the *karmic* result of those evil deeds. Or else," so I thought, "the Lāma must have perceived something in me whereby he knew that I would not be able to receive and practise the Doctrine. Or, again," I wondered, "was it that the Lāma did not regard me personally with liking or esteem? However it be," so I thought within myself, "without religion, the life of man is not worth living"; and I began to make up my mind to kill myself. At this moment, the Lāma's lady brought me her share of the offerings of consecrated food, and communicated her sincere condolences. But I had lost all relish, even for consecrated food, and wept on, the whole night through.

'Next morning, the Lāma himself came to me, and said, "Thou must complete both the buildings; then I will surely give thee the Instructions and the Truths."

'Going on with my building operations, I had almost completed the annexe, when another sore broke out on the small of my back; and, blood and matter pouring forth from all three sores, my whole back soon became nothing but one big sore. I showed it to my Reverend Mother; and, reminding her of the Lāma's promise to give me instructions, I asked her to plead for me with the Lāma, so that he might be pleased to vouchsafe me the Truths for which I thirsted. My Reverend Mother looked attentively at my sores, and, shedding profuse tears, promised to speak for me to the Lāma.

'So she went to the Lāma, and spoke thus: "Great Sorcerer hath done so much building work that his hands and legs are all cracked and bruised, and his back hath broken out into three large sores, from which ooze blood and matter. I have heard about sore-backed ponies and donkeys before this, and seen some, too; but never before have I heard of a sore-backed human being, much less seen one. What a disgrace it will be to thee if people come to hear of it! Thou who art such a highly respected and honoured Lāma, to be so cruel! Thou shouldst have some mercy on the lad. Moreover, thou didst promise to give him the Instruction he desireth so much, upon his completing the building." The Lāma answered, " I did, indeed, say so; I promised him that when the ten-storied building should be finished I would give him the Instructions, but where are the ten stories? Hath he finished them yet?" "But", urged my mediator, "he hath built an annexe far exceeding the ten-storied edifice in size." "'Much talk, little work,' as the proverb sayeth," retorted the Lāma. "When he hath completed the tenth story I will give him the Instructions— and not till then. But is his back really broken out into sores?"

'"O Reverend Father, thy being so despotic preventeth thy seeing it. Otherwise thou couldst not but have noticed that not only hath he a sore back, but that his whole back is nothing else but one big sore." This said in her severest manner, the Lāma's lady hurried away from him. But the Lāma called after her, saying, "Then let the lad come up to me."

'Accordingly, I went in to see him, greatly hoping that I was at last to be given the Instructions; but, instead, he only ordered me to show him my sore back. Upon my doing so, he looked at it very attentively, and said, "This is nothing to the trials and tribulations which were endured by my Lord Saint Naropa. He had to undergo in his own body twelve greater and twelve lesser trials, making twenty-four in all. I myself did not spare my wealth or consider my body's safety, but, sacrificing both ungrudgingly, followed and served my Teacher Naropa. If thou art really in search of the Truth, do not boast so about thy services, but continue waiting patiently and working steadily till thy building task is entirely finished." Once more my hopes were dashed to the ground.

'The Lāma, then, putting his robe in the shape of a pad, showed me how ponies and donkeys are padded when any of them getteth a sore back, and advised me to do the same for myself. When I asked him of what use a pad was when the whole of the back was one sore, he coolly told me that it would prevent the earth getting into the sore and making it worse; and added that I was to go on carrying clay and stones.

'Considering within myself that such was the wish of my *Guru*, I felt that I must go on and do as commanded. I therefore took up my loads and carried them in front of me now, and thus went about the work. The Lāma, seeing what I was doing, inwardly said, " Worthy of praise is that noble *shiṣhya* who un-grudgingly obeyeth his *Guru's* commands," secretly shedding tears of joy at seeing my sincerity and my faith in him.

'At length, as the sores grew more and more aggravated and inflamed, I suffered so much pain from them that I was unable any longer to go on working; and I asked the Lāma's lady to plead for me again, that I might be given the Truths. But even if this should be refused, I craved permission to rest awhile until I should be able to resume the work. She did so, but the Lāma only said, " Teaching or Instructions he cannot have until he hath finished the buildings; but rest he may if he be unable to work, since this cannot be helped. In any case, let him do as much work as is possible for him to do." Whereupon my Reverend Mother allowed me to rest and get my sores healed.

'When they were partly cured, the Lāma, making no men-tion of Instructions whatever, said to me, " Great Sorcerer, thou hadst better resume thy building work and get on with it quickly." I was on the point of doing as bidden, when my Reverend Mother said privily, " Let us do something that will make him give thee the Teachings."

'After she and I had consulted together, we decided that I should sally forth with all my worldly goods [my books and so forth], together with a small bag of barley flour, tied on my back; and that thereupon I should say to her, " Oh, let me go, let me go!" at a spot on the road where I should be visible [and audible] to the Lāma from where he [habitually] sat. This was to be by way of pretending that I was going away, while she was to detain me, saying, " Do not go away, do not go away; I will do mine utmost to get the Instructions for thee."

'When this little play was thus enacted within the range of the Lāma's eyes [and ears], he called, " Damema (One Without Egotism), what comedy is this ye two are acting?" His lady replied, " Great Sorcerer sayeth that he hath come from a far distant country, trusting to obtain from thee, his *Guru*, a know-ledge of the Saving Truths. However, instead of obtaining them, he hath only incurred thy displeasure and procured himself a number of beatings. And now, fearing lest he die without having learned the Truths, he wisheth to go elsewhere in quest of them; and I am assuring him that I will do mine utmost to obtain the Truths for him, and am trying to detain him." " I see," said the Lāma; and down he came from his seat, and, giving me several blows, cried, " When first thou didst come to me, didst thou not offer me thine entire self—body, speech, and mind? Where dost thou wish to go now? Thou belongest to me altogether. If I liked, I could chop thy body into a hundred bits; and no one could hinder me. And even if thou do intend to go away, what business hast thou to carry away flour from my house?" And with that, he knocked me down on the ground, and gave me a violent beating; then he took the bag of flour back into the house.

' On this, I was pierced to the heart with grief, as great as that of a mother who hath lost her only son. But, at the same time, I was awed by the imperious dignity of the Lāma, and by the thought that the whole occurrence was the outcome of my consultation with the Lāma's lady. I could do no otherwise than return and lie down weeping. My Reverend Mother said it was evident that the Lāma would not be moved to grant my request for the Truths by any of our prayers, entreaties, stratagems, and the like. " But rest assured," she said, " he will surely grant them at last. Meanwhile, I will venture to teach thee something." And she kindly taught me the method or system of meditation upon Dorje-Pa-mo,[1] which greatly appeased the yearning of my heart, albeit I did not attain to the entire boon of " The Realization of Knowledge ".[2] But for what I did receive I was very grateful indeed

---

[1] Text: *Rdorje-Pʻag-mo* (pron. *Dorje-Pa-mo*): Skt. *Vajra-Vārāhī*, meaning ' Immutable (or Thunderbolt) Sow ', an Indian Goddess, whose sow-form is a mystic symbol. The Brāhmanical conception of Vārāhī is contained in chapter xxiii of the *Tantra-rāja* (see *Tantrik Texts*, ed. by A. Avalon, vol. xii), and her *Dhyāna* (or way in which to meditate upon her) is contained in the English Introduction (p. 43) of the same volume. She is described as *Janakātmukā*, that is, she possesses the nature of the Father (*Janaka*). According to Tibetan belief, Dorje-Pamo is now incarnate in the Abbess of the famous Sam-ding Monastery. As such, this Abbess is the only female incarnate deity in Tibet.

[2] That is, the Realization of the Truths, born of practising them under a competent *Guru*.

to my Reverend Mother.  I thought that as she was the wife
of my *Guru*, such Truths as were received from her would
help to wipe out mine evil deeds.  So I tried to show my gratitude to her by doing little services for her comfort, such as
making a seat for her to sit on when she should be milking the
cows in the summer time, and another for her use when she
should be roasting barley in the yard in front of the house.

' About this time, I began seriously to make up my mind to
go and seek another *Guru*.  But, pondering the matter over
again, I came to the conclusion that as regardeth the Doctrine
whereby I might obtain perfect Emancipation in this very lifetime, my present *Guru* was the only one possessing it.  I saw,
too, that, unless I obtained Emancipation in this lifetime, the
evil deeds which I had committed would be enough to cast
me into one of the Hells.  Thus I resolved to do mine utmost
to emulate Naropa in his severe trials and endurance, as well
as in his unwearied perseverance in search of the Saving Truth,
and thus to secure mine Emancipation.  So minded, I went on
with my building work, stacking stones and heaping up earth
with which to make mud.

' Then came Ngogdun-Chudor, of Zhung, bringing valuable
presents, and accompanied by a large retinue, to receive the
Grand Initiation into the *Maṇḍala* [or Rite] of Gaypa-Dorje.[1]

' Thereupon, the Lāma's lady spoke to me saying, " If the
Reverend Father is still dissatisfied with the great devotion
and obedience thou hast shown in building these houses single-
handed, and must have some pecuniary offerings as his initiation fee, let us give him something in order to make sure of
thy participating in this initiation ceremony at all events.
Offer him this, and take the initiation ; and, if he demur,
I will add my prayers to thine.  So saying, she put in my
hands a valuable turquoise, of a deep blue shade, which was
her own personal property.

' I went, then, and offering it as mine initiation fee, took my
seat among those who were going to participate in the ceremony.
The Lāma took the turquoise ; and, turning it over and over,

---

[1] Text : *Dgyes-pa-rdorje* (pron. Gay-pa-Dorje), the Tibetan name of a Tantric
deity, and also of a series of *Tantras* in eight volumes : Skt. *Hé-Vajra*.

and examining it carefully, at length said to me, "Great Sorcerer, how didst thou come by this turquoise?" I replied, "The Reverend Mother gave it to me." He smiled, and said, "Call Damema here." When the Reverend Mother had come, he said, "Damema, how did we get this turquoise?" She prostrated herself several times before him and answered, "Reverend Father, this turquoise is in no way our common property. It is a special piece of private property given to me by my parents upon our marriage. Seeing that Thy Reverence was rather short-tempered, it was feared that we might fall out. So the turquoise was intended to serve as a provision for me in the event of our separation; and I was to keep it in secret as a piece of entirely private property. But noting how eager this poor boy is to obtain the Doctrine, I could not help producing it and giving it to him. Please accept this turquoise and grant him the Initiation. He hath suffered much agony of mind from having been turned out of the Sacred Circle several times already. Permit me, then, to pray that thou wilt have mercy on him. And ye, too, my sons, Ngogdun and ye others, I request you, in this, to add your prayers to mine." Having finished, she again prostrated herself several times before the Lāma.

'Knowing the Lāma's short temper, Ngogdun and the others dared not say anything, but simply rose and bowed down, repeating, "Yes, let it be as our Reverend Mother sayeth." But the Lāma—the turquoise on his necklace now—only said, "Damema, thy folly had very nearly lost me this valuable turquoise; it might have been lost altogether. Do not be silly, please! When thou thyself belongest altogether to me, the turquoise, of course, is mine. Great Sorcerer, if thou have any property of thine own, thou mayst bring it here, and I will bestow the Initiation upon thee. This turquoise is mine own property."

'Seeing that the Reverend Mother had made him an offering of the valuable turquoise, I thought that perhaps he might be softened into allowing me to share in the Initiation; so I stayed on for a little time. At this, the Lāma lost his temper, and rising, [apparently] in fierce anger, shouted, "Thou impertinent fellow, why dost thou not get out when I tell thee? What right hast thou to remain in my presence?" Thereupon, with stunning force, he felled me to the ground, face downward. Then, picking me up, he threw me down again on my back, with great violence. He was next taking up his stick to beat me, when Ngogdun intervened and caught him. Meanwhile, in mine extreme terror, I jumped out of a window, which made the Lāma anxious, though he still pretended to be angry.

'The leap did me no harm, but I was so grieved and hurt at heart that I resolved to kill myself. But again my Reverend Mother came to me, bringing me solace, and saying, "Great Sorcerer, do not take it so much to heart. There cannot anywhere be a dearer or more faithful pupil than thyself. If, after all, thou should have to go and look for another *Guru*, I will help thee myself with the necessary presents and means for thine expenses." Thus she sought to console me, remaining with me and weeping throughout the entire night, neglecting entirely her duty to be present and assist at the Lāma's evening devotions.

'Next morning, the Lāma summoned me into his presence. I went, in the hope that he was now going to fulfil my dearest wishes. He asked me whether his refusal to initiate me the previous day had shaken my faith in him or inspired me with dislike. I answered, "It did not shake my faith in thee, for I considered that it was my great evil-doing which debarred me from sharing in the ceremony, and I am pierced with remorse." Saying this, I burst into tears, whereupon he ordered me out, exclaiming, "What reason hast thou, by thy weeping, to blame me in this manner?"

'As I came out, I felt as if my heart were almost breaking; a perfect whirlwind seemed tearing at its very roots. I thought of the gold I had possessed at the time when I set out on my career of evil-doing, and deplored the fate which deprived me of it now, when I wished to set out on the path of righteousness. Oh, how I wished that I had but half of it now! I should then be able to obtain Initiation and the Doctrine. But without gold, I saw that this Lāma would never give me either. I should always require to have something for a present, even if I should go elsewhere to obtain the Doctrine; nothing could be done without it. Not possessing any worldly wealth, I should have to die unemancipated, having failed to obtain the saving Doctrine. It were better for me to end my life at once than to go on living without it. What should I do? Oh, what should I do? Should I go and make myself the servant of some rich man and, saving up my wages, get together enough gold to pay mine initiation fees and to support me during the period of penance and meditation? Or should I go home and see my mother? Perhaps I might get some money there somehow; but, then, I had worked such sad havoc among the folk of my district by my wickedness and my Black Art! One of two things, however, must be done at once. I must go forth in search either of gold or of the Doctrine. But go I must!

' So, taking my books, and leaving behind the bag of flour, for fear of incurring the Lāma's displeasure, I set forth without even telling my Reverend Mother of mine intention. When I had gone about four or five miles on my way, I was overcome by an intense longing to see her just once, and by remorse at mine ingratitude in thus leaving the kind lady without a word. It was time for the morning meal, so I collected a little barley-flour by begging, borrowed some vessels, gathered some fuel, and cooked my food. By the time I had eaten, it was past noon. The thought then came to me, that in getting my food from the Lāma I had been paid at least half my wages for the work I had done for him. And then reflecting on the trouble I had experienced in procuring just this one morning's meal, and comparing it with the rich living I had enjoyed at the Lāma's house, all ready prepared for me by his lady—tasty, steaming hot dishes every day—I thought myself very ungrateful indeed in coming away without first bidding the kind lady farewell! I had half thoughts of going back, but was unable quite to make up my mind to do so.

' As I was on my way to return the vessels I had borrowed, an old man stopped me, and said, "Dear me! thou art quite a young man, able to work; why dost thou beg? Why dost thou not earn thy food by reading the Scriptures, if thou can read? Or, if thou can not read, why dost thou not work at

something? Thou wouldst earn thy food and a little money,
too. Canst thou read or not?" I replied, telling him that I
was not a professional beggar, and that I was able to read.
The old man then said, "Very well; come and stay in my
house and read the Scriptures for me, and I will pay thee
handsomely."

'I was only too glad to accept the offer, and was soon engaged in reading the abbreviated version of the *Prajñā-Pāramitā* in eight thousand verses.[1] In the course of my reading,
I came to the history of an *Arhant* called Taktūngoo (Ever-
Weeping), in which it was narrated that this *Arhant*, being
penniless, had sold the very flesh off his body for the Doctrine.
Nothing can be dearer to a man than his own heart, yet even
this he determined to sell. Though the immediate consequence
would be death, that did not turn him from his purpose. As I
compared my trials with those of the *Arhant*, they seemed to
dwindle away to nothing. Thereupon, a hope sprang up in
me that, at last, the Lāma might impart to me the teaching
for which I longed. "But even if he do not," I reflected, "hath
not my Reverend Mother promised to help me to find another
*Guru*?" So back I went to him.

'To return to what happened at the time I left the Lāma.
When the Lāma's lady perceived that I had really gone away,
she went to the Lāma, and said, "At last, Reverend Father,
thine implacable foe hath left thee. Art thou satisfied now?"
"Whom dost thou mean?" he asked. And she replied, "Was
it not poor Great Sorcerer whom thou didst treat as thy dead-
liest enemy?" The Lāma frowned, but could not repress a
tear. "O *Gurus* of the Kargyütpa Deities, and Guardian
Spirits," he exclaimed, "bring back my destined pupil." This
said, he wrapped up his head in his mantle, and remained
silent for a long time.

'Upon my coming back and doing obeisance to the Lāma's

---

[1] The *Prajñā-Pāramitā* (Tib. *S'er p'yin*), or 'Transcendental Wisdom', in
twenty-one volumes, forms the third great division of the Northern Buddhist
Canon known as the *Kah-gyur*, and corresponds to the *Abhidharma* (Tib. *Ch'os-
non-pa*), or Metaphysical Part of the Southern Buddhist Canon known as the *Tri-
Piṭaka* (or 'Three Baskets [of the Law]'). Owing to its great bulk in the original,
there are various epitomized versions of it, such as this mentioned in our text.

lady, she was greatly rejoiced, and said, "Really, that was the best thing thou couldst have done. I think the Lāma will now, at last, favour thee with some teaching, for on mine informing him of thy departure, he shed tears and cried, 'Let my destined and gifted pupil be brought back!' And I think thou hast been brought back by the grace of the Lāma."

'I, however, thought to myself that the Reverend Mother was only saying this with a view to encouraging me; for I judged that to wish me back and call me his gifted pupil, and all that, hardly tallied with his refusing to give me even the least morsel of spiritual teaching. If he had, indeed, called me gifted, it would be something to rejoice over; but his refusal to give me any teaching in the Doctrine himself, or to allow me to go to any one else for it, filled me with grave apprehensions of more trouble.

' The Reverend Mother now went in and said to the Lāma, "O Reverend Father, Great Sorcerer hath not been able to forsake us. He hath come back. May I give him permission to come in and do obeisance to thee?" "Oh, it is not out of love for us, but for himself," said the Lāma; "but thou mayst let him come in and pay his respects." Upon my entering where he was, the Lāma spoke to me, saying, "Great Sorcerer, do not be vacillating in thine aims. If thou be really in earnest to obtain the Doctrine, thou must be prepared to sacrifice life itself for it. Now be gone; and, first of all, complete the three remaining stories of the building; and then thy wishes shall be granted. But if thou think otherwise—why, I am only throwing away food on thee; and thou canst go wherever thou wishest."

'I left the Lāma's presence without venturing to utter a word; but I said to the lady: "Reverend Mother, I have a great desire to see my mother once again, and I feel sure that the Lāma will not give me the Teachings. If I were sure of obtaining them when I had completed the building, I should be very content to go on and finish it. But I see very well that the Lāma will only raise one objection after another, as excuses for not giving them to me. I feel sure that I shall not get them, even though I do complete the building. So please allow me to return home. I wish health and long life to you both."

'I bowed down to her, and was coming away, when she said, "Thou are quite right. I have promised to find thee a *Guru*. Now there is a pupil of the Lāma, named Ngogdun-Chudor, who hath the same precepts and teachings as the Lāma; I will do my best to arrange that thou receive the Teachings thou desirest from him. Stay here a little while longer, and for a few days act as if thou wert working." Delighted at the prospect of obtaining my wish, I worked with a will for several days.

'It seemeth that the great Paṇḍit Naropa, while he lived, had been in the habit of observing the tenth day of every month as a grand day of worship, and so Marpa, too, was accustomed to do the same. Upon the occasion of this celebration of the holy day, the Reverend Lady practised a stratagem at his expense after this fashion. Three large vessels, each holding twenty measures of *chhang*, had been fermented for the occasion. These she strained; and, drawing off the first brew into one vessel, she had the *chhang* from that vessel served to him by various assistants (among them both herself and me), who filled his bowl with it again and again. The second brew was served to the pupils. And of the third brew, the lady herself sipped, and that only a little. I followed her example, and escaped becoming affected. All the rest of the pupils, however, became more or less affected. As for the Lāma, he having been plied so often with the over-strong brew fell sound asleep.[1]

---

[1] It should be noted here that this over-indulgence arises, in the first instance, from a ritualistic usage, not unlike that in connexion with libations and Holy Communion in other religions; and that, secondly, as it was due wholly to a woman's artifice, the Lāma himself is not morally responsible. As more fully explained in our Introduction, Marpa represents merely a transitional development in Tibetan Buddhism. His illustrious successor, Milarepa, was a reformer, more thoroughgoing even than Tsong-khapa, the Reformer of the Gelugpa, or Established Church of Tibet. Whereas Marpa was married and lived in the world, being a scholar more than a saint, Milarepa taught, and illustrated by his own later life, that the higher ideal is renunciation absolute—asceticism unqualified. In one of his Hymns (p. 191, following) he has put on record his opposition to the use of all stimulating beverages, not only those containing alcohol, but even tea.

While he thus lay asleep, his lady abstracted from his room certain articles, including Naropa's garlands and rosary of rubies. Then producing a letter in my *Guru's* name, which she had all ready, and enclosing therein the garlands and the rosary as a gift from the Lāma, after wrapping it up in a costly scarf and sealing the letter with the Lāma's seal, she directed me to go to the aforementioned Ngogdun-Chudor and hand it to him. The main purport of the letter was a command to Ngogdun to give the Great Sorcerer the Teachings. Thus was I sent by her in the direction of the Central Province of Tibet, to learn the Doctrine ; and I went to Ngogdun with full confidence in his ability to teach me the Saving Truths.

' Some two days after my departure, the Lāma asked his lady what I was doing. She replied that I was probably on the road, but exactly where she was unable to say. " Where hath he gone, and when ? " asked the Lāma. And she replied, " Oh, he was saying that though he had done so much work for thee, still thou wert not disposed to give him the Teachings, but only scoldings and beatings, so he would go and look for another *Guru* elsewhere. And as I should only have won him another beating by coming to tell thee of his intention, I pre-ferred not to do so. I did mine utmost to induce him to stay, but I could not hold him ; he left yesterday."

' On this piece of news, the Lāma's face turned black as night. " When did he leave ? " he asked. " Yesterday," replied his lady. For some time he sat silent. Then he said, " My pupil cannot have got very far away yet."

' Meanwhile, I had arrived at Riwo-Kyungding, in the Central Province of Tibet, and found Ngogdun—himself a Head Lāma by this time—expounding the Double Analysis [1] to a large body of his pupils. He was just dealing with the passage, " I am the Expounder and I am the Truth. I am the Hearer. I am the Teacher of the World, and I am the Devotee. I am the Being Who hath passed beyond all states of worldly existence, and I am the Blissful One," when I approached, and, at a distance, prostrated myself. The spot came to be known as Chag-tael-Kang (The Hill of Obeisance). Lāma

[1] Text : *Tak-nyi*, a philosophical treatise somewhat like the *Bhagavad-Gītā*.

Ngogdun, taking off his hat, returned my salutation, observing that from my mode of salutation I seemed to be one of the pupils of Marpa the Translator, and that the fact of mine arrival whilst he was expounding those particular stanzas seemed highly auspicious—so auspicious, indeed, that he predicted, from this simple occurrence, that I should one day become a master of all religious lore. He sent one of those about him to inquire who I was. The person sent recognized me, and asked, "What bringeth thee here?" I replied that our *Guru*, Lāma Marpa, being too busy to look after my private tuition, had sent me to attend the lectures here. I told him also that I had brought with me Naropa's garlands and ruby rosary as a token from the Lāma.

'When the man went back to Lāma Ngogdun and told him these things, and that I was Great Sorcerer, he was greatly delighted, so much so that he exclaimed, "Of a truth, rare are the occasions of enjoying such a favour as this. My humble monastery to be blessed and honoured by the presence within its doors of such precious and sacred reliques of our Great Teacher, Naropa! Such an occasion is as rare as the Udumvara blossom.[1] We must receive it with all the respect due to such a rare event." Thereupon, he broke off his exposition at the auspicious passage mentioned, and sent some of the monks to fetch banners, ceremonial umbrellas, and pendants, while various musical instruments were sounded in honour of the reliques I had brought.

'When I reached his dwelling, I prostrated myself, and offered the letter-packet and the reliques; and he, upon receiving them, was profoundly moved. Tears came from his eyes; and, taking off his hat, he put the reliques on the top of his head, praying that grace might be vouchsafed him. Then he put them in the holy of holies of his altar.

'The letter, which he now read, ran thus:[2] "I am just about to enter upon a close retreat, and as Great Sorcerer is im-

---

[1] The Udumvara (*Ficus Glomirata, Rox.*) is said to blossom only upon the birth of a Buddha in this world.

[2] Following M. Bacot's version (p. 120), this letter begins thus: 'To the Immutable Ngogdun, Realizer of *Nirvāṇa*.' In our version this address is lacking.

patient and eager to have the Teachings, I send him to thee
for the Initiation and Consecration.  Do thou, therefore, grant
him these, and teach him the Truths.  I authorize thee to do
so ; in token, whereof, I send thee herewith Naropa's garlands
and rosary of rubies."

' Having finished reading the letter, Ngogdun said that, as
ordered by the Lāma, he would surely give me the Initiation
and the Consecration.  He had been thinking of sending for
me, but now that I was come myself, it was very good, indeed,
and due to the Lāma's benediction and grace.  He said, further,
" I have a number of pupils who come from Kham, Tagpo,
Kongpo, and Yarlung, but on their way hither, through the
depredations of those lawless folk, the Yepo and Yemo, of Döl,
they are stripped of the scanty store of gear with which they
set out for this place in order to pursue their studies.  I therefore request thee to go and punish those lawless folk by
launching a hail-storm upon their lands.  When thou hast done
this, I will bestow upon thee the Initiation and Consecration
thou desirest."

' I now bitterly repented the fate that had put such an
accursed power into my hands, making me the means of
wreaking vengeance by doing hurt to life and property.  I had
come here in search of the Saving Truth, and here I was again
being asked to work harm and do an evil deed.  If I refused,
I should be disobeying a *Guru*, or, at least, one whom I intended to take for my *Guru*—almost as heinous a sin as to
refuse to obey an actual *Guru* ; and, in addition, I should lose
all opportunity of obtaining the Teachings.  And so I decided
that I must go, that I had no choice.

' Accordingly, I set forth, provided with the necessary appurtenances ; and, reaching the scene of my intended deed,
I took lodgings in the house of an old woman, in the Yepo
country.  Just as the hail-storm was about to burst, as the
lightnings flashed and the thunder growled and the first hail-
stones were about to fall, the old woman, my hostess, began to
beat her breast and weep, saying, " Alas !  What shall I have
to live on if my crops are destroyed by the hail ? "

' This was too much for me.  I could not bear to be so cruel

to this poor old woman, so, at imminent risk to myself, I requested her quickly to draw me a plan of her field. "Oh, my
field is like this," she cried in a despairing tone, at the same
time describing a triangular figure with an elongated end.
I immediately covered the figure with an iron pan, in my mind
shielding it from the hail, so that it escaped destruction, all
except a tiny corner, which, protruding beyond the covering-
pan, was devastated by a gust of wind.

'When the storm was over, on going out to look at the
country, I saw the slopes above the valley all furrowed into
ravines, the erstwhile luxuriant fields utterly laid waste, all
except the old woman's field, which was quite fresh and green.
But that corner of the field, corresponding to the corner of the
plan which, protruding beyond the covering-pan, had been
devastated by wind, was damaged by the hail and flooded with
water. Ever afterward, this field—except for its protruding
corner which had been flooded—escaped any hail-storm which
visited that neighbourhood. And it is said that the old woman
was thus exempted from payment of the hail-tax [1] on all of
the field save that corner.

'On my way back [to my new *Guru*], I met an old shepherd
and his child who had lost their herds in the flood. By them
I sent word to the people of the countryside, enjoining them
to refrain thenceforth from ill-treating or robbing Lāma Ngogpa's [2] disciples or adherents, on pain of being visited constantly
by similar hail-storms, thus revealing to them who had caused
the destruction. After this, the people of those two places
were so profoundly impressed with the phenomenal power of
Lāma Ngogpa, that they became his devoted followers and
faithfully served him.

'As I came along the way, I picked up some dead birds,
which I found all by themselves under a bramble bush, and
numbers of other birds, and some rats, which I found dead on
the road, until I had my cap and the lap of my robe full.
These I laid in a heap before Lāma Ngogpa, and appealed to

---

[1] A tax imposed on behalf of the hail-exorcizing *lāmas*. (See p. 50[1].)

[2] Lāma Ngogpa (or the Lāma living at Ngog) is a shortened form of the name
Lāma Ngogdun-Chudor.

him thus : "O Reverend Teacher, I came here expecting to
find the Holy Doctrine, but have been compelled to heap up
sin upon sin. Have pity on such a terrible sinner ! " and I burst
into bitter tears.[1]

' To this, the Lāma replied, " Be not despairing ; there is no
cause whatsoever for such abject fear. We, the followers of
Naropa and Maitrī,[2] possess those Truths which can save the
greatest of sinners in the twinkling of an eye—just as one
single stone flung from a sling serveth to frighten a hundred
birds simultaneously. All those sentient creatures, and these
birds and beasts which have been killed on this occasion by
the hail-storm shall be born again as thy foremost disciples
when thou shalt attain to Buddhahood.[3] Till that time cometh,
I shall put forth my power so as to prevent their falling into
Hell or [degenerating] into lower states of being. Therefore,
be at ease. But if thou still doubt, let me prove the truth of
what I say, thus." For a few moments, he sat silent with
closed eyes, then he snapped his fingers. In a trice, all the
dead birds and rats [which I had collected] revived, and made
off to their several nests and holes. I now perceived that the
Lāma himself was a Buddha. How delightful ! How blissful !
I should have rejoiced had many more creatures enjoyed the
privilege of dying on such an occasion.

' Thereafter, I was initiated into the *Maṇḍala* [or Rite] of
Gaypa-Dorje.[4] I had found a cave facing south, from which
I could see my *Guru's* residence ; and, having made it habitable
by the expenditure of a little labour, I shut myself up in it,
leaving only a small aperture in the side, for the passage of
food and water, and so forth.[5]

---

[1] Among Christians, it is only the taking of human life which is considered to
be wrong ; but among Buddhists, as among Brāhmins and Jains, the precept
' Thou shalt not kill ' applies to all living creatures.

[2] Maitrī (' Love '), like Naropa, is an Indian *Yogī*, or Saint, upon whose doctrines the Kargyütpa Sect is, in part, founded.

[3] That is, in future ages they shall have evolved to the state of man, and receive
the Saving Doctrine from Milarepa, who, by then, will have attained Buddhahood.

[4] See p. 108[1].

[5] It is the usual procedure for devotees of the Kargyütpa School thus to enclose themselves in a chosen retreat and remain there in solitary meditation for

'My *Guru* had explained to me the methods of meditation, and I persevered in their practice ; but, despite all the assiduity on the *Guru's* part, and perseverance on mine own, owing to my not having obtained the assent of Marpa, I experienced no spiritual development.

'One day, my *Guru* came and asked me if I had had such and such an experience. I replied that I had experienced nothing [of like nature]. "How is that?" he asked. "In this line of development there ought not to be, and there never hath been, any who have not within a very short time made fresh progress in spiritual development, except when there hath been something standing directly in the way of it. What can it be here? It cannot be that our Head *Guru* hath not given his assent to thine Initiation, or else he would not have sent the tokens and the letter. Well, anyway, proceed with thy meditation."

'I was a little alarmed at this encounter, and for a moment thought of confessing to the deception [I had practised], but my courage failed me. Now, more than ever, was I impressed with the necessity of propitiating my Head *Guru*, the Lāma Marpa ; but I went on practising meditation to the best of mine ability.

'About this time, Lāma Marpa, having had the remaining portion of his son's residence completed, wrote to Lāma Ngogpa requesting him to send him so many loads of small branches for the house.[1] The letter added, that upon the completion of the ornamental spires and the cornice, Lāma Ngogpa was to come in person and assist both in the consecration [of the house] and the ceremony to be performed [at the same time] to celebrate the coming of age of Doday-Bum [2] [Marpa's

the period of time prescribed by the *Guru*, their sustenance being passed in to them. In some remarkable instances, such devotees have not once left their cell during long periods of years. Similar austerities, probably derived from the example of Oriental asceticism, were practised by the early Christian *yogīs* who dwelt in the deserts of Egypt and Palestine.

[1] The tops of religious edifices and of dwellings of *lāmas* in Tibet are commonly fringed with twigs placed flat with ends projecting and trimmed evenly with the line of the walls so as to form a sort of frieze.

[2] This is another name for Marpa's son, who, as above (on p. 95), is also known as *Darma*-Doday. *Bum*, which here replaces *Darma*, is the popular name

son]. The letter also intimated that Lāma Marpa had heard
about my being with Lāma Ngogpa, reference being made to
me as a " wicked person ", and it requested that I should be
brought back to him at the same time.

'Lāma Ngogpa came to the aperture of my cave and read
me the letter, observing, " From the manner in which the Lāma
speaketh of thee, it would appear that thou hast not obtained
his permission in regard to the bestowal of the Truths." I
replied, " The Lāma himself did not give his consent ; but his
wife furnished me with the letter and the accompanying tokens,
with which I was directed hither." " Ah ! " he said, " so we
have been engaged in profitless work. Thou surely must have
known that it is vain to hope for spiritual growth without the
*Guru's* hearty co-operation and approval. It is no wonder thou
dost not develop any of the signs. However, he ordereth thee
to return. Dost thou wish to go or not ? " I prayed that
I might be taken with him as his attendant. He replied that
the branches had been sent by carriers, and that, until these
had returned and the exact date of the festival was known,
I was to remain in my retreat.

'Upon the return of the carriers, he again came to the aperture of my cell ; whereupon we had a long conversation about
our *Guru's* approaching ceremonial of consecrating the building and bestowing it upon his son, who was also to have a
distinction conferred upon him. In the course of our talk,
I inquired whether any mention had been made of myself.
" Yes," said Ngogpa, " our Lāma's lady asked the carriers
what thou wert doing. Being told that thou wert in retreat,
she asked what else thou wert doing there. Being told that
thou didst always cling to solitude, she set it down to thy
having left this die behind, at the same time giving it to the
man and helping him to tie it up in his waist-cloth, and
charging him to deliver it safely into thy hands." Ngogpa
then handed me a die made of clay. I took it from his hand

given to the first twelve volumes of the *Prajñā-Pāramitā* (see p. 112[1]), and to
the abbreviated version of the *Prajñā-Pāramitā* in 100,000 slokas. As applied to
Marpa's son, *Bum* may, therefore, be either an initiatory (or religious) appellation or a name given to him upon his coming of age. He is also called *Doday-
Bum* at the end of Chapter VII.

reverentially, and, deeming that it had been hallowed by the touch of my Reverend Mother, I put it on my head.

'When he had left me, I was taken with a desire to throw the die and play with it. But, after a few moments, the thought occurred to me that I had never manifested any weakness for dice-playing in the lady's presence, and I asked myself what she could mean by sending me a thing that had led to the impoverishment of some of mine ancestors. Was it not meant to show that I was an object of contempt to her? The thought was infuriating. In a rage, I threw the die on the ground with such force that it split asunder and revealed a small roll of paper wrapped up inside. I picked this up and read its message, which ran thus: " Son, thy *Guru* is now disposed to bestow upon thee the necessary Initiation and Scriptures. Therefore come with Lāma Ngogpa." This was such welcome news to me that I actually pranced up and down my little cave, and danced for very joy.

'Lāma Ngogpa then came and said, " Brave Grand Sorcerer, prepare thyself for the journey"; and I did so with alacrity. The Lāma himself collected everything he possessed for an offering, except what had been given him by Marpa himself. These possessions consisted of images, books, reliques, gold, turquoises, cloth, silk, plate, vessels, live stock, and so on. Of the latter, he drove off every sheep and goat in his possession, leaving behind but one lame old she-goat, which, on account of its lameness, was unable to keep up with the rest of the herd, and, so perforce, had to be left behind. Everything else he possessed he was preparing to take with him as an offering to his *Guru*. He was kind enough to acknowledge the service I had rendered to him, and gave me a silk scarf as mine own personal offering to Lāma Marpa. His wife added to it a bag full of powdered cheese, which was to serve as mine offering to Marpa's lady, Damema.

'Then Lāma Ngogpa, together with his wife, and myself, and a large retinue, set out for Dowo-Lung [Marpa's monastery]. When we had arrived at the foot of the hill, on which Dowo-Loong stood, the Lāma requested me to go in advance and inform Lāma Marpa and Damema of his approach, and to see if they would not send out some *chhang* for him. Accordingly, I went up towards Marpa's dwelling and there encountered his lady first. I presented her with the bag of cheese, and saluted her with reverence. I then informed her of the approach of Lāma Ngogpa, and asked her to send some refreshments to meet him on his approach. She was delighted to see me, and told me to go and pay my respects to Lāma Marpa, who was inside, and to tell him of Lāma Ngogpa's approaching arrival.

'I then entered the dwelling and found Lāma Marpa sitting in meditation on the topmost story of the house. I presented the silk scarf to him, and bowed down before him, he being seated facing the East. He turned his face to the West. Then I bowed down from the West, but he turned round towards the South. Then I spoke, and said, "Reverend *Guru*! Although out of displeasure thou refuse to accept mine obeisance, Lāma Ngogpa is coming here with all he possesseth of images, books, gold, turquoises, cattle, and such like, as an offering to thee. He surely deserveth some suitable reception befitting his state; I therefore pray that thou wilt be kind enough to send some *chhang* and refreshments out to him, on his way hither."

'Apparently bursting out in rage, the Lāma snapped his fingers and shouted, "What! Who gave me a reception when I came plodding home with the load of the precious teachings on my back from India? When I brought home the precious gems of the quintessence of all the four divisions of Buddhist Doctrine, did so much as a lame bird come out to greet me or receive me? And must I, a great translator, go and receive Ngogpa just because he is bringing me a few straggling cattle? No, it cannot be. If that be what he expecteth, he had better go back whence he came."

'I left the Lāma's presence and went and told his lady what he had said. "Oh," she said, "thy *Guru* is very testy. Ngogpa is a great man, and must be received in a befitting manner. Let us both go and meet him." I said, "Lāma Ngogpa doth not expect thee to go and meet him. Only give me a little *chhang* and I will run back with it to him." "No; I will go

and meet him," she said ; and, ordering some pupils to bring
a generous quantity of *chhang*, she went out personally to receive Lāma Ngogpa.

'Now all the people of Lhobrak had assembled together to
celebrate the coming of age of Marpa's son, Darma-Doday,
and to witness the ceremony of consecrating the house which
had been built for him. There was a general feast, and Lāma
Marpa raised his voice and sang the benedictory psalm as a
blessing upon the congregation and the occasion. It ran as
follows :

'I supplicate the Gracious *Guru*.

'On this, the glorious Sect of my Line,
   Resteth the blessing of stainlessness ;
   May the benediction of that blessing here alight.

'On the short path-way of my Truths profound,
   Resteth the blessing of unerringness ;
   May the benediction of that blessing here alight.

'On myself, Marpa the Translator,
   Resteth the blessing of learning deep ;
   May the benediction of that blessing here alight.

'On *Guru*, *Deva*, and *Ḍākinī*,
   Resteth the blessing of grace and favour ;
   May the benediction of that blessing here alight.

'On my spiritual sons and *shishyas* gathered here,
   Resteth the blessing of staunch and true faith ;
   May the benediction of that blessing here alight.

'On all my lay-disciples, far and near,
   Resteth the blessing of charity and merit ;
   May the benediction of that blessing here alight.

'On all pure deeds and actions,
   Resteth the blessing of altruism and Emancipation ;
   May the benediction of that blessing here alight.

'On good and evil spirits of this transient world,
   Resteth the blessing of great merit or great punishment ;
   May the benediction of that blessing here alight.

'On these Lāmas and these laymen gathered here,
Resteth the blessing of gladness and good wishes;
May the benediction of that blessing here alight.'

'When Marpa had ended, Lāma Ngogpa rose up and offered his gifts; after which he addressed Marpa in the following words: "Precious and Reverend *Guru*, I do not need to
say that all I have and am is thine. On this present occasion,
however, I beg leave to announce to thee that everything
I possess, save one lame old she-goat, too lame and too old to
keep up with the rest of the herd, which, therefore, had to be
left behind, hath been brought hither as an offering to thee, in
return for which I pray that thou wilt confer upon me, thine
ever devoted *shishya*, the Most Precious Initiations and the
Deepest Mystic Truths, and, above all, the scrolls containing
those [Esoteric] Truths that are to be whispered in the ear
only."

'So saying, he prostrated himself before the well-pleased
Marpa, who now spoke as follows, "Well, if this be so, I, in
turn, have to inform thee that the Truths and Scriptures I possess are among the rarest and most efficacious. They belong
mostly to that class of Truths called the 'Short-Cut of the Immutable Path',[1] by means of which it is possible to attain to
*Nirvāṇa* in this very lifetime, without having to wait for countless ages. Such are the surpassing virtues of these Truths.
But there is more; the Truths contained in the scrolls of which
thou speakest are attended by certain very strict conditions of
the *Guru's* requiring. So, unless thou bring up the last she-
goat, despite all her lameness and old age, thine acquisition of
that Scripture will be a matter of some difficulty. As for the
others, thou hast already received them." This last require-
ment evoked hearty laughter from all present, but Lāma
Ngogpa gravely asked if, when the old she-goat were brought
up, he would be given the Scripture he desired. To this Marpa
replied, "Yes; if thou go thyself and fetch it."

'The assembly then broke up for the day; and, next morn-

---

[1] That is, the short method of attaining Enlightenment by treading the Immutable (or Infallible) Path, or *Vajra-Yāna*.

ing, Lāma Ngogpa set forth by himself to get the lame she-
goat; and, bringing it on his own back, he offered it to Marpa,
who, much pleased, said, " A really devoted and faithful follower of the Mystic Truths should be like thyself. I have truly
little use for a lame old she-goat. I only made requisition for
it in order to illustrate the greatness and value of religious
truths." He then promised Lāma Ngogpa that he would initiate him into various Mystic Truths and *Maṇḍalas*, and, a
short time after, did so.

' One day [later on], during a feast given to some of his disciples from the most distant parts and to the members of his
own family, Lāma Marpa sat, with a long staff by his side,
looking with fierce eyes at Lāma Ngogpa, who was one of
those present. After a time, pointing at him with his finger, he
said, " Ngogdun Chudor, what explanation hast thou to give
in the matter of thy having conferred Initiation and the Truths
upon this wicked person, Thöpaga ? " And, as he spoke, he
kept casting glances at the stick.

' Lāma Ngogpa was terrified. " Precious *Guru,*" he stam-
mered, " Thy Reverence enjoined me under thine own hand
and seal to initiate Thöpaga. Along with the letter, Thy
Reverence sent Naropa's garlands and rosary of rubies as a
token of its genuineness, and I obeyed Thy Reverence's command. In this I have nothing with which to reproach myself;
so be pleased to abate Thy Reverence's displeasure with me."
As he spoke, he kept looking round about uneasily.

' Marpa then turned his angry finger on me, and asked,
" Where didst thou get these things ? " By this time I felt as
if my heart were being torn out of my body, and was in such
a state of terror that I could scarcely articulate. All trembling,
I faltered out that the Lady Mother had given them to me.

' At that, Marpa jumped up abruptly from his seat and
made towards his wife apparently with intent to belabour her
with the staff. But she, apprehensive of such a thing, had risen
and moved herself some distance from him. She now ran into
the chapel and shut the door. The Lāma made several attempts to open it, but, failing, came back and resumed his seat,
calling out, " Thou, Ngogdun-Chudor, who hast been doing

something thou wert not asked to do, I command thee to go and bring me Naropa's garlands and rosary instantly." This said, he wrapped up his head in his mantle, and so remained.

'Lāma Ngogpa bowed, and retired immediately to get the articles required.  As soon as he came out, I, having run out of Marpa's presence at the same time as the lady, saw him from a corner, where I sat weeping ; and I prayed him to take me with him.  But he said, " If I take thee again without the *Guru's* express command, the outcome will only be a similar scene, which will be painful to us both. Remain here for the present.  If our *Guru* refuse to be gracious to thee, I will then do what lieth in my power to help thee ? "

'Then I rejoined, "On account of my much evil-doing, not only do I myself suffer, but I involve thee and my Reverend Mother in a share of my troubles.  I have lost all hope of obtaining the Doctrine in this life.  Day by day I am only heaping up one great sin upon another.  It is much better that I cut short this life.  All I ask of thee is that by thy grace thou procure that my next birth shall be among [well-endowed] human beings,[1] and be a birth in which I shall have the opportunity to obtain the Truths."

'I turned away, intending to commit suicide on the spot, but Lāma Ngogpa, bursting into tears, caught hold of me and said, " Brave Grand Sorcerer, do not so !  Our Mystic Doctrine, which is the essence and ultimate meaning of the Blessed Conqueror's injunctions, declareth that all our various bodily principles and faculties are divine.[2]  If we presume to close their present career before their natural period [of dissolution], we incur the guilt of killing the divine in ourselves, and must face the due punishment for the same.  There is no greater sin than

---

[1] Birth as a well-endowed human being is, by all Buddhists, regarded as affording the supreme opportunity of reaching Enlightenment.  It is here in this world that the Path to Buddhahood must first be entered upon ; it cannot be entered upon in any of the after-death states, although once sufficient progress has been made upon it here, the Goal to which it leads may be realized in the highest of the Paradise Realms.

[2] 'Brāhmanism also teaches this, and makes any person who attempts suicide subject to punishment and to purification by expiatory rites (*Prāyash-chitta*).  The *Kūlārṇava Tantra* is very emphatic about the necessity of preserving one's life.'— Sj. Atal Bihari Ghosh.

suicide. In the *Sūtras*, too, suicide is spoken of as a most heinous sin. Understand this well, and abandon all thought of self-slaughter. After all, our *Guru* may still be pleased to confer the Truths upon thee. But, even if he do not, there will surely be found some one who will give thee them."

'Thus did Ngogpa seek to comfort me. Other of the disciples also sympathized with me, some running in to see if Marpa were yet in a mood to be addressed with safety, and some sitting down by me and trying to bring me solace. But either my heart was made of iron, or else the time had come for it to break, so acute were my sufferings. It was because of my having committed such terribly wicked deeds in the earlier part of my life, that now I had to suffer such excruciating and indescribable tortures at the very outset of my search for a Faith and Doctrine to emancipate me.'

At the hearing of this narration, none present was able to withhold tears of sympathy with the narrator ; and some there were who even swooned away with excess of emotion.

This is the story of the Second Meritorious Act of Milarepa, which treateth of his chastening and his purification from sin by means of trials and tribulations, both bodily and mental.

CHAPTER VI

# THE INITIATION

*Telling of the Completion of Jetsün's Probation; of Jetsün's Initiation; and of Marpa's Predictions concerning Jetsün.*

AGAIN Rechung addressed Jetsün, and asked him how, and under what circumstances, Lāma Marpa had favoured him afterward.

Jetsün continued: 'The other pupils, as I have said, were running up and down. After a while, Marpa recovered from his sulking and became quite mild. He said, " Now let Damema be requested to come here." Somebody having gone for her, he next inquired, "Where are Ngogdun Chudor, and the other pupils?" Some one said, " Thy Reverence having commanded Ngogdun to go and fetch Naropa's garlands and the rosary, he started forth ; but, meeting Great Sorcerer, just as he came out, he is even now engaged in consoling him." And the occurrence was fully related to Marpa. At this, his eyes were filled with tears, and he said, "It is necessary for disciples of the Mystic Truths to be so ; and he hath turned out exactly what is wanted. Now I pity my pupils, so go and call them."

'One of the pupils went to Lāma Ngogpa, and told him, " Now our Lāma hath become mild, and he hath sent me to call thee." I thereupon deplored my luckless condition, and envied the happy lot of those fortunate beings who enjoyed the *Guru's* grace and favour. "As for poor miserable me," said I, " I am debarred from the *Guru's* presence even when he is mild, for my very presence irritateth him and procureth me only his displeasure and beatings." And then I wept bitterly. Lāma Ngogpa stayed with me, and requested the same pupil to go and relate my case to the *Guru* and to find out whether I might be allowed to approach him, adding, "If I do not remain here, this desperate person may do something rash."

'The pupil went up and represented matters to Lāma Marpa, who said, " Formerly he would have been right, but to-day it shall not be so. The chief guest now is to be Great Sorcerer.

Damema, go thou and invite him." She came, all smiles, and said, "Great Sorcerer, at last, I think thy *Guru* is going to favour thee, for he said just now that thou wert to be the chief guest, and that I was to go and call thee. I take it to be a sign of an entire change on his part in thy favour. He was not angry with me either. Now rejoice and let us go in."

'I was still doubtful, and went in rather diffidently. Having taken my seat. Lāma Marpa said, "When we come to think well over matters, no one seemeth to deserve blame. Wishing that Great Sorcerer might be absolved from his sins, I caused him to build the edifices single-handed. Had it been for my selfish purpose, why I could have got on much better by coaxing and by gentle means than otherwise, hence I was not to blame. As for Damema, she being a woman, and possessing a more than usual share of maternal sympathy and pity, could not bear to see me ill-treat poor Great Sorcerer, who seemed so willing, obedient, and patient. So who could blame her for furnishing him with the forged letter, and the accompanying tokens, although it was a rather serious thing to do? As for thee, Ngogdun-Chudor, thou art not to blame, as thou hast thyself said. I would, however, request thee to bring the reliques back for the present occasion, but they shall be restored to thee. As for thee, Great Sorcerer, thou art quite right in trying to obtain Religious Truths by every possible means. Not having heard of the dispatch of the forged letter to Ngogdun, who had, in accordance with it, conferred the Initiation and the Sacred Truths upon Great Sorcerer, I was thus deprived of the chance of filling Great Sorcerer with despair, as I, [bound by duty], should have done. Therefore was I angered; and, although my anger recoiled on me like a wave of water, yet it was not like vulgar worldly anger. Religious anger is a thing apart; and, in whatever form it may appear, it hath the same object—to excite repentance and thereby to contribute to the spiritual development of the person. Should there be any one amongst you who are seated here, who, not understanding the religious motive, feeleth shocked at these things, I exhort him not to be shaken in his faith and belief. Had I had the chance of plunging this spiritual son of mine nine times into utter

despair, he would have been cleansed thoroughly of all his sins.
He would thus not have been required to be born again, but
would have disappeared totally, his physical body being forever
dissolved; he would have attained *Nirvāṇa*. That it will not
be so, and that he will still retain a small portion of his demerits, is due to Damema's ill-timed pity and narrow understanding. However, he hath been subjected to eight deep
tribulations, which have cleansed him of the heavier sins; and
he hath suffered many minor chastenings, which will purify
him from minor sins. Now I am going to care for him and
give him those Teachings and Initiations which I hold as dear
as mine own heart. I myself will provide him with food while
he is in retreat, and with mine own hands will enclose him in
the place of meditation.[1]   Henceforth rejoice."

'I was not sure whether I was awake or dreaming. If dreaming, I wished the dream to continue, and that I should not
awake, such was mine inexpressible joy. I wept from very
delight, and made obeisance. It was upon this occasion that
Lāma Ngogpa, and Mother Damema, along with the others
assembled there, did not know which to admire most in my
*Guru*—his sternness and inflexibility while chastening me, or
his mercy and kindness in undertaking the care of me, or his
wisdom and sagacity in all his deeds. They recognized him
to be a Buddha Himself, and were strongly confirmed in their
faith and belief. They regarded him with affection, and shed
tears, and again rose up and bowed down in gratitude for the
kindness shown to me. All were beaming with smiles and laughter, and in this happy mood all partook of the sacrificial cakes.

'That very night, offerings were laid on the altar; and, in
the presence of the assembly, my hair was cropped, and I was
ordained a priest, my dress being changed [for the priestly
robe]. Marpa said that in the dream-vision which he had had,
his *Guru* Naropa had given me, at the very beginning, the
name Mila-Dorje-Gyaltsen (Mila, Diamond Banner). I was
required to observe the vow of a *Ge-nyen* (lay-brother) and
enjoined to follow the vows of those who aspire to be Teaching
Buddhas [or Bodhisattvas].

[1] See p. 119[5].

'When Marpa blessed the wine of the Inner Offering, every one saw a rainbow-like halo emitted from the skull-cup [1] which contained the wine. With the sacrificial wine, he worshipped his Masters and Tutelary Deities, and then, partaking of it himself, gave me the remainder, which I drank entirely. My *Guru* said, "It is a good omen. Although the wine-offering of mine Inner Worship is superior to the Rite of Complete Initiation of any other sect, yet will I also give thee to-morrow morning the Complete Initiation [of our Sect], which will tend to ripen the seeds of the Mystic Truths that shall be sown in thy heart."

'Then he erected the *Dēmchog Maṇḍala* of sixty-two Deities,[2] and proceeded to explain it. He pointed to the dust-painted ground plan of the *Maṇḍala* and said that it was called the symbolical and figurative diagram.[3] Then, with his finger, he pointed to the firmament above, and said, "Look, those are called the *Maṇḍala* of the Actual Realities."

[1] A ceremonial cup made of a human skull, symbolizing the impermanence of man's life on Earth, and, also, renunciation of all *sangsāric* existence.

[2] That is, he prepared the Magic Circle, or *Maṇḍala*, for the reception of the sixty-two principal deities invoked in the ritual of the god Dēmchog (Skt. *Shamvara*), 'The Chief of Happiness'. See the late Lāma Kazi Dawa-Samdup's translation of the *Dēmchog Tantra*, edited by Arthur Avalon, *Tantrik Texts*, vol. vii (London, 1919).

[3] This, as indicated, is a geometrical diagram outlined with dust or sand, commonly of different colours, either on a floor, if the initiation be in a temple or house, or on the bare rock or earth, if the initiation be in a cave or in the open air. Then the Deities are invoked, usually by intoning their secret *mantra*, a special place within the diagram being assigned to each of them. *Siddhas* (or *Yogīs*) possessed of clairvoyant vision say that when the invocation is properly performed, by a highly developed human *Guru*, the Deities appear, each in the place assigned in the *Maṇḍala*, and make the Mystic Initiation very real and effective psychically, the neophyte at once becoming affected with divine vision and ecstatic joy. Thence come the mystic regeneration and the true baptism in the fire of the spirit, and the conferring of the new name, which invariably suggests the chief spiritual qualities of the neophyte receiving it. Milarepa's initiation being of the most exalted character, he beholds various psychic centres, and the Deities invoked, as though they were in the ethereal spaces directly overshadowing the *maṇḍala* on the Earth.

The *Kūlārṇava Tantra* (see *Tantrik Texts*, vol. v, ch. xiv, ed. by A. Avalon) refers to various kinds of Initiation (*Dīkṣā*). The degree of competency of the candidate determines the degree of the Initiation. Thus by the *Vedha-Dīkṣa*, the *Guru* transfers spiritual power to the *Shishya* directly. It is said that in this way Rāma-Kṛishṇa Paramahangsa initiated his chief disciple, Swāmī Vivekānanda.

'[And lo, there] I beheld, very distinctly, the Twenty-Four Holy Places, the Thirty-Two Places of Pilgrimage, the Eight Great Places of Cremation,[1] and Dēmchog,[2] with all the Deities inhabiting these different Holy Places seated round about him. The Deities, uniting their voice with the voice of my *Guru*, in one grand chorus, conferred upon me the initiatory name of *Pal-Zhadpa-Dorje* (Glorious Full-Blown Immutable One, i.e. Bearer of the Mystic Symbol[3]) : Skt. *Shrī-Vikasita (Hasita) Vajra.*

' My *Guru* next gave me free permission to go through the [Mantrayānic] *Tantras.* He also gave me detailed explanations of various works on meditation [or *Yoga*], and of their methods and systems in full.[4] Then, placing his hand upon the crown of my head, he said, " My son, I knew thee to be a worthy *shishya* from the very first. The night before thine arrival here, I had a dream which predicted that thou wouldst be one who would serve the Cause of Buddhism very efficiently. My Damema had a similar dream, which corroborated mine. Above all, both our dreams, showing the temple to be guarded by a female, predicted that the Guardian Deity of thy Teaching would be a *Ḍākinī.* Thus thou art a *shishya* whom my *Guru* and my Guardian Goddess have given me as a boon. Such being the case, I really had gone to meet thee, on the pretence of ploughing my field. Thy drinking up all the *chhang* which I there gave thee, and thy ploughing up the field entirely, predicted that thou wouldst be a worthy *shishya*, who would imbibe the whole of the Spiritual Truths which I had to impart to thee. Furthermore, thine offer of the four-handled copper vessel predicted my having four famous disciples. The vessel's

---

[1] See p. 36[2] concerning these various places of special sanctity.

[2] Text : *Dpal-hkhor-lo-sdom-pa* (pron. *Pal-Khor-lo-Dom-pa*), another name of Dēmchog (*Bde-mch'og*), ' The Chief of Happiness ', one of the Tutelary Deities of the Kargyütpa Sect : Skt. *Shamvara.*

[3] This rendering of the Initiatory Name follows that by M. Bacot, in his Version (p. 137).

[4] The Initiation being a Complete Initiation into the *Dēmchog Maṇḍala*, the underlying esoteric interpretation of the very profound *Dēmchog Tantra*, and of similar *Tantras* of the Mantrayānic School, is given to Milarepa ; and, also, the Secret *Mantras*, or Words of Power (see p. 37[2]). In addition, there are expounded to him various complementary treatises of an occult character concerning *yogic* systems of meditation.

being quite devoid of any dirt predicted thine entire freedom from worldly passions, and that thy body would gain complete control over the Vital Warmth.[1] The offering of thy vessel empty, predicted that when thou meditatest hereafter thou wilt suffer from want. But so that thou mightest enjoy plenty in thine old age, and that thy followers and disciples might be filled with the Elixir of Spiritual Truths, I filled thy vessel with melted butter for altar-lamps. With a view to making thy name famous, I rang the handle rings as loudly as possible. And it was with a view to cleansing thee from thy sins that I had thee to work so hard upon the four houses. The houses themselves symbolize the nature of the four types of action, each house representing one of the four, namely, the peaceful, the powerful, the fascinating, and the stern, respectively.[2] I purposely wanted to fill thy heart with bitter repentance and sorrow, verging on despair, by turning thee out ignominiously. And thou, for having borne all those trials with patience and meekness, without the least change in thy faith in me, shalt

[1] This is a peculiar bodily warmth acquired by *yogic* control of the breathing process and the vital forces of the body, whereby the *yogī* becomes immune to coldness. In the high snowy altitudes of Tibet, where Milarepa passed his life, fuel of all sorts, for producing fire, is rare and costly ; and the Vital Warmth is a very necessary acquirement for *yogīs* in hermitage there, and all practising hermits of the Kargyütpa Sect are enjoined by their *Guru* to become proficient in acquiring it. Deep breathing, as known to Europeans, forms part of the practice. The Editor possesses an English version of the process, which he worked out in collaboration with the late Lāma Kazi Dawa-Samdup, and which he anticipates publishing, along with other translations of Tibetan texts on *Yoga*. (See p. 144[2], following.)

Sj. Atal Bihari Ghosh has added here the following : ' Before the *shishya* can practise *yoga* in its highest form, in *Rāja-Yoga*, he must perfect his material body by means of *Haṭha-Yoga*, so that it becomes "beyond contraries" (Skt. *Dvan-dvātīta*)—heat and cold, dampness and dryness, and all similar physical opposites. To this end are necessary the various *yogic* processes prescribed for purifying the body (Skt. *Dhauti-Shodhana*), the various bodily postures (Skt. *Āsana* and *Mudrā*) and control of the breathing (Skt. *Prāṇāyāma*). The *Gheraṇḍa-Sanghitā* and the *Haṭhayoga-Pradīpikā* describe *Haṭha-Yoga* as the staircase leading to *Rāja-Yoga* ; and through *Rāja-Yoga*, the *yogī* becomes *Dvandvātīta* in a higher sense—praise and blame, pleasure and pain, and all similar mental or intellectual and psychic opposites becoming undifferentiated to him   Under *Haṭha-Yoga* is classified *Mantra-Yoga*, which, too, is preparatory to *Rāja-Yoga*.'

[2] The geometrical forms of the four structures are also symbolical, thus : the Circle symbolizes the Element Water ; the Crescent, the Element Air ; the Triangle, the Element Fire ; and the Square, the Element Earth.

have, as the result, disciples full of faith, energy, intelligence, and kind compassion, endowed from the first with the qualifications essential to worthy *shishyas*. They shall be devoid of carnal and worldly longings, patient, hardy, and painstaking in the time of their meditation.  Lastly, they shall be blessed with Realization of Wisdom, and be filled with grace and truth, so that every one of them shall be a perfect Lāma, and this Hierarchy of the Kargyütpa Sect be rendered as eminent and conspicuous as the waxing moon.  Therefore rejoice."

'Thus it was that my *Guru* encouraged, praised, and gladdened me, and that my happy days began.

'This is the Third [Meritorious] Act—the Act of mine obtaining the anxiously sought Initiation and Truth.'

## CHAPTER VII

# THE PERSONAL GUIDANCE BY THE *GURU*

*Telling of the Fruits of Jetsün's Meditation and Study; of
Marpa's Last Journey to India; of Jetsün's Prophetic Dream
and its Interpretation by Marpa; and of Marpa's special charge
to each of his Four Chief Disciples.*

RECHUNG then asked, 'Master, didst thou set off at once to
the wild solitudes after receiving the Truths, or didst thou continue to live with thy *Guru*?'

And Jetsün made reply, 'My *Guru* commanded that I should
continue there, saying that he would supply me with food and
other necessities, which he did most liberally; and I retired to
meditate in a rock-cave called Lhobrak-Tak-nya, with an
ample supply of provisions. There I used to sit in a rigid posture, with a lighted lamp on my head, without moving till the
light went out, were it night or day. Eleven months went by.
Then my *Guru* and his lady came to see me, bringing food
for the purpose of holding a religious feast. The *Guru* said,
"My son, it is very creditable that thou shouldst be able to
meditate for eleven months, without the [meditation] cushion
losing warmth. Now thou mayst pull down the wall [enclosing
thee], and come to thine old father for a little rest, as well as
to recount to me what thou hast experienced."

'I did not much care about relaxing my meditation, but,
seeing that my *Guru* had thus commanded, I was bound to go.
I proceeded to demolish the wall, though it seemed to be
a pity to have to do so, and was delaying a little. Thereupon,
the *Guru's* lady came up, and asked me, "Son, art thou
coming?" "I feel reluctant to pull down the wall," I answered.
She replied, "Oh, never mind that. Thou knowest that the
Profound Mystic Omens are very important. Besides, the
Lāma's temper is quite short; and should there occur any bad
omens through this delay, it will never do. So I will help thee
to pull down the wall and to come out quickly." With that
she pulled it down;[1] and I went out feeling altogether lost.

[1] The wall by which Milarepa was enclosed in his place of meditation was

'My *Guru* said, "While we two, father and son, shall be occupied in some rituals connected with this Meditation, do thou, Damema, prepare food." Then, while we were eating the meal, he asked, "My son, what beliefs or convictions hast thou arrived at regarding these Truths; what experiences, what insight, and what understanding hast thou obtained?" And he added, "Take thy time and recount them to me."

'Upon this, with deep and sincere humility, I knelt, and joining the palms of my hands, with tears in mine eyes, extemporaneously sang to my *Guru* a hymn of praise, offering him the sevenfold worship—as a prelude to submitting the narrative of mine experiences and convictions:

1

' "To the impure eyes of them Thou seekest to liberate,
Thou manifestest Thyself in a variety of shapes;
But to those of Thy followers who have been purified,
Thou, Lord, appearest as a Perfected Being; obeisance to
Thee.

2

' "With Thy Brahma-like voice, endowed with the sixty vocal
perfections,
Thou preachest the Holy Truths to each in his own speech,
Complete in their eighty-four thousand subjects;
Obeisance to Thy Word, audible yet inseparable from the
Voidness.

3

' "In the Heavenly Radiance of *Dharma-Kāya* Mind,[1]
There existeth not shadow of thing or concept,
Yet It prevadeth all objects of knowledge;
Obeisance to the Immutable, Eternal Mind.

4

' "In the Holy Palace of the Pure and Spiritual Realms,
Thou Person illusory, yet changeless and selfless,
Thou Mother Divine of Buddhas, past, present, and future,
O Great Mother Damema, to Thy Feet I bow down.

a loose structure made of rough stones held together with mud, and therefore not difficult to pull down.

[1] See p. 36[5].

## 5

'"[O *Guru*], to Thy children spiritual,
To Thy disciples who Thy word obey,
To each, with all his followers,
Obeisance humble and sincere I make.

## 6

"Whate'er there be, in all the systems of the many worlds,
To serve as offerings for the rites divine,
I offer unto Thee, along with mine own fleshly form;
Of all my sins, may I be freed and purified.

## 7

'"In merits earned by others, I rejoice;
So set the Wheel of Truth in motion full, I pray;
Until the Whirling Pool of Being emptied be,
Do not, O Noble *Guru*, from the world depart.

'"I dedicate all merit from this Hymn,
Unto the Cause of Universal Good."

'Having, as a prelude, sung this hymn of seven stanzas,
I then continued: " Inseparable from Dorje-Chang [1] Himself
art thou, my *Guru*, with thy consort, and thine offspring. In
virtue of thy fair and meritorious deeds, and of the power of
the waves of grace proceeding from thy boundless generosity,
and of thy kindness beyond repayment, I, thy vassal, have
imbibed a little knowledge, in the sphere of understanding,
which I now beg to lay before thee. Out of the unchanging
State of Quiescence of Eternal Truth, be pleased to listen unto
me for a little while.

'"I have understood this body of mine to be the product of
Ignorance, as set forth in the Twelve *Nidānas*,[2] composed of

---

[1] Or, Skt. *Vajra-Dhara*; see pp. 10, 39[5].

[2] These are the twelve interconnected causes, as taught by Buddhism, which
keep the Wheel of Birth and Death revolving. First there are the Past Causes:
(1) *Avidyā* (Ignorance), due to non-realization that *sangsāric* existence—in
worlds, hells, and even in heavens—is illusory and undesirable, that the One
Reality is beyond all conditioned states of being, beyond the realm of things,
of sensation, beyond Nature; that it is the Unbecome, Unborn, Unmade, Unformed—*Nirvāṇa*; (2) *Sangskāra* (Mental Activity), arising from the Ignorance.
Then come their Present Effects: (3) *Vijñāna* (Mundane Consciousness) within

THE SUPREME *GURU*

THE ĀDI-BUDDHA VAJRA-DHARA

Described on pages xxvii–xxviii, 8–10

flesh and blood, lit up by the perceptive power of consciousness. To those fortunate ones who long for Emancipation, it may be the great vessel by means of which they may procure Freedom and Endowments ; but to those unfortunate ones, who only sin, it may be the guide to the lower and miserable states of existence. This, our life, is the boundary-mark whence one may take an upward or downward path. Our present time is a most precious time, wherein each of us must decide, in one way or the other, for lasting good or lasting ill. I have understood this to be the chief end of our present term of life. Here, again, by holding on to Thee, O powerful Lord and Saviour of sentient beings like myself, I hope to cross over this Ocean of Worldly Existence, the source of all pains and

the *Sangsāra* ; (4) *Nāma-Rūpa* (Name and Form) concomitant with *sangsāric* existence ; (5) *Shaḍāyatana* (Sixfold Organ) of the *sangsāric* body, leading to (6) *Sparsha* (Contact) and (7) *Vedanā* (Sensation). These are linked with Present Causes : (8) *Tṛishṇā* (Desire) for *sangsāric* sensation ; (9) *Upādāna* (clinging) to *sangsāric* sensation ; and (10) *Bhāva* (*Sangsāric* existence itself). Finally, there result the Future Effects of these ten *nidānas* : (11) *Jāti* (Birth) ; and (12) *Jarā-maraṇa* (Old Age and Death). This is one aspect of the Twelve *Nidānas*, or Twelve Links of the Chain of Causal Nexus. (Cf. The Earl of Ronaldshay, *Lands of the Thunderbolt*, London, 1923, pp. 53-6.) Another aspect, derived from the pictorial Wheel of Life, as found in Tibetan monastic art, may be outlined as follows : (1) *Avidyā* (Unconscious Will), as in the state of passing from death to rebirth ; (2) *Sangskāra* (Conformations), as in the womb-state, preceding birth ; (3) *Vijñāna* (Consciousness), at birth ; (4) *Nāma-Rūpa* (Self-Consciousness), as personality develops and makes distinction between self and others, by name (*Nāma*) and form (*Rūpa*) ; (5) *Shaḍāyatana* (Sense-Surfaces and Understanding) in the outside world, as developed in the growing child ; (6) *Sparsha* (Contact), the exercise by the youth of the sense organs ; (7) *Vedanā* (Feeling), the resultant mental and physical sensations experienced ; (8) *Tṛishṇā* (Desire), developed as a result of the sensations thus experienced ; (9) *Upādāna* (Indulgence) of the desire, leading to clinging and greed and desire of an heir to inherit worldly possessions ; (10) *Bhāva* (Fuller Life), in mature and married life, with means of obtaining an heir ; (11) *Jāti* (Birth) of heir ; (12) *Jarā-maraṇa* (Decay and Death) as the Cycle of Life completes itself. Thence the Wheel turns until out of death there come another rebirth, through *Avidyā*, the first of the *Nidānas*. (Cf. L. A. Waddell, *The Buddhism of Tibet*, London, 1895, p. 110.)

These two aspects are complementary to one another, and both are here given in order to help the student to grasp the inner significance of one of the most essential doctrines of all Schools of Buddhism. It is by treading the Noble Eightfold Path (as described on p. 140[2], following) that the Chain of Enslavement to the *Sangsāra*, to Nature, is broken, and the Slave set free in *Nirvāṇic* Bliss, all *karmic* necessity for further birth and death forever ended. And it is this Supreme Goal which Milarepa is believed to have won.

griefs, so difficult to escape from. But to be able to do so, it is first of all necessary for me to take refuge in the Precious Trinity,[1] and to observe and adopt in a sincere spirit the rules prescribed. In this, too, I see the *Guru* to be the main source and embodiment of all good and happiness that can accrue to me.

' " Therefore do I realize the supreme necessity of obeying the *Guru's* commands and behests, and keeping my faith in him unsullied and staunch. After such realization, then deep meditation on the difficulty of obtaining the precious boon of a free and well-endowed human birth, on the uncertainty of the exact moment of death, on the certain effect of one's actions, and on the miseries of *sangsāric* being, cannot fail to compel one to desire freedom and emancipation from all *sangsāric* existence ; and to obtain this, one must cleave to the staff of the Noble Eightfold Path,[2] by which only may a sentient being obtain that emancipation. Then, from the level of this Path, one must pass on, by degrees, to the Higher Paths, all the while observing one's vows as carefully as if they were one's own eyes, rebuilding or mending them should they become in the least impaired. I have understood that one who aimeth at his individual peace and happiness adopteth the Lower Path (the *Hīnayāna*). But he, who from the very start, devoteth the merit of his love and compassion to the cause of others, I understand belongeth to the Higher Path (the *Mahā-yāna*). To leave the Lower Path and to enter upon the Higher Path, it is necessary to gain a clear view of the goal of one's aspirations, as set forth by the unexcelled Immutable Path (the *Vajra-Yāna*).

' " Again, to gain a clear view of the Final Goal, it is essential to have a perfectly well-accomplished *Guru*, who knoweth every branch of the four kinds of initiatory rites without the slightest misunderstanding or doubt regarding them ;

---

[1] Namely, the *Buddha*, the *Dharma* (or Doctrine), the *Saṅgha* (or Priesthood).

[2] This is the *Bodhi* Path, as taught by the Enlightened One. It may be verbally described as (1) Right Belief, or Right Seeing ; (2) Right Aims, or Right Aspiring ; (3) Right Speech ; (4) Right Actions ; (5) Right Means of Livelihood, or Right Living ; (6) Right Endeavouring ; (7) Right Mindfulness, or Right Remembering ; and (8) Right Meditation.

he alone can make the Final Goal thoroughly explicit to a *shishya*. The ceremony of initiation conferreth the power of mastering abstruse and deep thoughts regarding the Final Goal. In meditating on the Final Goal, step by step, one hath to put forth all one's energies, both of grammatical and logical acumen; as well as, through moral and mental reasoning and internal search, to discover the non-existence of the personal Ego and, therefore, the fallacy of the popular idea that it existeth.[1] In realizing the non-existence of the personal Ego, the mind must be kept in quiescence. On being enabled, by various methods, to put the mind in that state as a result of a variety of causes, all [thoughts, ideas, and cognitions] cease, and the mind passeth from consciousness [of objects] into a state of perfect tranquillity, so that days, months, and years may pass without the person himself perceiving it; thus the passing of time hath to be marked for him by others. This state is called *Shi-nay* (Tranquil Rest). By not submitting oneself to the state of total oblivion and unconsciousness [of objects], but by exerting one's intellect or faculty of consciousness in this state, one gaineth the clear ecstatic state of quiescent consciousness.

' "Although there be this state, which may be called a state of superconsciousness (*Lhag-tong*), nevertheless, individuals, or ego-entities, so long as they are such, are incapable of experiencing it. I believe that it is only experienced when one hath gained the first [superhuman] state [on the Path to Buddhahood]. Thus, by thought-process and visualization, one treadeth the Path. The visions of the forms of the Deities upon which one meditateth are merely the signs attending perseverance in meditation. They have no intrinsic worth or value in themselves.[2]

1 ' "Five things there are," said a sage in India, "namely, Being, Light, Bliss, Name, and Form. The first three are of the Supreme, the other two are of the [material] world." '—Sj. Atal Bihari Ghosh.

2 The objective forms of deities—like the illusory visualizations produced by practices of meditation upon them and frequently outwardly projected as hallucinatory images—are, in the last analysis of the Enlightened Mind, nonexistent, being no more real than the objective forms of human beings or of any other objects of Nature. In the *Bardo Thödol* (see the Sixth Day) it is said, 'The deities . . . exist from eternity within the faculties of thine own

' "To sum up, a vivid state of mental quiescence, accompanied by energy, and a keen power of analysis, by a clear and inquisitive intellect, are indispensable requirements ; like the lowest rungs of a ladder, they are absolutely necessary to enable one to ascend. But in the process of meditating on this state of mental quiescence (*Shi-nay*), by mental concentration, either on forms and shapes, or on shapeless and formless things, the very first effort must be made in a compassionate mood, with the aim of dedicating the merit of one's efforts to the Universal Good. Secondly, the goal of one's aspirations must be well defined and clear, soaring into the regions transcending thought. Finally, there is need of mentally praying and wishing for blessings on others so earnestly that one's mind-processes also transcend thought. These, I understand, to be the highest of all Paths.

' "Then, again, as the mere name of food doth not satisfy the appetite of a hungry person, but he must eat food, so, also, a man who would learn about the Voidness [1] [of Thought] must meditate so as to realize it, and not merely learn its definition. Moreover, to obtain the knowledge of the state of superconsciousness (*Lhag-tong*), one must practise and accustom oneself to the mechanical attainment of the recurrence of the above practices without intermission. In short, habituation to

intellect.' That is, they so exist only when man is regarded as the microcosm of the macrocosm.   Likewise, the *Dēmchog Tantra*, into which Milarepa has been initiated, says that the ' *Devatās* are but symbols representing the various things which occur on the Path, such as the helpful impulses and the stages attained by their means'; and that 'should doubts arise as to the divinity of these *Devatās*, one should say "the *Ḍākinī* is only the recollection of the body", and remember that the Deities constitute the Path'. (Cf. A. Avalon, *Tantrik Texts*, London, 1919, vol. vii. 41.)

[1] Text : *Tong-pa-nyid* : Skt. *Shūnyatā*, here meaning Voidness [of Thought], with reference to a transcendental or *Nirvāṇic* state of unmodified or primordial consciousness. As in Patanjali's definition of *Yoga* (in his *Yoga Aphorisms* i, 2), as 'the suppression of the transformations of the thinking principle' or, as otherwise translated, as 'the restraint of mental modifications', this Voidness [of Thought] is not the voidness of nothingness, but a state of supramundane mind only capable of being known—as Milarepa explains—by the Perfected *Yogī* who has realized it. It is the indescribable state wherein the limited personal consciousness becomes merged, but not lost, in the unlimited cosmic All-Consciousness—like a raindrop merged in an infinite ocean, or like the light of a lamp merged in the light of the sun.

the contemplation of Voidness, of Equilibrium, of the Indescribable, and of the Incognizable, forms the four different
stages of the Four Degrees of Initiation,—graduated steps in
the ultimate goal of the mystic *Vajra-Yāna* [or Immutable
Path]. To understand these thoroughly, one must sacrifice
bodily ease and all luxuriousness, and, with this in mind, face
and surmount every obstacle, being ever willing to sacrifice
life itself, and prepared for every possible contingency.

' " As for myself, I have not the means to recompense thee,
my *Guru* and the Reverend Mother,—my benefactors ; your
loving kindness is beyond my power to repay by any offer of
worldly wealth or riches. So I will repay you by a lifelong
devotion to meditation, and I will complete my final study of
your Teachings in the 'Og-min Heaven.[1]

' " To my *Guru*, the Great Dorje-Chang,
 To Damema, the Mother of all Buddhas,
 And to all Princes Royal, the *Avatāras*,
 I make as offering, to Their ears, this essence of my learning
  gleaned.

' " If there be heresy or error in my speech,
 I pray that They will kindly pardon it,
 And set me then upon the Righteous Path.

' " Lord, from the sun-orb of Thy Grace,
 The radiant Rays of Light have shone,
 And opened wide the petals of the Lotus of my Heart,
 So that it breatheth forth the fragrance born of Knowledge,
 For which I am for ever bounden unto Thee ;
 So will I worship Thee by constant meditation.

' " Vouchsafe to bless me in mine efforts,
 That good may come to every sentient being.
 Lastly, I ask forgiveness, too, for any lavishness of words."

' My *Guru* was delighted, and said, " My son, I had ex-

---

[1] This, the Heaven of the Ādi-Buddha, is the last outpost of the *Sangsāra* (i. e.
the Universe of Nature). Within the 'Og-min Heaven, as the text suggests, it is
possible, as it is on Earth, to realize *Nirvāṇa*, and thus escape the *Sangsāra*
wholly, and for ever. (See p. 44[1], above.)

pected much from thee; my expectations have been fulfilled."
Next the lady said, " I knew that my son had the will and intellect to succeed." Both were highly gratified, and we conversed on religious topics for a long time. Then my *Guru* and
his lady took leave of me, and I resumed my meditations in
the close retreat.

'About this time, my *Guru*, being on a pastoral tour in the
North Uru villages, was performing a religious ceremony in
one Marpa Golay's house when he had a vision. In it the
*Ḍākinīs* appeared, and reminded him of some enigmatical
hints of his *Guru* Naropa, which, when given, he had not
understood; and these the *Ḍākinīs* interpreted and explained
to him. The outcome of this led him to go to India to see
Naropa.

' Then, one night, some days after my *Guru* had returned
to Wheat Valley, I dreamt that a woman of somewhat dark
blue colour, dressed in silks and beautifully adorned with the
six bone ornaments, having eyebrows and eyelashes of a golden
hue, appeared to me, and said, "Son, by long continued application to meditation thou hast obtained the Truths of the
Great Symbol,[1] which will enable thee to attain *Nirvāṇa*.
Thou hast also obtained the Six Doctrines.[2] But thou lackest

---

[1] Tib. *Phyag-rgya-ch'en-po* (pron. *Chag-gya-ch'en-po*): Skt. *Mahā-Mudrā*:
'Great Symbol'. This is one of the chief systems of *yogic* meditation of the
Kargyütpa School. Judging from an English translation of a text of this *Yoga*,
which the Editor and the late Lāma Kazi Dawa-Samdup worked out together,
in Gangtok, Sikkim, it is a system developed under Tibetan influences, but
essentially Indian by origin.

To an Indian *yogī*, *Mahā-Mudrā* denotes a *yogic* posture, but here, in this
Tibetan sense, a state attained by *yoga* practices, whereby, as the text of
*The Great Symbol* explains, 'one obtaineth the highest boon of The Great
Symbol, . . . *Nirvāṇa*'.

[2] Tib. *Chos-drug* (pron. *Cho-dug*): ' Six Doctrines (or Truths')'. This, like the
*Great Symbol*, is a treatise expounding the practical application of various *Yogas*,
more or less of Indian origin. An old block-print copy of the Tibetan text of the
*Six Doctrines*, with English translation by the late Lāma Kazi Dawa-Samdup
and the Editor, gives the Six Doctrines as follows: (1) *Gtum-mo* (pron. *Tummo*): 'Vital Warmth (or Psychic Heat)', the acquisition of which is necessary
for the sake of physical comfort in Tibet and, also, as a driving force for the
devotee seeking spiritual development; (2) *Sgyu-lüs* (pron. *Gyu-lü*): 'Illusory
Body', a teaching whereby the *yogī* realizes that his own body and all objects
of Nature, being *sangsāric*, are illusory; (3) *Rmi-lam* (pron. *Mi-lam*): ' Dreams ',

the precious teaching of the *Drong-jug* [1] by which thou mayst attain Buddhahood in an instant; and this thou must procure."

'I thought over the dream, and concluded that the woman was a *Ḍākinī*, since she had all the appearance of one. Nevertheless, I was doubtful whether the vision was an intimation from the *Ḍākinīs* of some coming event or a temptation from Māra. [2] Anyway, I was firmly convinced that my *Guru*, the Embodiment of the Buddhas, past, present, and future, would certainly be able to tell me, since there could be nothing which he did not know. Especially as regarded knowledge, I knew that his understanding embraced its whole extent, from the Sacred Truths above-mentioned [whereby *Nirvāṇa* is obtained] to the science of patching broken earthenware. And if he took it to be a premonitory revelation, I should have to obtain the *Drong-jug*. So I pulled down the partition, plastered together with mud, and went to my *Guru*. He seemed shocked, and said, "Why hast thou come, instead of remaining in close retreat? Thou runnest the risk of incurring some mishap." I informed him of my dream and said I wanted to be assured whether it was a revelation or a temptation; if the former, I begged that he should bestow on me the revealed science for which I had come. He sat in silence for some time, and then said, "Yes, that was a revelation from the *Ḍākinīs*. When I was about to return from India, my *Guru*, the great

a teaching whereby the *yogī* realizes that even as dreams are illusory so are all *sangsāric* experiences, in the waking state and in the sleeping state equally; (4) *Hod-gsal* (pron. *Öd-sal*): 'Clear Light', defined, in the text, as follows: 'It hath been said that the unmodified, phenomena-transcending mind (or mind in the *yogic* state of non-thought)—which is the Thatness of all things and inseparable from the Voidness, the Ultimate—while experiencing the thought-transcending Great Bliss [of Ecstatic Illumination] is the Clear Light'; (5) *Bar-do*: 'Intermediate State' [between death and rebirth], which teaches the *yogī* how to traverse death and rebirth without break of consciousness; and (6) *Hpho-va* (pron. *Pho-wa*): 'Transference', the science of voluntarily transferring, from body to body or from place to place, the principle of consciousness. Cf. pp. 154-6.

[1] This, too, is a *yogic* treatise, but the Editor has not made a study of it.

[2] Māra is here the Evil One, the Devil-Tempter of Buddhism. As the Devil tempted the Christ ('The Anointed One') in the Wilderness, so Māra tempted the Buddha ('The Enlightened One') under the Bo-Tree at Budh-Gaya, when He was attaining Enlightenment.

Paṇḍit Naropa, spoke about this same *Drong-jug*, but I do not recollect having obtained it. I will look over all mine Indian manuscripts and search for it."

'Thereupon, both of us spent a whole day and night in ransacking the whole collection of manuscripts, searching for the *Drong-jug*. But although we found several treatises on *Pho-wa*,[1] not a single letter regarding *Drong-jug* was to be found. So my *Guru* said, "Ah, the dream which I had in North Uru is likewise a sign directing me to go and obtain this same work [on *Drong-jug*]. Besides, I know not how many other works there may be to procure. Therefore I shall go to India to obtain them."

'In spite of entreaties and expostulations, urging his age as obstacles to this toilsome journey, my *Guru* was resolved on undertaking it. His disciples contributed liberally towards his travelling expenses; and, the offerings being converted into a cupful of gold, with this he set out for India, where he arrived just about the time of Naropa's disappearance.[2] He had made

---

[1] A manuscript text of this, fuller than that contained in the *Six Doctrines*, with English rendering by the Editor and the late Lāma Kazi Dawa-Samdup, shows it to be another treatise on *Yoga*—the *Yoga* of transferring the principle of consciousness from one's own body to another's (as in spirit obsession), or, in one's own subtle body, to any place on Earth, or to any world, heaven, or hell of the Universe. The *Drong-jug* appears from the present passage to be a *yogic* treatise of like nature, except that the transference is not limited, as in the *Pho-wa*, to the Universe (or *Sangsāra*), but comprises in its scope *Nirvāṇa* (which is the Unbecome, Unformed, Unmade, beyond the *Sangsāra*), whereby the mundane consciousness is transmuted into the supra-mundane consciousness— *Nirvāṇa* not being a place, but a state of Perfect Enlightenment. In this sense, then, the *Pho-wa* treats of the *yogic* transference of the mundane consciousness, and the *Drong-jug* treats of the *yogic* transmutation of the mundane (or *sangsāric*) consciousness of objects (of Nature) into the supra-mundane consciousness, wherein all component things are realized to be illusion (or *Māyā*). Hence the importance which Marpa attaches to the *Drong-jug* and his insistence that Milarepa should obtain a copy of the text and master it.

[2] According to some traditions, current among Tibetan Lāmas, Naropa, being a Perfected *Yogī*, did not die, but merely entered into the subtle form by direct transmutation of the grosser physical body. The Biblical translation of the old Jewish Prophet Elijah, as it is said in symbol, 'in a chariot of fire', to Paradise, and the theory that Jesus rose from the dead in the spiritual body, leaving no corpse in the Tomb, illustrate the same belief, which has been current among many peoples in all historical ages. Milarepa, too, passes in a similar mystical way, as will be seen in chap. xii. Other traditions say that Naropa is still alive

up his mind to sacrifice life itself in attempting to obtain an interview with his *Guru* ; and various hopeful signs and omens he interpreted as predicting his final success and the fulfilment of his wish.

'Seeking his *Guru* with fervent prayers, he at last met him in a jungle ; and, taking him to the monastery of Phulahari, asked of him the science of *Drong-jug*. Thereupon Saint Naropa asked Marpa, " Didst thou recollect this thyself, or didst thou receive a revelation ? " Marpa replied, " I did not recollect it myself, nor was a revelation vouchsafed to me personally. I have a disciple named Thöpaga to whom the revelation was granted, and it was on that account that I came." " Excellent," said Naropa, " there are in the benighted land of Tibet some bright spirits, like the sun illuminating the mountain peaks."

in India, being one of the Great *Siddhas*, that is to say, a human being made perfect on Earth, who, as such, having control over all processes of Nature, can live or die at will, and reincarnate at will in a new body by submitting to the process of womb-birth. The same claim of *yogic* power to reincarnate is made for the Dalai Lāma, the God King of Tibet and Pope of Northern Buddhism, and for his colleague in spiritual authority, the Tashi Lāma, the former being the incarnation of the National Divine Protector of Tibet, the All-Compassionate One, Avalokiteshvara, and the latter of Amitābha, the Buddha of Boundless Light.

A remarkable example of conscious reincarnation, which the Editor takes to be worthy of at least provisional credence, is actually exhibited by the Burmese boy Maung Tun Kyaing, a picture of whom is in the Editor's possession. According to trustworthy report, Maung Tun Kyaing is able, without having been educated in this lifetime, to deliver learned discourses on the most abstruse metaphysics of Buddhism and to read and correct errors in classical Burmese and Pali, and to remember his incarnation immediately prior to his present incarnation, wherein he was the head of the Yunkyaung Monastery, near Pantanaw, Burma, and named U. Pandissa. Recently he is said to have been preaching to immense audiences throughout Burma.

Sj. Atal Bihari Ghosh tells me that Trailanga Swāmī, who passed away within recent times, is known to have been in Benares long before the advent of the British in India. Learned paṇḍits regularly sought the aid of the Swāmī in their numerous scholarly and religious problems, but none of them had lived long enough to remember when he first appeared in the Holy City. Govinda-Bhagavat-Pādāchārya, the *Guru* of Shangkarāchārya, the great monistic expounder of the Vedānta, is believed to be yet alive. This *Guru's* fame rests not only on his profound understanding of the Vedāntic philosophy, but on his knowledge of chemistry as well ; and some of his very remarkable works on chemistry are just being brought to light.

' It is said that Naropa, then holding out his hands in prayer, chanted as follows :

' " In the gloomy regions of the North,
Like the sun illuminating the mountain peaks,
Dwelleth he who is called Thöpaga ;
Obeisance to that Great Being."

' Then Naropa closed his eyes reverently, and nodded his head thrice towards Tibet ; and all the Indian mountain-tops and the trees also nodded thrice towards Tibet. It is said that even until to-day the hill-tops and the tops of trees round about Phulahari incline towards Tibet.[1]

' Having transmitted the whole of the *Ear-Whispered Tantra of the Ḍākinīs*,[2] Saint Naropa interpreted certain omens as predicting future events. The manner of Marpa's obeisance, for example, foretold the failure of Marpa's own offspring, but predicted the perpetual continuance of the Hierarchy through me ; and after Marpa returned to Tibet he lost his son, Darma-Doday, just as had been predicted at the premonitory ceremony of his obeisance.

' On the anniversary of his son's death, after the completion of the ceremony [in commemoration of it], as Marpa sat amidst the assembly of all his disciples they addressed him in a body, representing to him his advanced age and the unfortunate loss of his saintly son, who was the very embodiment of the Buddhas of the past, present, and future, and who, had he lived, would have been a worthy successor. They said, " Now we must first of all consider the best method of rendering our Kargyütpa Hierarchy as enduring and eminent as possible. We also pray that thou wilt be pleased to leave special directions to each of us, thy *shishyas*, as to what particular branches of doctrine each should adopt, and what particular lines of prac-

---

[1] This is obviously a folk-legend to account for natural phenomena in the Phulahari country—the dip of mountains, and the inclination of trees caused by the direction of the prevailing winds.

[2] Text : *Mkah-'gro-nyen-rgyud* (pron. *Kah-'gro-Nyen-Gyüd*) : Skt. *Ḍākinī Karṇa Tantra*, meaning *Ear-Whispered* (i. e. Esoteric) *Tantra of* (or *inspired by*) *the Ḍākinīs*. Judging from the source and manner of the transmission to Marpa, it seems to be one of the most esoteric of the orally-transmitted teachings preserved by the Kargyütpa Initiates.

tice each should pursue." [1] The *Guru* said, "I, the spiritual disciple of the Great Pandit Naropa, rely upon occult directions by omens and dreams. The Kargyütpa Hierarchy hath the blessings of the Saintly Naropa. Do ye, my chief *shishyas*, go and await your dreams and report them to me."

'Accordingly, the chief disciples concentrated their minds upon their dreams and reported the results. All or nearly all were more or less good, but none of them were revelations regarding the future of the Hierarchy. I, however, had a dream of four great pillars, which I reported to the *Guru* in the following verses:

'"Obedient unto Dorje-Chang's command,
   The dream of yesternight I now narrate,
   Exactly in the manner it was dreamt;
   Be pleased [O *Guru*] to vouchsafe Thine ear awhile.

'"In the ample regions of the World's North,
   I dreamt there stood a mountain grand,
   Its summit touching the very skies.
   Around this summit moved the sun and moon,
   Their rays illumining the heavens above.
   The base of the mountain covered the Earth;
   From its four sides flowed four perennial streams,
   Quenching the thirst of every sentient being.
   Their waters fell into an ocean deep,
   And on their shores bloomed varied flowers.
   Such was the general purport of my dream,
   Which to my *Guru*, the Eternal Buddha,[2] I narrate.

'"Eastward of that glorious mountain,
   Of a pillar high I chiefly dreamt.
   Upon the pillar's top a lion ramped;
   The mane of the lion was luxuriant,
   His four outstretched paws clawed the mountain-side,
   His eyes upturned were looking heavenward.

---

[1] It is the duty of the *Guru* to set each of his *shishyas* upon that path of spiritual development which is best suited to the *shishya*, one on one path, one on another, according to the *Guru's* insight into the innate tendency of each. (Cf. pp. 154-5.)

[2] Or 'Buddha of the Three Times (the Past, Present, and Future)'.

[Then] over the mountains the lion roamed free.
This to my *Guru*, the Eternal Buddha, I narrate.

'" Southward [of the mountain] stood a pillar high ;
Upon the pillar's top a mighty tigress roared ;
The stripes of the tigress were beautiful,
The inner stripes were triple and bold,
Her four paws clawed the jungles deep,
Her eyes upturned were looking heavenward.
[Then] through the jungles the tigress roamed free,
And passed through the groves of wood and plain.
This to my *Guru*, the Eternal Buddha, I narrate.

'" Westward [of the mountain] stood a pillar high ;
Above the pillar's top an eagle soared ;
The wings of the eagle were wide outspread,
The horns of the eagle pierced the skies,
The eyes of the eagle gazed heavenward ;
Then it soared on high, in the blue above.
This to my *Guru*, the Eternal Buddha, I narrate.

'" Northward [of the mountain] also stood a pillar high ;
Above the pillar's top soared a vulture bold ;
The wings of the vulture were wide outspread,
Upon a rock the vulture's nest was perched,
And I beheld it had a young one fledged,
And that the skies were filled with smaller birds.
The vulture turned its eyes heavenward,
Then soared away to the regions high.
This to my *Guru*, the Eternal Buddha, I narrate.

'" Deeming these to be auspicious signs,
Foreboding good and virtuous deeds,
With joy ecstatic was I thrilled ;
I pray Thee, tell to us their meaning."

' On my recounting the above, my *Guru* was highly pleased,
and said, " The dream is excellent." Then, addressing his lady,
he said, " Damema, prepare an ample meal." When she had
done so, all the pupils and disciples were invited to it. The

*Guru* then addressed the meeting, and said, " Mila-Dorje-Gyaltsen[1] hath had such and such a dream, which is an excellent sign." The chief disciples asked him to interpret the dream and to unravel the mysterious signs. Then [our saintly *Guru*], the Great *Avatāra* and Translator, sang extemporaneously the interpretation of the dream, foretelling the future destiny of the Kargyütpa Hierarchy to his disciples, as follows :

' " Lord, Refuge of all Sentient Beings, Thou, the Eternal
    Buddha,
  O Saintly Naropa, I bow down at Thy Feet.

' " O ye, my *shishyas*, in assembly seated here,
  Give ear attentively unto the meaning of this wondrous and
    prophetic dream,
  Which to you I will now interpret.

' " The ample regions of the World's North
  Symbolize the Buddhist Faith in Tibet prevailing.
  The mountain grand signifieth the Kargyütpa Sect,
  Founded by my agèd self, Marpa the Translator,
  And by my followers and all the Hierarchy.
  The mountain's summit touching the skies
  Symbolizeth our Peerless Goal ;
  The sun and moon revolving
  Are full Enlightenment and Love ;
  Their rays illumining the heavens above
  Are Grace enlightening Ignorance ;
  The base of the mountain covering the Earth
  Showeth how our deeds will fill the World ;
  The four streams from the four sides issuing
  Symbolize Rites of Initiation and the Truths ;
  Their waters quenching the thirst of every being
  Portend that every living thing shall ripen and be saved ;[2]

---

[1] Here Milarepa is called by the family name of Gyaltsen, after that of his father, Mila-Sherab-Gyaltsen.

[2] It is thus that Buddhism, in teaching that every living thing will ultimately reach Enlightenment, repudiates the Semitic doctrine of Eternal Damnation ; all *karmic* suffering, even in Hell, must at last run its course and end. Nothing *saṇgsāric*, whether worlds, hells, or heavens, or existence therein, is permanent —all is subject to change, decay, and dissolution, even Brahmā and all the Gods ; and Evil must eventually be transmuted or swallowed up in Good.

Their waters falling in an Ocean Deep
Are the blending of the Inner with the Outer Light ; [1]
The varied blossoms blooming on the shores
Are Fruit Immaculate, Truths Realized.
O ye, my *shishyas*, in assembly seated here,
The dream entire is good, not ill.

' " The great pillar eastward of the mountain grand
Is Tsurtön-Wang-gay, of Döl.
The lion ramping on the pillar's top
Showeth Tsurtön to be in nature lion-like ;
The lion's mane luxuriant, showeth how
With the Mystic Truths he is imbued ;
The lion's four paws clawing the mountain-side
Show him endowed with the four boundless motives ;
The lion's eyes turned heavenward
Show he hath bidden farewell to *sangsāric* life ;
The lion's roaming free o'er the mountains high
Showeth that he hath gained the Realms of the Free.
O ye, my *shishyas*, in assembly seated here,
The dream regarding the East is good, not ill.

'" The great pillar southward of the mountain grand
Is Ngogdun-Chudor, of Zhung ;
The tigress roaring on the pillar's top
Showeth him to be in nature tigress-like ;

---

[1] Tib. *Chös-nyid-ma-bu* : Skt. *Dharmatā-Mātri-Putra* : ' Mother and Offspring Reality', or 'Inner and Outer Light'. The Offspring Reality (or Truth, or Light) is that realized in this world through practising deep meditation (Skt. *Dhyāna*). The Mother Reality is the Primal or Fundamental Truth, experienced only after death, in the Intermediate (or *Bar-do*) State at the moment when the consciousness-principle quits the body and before *karmic* propensities have begun to burst forth into activity. There is then momentarily a glimpsing of Reality, of Supramundane All-consciousness, in a state of quiescence of the primordial or unmodified mind – a foretaste of *Nirvāṇa*. Numerous are the records of great saints and seers, in various ages and lands, and of many races and Faiths, who when dying have seen this Light, the Pagan calling It the Light of the Gods, the Christian the Light of Christ, or the Buddhist the Light of Truth. If, when the Inner and Outer Light thus dawn in at-one-ment, the percipient has the *yogic* power to hold fast to the transcendental experience—and usually he has not—all *karmic* clingings to the *Sangsāra* being cut off, the Complete Illumination of Buddhahood is won.

The stripes appearing well-defined and beautiful
Show him well imbued with the Mystic Truths;
The triple all-encircling stripes
Show that he hath, within himself, realized the Trinity;
The four paws clawing the jungles deep
Show that by him the Duties Four [1] will be fulfilled;
The eyes of the tigress turned heavenward
Show that he hath bidden farewell to *sangsāric* life;
The tigress roaming the jungles free
Showeth that he hath attained Salvation;
The tigress traversing the groves of wood and plain
Showeth that his Hierarchy will be continued through his
    progeny.
O ye, my *shishyas*, in assembly seated here,
The dream regarding the South is good, not ill.

'" The great pillar westward of the mountain grand
Is Metön-Tsönpo, of Tsang-rong;
The eagle soaring above the pillar's top
Showeth him to be in nature eagle-like;
The wings of the eagle wide outspread
Show him well-imbued with the Mystic Truths;
The eagle's horns piercing the skies
Show that he hath passed meditation's pitfalls; [2]
The eyes of the Eagle turned heavenward
Show that he hath bidden farewell to *sangsāric* life;
The flight of the eagle in the blue above
Showeth that he hath passed to the Realms of the Free.
O ye, my *shishyas*, in assembly seated here,
The dream of the West is good, not ill.

'" The great pillar northward of the mountain grand
Is Mila-Repa, of Gungthang;
The vulture soaring above the pillar's top
Showeth him to be in nature vulture-like;
The wings of the vulture wide outspread
Show him well-imbued with the Mystic Truths;

---

[1] See p. 36[4].
[2] That is, the dangers, physical and psychical, and the numerous impediments or temptations attendant upon the practice of meditation, or *Yoga*.

The vulture's nest perched on a rock
Showeth his life to be enduring as the rock ;
The vulture's bringing forth a chick
Showeth that he will have a peerless [spiritual] son ;
Small birds filling the heavens wide
Show the spread of the Kargyütpa Sect ;
The vulture's gazing heavenward
Showeth that he hath bidden farewell to *sangsāric* life ;
The flight of the vulture in the regions high
Showeth that he hath attained the Realms of the Free.
O ye, my *shishyas*, in assembly seated here,
The dream of the North is excellent.

' " Now is the duty of my life fulfilled ;
On you my mantle now hath fallen.
And if my words prophetic be,
Then shall the Kargyütpa Hierarchy
Attain pre-eminence and glorious growth."

' When the *Guru* had uttered these prophetic words, each of the *shishyas* was filled with joy. Then he opened out to them his treasures of religious books and scrolls of Mystic Truths and Sciences. By day he gave them instruction, by exposition, lecture, and sermon ; by night he encouraged them to meditation. Thus each made good progress in spiritual development.

' One night, during a special Initiation Rite of the *Yūm* (Mother Text), the Lāma thought that he would find out, by the aid of his clairvoyance, what particular line of study and truths was most suitable for each of his four chief disciples, so that he might give to each just those texts of the Scriptures which would be most useful. So he resolved to observe the omens of the dawn. Accordingly, at daybreak next morning he regarded all his principal disciples with his clairvoyant vision. He saw Ngogdun-Chudor, of Zhung, engaged in explaining and elucidating the rituals of *Gaypa-Dorje*.[1] Tsurtön-Wang-gay, of Döl, was engaged in meditating on *Pho-wa* (Transference—of the Principle of Consciousness) ; Metön-

---

[1] See p. 108[1].

Tsönpo, of Tsang-rong, was engaged in meditating on *Öd-Sal* (Clear Light),[1] and I myself had been observed meditating on *Tüm-mo* (the science of generating Vital Heat).[2]

'Thus was he occultly apprised of the innate aptitude of each of his chief disciples for mastering that particular line of study which would be most profitable and into which he should confer initiation.

'Accordingly, he favoured each of us with the gift of his last and best teachings. To Lāma Ngogpa he gave the text categorically explaining the *Gyüd* (*Tantras*), according to the four methods and the six aims, which set forth the explanations so clearly and methodically that it may be said to resemble a row of pearls strung upon a thread. To this he added the six ornaments, the sacrificial spoon, and the ruby rosary which were originally Naropa's. He also gave to him the Indian commentaries on the texts already given, and exhorted him to serve the universal aim by preaching to all sentient beings.

'To Tsurtön-Wang-gay, of Döl, Marpa gave the text on *Pho-wa* (Transference—of the Principle of Consciousness), which is to be likened to a bird flying out of an open skylight.[3] This was accompanied by the reliques of Naropa's hair, nails, and medicinal pills,[4] and ritual head-dress illuminated with

[1] See p. 145[n].

[2] Ibid. In addition to its resultant physical warmth, this *yogic* practice also produces very marked effects psychically, and so greatly assists the Tibetan *yogi* in solitary meditation.

[3] The open skylight is the Aperture of Brāhma (Skt. *Brahma-randhra*), situated on the crown of the head at the sagittal suture where the two parietal bones articulate, opened by means of the *yogic* practice of the *Pho-wa*. The bird flying out of it is the consciousness-principle going out; for it is through this Aperture that the consciousness-principle quits the body, either permanently at death, or temporarily during the practice of the *Pho-wa*, or Transference of the consciousness-principle. The process is a part of *Kuṇḍalinī Yoga* (see p. 34[2]).

[4] These are not pills for curing fleshly ills, but pills which have been occultly compounded and psychically infused with virtue by Naropa for the cure of Ignorance (*Avidyā*)—the Cause of Death and Rebirth. Their ingredients, which are kept secret from the laity, are commonly spices and drugs, so compounded by a Saint or Holy Lāma that they are believed to be *yogically* charged with his grace-radiations and auric blessing and thus capable of conveying these to the patient. The Editor possesses a treatise in Tibetan, with English translation, giving a recipe for manufacturing such spiritually-potent pills as are still made and sold by the *lāmas*—even by the Dalai Lāma himself. (Cf. p. 258[4].)

paintings of the Five Dhyānī Buddhas,[1] and the injunction to
practise *Pho-wa*.

' To Metön-Tsönpo, of Tsang-rong, he gave a text on the
*Öd-sal* (Clear Light), which is like unto a lighted lamp illuminating the gloom of night,[2] along with Naropa's *lāmaic*
sceptre (*dorje*) and bell, small double-drum (*damaru*), and
oyster-shell libation-cup, with the exhortation that he should
take the short path across the *Bar-do* (the Intermediate State—
between death and rebirth).

' To myself Marpa gave a text on *Tŭm-mo* (the science of
generating Vital Heat), which is like unto a blazing faggot,
with Maitrī's[3] hat and Naropa's raiment, and commanded me
to meditate in various solitudes—on mountain peaks, in caves,
and in wildernesses.

' Then, before a vast assembly [of disciples], Marpa [chiefly
addressing the four disciples named] said, " I have given to
each of you those Texts and Branches of the Truth by which
ye will be most benefited ; and I foretell that these same
Teachings shall be the best adapted to the followers of each
of you. I have no longer my son, Doday-Bum. Therefore,
I entrust to you the entire charge of all my sacred Kargyütpa
texts and reliques. May you prove to be devoted guardians
of the Faith, that it may flourish and expand." Thereupon,
[three of] the chief disciples departed, each to his own country.

' To me he said, " As for thee, stay a few years longer with
me. I have several more Teachings and Initiations to impart ;
besides, thine understanding should develop well in thy *Guru's*
presence."

---

[1] Such a head-dress consists of five pieces—usually of thickened Tibetan manu-
script-paper shaped like a pointed pear—on each being a painted image of one
of the Five Dhyānī Buddhas, often illuminated with gold and silver. With the
points upward, the pieces are fastened together side-wise so as to form a circular band which fits round the head leaving the top of the head uncovered, and
when worn appear like a gorgeous crown.

[2] That is to say, the experiencing of the Clear Light implies an ecstatic state
wherein the gloom of Ignorance (*Avidyā*), which is the ' gloom of night ', is
illuminated—in a super-conscious glimpsing of *Nirvāṇa*, or Enlightenment.

[3] The hat worn by the Kargyütpa *yogīs* on ceremonial occasions symbolizes
this relique, the original hat of the Great Indian *Yogī* Maitrī ; and bears a mystic
mark like a St. Andrew's Cross (X).

'Thus, according to Marpa's command, I shut myself up in close retreat in the *Zang-phug* (Copper Cave)—a cave prophesied of by Naropa. Both my *Guru* and his lady ever sent me a share of any food of which they partook, and a part of the offerings from every religious ceremony—even the smallest —which they celebrated.

'In this wise did I pass my time in delightful meditation, developing mine understanding in the presence of my *Guru* for some years, until the shoots of Spiritual Wisdom shot up in my heart.'

[This constituteth Milarepa's Fourth Meritorious Act.]

## CHAPTER VIII

# THE PARTING FROM THE *GURU*

*Telling of how Jetsün, led by a Dream, left his Hermitage, and, going to his Guru, secured permission to visit Tsa, Jetsün's Birthplace; of the Guru's Final Instructions and Admonitions; of the Sorrowful Parting; and of how Jetsün reached Tsa.*

THEN Rechung asked Jetsün, 'What led to thy coming away from Marpa's presence? How many years didst thou stay in retreat?'

And Jetsün said, 'I did not stay there many years, and the circumstances which led to my returning home were these. While in retreat I was making satisfactory progress. Usually I never slept; but one morning it happened that I had slept very long, and had a dream. This dream showed me that my house, called "Four Columns and Eight Pillars", was in such a broken and dilapidated condition that it looked like an old donkey's ears. The books of Scripture appeared damaged by the leakage. The field called "Worma Triangle" appeared to be overgrown with weeds. My mother was dead, and mine only sister was roving friendless in the world. The grief I experienced at not having met my mother again since our parting under the aforesaid unhappy conditions so many years before, was heart-rending; and I was calling upon my mother's and sister's names and weeping bitterly. On waking up, I saw that my pillow was quite wet with my tears. When I attempted to think, the longing to see my mother only increased more and more. I could not help shedding tears again; and I made up my mind to go and see mine aged parent once again by any possible means.

'At dawn, demolishing the wall enclosing me in my retreat, I went to ask leave of my *Guru*. When I got there he was sound asleep, but sitting near the head of his bed I meekly and humbly chanted to him this appeal:

'"O Lord Compassionate, Thou the Immutable,
Pray let me as a mendicant go to my home once more.
Of the inhospitable land of Tsa,
A family of three members, harassed by hostile relatives,

Have now for many years been parted;
No longer can I bear the pain of separation.
So let me go and see my mother but this once,
And quickly, then, will I return."

'Just as I had finished this appeal my *Guru* awoke. The
sun's rays shot through a chink above his pillow and like
a halo of glory lit up his venerable head, and at the same
moment his lady brought in the morning meal. These three
events occurred simultaneously; they were a combination of
events with which several future happenings were inseparably
connected. My *Guru* at once addressed me, saying, " My son,
how dost thou dare to come out of retreat so suddenly? Why,
thou runnest the risk of being possessed by the Demon (Mārā).
And thou also incurrest great personal danger. Back again to
thy retreat, this very moment!" But once more I urged upon
him what I had dreamt, in the following verses:

' " O Lord Compassionate, Thou the Immutable,
Permit this mendicant but once again to see his home,
In the wretched glen of Tsa.

' " Though of wealth not much remaineth,
Yet there are these to cause anxiety:
My house called ' Columns Four and Pillars Eight';
I fain would see if it be fallen in ruin.
My library of Sacred Scriptures;
I fain would see if it be ruined or not.
My well-known field, the ' Worma Triangle';
I fain would see if it be overgrown with weeds or not.
My mother, the vessel that held my form;
I fain would see if she be yet alive in health.
Mine only sister, Peta Gönkyit;
I fain would know if she hath strayed or not.
My Zesay, who was betrothed to me in youth;
I fain would see if she be fit to wed.
My neighbour and mine uncle, Yung-gyal;
I fain would see if he still liveth.
My cruel aunt, the Tiger-Demon;
I fain would see if she be dead or not.

My family pastor, Kunchog-Lhabum ;
I fain would know if he liveth now or not.
And more than all, my dear old mother ;
I long to see her, oh so anxiously.
The anguish now hath grown unbearable ;
Therefore, I beg Thee, Lord,
Let me go home but once,
And quickly I'll return."

'Then my *Guru* replied, "My son, when first thou didst
come here to me, thou didst say that thou shouldst have no
reason to yearn for thy relatives or home, but now thou
yearnest for many things besides. Even though thou wert to
go home, it is not likely that thou wouldst find thy mother
alive ; and, as for the others, thou canst not be quite sure of
finding any of them in good health. Thou hast passed some
years in Ü and Tsang, and here also thou hast been for these
many years. But if thou desire to go, I grant thine appeal. If
thou count on coming back here, know that finding me in sleep
when thou didst come to address me is an omen that we two
shall not meet again in this life. But the rays of the rising sun
shining upon my dwelling-house is a sign that thou wilt be
a shining light amongst the Buddhist hierarchies, and that
thou wilt glorify the Faith. And the sun's rays enhaloing my
head is a sign that this Sect of meditative Kargyütpas will
flourish and spread far and wide. Further, Damema's bringing
in the morning meal just then showeth that thou wilt be sus-
tained by spiritual food. Now I can let thee go. Damema,
deck the altar with offerings."

'My Teacher set himself to prepare the *maṇḍala* diagram,
while his lady decked the altar. Then, having conferred upon
me the last and highest Initiations, and the Mysteries of the
Dream Symbols,[1] and the *Tantras* whispered in the ear of the

---

[1] As referred to in the treatise on the *Six Doctrines* ; see p. 144[2], above. There
is, too, a system of *Yoga* whereby the *yogī* is taught to enter the dream-state at
will, in order to explore scientifically its characteristics as compared with the
waking state, and then to return to the waking state without breaking the stream
of normal consciousness. Thus is realized the illusory nature of both states. The
practice also enables its master to die and to be reborn without loss of memory—
death being the entry into a dream-state and birth the awakening.

*Shishya* by the *Guru*,[1] he said, "Fix well thine attention ; upon thee alone I confer these Texts, Mysteries, and Initiations, because I have been so commanded by my Lord Naropa. Thou in thy turn shalt confer them upon such of thy disciples as the Deities shall indicate. And I command thee to confer them thus, with the condition that they shall be handed down from one *guru* to one *shishya* for thirteen generations. If these Truths be exchanged for worldly vanities or for the currying of favour, thereby will the displeasure of the Deities be incurred, and dire will be the effect ; therefore, guard them with the utmost care. If any *shishya* manifest innate aptitude for receiving these Truths, let them be given him,[2] although he be unable to present any worldly wealth as the offering. Take all such *shishyas* in thy special care, watch and guard over them ; develop them ; and let them enhance the glory of the Faith. The method adopted by Tilopa in disciplining Naropa, and by me in converting thee, will not be very suitable for degenerate beings of the future, who will be narrow of heart, and incapable of understanding the sublimest of the Truths. Therefore, beware of adopting that method of instruction.

'"In India there exist nine texts of this character, though somewhat lighter conditions than these are sometimes attached to them. Four of them I have given to thee. So there are five more to be obtained from India ; one of my disciples will journey to India and obtain these from one of the disciples of Naropa's other disciples. Thou, too, shouldst try thine utmost to obtain them ; they are certain to be of the greatest use to humanity. And now, if thou entertain any thought that because thou art unable to offer me worldly goods I may still have other texts secreted from thee, divest thy mind of such thought ; for it is not worldly vanities alone that will satisfy me. Much more am I satisfied with thy sincere devotion and energy.

---

[1] That is, the esoteric (or ' ear-whispered ') teachings, which are never committed to writing, being handed down orally from *guru* to *shishya*.

[2] 'In the *Nityāshoḍashikārṇava Tantra* (iv. 4) there is recorded the following parallel command : " Let not affection, greed, or fear prompt thee to reveal the Great Mystery to the unworthy. Reveal it only to the deserving." The *Shruti* (Vedic Texts) likewise enjoin secrecy regarding *Brahmavidyā* (knowledge of the Supreme Brahma).'—Sj. Atal Bihari Ghosh.

Therefore, raise aloft the Banner of Zealous Devotion and Meditation.[1]

' " I have conferred upon thee the Supreme, Mystic, Ear-Whispered Truths, as revealed by the Deities and transmitted to me by my Lord Naropa. To no other of my disciples have I imparted them; nay, not even to the foremost. To thee I have handed them on in an entire and perfect manner, like unto a vessel filled to the very brim."

' Then he invoked the Tutelary Deities to bear witness to the truth of these statements.

' The *Guru* having delivered this deeply impressive discourse sang the following song extempore:

' " Obeisance! Adoration to the Kind and Gracious Lord!
To meditate upon His Acts is of itself a holy text.[2]

' " To desire much, bringeth a troubled mind;
[So] store within thy heart [these] precepts wise:
Many *seeming* ' Thats ' are not *the* ' That ';
Many trees bear nought of Fruit;
All Sciences are not the Wisdom True;
Acquiring these is not acquiring Truth.
Much talking is of little profit.

' " That which enricheth the heart is the Sacred Wealth;
Desirest thou wealth? then store thou this.
The Doctrine which subdueth passions vile is the Noble
    Path;
Desirest thou a safe path? then tread thou this.
A contented heart is the noblest king;
Desirest thou a noble master? Then seek thou this.

' " Forsake the weeping, sorrow-burdened world;
Make lonely caves thy home paternal,
And solitude thy paradise.
Let Thought riding Thought be thy tireless steed,
And thy body thy temple filled with gods,
And ceaseless devotion thy best of drugs.

---

[1] Literally, ' Banner of *Sādhanā* '.

[2] Marpa's prayer is addressed to his own *Guru* Naropa; while Milarepa's is to his *Guru*, Marpa. Each *Guru* is visualized as being a Divine Being.

'" To thee, thou energetic one,
 The Teaching that containeth all of Wisdom I have given;
 Thy faith, the Teaching, and myself are one.
 And may this Perfect Seed of Truth, thus to my son en-
  trusted,
 Bring forth its foliage and its fruit,
 Without corruption, without being scattered, without wither-
  ing." [1]

' Having sung this, the *Guru* placed his hand upon my head,
and said, " My son, thy going away breaketh my heart; but
since all composite things are alike liable to dissolution it cannot be helped. Yet remain with me a few days more; examine
thy texts, and if thou find in them uncertainties, have these
cleared." I obeyed, and on my remaining for some days my
uncertainties touching the texts were cleared up.

' Then the *Guru* commanded his lady to deck the altar with
offerings for a ceremony, which she did upon a grand scale,
placing offerings for the Tutelary Deities, sacrificial cakes for
the *Ḍākinīs*, and a splendid feast for the brotherhood. During
the assembly, my *Guru* showed himself in the form of Gaypa-
Dorje and in various other divine forms, with the various
symbolic implements associated with these Deities, such as
*dorjes*, bells, wheels, gems, lotuses, swords, and all the others.
He also showed the mystic [*mantric*] letters *Ōm, Ăh, Hūṃ* in
different colours. Having manifested these signs of a Master
of the Occult Sciences, he said, " These are called psycho-
physical powers, which ought never to be exhibited in a spirit
of mere bravado; I have shown them as my parting gift to
thee, Milarepa."

' Thus did I see that my *Guru* was as infallible as the
Buddha Himself; and rejoiced beyond measure at it, and
resolved within myself to emulate my *Guru* and obtain occult
powers of like nature.

' Then my *Guru* asked me, " Son, hast thou seen, and dost
thou believe?" I replied, "Yes, Lord and *Guru*, impossible

[1] The sense of this last stanza being somewhat uncertain in the late Lāma
Dawa-Samdup's translation, M. Bacot's version has in part been followed here.

is it not to believe; I myself will emulate Thee in devotion, till I, too, obtain these powers."

'He answered, "That is well, my son. And now thou art fitted to take thy departure, for I have shown to thee the mirage-like nature of all existing things. Realize this fact for thyself, going into retreat in mountain recesses, lonely caves, and the solitudes of wildernesses. Amongst mountain recesses, that known as Gyalgyi-Shrī-La (Holy Mount of Glorious Solitudes) hath been blessed by the feet of many a great Indian saint and *yogī*, while the Tisé Peak (Mount Kailāsa) hath been mentioned by the Lord Buddha Himself as the Great Mountain, the abode of Dēmchog (Shamvara), and a fit place for meditation. Do thou meditate there. The Lapchi-Kang is the most sacred amongst all the Twenty-Four Places of Pilgrimage, being the Godavari of the Scriptures. And Riwo-Palbar, and Yölmo-Kangra, in Nepal, are mentioned in the *Lalita-Vistara*. Meditate there. Chūbar, in Brin (Drin), is a spot sacred to the *Dākinīs*, and any solitary cave, with fuel and water close at hand, should be a suitable place for meditation and for raising the Banner of Devotion. Devi-kot and Tsari, near each other, lie in the East, but the time hath not come yet for the opening of them. A disciple of thy succession will open these sacred places of pilgrimage and guard them. Thou thyself shalt devote thy whole life to meditation, taking up thine abode in these places as foretold. If thou do so earnestly, thou shalt satisfy thy *Guru* and repay thy parent's kindness and love, and thereby serve the Cause of Universal Good. But if thou fail in devotion, then thy life, though long, shall be but an occasion for heaping up demerits. Renounce, then, all the ambitions of this life; waste not thy time in vain talk with the multitude, who seek only to attain the aims and ends of worldly existence, but at once devote thyself to meditation."

'Tears filled the *Guru's* eyes and ran down his cheeks, as he continued, "Now, my son, we shall not see each other again in this life. I will bear thee in my heart, and thou wilt bear me in thine. We shall without doubt meet again in the pure celestial regions of the life beyond, so rejoice.

'"At some period of thy devotions, I foresee that thou wilt

be assailed by a very great physical danger; when that cometh, look thou into this, but open it not till then." And thereupon he handed to me a sealed scroll. Every word that my *Guru* uttered at this time produced a deep and lasting impression upon my heart, and each word helped me in my subsequent devotion.

'Then the *Guru* said, "Damema, Milarepa is going to-morrow, make suitable preparations for the occasion; though it is sure to depress my spirits, I must go some distance to see him off." To me he said, "Sleep thou near me this night. We two, father and son, shall converse." And I did so. My *Guru's* lady, upon coming to join us, at once began to sob and weep. The *Guru* said to her, "Damema, why weepest thou? Seeing that my son hath received the Precious Truths in full, and goeth to meditate on them in solitude, what cause is there here for tears? If thou consider how all sentient creatures, though potentially Buddhas, through ignorance of their high origin and destiny suffer pain and sorrow and die in anguish, and more especially how human beings, once having won [in virtue of their human birth] the mighty opportunity of bettering their condition, forgo it, and die without Enlightenment, then indeed mightest thou weep, yea, even unceasingly."

'The lady replied, "Thou speakest truly, but difficult is it to hold fast to compassion such as that. I weep now because I cannot help it. I was deprived by Death of a son, perfectly accomplished in both temporal and spiritual affairs, who would have fulfilled the wishes both of himself and of others. And now this son, so faithful, energetic, and intelligent, so kind-hearted, willing, and faultless from every point of view, is going to be separated from me while yet living. How can I help weeping?" And she wept still more bitterly as she said this. I, too, was overwhelmed with weeping, and my *Guru* likewise.

'The night was passed in similar expressions of sorrow, and we had no really serious talk. The next morning the whole party, consisting of thirteen persons, came to see me off, up to a distance of about four or five miles. All were sad, and expressed their sorrow in words and tears. When we came upon a hill-top called Chhö-la-Gang (Hill of Religion), which commanded a good view of the country all round, we halted and took our meal. This over, my *Guru* held my hand, and said, "My son, I should have liked to send thee in the company of some reliable comrades, because thou art going through Ū and Tsang, and it is said that robbers infest the Silma Pass in Tsang, but I see that thou are destined to go alone. But I will pray for thee, and entreat the Tutelary Deities to watch over thy safety as thou goest. Be thou very wary on the way. Go thou hence to Lāma Ngogpa, and compare notes with him regarding the sacred texts thou hast received, noting all differences. Having done this, thou mayst proceed straight to thy home. Spend no more than seven days there. Then proceed at once to the wilderness to meditate and carry on thy devotions, which thenceforth must be thine only duty. By that alone wilt thou benefit thyself and all living creatures."

'Then I sang to my *Guru* these verses of an extempore psalm :

'"O Lord, Thou the Immutable, O Dorje-Chang,
For the first time, as humble mendicant, I go to Tsang,
For the first time, as Thy Humble *Shishya*, to my home I go.
O Kindly Lord and Father, Thy Gracious Love provideth,
On Silma's Pass, an escort of twelve mountain goddesses ;
Adoration unto Thee, O Gracious Lord.

'"Trusting to the power of the Precious Trinity,
Escorted by hosts of *Ḍākinīs*,
And by a pure and sincere heart accompanied,
I go, guarded by Divinities ;
What need have I of fear of mortal foes ?

'"I have, howe'er, a prayer to urge :
That Thou wilt be my Constant Guide
In this as in the future life ;
Bless Thou my body, speech, and mind,
And safely keep them from temptation.

"Grant Thine Approval to my prayer,
And seal it by Thy Spiritual Power ;
Make me to realize the Truths Profound.

[Likewise] I crave Thy Blessing for a long and healthy life.
Thy suppliant's fate lieth in Thy Hands ;
Bless him, that he shall steadfastly remain in solitude."

'When I had offered up this prayer, my *Guru* said, "My
son, thy words are sweet. Now shall I impart to thee my best-
prized and last instructions ; bear them ever in thy heart."
Then, placing his hand upon my head, he sang to me the following hymn :

'"Obeisance unto all the *Gurus*!

'"High-minded, noble, righteous son,
May thou the *Dharma-Kāya* gain ;
May thy nectar-like and prayerful speech
In the *Sambhoga-Kāya* reach perfection full ;
May thy righteous heart, so pure and grateful,
The *Nirmāna-Kāya* realize.[1]

'"May these, my last and precious words,
Unerring as the Eternal Law,
Sink deep and rest within thy heart ;
And may the benedictions of the *Devas* and the *Dākinīs*
Invigorate thy life and mind,
And the Protecting Spirits watch o'er thee.

'"May this, my prayer, bear speedy fruit :
By pious ones mayst thou be ever loved,
And may the escort of twelve goddesses
Attend thee o'er the Silma Pass,
And Guardian Angels guard thy path
Throughout thy journey of the following days.

---

[1] This stanza is based upon the Mahāyānic doctrine of the Three Bodies (Tib.
*Sku-gsum*—pron. *Kū-sum* ; Skt. *Tri-Kāya*). Of these, the first is the Divine Body
of Truth (or *Dharma*), the *Dharma-Kāya* (Tib. *Chos-sku*—pron. *Chö-ku*), which is
the Body of all Buddhas ; being beyond all concepts of the mundane mind, it
is the Voidness (Skt. *Shūnyatā* ; Tib. *Tong-pa-nyid*), the Unformed, Unmade,
*Nirvāna*. The second is the Divine Body of Perfect Endowment, the *Sambhoga-
Kāya* (Tib. *Longs-spyod-rzogs-sku*—pron. *Long-chöd-zo-ku*), which is the body
of all Bodhisattvas in Heaven-Worlds ; it is the first reflex of the Divine Body
of Truth. The third is the Divine Body of Incarnation, the *Nirmāna-Kāya* (Tib.
*Sprul-pahi-sku*—pron. *Tül-pai-ku*), of *Avatāras*, or Great Teachers, on Earth.
The first Body is Transcendental *Bodhi* ; the second, Reflected *Bodhi* ; the third,
Practical *Bodhi*.

' " In the sad sight of thy home and fields
    There is a preacher of ' 'tis vanity '.

' " Among thy sister, aunt, and kith and kin
    There is a tutor who'll dispel fond dreams [of family ties].

' " Amid the lonely solitudes of caves
    There is a mart wherein thou canst exchange
    This whirlpool life for bliss eternal.

' " Within the temple of thy form inspired
    There is a meeting-hall of deities.[1]

' " Within the wholesome feast of nettle soup [2]
    There is nectar pleasing to the gods.

' " Within the scientific system of thy texts
    There is a harvest yielding precious fruits.

' " Within the hatred and contempt awaiting thee at home
    There is incentive to immediate devotion.

' " Within the close confinement of a solitude,
    By noise of men and dogs untroubled,
    There is the boon of quickly gaining *Siddhi*.[3]

' " Within the freedom of one's self-support
    There is the heavenly blessing of a peaceful heart.

' " Within a region undefiled, about a sacred temple,
    There is the pleasing prospect of success.[4]

' " Within sincerity of faith devout
    There is the virtue born of zealous effort.

' " Within the sacred Garden of Obedience [5]
    There is a mine of all success.

[1] The ' meeting hall ' is the ' Thousand-Petalled Lotus ', wherein Shiva (as the *Deva* or *Shakta*) and Kuṇḍalinī (as the *Devi* or *Shakti*) in union produce in the *yogī* the ecstatic state of Illumination. (See pp. 34[2], 169[5].)

[2] It was nettle soup, as will be seen in Chapter X, which constituted Mila-repa's chief food while he was practising *Yoga* in the solitudes.

[3] *Siddhi* literally means ' accomplishment ', or 'fruition of *Sādhanā*'. Here it refers to success in gaining *yogic* or super-normal powers.

[4] The magnetic or psychic influences which a sacred centre naturally radiates— if it be undefiled by the auric emanations of towns or villages inhabited by worldly-minded multitudes—favour success in *Yoga*.

[5] That is, obedience to the commands of the *Guru*.

' " Within the Vital Truths by *Ḍākinīs* revealed
There is the boundary between *Sangsāra* and *Nirvāṇa*.[1]

' " Within the School of Marpa the Translator
There is the hope of endless fame.

' " Within the zeal and energy of Milarepa
There is a pillar of the Buddhist Faith ;
Upon the Being[2] who holdeth that Pillar [may there rest]
The blessings of the Noble Succession,
The blessings of the Kargyütpa Saints,
The blessings of the Deities Divine,
Dēmchog, Gaypa-Dorje, and Sang-dü,
The blessings of the Noble Truths,
The blessings of the Vital Truths by the *Ḍākinīs* revealed,
The blessings of the Gracious *Ḍākinīs*,
The blessings of the Dwellers in the three Abodes,[3]
The blessings of the Noble Guardians of the Faith,[4]
The blessings of the Mother Kālī,[5]
The blessings of the noble brethren in the Faith.

' " [Let there be] blessings on thine efforts, of obedience born,
And blessings on thy lineal followers ;
And infallible may mine own blessings be.

---

[1] That is, the Vital Truths enable the devotee to differentiate the *Sangsāra* from *Nirvāṇa* ; and also to realize—in the Supra-mundane Consciousness of Buddha-hood—that the one is inseparable from the other.

[2] The Being is Milarepa.

[3] ' Dwellers in the Three Abodes' is probably a reference, esoterically worded, to adepts in the science of *Kuṇḍalinī Yoga*, the ' Three Abodes' being, in this esoteric sense, the Heart Psychic-centre (Skt. *Anāhata-chakra*), the Throat Psychic-centre (Skt. *Vishuddha-chakra*), and the Brain Psychic-centre (Skt. *Sahasrāra-Padma*). (Cf. p. 34[2].)

[4] These are the deities called in Sanskrit the *Dharma-pālas*, i. e. ' Guardians of the *Dharma*' ; in Tibetan they are called *Ch'os-skyong*.

[5] Kālī is the Great Wrathful Mother-Goddess Kālī (or Durgā) ; here she symbolizes the *Shakti* or Primordial Negative (or Female) Energy of the Universe, being the Spouse of *Shiva*, who is the personification of the Primordial Positive (or Male) Energy.

Sj. Atal Bihari Ghosh has added here the following : ' In another aspect, Kālī is the Ever-youthful Mother (*Ādyā Prakṛiti*) ; for she is not always of wrathful aspect, but appears benign or terrific in accordance with the devotee's *karmic* deserts. She is called Kālī because she devours (*kalanāt*) Time (*Kāla*), who devours all things.' (Cf. *Tantra of the Great Liberation*, ch. iv, as edited by Arthur Avalon, London, 1913.)

' " Bear these [my final admonitions] in thy heart and realize
    them."

'Having sung this, Marpa was filled with great gladness.
Then the Reverend Mother, my *Guru's* lady, presented me
with substantial presents, including clothes, boots, and provisions, saying, " My son, these are a few articles for the time
being, as a small token of regard from me. They are my last
parting gift to thee, my son. I wish thee a happy journey;
and may we meet again in the blessed and holy paradise of
Urgyen. Forget not these last spiritual gifts, and this sincere
prayer from thy mother, which I now utter " ; and, giving me
a human skull filled with oblation-wine, she sang the following
hymn:

' " Obeisance to the Feet of Gracious Marpa!

' " My patient son, so energetic,
    Constant, and long-suffering,
    O son of highest destiny,
    Drink deeply of the nectar of thy *Guru's* Divine Wisdom;
    In perfect peace and safety go thy way;
    And, as friends, in future may we meet
    In the blessed Holy Realm.

' " Forget thou not thy parents spiritual;
    Oft and ever pray to them;
    Eat all thou canst of heart-sustaining
    Sacred texts and sermons deep;
    In perfect peace and safety go thy way;
    And, as friends, in future may we meet
    In the blessed Holy Realm.

' " Forget thou not thy parents spiritual;
    In grateful memory hold them ever,
    And of their kindly care oft think;
    The warming breath of angels wear,
    As thy raiment pure and soft;[1]
    In perfect peace and safety go thy way;
    And, as friends, in future may we meet
    In the blessed Holy Realm.

    [1] This refers to the Vital Warmth acquired by *yogic* practice.

'"Thinking of the helpless beings [of *Sangsāra*],
    Train thy heart to selflessness;
    The burden of the Higher Path (the *Mahāyāna*)
    Bear thou e'er with faithful fortitude;
    In perfect peace and safety go thy way;
    And, as friends, in future may we meet
    In the blessed Holy Realm.

'"Damema, of noble destiny,
    Unto her son her last injunctions giveth,
    And may he e'er retain them in his heart;
    Thee [O son] thy loving dame shall cherish;
    May we, the loving son and mother,
    As friends, in future meet
    In the blessed Holy Realm.

'"May these good-wishes bring forth fruit,
    And may devotion pure repay them."

'As she sang these verses, tears choked her voice, and the long-pent-up grief of the others burst forth in torrents of tears and sobs. I bowed down to my spiritual father and mother for the last time, and moved backward, keeping my face towards them as long as my *Guru's* countenance was within view. I saw them standing there with tearful faces, and strong was mine inclination to go back. But when I passed out of their sight, I walked in the usual manner till I came to a knoll whence I could again see them, as a dim grey group. My heart yearned to rejoin them, and it was with a most painful effort that I tore myself away. I thought to myself that I had now obtained the Truths in their entirety, and that henceforth I would commit no irreligious act. As for my *Guru*, I could always meditate on him [as if he were enhaloed] above the crown of my head [1] as long as I should live; and as for the next life, he had promised that we should meet again in the Holy Regions. Besides, I was only going away for a short while, to

---

[1] This refers to the *yogic* practice of meditating on the *Guru* as being in the contemplative posture (or *āsana*) and overshadowing the Brāhmanic Aperture, whence the consciousness-principle goes out of the body. The practice is said to help in awakening the Kundalini or Serpent Power.

see my mother who had given me birth, and I could hurry back to my *Guru*.

'Thus I went on communing with myself, in a sorrowful mood, until I reached Lāma Ngogdun-Chudor's house. There, after we had duly compared notes with each other, I found that he exceeded me in the exposition of the *Tantras*, but that in the actual practice of the rites and rituals pertaining to the Doctrine, and in their application to daily life, I was not far behind him, while I exceeded him in some respects, as possessing the divinely-inspired esoteric teachings which are ear-whispered.[1]

'Having done this, I paid him due worship, and expressing a wish for a future meeting started for home. I reached there after three days, feeling somewhat elated at the development in the art of controlling the breath which this betokened.[2]

'Thus did all come about—mine obtaining the Truth in its entirety, my thorough study of it, and, while thus engaged, my being impelled by a significant dream to take leave of my *Guru* and return home.'

Thus endeth [the narrative which constituteth Milarepa's] Fourth Meritorious Act.[3]

[1] Literally, ' the Sacred *Dākinī Karṇa Tantras*'. (Cf. p. 161[1].)

[2] M. Bacot (p. 177) here notes that ordinarily, that is by normal means, the ourney would have taken several months, whereas by super-normal means Milarepa accomplished it within three days.

[3] Here and onwards the textual numbering of the chapters has been made to conform to the numerical rearrangements by the Editor, this chapter in the Tibetan being numbered the fifth.

## CHAPTER IX

# THE RENUNCIATION

*Telling of the Disillusionment which Jetsün met when he had reached his Home; and of his Vows to live the Ascetic Life and Practise Meditation in Solitude.*

AGAIN Rechung asked, 'Venerable *Guru*, when thou didst reach home, did the dream prove to be true, or didst thou find thy mother alive?' Jetsün replied, 'The inauspicious dream proved only too true; it was not my lot to see my mother.' Then Rechung said, 'Tell us, Venerable *Guru*, how thou didst enter thy house,[1] with whom thou didst meet, and in what spirit the people received thee.'

Thereupon Jetsün continued: 'I saw a number of shepherds at a place high up in the glen whence my house was visible; and, feigning ignorance, I asked them the names of places, houses, and their occupants, upon which they told me everything in detail. Then, finally, pointing towards mine own house, I asked them the name of the place and its occupants. They told me that the house was called "Four Columns and Eight Pillars", but was at present occupied by ghosts only, as there were no living occupants. On asking them how it came to be empty, and what had happened to the inmates, whether they had gone elsewhere or died, I was told, "Formerly, there was a very well-to-do family in that house, who had a single son. Owing to the early death of the father, and a mistake in the manner of his making his will, after the father's decease the paternal relatives usurped all the property of the minor son. When the son had attained his majority, he asked for the restoration of his property; and, failing to get it, had recourse to black magic. Launching curses and hail-storms on this place he did much mischief here. Now we are all so very afraid of his Tutelary Deities that not one of us hardly dareth even to look in that direction, let alone go there. On this account, the house

---

[1] The sense apparently is, 'in what condition thou didst find thy house'.

holdeth the corpse of the mother of the only son, and some evil spirits. He had one sister, who, abandoning the mother's corpse, hath gone away begging somewhere, and not come back. The son, too, must be dead, as nothing hath been heard of him. If thou dare to go there thyself, O Pilgrim, thou mayst get some books in the house." I asked the speaker how long ago all this had happened, and he said that it might be about eight years since the mother's death; but concerning the launching of the hail-storms and the other havoc wrought by the son's black magic he could barely recollect them as a child. And about the happenings previous to that he had only heard from others.

' This assured me that the villagers were so afraid of my Tutelary Deities that they would not dare to harm me. The news of the death of my mother and the disappearance of my sister filled my heart with despair and sorrow. I hid myself in a nook till past sunset, where I wept bitterly. After sunset I went to the village, and lo ! I beheld my house exactly in the condition I had seen in my dream. The fine house, which used to be like a temple, was in a most dilapidated and ruinous condition. The set of sacred volumes had been damaged by the rain leaking in, and thick layers of dust and earth fallen from the [ruined] roof covered them; they were serving as nests and sleeping-places for birds and mice. Wherever I looked, desolation and ruin met me, so that I was overwhelmed with despondency. Then groping my way towards the outer rooms I found a heap of earth and rags, over which a large quantity of weeds and grass had grown. On shaking it up I found it to be a heap of human bones, which instinctively I knew to be my mother's. A deep and unutterable yearning seized me. So unbearable was the thought that I should never more see my mother that I was about to lose consciousness, when I remembered my *Guru's* Teachings; and, communing spiritually with my mother's spirit and the divine spirits of the saints of the Kargyütpa Sect, I made a pillow of my mother's bones and remained in an undistracted state of tranquillity, in clear and deep meditation, whereby I realized that it was indeed possible to save both my father and mother from the pain and miseries of *sangsāric* existence.  After passing seven days and nights thus, I rose from the *samādhi.*[1]

'Thence, upon reflection, I came to the conclusion that there was no permanent benefit to be obtained in any state of *sangsāric* existence.  So I made up my mind to dispose of my mother's bones in the approved way, namely, to have them pulverized and mixed with clay and then moulded into miniature reliquaries, called *tsha-tshas.*[2]  I would offer the volumes of Scripture in payment for having this done; and, as for myself, I would go away to the Dragkar-Taso Cave[3] and there pass my whole time in constant meditation.  I determined to sit there night and day, till death should put an end to my life. I vowed that if any thought of worldly ambition should allure me, I would commit suicide rather than allow myself to be overcome by it.  I prayed to the Tutelary Deities and *Ḍākinīs* to cut short my life if ever I should come to think of an easy sort of devotion.

'Making these mental resolves over and over again, I gathered up my mother's bones; and then, upon removing the heap of dust and dirt that had accumulated upon the volumes of Scripture, I saw that their letters were still clear.  Carrying the volumes on my back and my mother's bones in my lap, I started forth.  An unutterable anguish wrung my heart to its very core.  Henceforth, the world had nothing to tempt me or

[1] All Tantric *yogīs* are exhorted by the *guru* to practise meditation in cemeteries and in places where corpses are cremated or else thrown to the birds of the air to be devoured, in order to overcome the dislike or horror, universal among human beings, of such environments, and to realize the transient nature of worldly existence.  In some rituals, it is necessary for the *yogī* to sit in solitary meditation upon a corpse, especially during the dark hours of the night; in other rituals, he is directed to make a pillow of the corpse, and, if need be, sleep in that posture. Accordingly, Jetsün practised such meditation, making of his mother's bones a pillow, and remained thus in *samādhi* for seven days and nights.

The following addition to this note has been made by Mr. Sri Nissanka : 'Seven days appears to be the period of time usually passed in *samādhic* trance.  The Buddha Gautama is said to have passed seven days of ecstatic bliss alternating with seven days of *Nirvāṇic* bliss during a period of seven weeks while seated beneath the *Bodhi* Tree at Budh Gaya.'

[2] Tib. *tsha-tsha* (pron. *tsha-tsha*), which is shaped like a miniature *stūpa*; it corresponds to the *Dharma-sharīra* of Indian Buddhism, and is still in use throughout Tibet.

[3] Or 'the Rock-Cave White as the Tooth of a Horse'.

to bind me to it. I repeated my vows to devote my life to a rigid course of asceticism in the realization of the Truth, and resolved to adhere to them firmly. In an almost frenzied mood I sang the following verses of firm resolution to myself:

'" O Gracious Lord, Thou the Immutable,
O Marpa the Translator, according to Thy Words Prophetic,
A teacher of the transitoriness of things I've found
Within my native land—prison of temptation;
And by Thy Blessing and Thy Grace, may I,
From this noble teacher, experience and faith obtain.

'" All phenomena, existing and apparent,
Are ever transient, changing, and unstable;
But more especially the worldly life
Hath no reality, no permanent gain [in it].
And so, instead of doing work that's profitless,
The Truth Divine I'll seek.

'" First, when my father lived, the [grown-up] son lived not;
Next, when I was born [and grown], my father did not live.
Had both together met, little would have been the profit,
    even then;
So I will go to gain the Truth Divine,
To the Dragkar-Taso Cave I'll go, to practise meditation.

'" When my mother lived, myself, the son, was long away;
When I come home, I find my mother dead.
Had both together met, little would have been the profit,
    even then;
So I will go to gain the Truth Divine,
To the Dragkar-Taso Cave I'll go, to practise meditation.

'" When my sister was at home, myself, her brother, was away;
When I, her brother, come back home, I find my sister
    gone astray.
Had both together met, little would have been the profit,
    even then;
So I will go to gain the Truth Divine,
To the Dragkar-Taso Cave I'll go, to practise meditation.

' " When the Scriptural Texts were there, no veneration had
   they;
When the veneration came, they lay damaged by the rain.
Had both together [earlier] met, little would have been the
   profit, even then;
So I will go to gain the Truth Divine,
To the Dragkar-Taso Cave I'll go, to practise meditation.

' " When the house stood firm, the master was away;
When the master came, the house was fallen in ruin.
Had both remained together, little would have been the
   profit, even then;
So I will go to gain the Truth Divine,
To the Dragkar-Taso Cave I'll go, to practise meditation.

' " When the field was fertile, the farmer was away;
When the farmer came, the field was choked with weeds.
Had both remained together, little would have been the
   profit, even then;
So I will go to gain the Truth Divine,
To the Dragkar-Taso Cave I'll go, to practise meditation.

' " Native land, and home, and all possessions,
I know you all to be but empty things;
Any thoughtless one may have you.
As for me, the devotee, I go to win the Truth Eternal.

' " O Gracious Father, Marpa the Translator,
May I succeed in meditation in the solitude."

' Having thus sung this, half song, half hymn, in a burst of
religious zeal, I went first to the house of my former private
tutor. I found him dead; but his son was living, and to him
I offered the volumes, asking him to cast the *tsha-tshas* of my
mother's bones. He was afraid, he said, that if he accepted
the books my Tutelary Deities would haunt his house, but he
kindly promised to cast the *tsha-tshas* for me. When I told him
that my Tutelary Deities would not haunt him, as I was
giving the books to him voluntarily, he consented to take them,
saying, " So be it, then." Thereupon he began to make the

*tsha-tshas*, I helping him. The casting of them having been finished, I saw the consecration rites performed [over them]. Then, having deposited them inside a *stūpa* (reliquary), I was preparing to depart, when my tutor's son proposed to detain me for a few days to talk over old times, saying that he would give me of his best; but I told him that I must hasten on to meditate at once, and had no time for talk. He insisted, however, on my spending at least the night with him, so as to allow him time to furnish me with a small quantity of provisions to serve me during my devotions.

'To this I agreed; and he, continuing the conversation, said to me, "In thy youth thou didst destroy thine enemies by black magic. Now, in thy maturity, thou hast become a religious devotee; this, indeed, is admirable. Thou wilt surely become a saint in the future. What *Gurus* hast thou sought, and what spiritual texts hast thou obtained?" He asked me these questions with interest; and in reply I told him that I had obtained the doctrine of the Great Perfection, and related to him how I had found Marpa. He congratulated me, and suggested that I should repair my house, marry Zesay, and settle down as a Ñingma Lāma. I told him that Marpa had married for the purpose of serving others, but that if I presumed to imitate him without being endowed with his purity of purpose and his spiritual power, it would be the hare's emulation of the lion's leap, which would surely end in my being precipitated into the chasm of destruction. And I added, "I have a general conviction that I do not want anything save a life of meditation and devotion, for I take no pleasure in the worldly life. To live as a hermit in solitude and devote my whole life to meditation is the essence of my *Guru's* command. Therefore will I aim to live the ideal life [of a Kargyütpa devotee],[1] thus satisfying my *Guru* as well as doing service to all sentient beings and serving the Cause of the Hierarchy. Thereby will I also rescue my parents [from *sangsāric* existence]; and,

---

[1] The hermit life such as Milarepa sought is, for the Kargyütpa devotee seeking Enlightenment, the highest life on earth; for by means of it the devotee may acquire true wisdom, and thereby preparation for returning to the world of mankind as a guide to salvation, not by repetition of intellectual formulas of 'I believe', but in virtue of knowledge of truth.

lastly, I shall even profit myself.  I know naught but meditation, and so am not likely to accomplish anything else; nor
do I aspire to other than this.  Moreover, after my having seen
the wretched ruins of the house and the remains of the
property which my deceased parents possessed, it hath been
indelibly impressed upon my heart that worldly pursuits are
worthless, and a burning desire to devote my life to meditation
hath been enkindled.  A life of ease may do for those who
have not suffered as I have, and to those to whom the thought
of death and hell hath not been brought forcibly home.  As
for myself, circumstances have convinced me most firmly of the
vital need of zealous devotion and deep meditation as long as I
live; yea, even unto death itself, despite starvation and poverty.'

'And with tears welling out mine eyes I sang the following
song:

'"Obeisance to Thy Feet, O Noble Marpa!
     May I, the mendicant, be purged of worldly clingings by
          Thy Grace.

'"Alas, alas, ye beings unfortunate,
     Who cling to worldly things,
     The deeper is my grief the longer that I think of you;
     The deeper is my sorrow the longer that I taste of yours.
     We whirl and whirl, till into Hell we fall;
     For them whose *karma* bringeth [sorrow's] heart-ache,
     Devotion of their life to Truth is, of all things, best.

'"Lord Dorje-Chang, Thou the Immutable,
     Grant that this mendicant, blessed by Thy Grace, may cling
          to solitude;
     The guests who loiter in this world—
     Illusory and transient as it is—
     Must needs be ill with [sorrow's] heart-ache.

'"My pasture-fields, where browsed my sheep and goats and
          cows,
     Amid the charming Gungthang plains,
     Are haunted now by evil spirits;
     This is a picture of Illusoriness,
     Which maketh me to seek the contemplative life.

' " My well-built house, ' Four Columns and Eight Pillars ',
Now looketh like a lion's upper jaw;
The tower of four sides, eight pinnacles, and roof that made
    these nine,
Now looketh like a donkey's ears:
These too are pictures of Illusoriness,
Which make me seek the contemplative life.

' " My fertile field, the ' Worma Triangle ',
Is now o'ergrown with weeds and grass;
My cousins and my kith and kin
Are ready now to rise as foes [against me] :
E'en these are pictures of Illusoriness,
Which make me seek the contemplative life.

' " My noble father, Mila-Shergyal,[1]
Hath left no trace of ever having lived ;
My fond and loving mother, Nyang-Tsa-Kargyen,
Is now nought but a heap of whitened bones :
E'en these are pictures of Illusoriness,
Which make me seek the contemplative life.

' " My household priest and private tutor, Kunchog-Lhabum,
Is serving now as menial under others ;
My sacred books, the Treasure of the Law,
Have served as lining for rats' holes and nests of birds :
E'en these are pictures of Illusoriness,
Which make me seek the contemplative life.

' " My relative and neighbour, uncle Yung-gyal,
Now sideth with mine enemies ;
Mine only sister, Peta-Gön-kyit,
Hath strayed, and no one knoweth where she be :
E'en these are pictures of Illusoriness,
Which make me seek the contemplative life.

' " O Gracious One, Thou the Immutable,
Bless Thou Thy Suppliant that he may cling to solitude."

' On my singing this melancholy song, my host sighed and
said, " Excellent ; thou art quite right." And his wife shed

---

[1] This is a shortened form of Mila-Sherab-Gyaltsen.

copious tears. The sight of the wretched condition of my home in ruins had affected me so deeply that I could not help giving utterance to several such resolutions to live the life of a hermit in solitary meditation. In mine own heart, too, I kept on repeating the resolution over and over again to myself that I would do so. And, in fact, I have no cause to blame myself for having practised meditation and devotion instead of having wasted my time in worldly pursuits.'

This constituteth the Fifth Meritorious Act, in which is related how Milarepa was driven to a religious life of energetic devotion by the sad circumstances described herein.

## CHAPTER X
# THE MEDITATION IN SOLITUDE

*Telling of how Jetsün entered into Solitary Meditation in the Mountain Solitudes; of the Outer Experiences, and of the Psycho-Physical Results which Ensued; and of his Songs Recording each Event.*

RECHUNG then asked Jetsün in what places he had meditated and practised penance and devotion.

In reply, Jetsün said : ' The next morning, my teacher's son provided me with a bag of flour and some seasoning of butter and cheese and other provisions, saying, " Let these serve thee as food during thy devotional seclusion, and pray for us, too." Provided with these, I started forth, and went and sat in meditation in a spacious cave which existed in the hill-side behind mine own house. The provisions being used rather sparingly—only as an admixture—my constitution became exhausted and very weak, but I made great progress in my devotions. Thus the food lasted for some months. When it was all exhausted, I was unable to go on long provisionless. So I thought that I should go and beg some butter and cheese and other provisions from the herdsmen who dwelt on the upper parts of the hills, and some grain or flour from the cultivators who lived on the lower parts. Thus I should not have to starve altogether, and could go on meditating.

' On going to the herdsmen to beg, I came to the entrance of one of those yak-hair tents, and begged the inmates to grant alms of seasoning, butter, and cheese to a devotee. As ill luck would have it, this turned out to be the tent of mine aunt, who at once recognized me. In displeasure, she let loose her dogs, which I kept off with a stick, pelting them with stones. Thereupon, she issued out herself, armed with a tent-pole, crying, " O thou disgrace to a noble father ! Thou seller of thy kindred's lives ! Thou destroyer of thine own country ! Why dost thou come here ? To think that thy noble father should have begotten a son like thee !" Saying this, she be- laboured me as hard as she could. I turned back in flight, but, weak from want of food, I stumbled against a stone and fell into a pool of water, and nearly died. She, however, continued raging. I got up as best I could, and, leaning my body against my staff, sang the following song to mine aunt :

' " At the Feet of my Kind Father Marpa I bow down !

' " In the unhappy home, amid the melancholy nook of Tsa,
  We three unfortunates—a saddened mother and two orphans—
  Were scattered far, as peas are by a staff.
  Were ye or were ye not the cause of this,
  Bethink yourselves, O ye aunt and uncle ?

' " Whilst I, as mendicant, was wandering afar,
  My mother died, by poverty's keen sword ;
  And, begging food and cloth, my sister strayed.
  Unable to destroy the longing to behold them,
  Unto this prison, mine own native land, I've come again.

' " Forever severed from me hath my loving mother been ;
  Because of sorrows hath my sister wandered off ;
  So was my heart with deepest anguish pierced.
  These miseries and sorrows which we three endured—
  Were they not due to you, our relatives ?

' " These sufferings unbearable have led me to the life religious ;
  Yet whilst I meditated, in the solitudes of lonely hills,
  Upon the Sacred Teachings of my Gracious Marpa,
  My provisions grown exhausted, no food had I to keep
    alive this transient form,
  And thus went forth to beg for alms.

' " Like a dying insect attracted to the entrance of an ant-hill,
  Here have I come, before mine aunt's door-way ;
  And thou dost set ferocious dogs against my weak, im-
    poverished body,
  And dost thyself join in the fierce attack.

' " By thy rude curses and thy threats,
  The grief, deep in my heart, thou stirrest anew ;
  By thy repeated strokes, made with thy tent-pole,
  Thou fillest my poor body full of pains and bruises,
  And hast almost deprived me of my life.

'"Good cause have I for anger 'gainst thee,
     But the commandments of my *Guru* I'm fulfilling;
     Be not so vengeful, O mine aunt,
     And food for my devotions give to me.

'"O Marpa, Lord! O Thou the Merciful!
     By the power of Thy Grace, cool down Thy suppliant's wrath!'

' On my singing this, half in song and half in weeping tones, a girl who had come behind mine aunt could not refrain from shedding tears. Mine aunt also was struck with remorse and shame, and she went inside and sent me a roll of butter and some powdered cheese-flour by the girl.

' Going round to the other tents to beg, I could not recognize any of the occupants, but they all seemed to recognize me. Staring hard at me, they each gave me a handsome quantity of alms, with which I returned to my cave. From mine aunt's behaviour I could judge what would be mine uncle's,[1] so I resolved that I would not go in his direction on any account. But happening to go to beg from the cultivators of the upper Tsa Valley, I chanced to come right on the door of mine uncle's new house, whither he had removed [after his disaster]. He, knowing me, rushed upon me, crying, " Though I be like an old corpse, yet thou art the very man I have wanted to meet." With deadly purpose, he flung at me a stone which nearly hit me. I turned and fled, but he flung at me as many stones as he could, with whatever strength he possessed. I continued my flight, but he came out armed with a bow and arrows, saying, "Thou trafficker in lives! Thou traitor![2] Hast thou not destroyed this country? O neighbours, countrymen, we have now got hold of our enemy; come out quickly!" With that he began shooting at me, while some of the youths of the place began to pelt me with stones. I, on my part, was afraid that I might fall a victim to their wrath and vengeance as a retribution for having employed black magic against them. So intending to intimidate them with my black-magical power, I cried out loudly: " O my Father, and ye *Gurus* of the Karg-

---

[1] This is the paternal uncle who robbed Jetsün of his inheritance, and whose house and wedding party Jetsün, in revenge, afterward destroyed by black magic.

[2] Literally, ' tripper up of feet '.

yütpa Sect ! O ye myriads of blood-drinking and faith-guarding Deities! I, a devotee, am pursued by enemies. Help me and avenge me. Although I may die, ye Deities are immortal."

'Thereupon, all of them were terror-stricken; and they caught hold of mine uncle, some who sympathized with me intervening and acting as mediators, while those who had stoned me asked my forgiveness. Mine uncle alone would not consent to give me any alms, but the rest gave me each a handsome amount, with which I returned to the cave. I thought that if I remained there any longer I should only be stirring the anger of the people; so I resolved to go elsewhere. But that night I had a dream which directed me to stay there a few days more, and this I did.

'Zesay (to whom I had been betrothed in my childhood), hearing about my being there, came with some nice food and drink to meet me. She wept copiously and embraced me. When she had told me of the manner of my mother's death and about my sister's straying, I was greatly saddened, and wept bitterly. I said to her, " How constant thou art, that thou shouldst not have married yet." She said, " People were so afraid of thy Deities that no one dared to ask my hand in marriage, nor would I have married even had any one proposed to me. That thou hast taken to this religious life is admirable; but what dost thou intend doing with thy house and field ?" I understood her desire, and thinking that since, by the grace of my *Guru* [Marpa the Translator], I had given up worldly life altogether, praying for her might suffice from a religious point of view, but that I should say something to her which might settle her doubts from a worldly standpoint. So I said to her, " If thou meet my sister, give them to her; until she cometh, thou mayst enjoy the field thyself; and, if my sister be dead, then thou canst have both the house and the field for thine own." She asked me, "Dost thou not want them thyself?" And I replied, " I shall find my food as the mice and birds do theirs, or I shall fast and starve, therefore I need not the field; and, as I shall dwell only in caves and lonely solitudes, I have no need of a house. I realize that even though I should possess the whole world, at my death I should have to give up everything; and so it will confer happiness in this and the next life if I give up everything now. I am thus pursuing a life which is quite opposite to that followed by the people of the world. Give up thinking of me as a living person."

'She then asked me, " Is thy practice also opposed to that of all other religious persons?" And I replied, "I am of course opposed to those hypocrites who have assumed a religious garb only for the sake of the honour attending it, and— their aim being merely the acquisition of wealth, fame, and greatness—have succeeded in getting by heart the contents of a volume or two; and who, having strong party feelings, strive for victory for their own party and defeat for the opposite party. But as for those who are sincere devotees, although they be of different sects and creeds, if their principle be not like the one mentioned above, then there cannot be much disagreement between the aim of the one or the other, so I cannot be opposed to any of them. On the whole, if they are not as sincere as myself, then they must, of course, be opposed to my creed."

'On this, she said, "Then how is it that thy practice is so poor and miserable—much worse than that of the meanest beggar? I have never seen any one like this before. To what particular doctrine of the Mahāyāna Sect dost thou belong?" I told her that it was the highest creed of the Mahāyāna; that it was called the Path of Total Self-Abnegation, for the purpose of attaining Buddhahood in one lifetime;[1] and that to attain Buddhahood thus we must scatter this life's aims and objects to the wind.

'She said, " Indeed, I see that the practice of thy doctrine and theirs is quite opposite; and from what I hear and see of thee it appeareth that the practice of the *Dharma* is not altogether a very easy matter; theirs would have been an easier path to

---

[1] It is one of the teachings peculiar to Mahāyāna Buddhism, as taught throughout *The Tibetan Book of the Dead*, that simultaneously with realization of the unreality of all *sangsāric* (i. e. worldly) existence Perfect Enlightenment, Buddhahood, dawns; and that this supreme attainment is possible for any *yogic* devotee sufficiently advanced on the Path to make the Great Renunciation and win the Great Victory in a single lifetime, as Milarepa is later on shown to have done.

tread." I replied, " The *yogī* who still retaineth a love of the world would not attain to mine ideal of a sincere devotee. I am of opinion that even those sincere Truth-seekers who still cling to the yellow robe retain a little love of worldly fame and honour; and even though they do not retain it, yet am I convinced that there is [between me and them] a vast difference in regard to the speed and efficacy of attaining Buddhahood. This, however, thou wilt not comprehend just now. So, if thou think thou canst, thou shouldst devote thyself to a religious life; but if thou feel unequal to the task, then thou canst enjoy the house and field as I have already said, and hadst better go home." She replied, " I cannot accept thy house and field which thou shouldst give to thy sister. I should like to be a devotee, but such a devotee as thou art I cannot be." Having said this she went away.

' Mine aunt, coming to learn that I did not care about my house and field, after a while began to think that since I professed a determination to adhere to my *Guru's* command, she might perhaps be able to obtain them for herself. So she visited me, bringing with her a quantity of barley-flour, butter, *chhang*, and other food, and said, " Some time ago I treated thee unkindly, being steeped in ignorance; but as thou, my nephew, art a religious person, thou must pardon me. If thou wilt allow me, I will cultivate thy field, and supply thee with food." To this I agreed, saying, " So be it; please supply me with the flour of twenty measures of barley per month; the rest thou canst enjoy; thou mayst cultivate the field." She went away delighted with the bargain. For two months she supplied the flour as agreed; then she came again and said, " People say that if I cultivate thy field perhaps thy Tutelary Deities may injure me because of thy magical power." When I satisfied her, saying, " Why should I practise sorcery now? Rather wilt thou be acquiring merit if thou continue to cultivate the field and supply me as thou art doing," she at once said, " In that case, wilt thou kindly reassure me by taking an oath that thou wilt not practise sorcery any more. Thou canst have no objection to doing so." I was not sure what she intended doing; but, as I considered it consistent with my calling to please others, I reassured her by taking the oath in accordance with her wish, at which she went away quite pleased.

'All this while, in spite of mine unremitting perseverance in meditation, I was unable to obtain signs of any improvement or growth in my knowledge or experience of Ecstatic Warmth ; and I was becoming anxious as to what I should do next. One night I dreamt that I was engaged in ploughing a very stiff and hardened plot of land, which defied all mine efforts ; and, despairing of being able to plough it, was thinking of giving up the task. Thereupon, my beloved *Guru* Marpa appeared in the heavens and exhorted me, saying, " Son, put forth thine energy and persevere in the ploughing ; thou art sure to succeed, despite the hardness of the soil." Then Marpa himself guided the team ; the soil was ploughed quite easily ; and the field produced a rich harvest. The dream gave me great pleasure on my waking up.

'Thereby the thought arose in me that dreams, being illusory reproductions of one's own thoughts, are not regarded as real even by stupid and ignorant boors, and that when I thus allowed a dream to affect my temper I must be more silly than the greatest fool. But as it seemed to be a sign that if I continued to meditate with zeal and perseverance mine efforts would be crowned with success, I was filled with pleasure, and in that mood I sang this song to impress the true interpretation of the dream clearly on mine own memory :

'" I pray to Thee, O Gracious Lord !
Grant that this mendicant may cling successfully to solitude.

'" I put upon the field of Tranquil Mind
The water and manure of a constant faith,
Then sow it with unblemished seed of a heart immaculate,
And over it, like pealing thunder, reverberateth sincere
    prayer;
Grace of itself upon it falleth, like a shower of rain.

'" Unto the oxen and the plough of Undistracted Thought
I add the ploughshare of [Right] Method and of Reason.
The oxen, guided by the undeluded person,
And with firm grasp of undivided purpose,

And by the whip of zeal and perseverance goaded on,
Break up the hardened soil of Ignorance, born of the Evil
    Passions Five,
And clear away the stones of the hardened, sin-filled nature,
And weed out all hypocrisies.

' " Then, with the sickle of the Truth of *Karmic* Laws,
The reaping of the Noble Life is practised.
The fruits, which are of Truths Sublime,
Are stored within the Granary to which no concepts can apply.

' " The gods engage in roasting and in grinding this most
    precious food,
Which then sustaineth my poor humble self
Whilst I for Truth am seeking.

' " The dream I thus interpret :
Words bring not forth True Fruit,
Mere expositions do not yield True Knowledge.
Yet those who would devote themselves unto the life religious,
In meditation must exert their utmost zeal and perseverance ;
And if they will endure hardships and strive most zealously,
And seek with care, the Most Precious can be found.

' " May all who are sincerely seeking Truth
Untroubled be by obstacles and interruptions on the Path."[1]

' Having sung this, I made up my mind to go and carry on
my meditation in the Dragkar-Taso Cave. As I was about
to start, mine aunt came up with sixty measures of barley-flour,
a ragged dress of skins, one piece of good cloth, and some
butter and grease mixed up into a ball, and said, " My nephew,
these are in payment of thy field, which thus is disposed of.
Take them and go away to a place far beyond my sight and
hearing, for the neighbours are saying to me, ' Thöpaga hath
wrought much mischief upon us before this ; and if thou must
still have dealings with him and serve him, we are certain that
he will do us more harm and perhaps kill the remaining
people of the place. Rather than this, we will kill both of you.'
So it is safer for thee to flee away into some other country.

---

[1] Or : ' in their quest for Truth '.

If thou do not go, why should they sacrifice me? But there is not the least doubt that they will kill thee."

'I knew that the people would not speak in that fashion, and so I said to her, "If I were not faithful to my religious vows, I would not refrain from practising sorcery to regain possession of my field, especially as I have not sworn to refrain from doing so under these circumstances. Being possessed of such magical powers, I could with the greatest ease stretch thee out a pale corpse in an instant; yet I will not do so, for on whom should I practise my patience if not on those who have wronged me? If I should die to-night, what could I do with the field, or with these few articles themselves? Patience is said to be the shortest path to obtain Buddhahood, and thou mine aunt art the very person on whom I must practise my patience. Moreover, ye, mine aunt and mine uncle, have been the means of bringing me to this life [of renunciation]. I am sincerely grateful to both of you, and in return for these deeds of yours I will ever pray for you, that ye may obtain Buddhahood in your future lifetime. Not only can I give to thee the field, but the house, too." Then I explained to her everything explicitly, and ended by saying, "As for me—whose life is devoted to the search for Truth—I require only my *Guru's* instructions and nothing more; so thou art welcome to both the field and house." And I sang to her the following song:

'"O Lord, my *Guru*, by Thy Grace do I the life ascetic live;
    My weal and woe are known to Thee!

'"The whole *Sangsāra*, being e'er entangled in the Web of *Karma*,
    Whoever holdeth fast to it severeth Salvation's Vital Cord.

'"In harvesting of evil deeds the human race is busy;
    And the doing so is to taste the pangs of Hell.

'"The affectionate expressions of one's kith and kin are the
        Devil's Castle;[1]
    To build it is to fall into the Flames [of Anguish].

---

[1] That is, exclusive attachment to one's own family is selfish, the true and only family being Humanity, and for this family alone should the Bodhisattva labour. Cf. *Matthew* x. 36-7: 'And a man's foes shall be they of his own household. He that loveth father or mother more than me is not worthy of me; and he that loveth son or daughter more than me is not worthy of me.'

' " The piling up of wealth is the piling up of others' property ;
What one thus storeth formeth but provisions for one's enemies.

' " Enjoying wine and tea in merriment is drinking juice of
aconite ;
To drink it is to drown Salvation's Vital-Cord.[1]

' " The price mine aunt brought for my field is things wrung
out of avarice ;
To eat them would entail a birth amongst the famished ghosts.[2]

' " The counsel of mine aunt is born of wrath and vengeance ;
To utter it entaileth general disturbance and destruction.

' " Whatever I possess, both field and house,
Take all, O aunt, and therewith happy be.

' " I wash off human scandal by devotion true ;
And by my zeal I satisfy the Deities.

' " By compassion I subdue the demons ;
All blame I scatter to the wind,
And upward turn my face.

[1] In the Buddhist view, all stimulants—alcoholic drinks, narcotic drugs, tobacco, and even the narcotic effects of strong tea and coffee—are not only demonstrably deleterious to the physical organism, but in exciting the nerves and the mind they give such control over the body to the lower or animal nature as to inhibit all influx of the elevating spiritual influences of the higher nature. Furthermore, sorrow, pain, and despair are to be regarded as potent means to awaken the human race to the fact that all *sangsāric* existence is, in the last analysis, inseparable from suffering, and therefore undesirable. Thus, if stimulants are used to drown all unhappiness and an artificial and deceptive feeling that everything is well with the world be engendered thereby, the opportunity of reaching the purely spiritual state of Supramundaneness, beyond the realm of sorrow, wherein there is the only true bliss, is lost—the Vital Cord of Deliverance, the golden link between the higher and the lower, is sundered, the sacred way to Olympus is closed, and human beings are left in the darkness of their unbelief, slaves to the animal within them.

Although Christianity does not, most unfortunately, prohibit the use of all such stimulants, as do Buddhism, the Higher Hinduism, and the whole of Islam, the old Jewish prophet Isaiah has approached the right view in these words : ' The priest and the prophet have erred through strong drink, they are swallowed up of wine, they are gone astray through strong drink ; they err in vision, they stumble in judgement ' (*Isaiah* xxviii. 7). Cf., too, Paul's *Epistle to the Ephesians* (v. 18) : ' And be not drunken with wine, wherein is riot, but be filled with the Spirit.'

[2] That is, in the world of famished (or unhappy) ghosts (Skt. *Preta-Loka*).

'"O Gracious One, Thou the Immutable,
Vouchsafe Thy Grace, that I may pass my life in solitude
    successfully."

'On my singing this, mine aunt said, "A truly religious person
should be like thee, my nephew; it is very praiseworthy."
And she went away satisfied.

'This circumstance affected me very painfully; but, on the
other hand, I felt relieved of the care of my field and house,
of which I had thus disposed. I resolved to carry out immediately my plan of going to the Dragkar-Taso Cave to
continue my meditation. As this cave had afforded me protection while I laid the foundation of *Samādhi* (the Quiescent
State), it came to be called Kangtsu-Phug (i. e. the Cave
wherein he [Milarepa] was set upon his feet in devotion, or
laid the Foundation). The next morning, I set forth with the
articles which mine aunt had brought me as the price of my
field and the little remnants of the former provisions, and came
to the Dragkar-Taso Cave, which I found to be very comfortable, and therein settled myself. Having provided myself
with a hard mattress seat, and spreading my bedding on it,
I took the vows of not descending to any village or human
habitation:

'"Until I have attained to *Siddhi*[1], unto this solitude will
    I hold fast;
Of starvation though I die, I'll not go to seek alms given in
    faith or dedicated to the dead,
For that would be to choke myself with dust.[2]
E'en though of cold I die, I'll not descend to beg for gar-
    ments.
E'en though of misery and sorrow I should die, I'll not
    descend to join in pleasures of the worldly life.
Though I fall ill, e'en unto death, I'll not descend to seek
    one dose of medicine.

[1] *Siddhi*, or occult powers, or transcendent or super-normal knowledge.
Immediately prior to attaining Buddhahood, Gautama while still a Bodhisattva,
as Milarepa is here, made similar resolutions (cf. the *Mahāpadāna Sutta*).
[2] That is, such food is unclean to a devotee, having been dedicated to a deity
or to the dead.

And not one movement of my body will I give to any
    worldly purpose ;
But body, speech, and heart I dedicate to winning Buddha-
    hood.

' " May the *Guru*, Gods, and *Ḍākinīs* enable me to keep my
    vows,
And may they bless mine efforts ;
May the *Ḍākinīs* and Faith Protecting Deities fulfil my
    wishes,
And render me all needed aid."

'[I added] : " Should I break these vows—seeing that it is
better to die than to live a life without seeking to acquire
Truth—may the Divine Beings, who protect the Faith, cut
my life short immediately, and may my *Guru's* and *Devas's*
grace combine in directing my next life to religious pursuits
and endow it with the firmness and intellect necessary to
enable it to surmount all obstacles [on the Path] and triumph
over them."

' Having thus vowed, I sang this song, consecrating my
vows :

' " Offspring of Naropa and of the Saving Path,
May [I], the hermit, cling successfully to solitude.

' " May pleasures of the world illusory not tempt me ;
But may Tranquillity of Meditation be increased ;

' " May I not lie steeped in Unconsciousness of Quietude ; [1]
But may the Blossom of the Superconsciousness bloom forth
    in me.

' " May various mind-created worldly thoughts not vex me ;
But may the foliage luxuriant, of Uncreatedness, burst forth
    in me.

---

[1] There are states of Unconsciousness, into which a *yogī* may fall, which do
not lead to Enlightenment. A like state, which, however, is not necessarily
a state of unconsciousness, is experienced in the *yogic* condition of suspended
animation or *yogically* induced hibernation. Although a practised *yogī* may
hibernate for very long periods—according to some *yogīs* for centuries—and
eventually revive in his physical form, it is not desirable that he should do so,
if he be aiming—as Milarepa was—at Deliverance from the *Sangsāra*.

'"May I, in hermitage, be troubled not with mental conflicts;
    But may I ripen fruit of Knowledge and Experience.

'"May Mārā and his hosts disturb me not;
    But may I find self-satisfaction in the Knowledge of mine
        own [True] Mind.

'"May I doubt not the Path and Method I pursue;
    But may I follow in the footsteps of my Father [Spiritual].

'"O Gracious Lord, Embodiment of the Immutable,
    Thy Blessings grant, that I [the mendicant], may firmly
        hold to solitude."

'This prayer finished, I continued my meditations, living on
just a little flour mixed up with whatever food came in my
way. I mentally acquired knowledge of the *Mahā-Mudrā*
(Great Symbol); but my body, being too weak, was unable to
control the Airs (Psycho-Physical nervous Power, or Fluid)[1]
of my system, so that I did not acquire the Ecstatic Internal
Warmth, and continued to be very sensitive to the cold.

'I prayed earnestly to my *Guru*; and, one night, I had the
following vivid dream, or rather vision in a superconscious
state. A number of women came carrying all sorts of food
with which they performed a *pūjā* (religious ceremony), saying
that they had been sent by my *Guru* Marpa to instruct me
in religious physical exercises.

'[Thus directed], I began to practise the three exercises of
Physical, Vocal, and Mental Culture, and developed the Ecstatic
Physical Warmth.[2] Thus a year went by, when, one day,
I had a desire to go about for a little recreation. I was about
to start forth, when I instantly recollected mine own vows, and
sang to myself the following song of self-reproof:

---

[1] Skt. *Vāyu*, which, being derived from the root *Vā* ('to breathe' or 'to
blow') refers to the motive power of the vital-force (Skt. *Prāṇa*).

[2] Here M. Bacot's version (p. 203) is more detailed, as follows: 'Then, in
the squatting posture [or *āsana*] which resembleth the "Six Internal Hearths",
I sought the well-being of my body. By means of the condition of the breathing
which giveth regularity, I sought rightness of speech. By the condition of
mine own liberation which controlleth the imagination, I sought calmness
of mind. After that I entered into meditation. Soon the internal heat began
to come over me.'

' " O Dorje-Chang Thyself, in Marpa's form !
Grant that this mendicant may cling to solitude.

' " O thou strange fellow, Milarepa !
To thee I sing this song of self-counsel.

' " Aloof thou art from all of humankind
Who might with thee sweet converse hold.

' " Therefore thou feelest lonely and wouldst seek diversion ;
No reason is there for thee thus to seek.

' " Excite not thus thy mind, but let it rest in peace ;
If thoughts it harbour, 'twill hanker after numerous im-
pieties.

' " To thy desire for these distractions give not way, but exert
thine intellect ;
If to temptation thou give way, scattered to the wind will
thy devotion be.

' " Walk thou not forth, but rest content upon thy seat ;
If forth thou walk, thy feet may strike 'gainst stones.

' " Raise not thy head, but bend it down ;
If it be raised, 'twill seek for vain frivolities.

' " Sleep not, but continue thy devotions ;
If thou fall asleep, the Poisons Five, of Ignorance, will
subdue thee." [1]

' Then, having sung this song of self-reproof, I continued
unceasingly my meditations for over three years, both night
and day, and I could feel my spiritual knowledge expanding
and improving greatly. But now my stock of barley-flour was
quite expended. I had resolved on the starvation diet of
twenty measures of barley-flour per year, and now even that
had run out. I might have died without being able to attain
Buddhahood ; this would have been a deplorable interruption

[1] Slothfulness and torpor are condemned as unbecoming a *yogī*. The vow
not to sleep is one of twelve austerities permitted by the Buddha. But an
esoteric meaning is also implied here, namely, that the devotee must not allow
the hypnotic glamour of the worldly life to affect him, lest the ' Five [or Six]
Poisons '—Pride, Jealousy, Sloth, Anger, Greed, and Lust—enslave him, as
they do the multitude, to *sangsāric* existence.

in mine eternal career. I considered that worldly people rejoiced over the acquirement of a *seeka* (one four-anna weight)
or two of gold and felt unhappy at losing the same. Compared
to that, my life, devoted as it was to the attainment of Buddhahood, was infinitely more precious. Were the entire universe
to be filled with gold, still the life devoted to the attainment
of Buddhahood was infinitely more precious. At the same
time, it would be preferable to die in the course of my devotional life rather than break my vows. What should I do?
Then the thought came to me that if I started forth in search
of some article of food to sustain my life, without descending
to human habitations to beg, I should not be breaking my
vows. Moreover, it would be in the interests of my devotion
to do so. Accordingly, I strolled forth beyond the front of my
Dragkar-Taso Cave ; and there discovering a sunny spot
with good springs of water, with plenty of nettles growing
round about—a delightful spot, commanding extensive views—
I removed to it.

'Living on nettle broth alone, I continued my meditations.
I had no clothes on the outside of my body, nor any wholesome food inside. My body became shrunken to a mere skeleton ; and it was greenish in hue, just like the nettle, and over
it grew a covering of greenish hair.

'I used to regard the scroll, which my *Guru* had given me,
with special veneration, sometimes putting it on my head, and
touching it with fondness; and this had the effect of soothing
my stomach, although I had nothing to eat. Sometimes I used
even to have belchings [as if I had eaten my fill of food].
Once or twice I was on the point of opening and reading its
contents ; but I had some signs telling me that the time for
doing so had not yet arrived; accordingly, I kept it by me.

'About a year after that, some hunters from the Kyeedrong
mart chanced to come strolling my way, having failed to
obtain any sport. At first they ran away, saying they had
seen a *bhūta* (an evil spirit). On mine assuring them that I was
a human being and a devotee, they said I did not look like
one, but anyhow came to look well at me. They came up and
pried into every nook and corner of my cave. At last, they

said, " Where are thy food-stuffs? Let us borrow some, and we will repay it liberally; otherwise we will kill thee." Thus they threatened me. I told them I had only nettles, and even if I had other things—seeing that they were rude enough to insult me by lifting me up—they should not obtain them by using force. They replied that they were not going to rob me; and, as for insulting me, what should they gain by it? I said that they might possibly acquire merit. Thereupon they said, " All right; we will lift thee up again." And they picked me up and let me fall on the ground several times over. This filled my poor weakened body with much pain; but, in spite of it, I pitied them sincerely,[1] and shed tears. One of them, who refrained from this heartless deed, said, " O ye fellows, this man seemeth to be a real Lāma, and even if he be not one, ye will not gain glory by ill-treating such a weak person. He hath not compelled us to be hungry. Do not act so." And to me he said, " Hermit, it is admirable of thee to stand such ill-treatment. As for me, I have done nothing against thee; therefore remember me in thy prayers." The others added, in fun, " As we have lifted thee up, remember to put us, too, under thy prayers' protection." The other one said, " Ay, ay, that he will do, ye may be quite sure—only in a different way!" They went away laughing boisterously. I had no intention or thought of cursing them; but it seemeth that divine retribution overtook them, for I came to learn afterward that the hunters had been arrested by the Governor of the Province. The leader was killed, and all, except the person who refrained from offering indignities to me, had their eyes put out.

' About a year after that, all my clothes were worn out, and only some rags of the cloth which mine aunt had given me as the price of my field, and the sack in which the flour had been supplied, remained. I once thought of sewing the rags together and making them into a sort of bedding; and then I thought

---

[1] Milarepa here shows himself loyal to his Vow, it being essential to attainment of Nirvāṇic Enlightenment for the Bodhisattva to be perfected in the ' Four Brahma Qualities ', namely, Pity, Compassion, and Altruistic Love for every sentient being, and the Indifference of equanimity towards all states or conditions of sangsāric existence.

that if I died that very night what would be the use of sewing;
better far to go on with my meditation. So, spreading the
tattered skin dress underneath as bedding, I made it serve as
covering for the lower part of my body [by wrapping its ends
round me] as well as it could; while I covered the upper part
of my body with the ragged empty flour sack; and, with what
remained of the rags of the cloth, I covered those parts of my
body which required it most. At last, all these were far too
worn to be of any use at all to serve as coverings. Finally, it
seemed to me that this was too much of self-abnegation, and
that I must sew the rags together, but I had no needle or
thread, so I twined the rags about my body in three pieces,
knotted in three places, and kept in position by ends of rope
tied together to make a girdle. Under this, I passed the days
as well as I could; and, at night, the ragged sack and the
remains of the tattered skin dress afforded me some protection
from cold.

'Thus I continued meditating for about another year, when
one day there was a noise as of many people talking. On
peeping out, I saw another party of hunters, carrying large
quantities of meat, approach the entrance of my cave. On
seeing me, those in the front cried out, " Oh, there is a *bhūta* ! "
and ran away; those in the rear said that it was not probable
that there would be a *bhūta* about in broad daylight, and
added, " Look again, and see whether the *bhūta* is there still."
On being told that there it was still, even those old hunters
who had come last, in the rear, began to be afraid. I told them
that I was not a *bhūta*, but a hermit, who was reduced to this
plight for want of provisions. They wished to see for themselves, and ransacked the whole place, every nook and corner
being pried into. But seeing nothing but nettles, all of them
were moved to veneration. They left me the remainder of
their provisions, and a large quantity of meat, saying respect-
fully, "It is praiseworthy of thee to practise such asceticism.
Please pray for the absolution of the animals we have killed,
and for our own sins in killing them."

'I rejoiced at the prospect of having food such as ordinary
human beings eat, and, on partaking of the food, I enjoyed a

sense of bodily ease and comfort, and a cheerfulness of mind which tended to increase the zeal of my devotional exercises ; and I experienced keen spiritual happiness such as transcended anything I had known before. I thought that the merit acquired by those who offer a few scraps of food to the lonely hermits in the solitudes would surely exceed that of the most munificent gifts to those who are enjoying plenty and living amidst human society in towns and villages. The meat I used sparingly, till at last it was full of maggots. I once thought of clearing it of the maggots and using it ; but I considered that it was not intended for me to enjoy the meat, since I should have to dispute it with maggots, which would be robbery. And I thought that however nice it might be, it was not worth my while going to the length of committing robbery for a meal ; so I allowed the maggots to take the meat for themselves, while I fell back upon mine own nettle broth.

' One night, a person, believing that I possessed some wealth, came and, groping about, stealthily pried into every corner of my cave. Upon my observing this, I laughed outright, and said, " Try if thou canst find anything by night where I have failed by daylight." The person himself could not help laughing, too ; and then he went away.

' About a year after that, some hunters of Tsa, having failed to secure any game, happened to come strolling by the cave. As I was sitting in *Samādhi*, wearing the above triple-knotted apology for clothing, they prodded me with the ends of their bows, being curious to know whether I was a man or a *bhūta*. Seeing the state of my body and clothes, they were more inclined to believe me a *bhūta*. While they were discussing this amongst themselves, I opened my mouth and spoke, saying, " Ye may be quite sure that I am a man." They recognized me from seeing my teeth, and asked me whether I was Thöpaga. On my answering in the affirmative, they asked me for a loan of some food, promising to repay it handsomely. They said, " We heard that thou hadst come once to thy home many years ago. Hast thou been here all the while ? " I replied, " Yes ; but I cannot offer you any food which ye would be able to eat." They said that whatever did for me would do for them. Then I told them to make fire and to boil nettles. They did so, but as they expected something to season the soup with, such as meat, bone, marrow, or fat, I said, "If I had that, I should then have food with palatable qualities; but I have not had that for years. Apply the nettles in place of the seasoning." Then they asked for flour or grain to thicken the soup with. I told them if I had that, I should then have food with sustaining properties; but that I had done without that for some years, and told them to apply nettle tips instead. At last they asked for some salt, to which I again said that salt would have imparted taste to my food; but I had done without that also for years, and recommended the addition of more nettle tips in place of salt. They said, "Living upon such food, and wearing such garments as thou hast on now, it is no wonder that thy body hath been reduced to this miserable plight. Thine appearance becometh not a man. Why, even if thou should serve as a servant, thou wouldst have a bellyful of food and warm clothing. Thou art the most pitiable and miserable person in the whole world." I said, "O my friends, do not say that. I am one of the most fortunate and best amongst all who have obtained the human life. I have met with Marpa the Translator, of Lhobrak, and obtained from him the Truth which conferreth Buddhahood in one lifetime; and now, having entirely given up all worldly thoughts, I am passing my life in strict asceticism and devotion in these solitudes, far away from human habitations. I am obtaining that which will avail me in Eternity. By denying myself the trivial pleasures to be derived from food, clothing, and fame, I am subduing the Enemy [Ignorance] in this very lifetime. Amongst the World's entire human population I am one of the most courageous, with the highest aspirations. But ye!—born in a country where the Noble Doctrine of the Buddha prevaileth, yet have not so much as listened to one religious discourse, let alone devoting your lives to it; but, on the other hand, ye are striving your utmost to gain the lowest depths and the longest terms of an existence in the Infernal Regions! Ye are accumulating sins by the pound and stone, and vying with

each other in that! How foolish and perverted are your aims
in life! I not only rejoice in the prospect of Eternal Bliss, but
enjoy these things which give me contentment and self-appro-
bation."

' I then sang to them a song about my Five Comforts:

' " Lord! Gracious Marpa! I bow down at Thy Feet!
Enable me to give up worldly aims.

' " Here in the Dragkar-Taso's Middle Cave,
On this the topmost summit of the Middle Cave,
I, the *Yogī* Tibetan called Repa,
Relinquishing all thoughts of what to eat or wear, and this
    life's aims,
Have settled down to win the perfect Buddhahood.

' " Comfortable is the hard mattress underneath me,
Comfortable is the Nepalese cotton-padded quilt above me,
Comfortable is the single meditation-band which holdeth up
    my knee,[1]
Comfortable is the body, to a diet temperate inured,
Comfortable is the Lucid Mind which discerneth present
    clingings and the Final Goal;
Nought is there uncomfortable; everything is comfortable.

' " If all of ye can do so, try to imitate me;
But if inspired ye be not with the aim of the ascetic life,
And to the error of the Ego Doctrine[2] will hold fast,
I pray that ye spare me your misplaced pity;
For I a *Yogī* am, upon the Path of the Acquirement of
    Eternal Bliss.

' " The sun's last rays are passing o'er the mountain tops;
Return ye to your own abodes.
And as for me, who soon must die, uncertain of the hour of
    death,

[1] The meditation-band is placed so as to encircle the body and the *yogically*
postured legs and thus prevent the legs dropping when the *yogī* enters into
deep meditation—there being need to maintain the posture (Skt. *Āsana*), which
cuts off or short-circuits certain bodily forces or currents. *Āsanas* also make
the body pliant and capable of great endurance, eliminate unhealthy physical
conditions, and cure illnesses.

[2] The Doctrine of a personal Ego or Soul; see p. 38[1].

With self-set task of winning perfect Buddhahood,
No time have I to waste on useless talk ;
Therefore shall I into the State Quiescent of *Samādhi*
    enter now."

'On hearing the song, they said, " Thou art singing of various comforts, yet, in fact, thou dost really possess a very nice voice. As for us, we cannot rough it as thou art doing." Then they went off home.

'On the occasion of an annual feast-day in Kyanga-Tsa, they chanced to sing this song together. It happened that my sister Peta was also there, having gone to obtain some food and drink. She, upon hearing the song, said to them, " Sirs, the man who sang that must be a very Buddha himself." One among the hunters said, " Ha ! Ha ! see how she praiseth her own brother " ; and another said, " Whether he be Buddha or animal, it is thy half-starved brother's song ; he is on the point of death from hunger." On this, Peta said, " Oh ! my parents are dead long ago ; my relatives have become mine enemies ; my brother hath roamed away, and I myself am reduced to a beggar's life : what is the need of gloating over my miseries ? " And she burst out weeping. Zesay came up just then, and comforted her by saying, " Do not weep. It is quite possible that it is thy brother ; I also met him some time ago. Go thou to the Dragkar-Taso Cave, and find out if he be there still. If he be, then both of us will go to see him."

'Thus being led to believe the statement, she came to me at the Dragkar-Taso Cave with a jugful of *chhang* and a small vessel full of flour. On first seeing me from the entrance of the cave, she was frightened. My body was emaciated by the privations and hardships ; mine eyes were deeply sunken into the sockets ; my bones showed prominently ; my colour was of a bluish green ; my muscles were all shrunken and shrivelled ; a growth of bluish-green hair covered my skeleton-like form ; the hairs of my head were stiff, and formed a formidable wig ; and my limbs appeared as if they were about to break. Altogether, I was a sight which inspired her with such a dread-

ful fright that she took me to be a *bhūta*. But recollecting
that she had heard that her brother was on the point of death
from starvation, she half doubted whether it was really myself.
At last she mustered up courage, and asked me, " Art thou
a human being or a *bhūta*?" I answered, and said, " I am Mila
Thöpaga." She, recognizing my voice, came in and embraced
me, crying, " Brother, brother !" and then fainted away for
a while. I, too, knowing her to be Peta, felt both glad and
sorry at the same time. Applying the best means of restoring
her, I at last succeeded in doing so. But she put her head
between my knees, and, covering her face with both her hands,
gave way to another flood of tears, sobbing forth the following :
" Our mother died in great trouble with a keen yearning to
see thee. No one came near us ; and I, being unable to bear
the great privations and loneliness in our own house, left it to
go a-begging in distant lands. I thought that thou wert also
dead. I should, however, have expected that if thou were alive
to have found thee in better circumstances than these. But,
alas ! thy circumstances are such. Thou seest what mine own
destiny is ! Could there be any one on the earth more wretched
than ourselves ! " Then she repeatedly called upon the names
of our parents, and continued wailing bitterly. I tried my
best to console her. At last, I, too, felt very sad, and sang
this song to my sister :

' " Obeisance to my Lords, the *Gurus* !
Grant that this *Yogī* may hold fast to solitude.

' " O sister, thou art filled with worldly sentiments and feel-
ings ;
[Know thou that worldly] joys and griefs are all imper-
manent.
But I, alone by taking on myself these hardships,
Am sure to win Eternal Happiness ;
So harken thou unto thy brother's song :

' " To repay the kindness of all sentient beings,
They having been our parents,[1] to the life religious I did
give myself.

---

[1] So interminably, during inconceivable aeons, have evolution and transition,

' " Behold my lodgings ; like those of jungle beasts are they ;
Any other person would be timid in them.

' " Behold my food ; 'tis like the food of dogs and pigs ;
It would excite in others nausea.

' " Behold my body ; 'tis like a skeleton ;
Even an enemy would weep on seeing it.

' " In my behaviour, I am like a madman ;
O sister, thou art moved thereby to disappointment and to
sorrow ;
Yet if thou could observe my mind, 'tis the *Bodhi* Mind
itself ;
The Conquerors rejoice at seeing it.

' " Sitting upon this cold rock underneath me, I meditate with
zeal,
Enough to bear the tearing of my skin off or my flesh from
off its bones ;
My body, both inside and out, like nettles hath become ;
A greenish hue, which changeth not, it hath assumed.

' " Here in this solitary rocky cave,
Though with no chance of driving melancholy from my
mind,
Unchangedly I ever hold adoration and affection
For the *Guru*, True-Embodiment of the Eternal Buddhas.

' " Thus persevering in my meditation,
I doubtlessly shall gain Transcendent Knowledge and Experience ;

and rebirth, been going on, that all sentient beings have been our parents. The
respect for woman among Buddhists is based on this principle, which is highly
interesting in the light of modern biological sciences.

The Hindus, likewise, say that each creature normally experiences 8,400,000
sorts of birth ere attaining to the state of mankind. As in *The Tibetan Book of
the Dead* (p. 178), four kinds of birth are mentioned : birth by heat and moisture,
as in the lowest forms of organic life ; birth by egg ; birth by womb ; and super-
normal birth, such as that when the consciousness-principle is transferred from
the human to another realm of existence, either at death normally or by *yogic*
practices super-normally at any time.

And if, in this, I can succeed,
Prosperity and happiness is won within this lifetime, as I go
    along ;
And, in my next birth, Buddhahood I'll win.

' " Therefore, my sister, Peta dear,
To woeful sorrows give not way,
But also give thyself to penances, for religion's sake."

' When Peta had heard this, she said, " It would be admirable
were it as thou sayest, but it is difficult to believe it true.  For
were it as thou representest it to be, other devotees would practise
at least part of such hardships, even if they could not bear all
that thou hast borne.  But I have not seen even one who is
undergoing such privations and penances."  Saying this, she
gave me the *chhang* and the food she had brought.  I felt very
much strengthened and refreshed by partaking of it, and my
devotions during the night were more earnest and spiritual.

' The next morning, after Peta's departure, I experienced
a sharp feeling of excitement and physical pain ; and a variety
of pious and impious ideas and thoughts sprang up in my
mind.  I tried mine utmost to concentrate my mind upon meditation, but it was of no avail.  Some days after this, Zesay
paid me a visit, bringing some well-cured and seasoned meat
and butter, and a goodly supply of *chhang* and flour.  She was
accompanied by Peta.  They met me while I was going to
fetch water.  I being stark naked (for I had no clothes), they
were both ashamed ; and yet, despite their bashfulness, they
could not help weeping at mine utter poverty.  They offered me
the meat, butter, flour, and *chhang*.  While I was drinking the
*chhang*, Peta said, " O my brother, whichever way I observe
thee, thou dost not look at all like a sane human being.  Pray
have recourse to soliciting of alms, and do partake of the food
of men.  I will try to find some cloth and bring it over to
thee.  Zesay added, " Do have recourse to alms, begging for
your food, and I, also, will come to offer thee a cloth."  But
I said, " With the uncertainty of the time of death looming
over me, I see not the use of going a-begging for food, nor
could I afford to lose the time in doing so.  Even if I were to

die of the cold, it would be for the sake of Truth and Religion; and, therefore, I should have very little cause for regret.
I could not be satisfied with that show of devotion which is
practised amid a circle of merry relatives and friends, revelling
in unlimited quantities of food and drink, and clothed in fine
raiment—all obtained at the cost of real and sincere devotion.
Nor do I need thy clothes and visits. I will not pay heed to
thine advice of going a-begging for food." Peta said, " How
then, my brother, can thy heart be satisfied? It seemeth to
me that something more wretched than this would satisfy
thee, but even thine ingenuity seemeth to fail in devising anything more painful and abstemious." I replied that the three
Lower *Lokas* [1] are much more miserable than this; yet most
sentient beings are doing their best to obtain the miseries of
these three states of existence. As for me, I am satisfied with
these present afflictions. So saying, I sang the song of what
would constitute my Satisfactions:

' "Obeisance to the Body of my Lord, the *Guru*!
    O grant that I may cling successfully to solitude.

' "My happiness unknown unto my relatives,
    My sorrowing unknown unto mine enemies—
    Could thus I die, amid this Solitude,
    Contented would I be, I the devotee.

' "My growing old unknown unto my betrothed,
    My falling ill unknown unto my sister—
    Could thus I die, amid this Solitude,
    Contented would I be, I the devotee.

' "My death unknown to any human being,
    My rotting corpse unseen by birds [2]—
    Could thus I die, amid this Solitude,
    Contented would I be, I the devotee.

---

[1] Namely, the World of Sub-human Creatures (Skt. *Tiryaga-Loka*), the
World of Unhappy Ghosts (Skt. *Preta-Loka*), and the Hell-world (Skt. *Naraka-
Loka*).

[2] In most parts of Tibet it is customary to give a corpse to the birds to
devour—as the Parsees do.

' " My putrid flesh sucked by the flies,
    My dissolving muscles eaten by the worms—
    Could thus I die, amid this Solitude,
    Contented would I be, I the devotee.

' " With no human foot-print by my door,
    With no mark of blood within [the Cave] [1]—
    Could thus I die, amid this Solitude,
    Contented would I be, I the devotee.

' " With none to crowd about my corpse [or bier],
    With none to lament o'er my death—
    Could thus I die, amid this Solitude,
    Contented would I be, I the devotee.

' " With none to ask where I had gone,
    And with no place which one might point to as my goal—
    Could thus I die, amid this Solitude,
    Contented would I be, I the devotee.

' " Thus, may this prayer about the manner of my death
    Amid this uninhabited Solitude
    Bear fruit, and, for all beings good, be granted as I wish ;
    Then satisfied I'll die, I the devotee."

' On hearing this, Zesay said, " Thy first sayings and thy present actions agree. Therefore this song is worthy of admiration." Then Peta said, " Whatever thou mayst say, my brother, as for me, I cannot bear to see thee in such utter want of clothes and food. I will do my best to find a cloth for thee, and will come over with it. Thy devotion would not run away if thou shouldst have a sufficiency of good food and clothing ; but seeing that thou wilt not go to beg for alms, it is probable that thou wilt die without any one near thee, in this solitude, of starvation and cold, just as thou desirest.

---

[1] This refers to the Tibetan method of air-burial, whereby a corpse is given to the denizens of the Element Air, the birds and wild beasts, after having been dismembered. In addition—according to place, circumstances of death, and rank of the deceased—fire-burial, i. e. the giving of the corpse to the Element Fire, as in cremation ; water-burial, the giving of the corpse to the Element Water, by casting it into rivers or lakes ; and earth-burial, the giving of the corpse to the Element Earth, as among Christians ; and, also, mummification of the corpses of the Dalai and Tashi Lāmas and of great nobles, somewhat after the Egyptian fashion, are practised in Tibet. See *The Tibetan Book of the Dead*, pp. 25-7.

Should I, however, find that thou art not dead, I will come to bring thee some sort of a cloth, which I will try to get." Having said this, they both went away.

'On my partaking of the good food, my physical pains and my mental disturbances increased so much that I was unable to go on with my meditation. In this predicament, thinking that there could not be a greater danger than the inability to continue my meditation, I opened the scroll given me by my *Guru*. I found it to contain the manner of treating the present ailment, thus clearing the obstacles and dangers on the Path, and turning the Vice to Virtue, and increasing the Spiritual Earnestness and Energy. It was mentioned in the scroll that I should use good wholesome food at this time.[1] The perseverance with which I had meditated had prepared my nerves for an internal change in the whole nervous system, but this had been retarded by the poor quality of my food. Peta's *chhang* had somewhat excited the nerves, and Zesay's offerings had fully affected them. I now understood what was happening; and, on studying the contents of the scroll, I found it contained the accessory means and exercises [both physical and mental], which I at once began to practise. Thereupon, I saw that the minuter nerves of my system were being straightened out;[2] even the knot of the *Sushumṇā-Nāḍī* (median nerve) was loosening below the navel;[3] and I experienced a state of supersensual calmness and clearness resembling the former states which I had experienced, but exceeding them in its depth and ecstatic intensity, and therein differing from them. Thus was a hitherto unknown and transcendent knowledge born in me. Soaring free above the obstacles, I knew that the very evil [or danger] had been turned to good. What till now had been regarded as objective discrimination shone forth as the *Dharma-Kāya*. I understood

---

[1] As in the practice of Kuṇḍalinī Yoga, the devotee is directed to change his food as he progresses from one stage to another on the Path of Accomplishment.

[2] Literally, 'their knots were loosening'; see p. 34[2].

[3] The navel nerve-centre (*Maṇipūra-chakra*) is the centre of the Element Fire of the body. Next below it is the centre of the Element Water, the *Svādhishṭhāna-chakra*; and next below this is the centre of the Element Earth, the *Mūlādhāra-chakra*; see p. 34[2].

the *Sangsāra* and *Nirvāṇa* to be dependent and relative
states ;[1] and that the Universal Cause is Mind, which is distinct from the ideas of Interestedness or Partiality. This
Universal Cause, when directed along the Path of Disbelief
[or Selfishness], resulteth in the *Sangsāra*; while if it be
directed along the path of Altruism, it resulteth in *Nirvāṇa*.
I was perfectly convinced that the real source of both *Sangsāra* and *Nirvāṇa* lay in the Voidness [of the Supra-mundane
Mind].[2] The knowledge I now had obtained was born of my
previous energetic devotions, which had served as its main
cause ; and it only awaited the accident, at the crisis, of the
wholesome and nourishing food, and the timely prescription
contained in the scroll, to bring it forth. My belief in the
methods of the Mantrayānic doctrines, which teach that a real
transcendent knowledge can be obtained by proper care of the
body and without giving up nourishing food and comfortable
clothing, was thus firmly established. I also saw that Peta
and Zesay had greatly contributed to the final development
of the hitherto latent qualities, and therefore mine obligation
to them was great. So by way of proving my gratitude,
and to consecrate their pious deeds to an Eternal and Inexhaustible Purpose, I sang this hymn [of prayer], which
embodieth the Essence of the Dependence and Relativity of
Facts :[3]

' " Obeisance to the Feet of Marpa of Lhobrak !
Grant that this hermit may hold fast to Solitude successfully.

[1] *Sangsāra* and *Nirvāṇa* to the Enlightened Mind of a Buddha are, as the
Ultimate Opposites, inseparable—being but states of mind, the one the state
of the mundane mind, the other the state of the supra-mundane mind of the
*Dharma-Kāya*.

[2] Cf. pp. 35[1] and 36[5].

[3] The Translator, the late Lāma Kazi Dawa-Samdup, has here added the
following explanatory note : ' This somewhat abstruse phraseology means—as
far as can be understood—that this hymn was sung as a dedication of the merits
of Zesay's and Peta's pious gifts, in such a way that these gifts may become
eternal and inexhaustible sources of good *karmic* results to them, as their gifts
had tended to bring out and develop the latent qualities in Jetsün's own physical
system, and accelerated his spiritual growth and development. This accelera-
tion having been brought about by their gifts, it may be said that the result
depended on their gifts. So Jetsün wished to weigh their gifts, not according to
their value, but according to their result.'

' " Upon the charity of righteous laymen,
    Success for them and me dependeth ;
    This body, delicate and brittle, and difficult to gain,
    By meeting food, is nourished and sustained.

' " The life-sustaining principle, upsprouting from the earth,
    And ambrosial showers from the heavenly dome of blue,
    Join together and confer a blessing on all sentient beings ;
    And in a life religious this is employed the best.[1]

' " The transient body, nourished by one's parents,
    And the Sacred Teaching of the Sacred *Guru*,
    Join together and then favour the religious life ;
    Wherein, in Perseverance, lieth true success.

' " The rocky cave, amid the uninhabited solitude,
    And devotion zealous and sincere,
    Join together and bring forth the Issue of Success ;
    Of Knowledge Spiritual doth this consist.

' " In the stoical and patient fortitude of Milarepa's meditation,
    And the faith of beings of the *Lokas* Three,
    Lieth opportunity of Universal Usefulness ;
    Of this, the essence is Compassion.[2]

' " The *yogī* who, in rocky caves, doth meditate,
    And laymen who provide his sustenance,
    Do each thus win the chance of gaining Buddhahood ;
    Of this, the essence is the Consecration.[3]

---

[1] There is herein an underlying reference to the development of the Kuṇḍalinī (or Serpent) Power. From the Root-Support Lotus (the Earth) it rises ; from the Thousand-Petalled Lotus (the Sky or Heavens) falls the ambrosial showers, which confer Ecstatic Illumination.  (See p. 34².)

[2] The virtue of Milarepa's meditation and of the faith of the beings of the Three *Lokas* or Regions, viz., of Desire (*Kāma*), of Form (*Rūpa*), and of Formlessness (*Arūpa*), unite and produce a spiritual force helpful to all sentient beings throughout the *Sangsāra* (or Universe of Nature). Of this the essence is Compassion.

[3] The *yogī* meditating, and the layman providing him with food, both work for and attain Buddhahood, by means of consecrating the merits of their mutual helpfulness to the Cause of the Enlightenment of all sentient beings. (Cf. the first stanza above, after the Obeisance.)

' " In the Sacred *Guru's* grace,
And the active meditation of the zealous *shishya*,
Lieth opportunity to uphold the Truth [the Hierarchy];
Of this, the essence is the Purity of Faith.[1]

' " In the Rites Initiatory, which confer and bless with Occult
Power,
And in the prayer, earnest and sincere [of the devotee],
Lieth opportunity of meeting speedily [Spiritual Communion];
Of this, the essence is the Benediction.[2]

' " Lord Dorje-Chang, O Thou the Immutable,
The weal and woe of this mendicant Thou knowest."

' This hymn having been sung, I zealously persevered in my
meditations. At last, I began to feel that I had obtained the
power of transforming myself into any shape [desired], and of
flying through the air. By day, I thus felt that I could exercise
endless phenomenal powers; by night, in my dreams, I could
traverse the universe in every direction unimpededly—from
the summit of Mount Meru[3] to its base—and I saw every-

---

[1] Pure faith and devotion in the *shishya* and the divine grace of the *Guru*
combine to produce the Saints who uphold the Church of Truth Universal on
Earth.

[2] The benediction bestowed upon the Initiate and his fervent aspiration to
attain Realization of Truth combine and speedily lead to the Goal—True Wisdom
being won through direct communion with the superhuman *Gurus*, of whom
Vajra-Dhara (Tib. *Dorje-Ch'ang*) is, for the Kargyütpa School, the Chief.

[3] Mount Meru is the Great Central Mountain of Buddhist as of Hindu mythology,
round which the cosmos is disposed in seven concentric circles of intervening
seas and mountains. Rationally interpreted, Mount Meru is the centre of gravi-
tation of a universe such as ours; and, in the Buddhist scheme of Cosmology,
our Universe is but one in the infinity of space, each being separated from the
other by an iron-wall, which, like an egg-shell, encloses each universe, the iron-
wall symbolizing darkness. But here, in our text, Mount Meru, the hub of the
physical universe, has an esoteric significance. It symbolizes the Mount Meru of
the human organism, the spinal column (Skt. *Brahma-danda*), in the hollow of
which is the median-nerve (Skt. *Sushumnā-nādī*), the chief channel of psychic
forces in man regarded as the Microcosm of the Macrocosm. Round the *Brahma-
danda*, like the two serpents coiled round the wand of the messenger-god Hermes,
are the two complementary channels, the left-nerve (Skt. *Idā-nādī*) and the right-
nerve (Skt. *Pingalā-nādī*). The summit of Mount Meru is the Thousand-Petalled
Lotus of the brain nerve-centre, the *Sahasrāra-Padma*; the base is the Root-
Support nerve-centre of the *Sushumnā-nādī*, known as the *Mūlādhāra-chakra*,

thing clearly [as I went]. Likewise [in my dreams] I could multiply myself into hundreds of personalities, all endued with the same powers as myself. Each of my multiplied forms could traverse space and go to some Buddha Heaven, listen to the Teachings there, and then come back and preach the *Dharma* to many persons. I could also transform my physical body into a blazing mass of fire, or into an expanse of flowing or calm water. Seeing that I had obtained infinite phenomenal powers [even though it be but in my dreams], I was filled with happiness and encouragement at mine own success.

'Thenceforth, I persevered in my devotions in a most joyous mood, until, finally, I actually could fly. Sometimes I flew over to the Min-khyüt-Dribma-Dzong (Castle lying in Shadows to the Eyebrows)[1] to meditate; and there I obtained a far greater development of the Vital Warmth than ever before. Sometimes I flew back again to the Dragkar-Taso Cave.

'Once, while I was thus flying, I happened to pass over a small village, called Long-da, where a brother of mine uncle's deceased daughter-in-law happened to live. She had been one of those who had perished in the crashing of the house. He had also a son, and the father and son were engaged in ploughing a field [as I flew over]. The son was leading the team, while the father was guiding the ploughshare. The son saw me flying, and said, " See, a man is flying!" And he left his work to look at me. The father said, " What is there to marvel at or to be amused about in the sight? One Nyang-Tsa-Kargyen, a very mischievous woman, had a wicked son, named Mila. It is that good-for-nothing starveling. Move aside and do not allow his shadow to fall over thee, and go on leading the team." The father himself was bending his body about so as to avoid

---

situated in the perineum. In the Thousand-Petalled Lotus, Shiva (*Jñāna* : ' Divine Wisdom ') and Kuṇḍalinī (*Shakti* : ' Divine Power ') come together in union, and the *yogī* experiences Illumination. The *Tantras* teach that to know the Microcosm (Skt. *Piṇḍāṇḍa*) is to know the Macrocosm (Skt. *Brahmāṇḍa*)— that whatever is here is elsewhere, that whatever is not here is not elsewhere.

[1] This name may possibly also have esoteric significance. If so, the ' Castle lying in Shadows to the Eyebrows ' would be the *Ājñā-chakra*, whither Milarepa sometimes flew, i. e. centred his consciousness in practising *Kuṇḍalinī Yoga* (see p. 34[2]) and thus acquired the *siddhi* of levitation and flying.

falling under my shadow. But the son said, " If a man be able
to fly, I do not mind his being a good-for-nothing person;
there can be nothing more wonderful than a man flying." So
saying, he continued looking at me.

' Now I thought that I could efficiently help all sentient
beings if I liked, so I resolved to devote myself to helping
others; but I had a direct command from my Tutelary Deity
to go on devoting my whole life to meditation, as my *Guru*
had commanded. By that alone I should serve the Cause of
the Buddhistic Faith ; and, also, in serving all sentient beings
thereby, I could do no better; such was the command I received. Thereupon, I thought that by dedicating my whole
life to meditation, I should be setting an example to future
devotees, who would thus be led to spend their life in devotion,
after giving up all worldly aims and prospects ; and that would
conduce to the Cause of the Buddhistic Faith and to the benefit
of all sentient beings. So I resolved to spend my whole life
in meditation.

' Again, I thought that I had lived very long in the place,
during which I had been seen by several persons to whom I had
talked upon religious subjects ; and now, that I had obtained
transcendent knowledge and *siddhi* (super-normal powers), and
had been seen flying by human beings, if I continued here,
worldly folk would flock to me, praying for protection from
harms and the fulfilment of selfish desires.[1] This would be
courting the temptations of the Son of the Celestials.[2] Worldly
fame and prosperity might retard the progress of my devotion
and obscure my spiritual knowledge ; so I resolved to go and
carry on my meditation in the solitudes of Lapchi-Chūbar
(Between Rivers).[3] Accordingly, I started forth, carrying on

[1] This is one of the reasons why the Buddha and other of the Great *Rishis* ot
India prohibited the working of miracles except in cases of extreme necessity.

[2] That is, Indra's temptations, or worldly glory and prosperity.  Indra, now
King of the Celestials, although risen to his present state from the human state,
once having been a prince on Earth, is said to use these temptations against any
man who practises great *yogic* austerities, like those that he once practised, to
prevent such a one from becoming his rival.

[3] The Translator has thought that Lapchi-Chūbar may possibly be another
name for Mt. Everest, in the caves of which the followers of Milarepa, even till
now, practise the Kargyütpa system of *yogic* meditation. The Tibetan name

my back from the Dragkar-Taso Cave the earthen vessel in which I had been cooking my nettle-food. But as I had been long practising meditation and living upon such poor food, and quite naked most of the time, my soles having become hardened, and horny scales being upon them, I slipped upon a stone just beside my cave and fell down. The handle of the earthen pot breaking, the pot itself rolled away and broke, despite mine attempts to catch it. From within the broken vessel there rolled a perfect green image of it, this being the hardened encrustation of the nettle broth which had assumed the shape of the outer vessel. The mishap vividly brought home to me the impermanent nature of all worldly things. I also understood it to be a sort of exhortation to persevere in my devotions. Feeling the whole occurrence to be very wonderful, I sang the following hymn in a spirit of deep faith :

' " Even the earthen pot, by having once existed, and now by
        existing not,
    Demonstrateth the nature of all things [component] ;
    But more especially human life it symbolizeth.
    Therefore do I, Mila the Devotee,
    Resolve to persevere unwaveringly.
    The earthen pot, which constituted my sole wealth,
    By breaking, hath now become a *Guru*,[1]
    For it preacheth unto me a wondrous sermon on Imper-
        manence."

' While I was singing this, some hunters, who were coming towards my place for a meal, had heard it. They said, " O Hermit, thou possessest a very musical voice for singing. What art thou doing with the broken earthen pot and the inner pot of hardened encrustations of froth of nettle broth ; and how cometh it that thou art so emaciated and greenish in appearance ? " On mine explaining to them the reason of mine emaciation they were filled with wonder, and asked me to partake of their meal. While I was eating, one of the younger hunters

commonly given to Mt. Everest is Lapchi-Kang, and this name is used by Milarepa in his song to his sister (see p. 224).

[1] ' There is this precept among the Kaula Tantrics : " From Brahmā to a blade of grass all things are my *Gurus*." '—Sj. Atal Bihari Ghosh.

said, "Why, thou seemest to be a powerfully built man. Instead of undergoing such troubles and privations, if thou should take to a worldly career, thou wouldst, if things went well, be riding a horse like a lion ; and, accoutred in arms like a thorn-bush, thou wouldst be subduing thine enemies. By accumulating wealth thou wouldst be protecting thine affectionate kindred, and thou wouldst be happy. Or else thou couldst devote thyself to trade, in which line thou couldst earn sufficient to make thee happy. At the worst, thou couldst serve as a servant, and obtain good food and clothes ; as regardeth thy body and mind, thou wouldst be far better off than this. Hitherto, thou dost not seem to have known of this ; so set about it now." One of the older hunters said, "He appeareth to me to be a very good devotee, and it is not likely that he will mind our worldly counsel ; better keep quiet." Then to me he said, "Thou possessest a very fine voice. Please sing us a song, which will do good to our minds." To which I replied, "Ye all seem to think me very miserable, but there is no one in the world who is so happy as myself, nor one who can boast of greater sense or a nobler and more successful life ; but ye could not understand it. I enjoy the following things, which constitute my felicity, just as the best of you. Listen to me." So saying, I sang them the hymn of a *Yogī's* Race :

' " I bow down at the Feet of my Gracious Father Marpa !

' " Within the Temple of the Bodhi Hill, my body,
  Within my breast, wherein the Altar is,
  Within the chamber topmost and triangular within my heart,
  The Horse of Mind, moving like the wind, doth prance about.[1]

' " What Lasso must be used to catch this Horse ?
  And to what Post must It be tied when caught ?
  What Food is to be given It when hungry ?

---

[1] It is here assumed that the heart is the centre whence originate all mental impulses, which, when uncontrolled, are as unruly as a wild horse. The catching and tying up of the Horse are the first steps in the science of mind-control called *Yoga.* Once the mind processes are dominated, the bridled and saddled Horse carries its spiritually accoutred rider, the Youth of Intellect, to Buddhahood.

What Drink is to be given It when thirsty?
In what Enclosure is It kept when cold?

'"To catch the Horse, use, as the Lasso, Singleness of Pur-
    pose;[1]
It must be tied, when caught, to the Post of Meditation;
It must be fed, when hungry, with the *Guru's* Teachings;
It must be given to drink, when thirsty, of the Stream of
    Consciousness;
It must be kept, when cold, in the Enclosure of the Voidness.
For Saddle, use the Will, for Bridle, Intellect;
Attach to It, as Girths and Cruppers, Fixedness Immovable;
Around it pass, as Head-stall and as Nose-band, the Vital-
    Airs.

'"Its rider is the Youth of Intellect [Keen Watchfulness]:
The Helmet, which he weareth, is Mahāyānic Altruism;
His Coat of Mail is Learning, Thought, and Contemplation;
Upon his back he carrieth the Shield of Patience;
He holdeth, in his hand, the long Spear of Aspiration;
And, by his side, hangeth the Sword, Intelligence;
The smoothèd Reed of Universal Mind [or Cause],
Made straight by lack of wrath or hatred,[2]
Barbed with the Feathers of the Four Unlimited [Virtues],
Tipped with the Arrow-head of Intellect made keen,
Then placed within the pliant Bow of Wisdom Spiritual,
And fixed there, in the Aperture of the Wise Path and
    Right Method,
He draweth out to the full fathom of Communion Wide;
And shot forth thus, the arrows fall midst all the Nations.
They strike the Faithful Ones,
And slay the Sprite of Selfishness.[3]

[1] These verses describe progressive stages in *yoga* practice, beginning with
*Ekāgratā*, 'Singleness of Purpose', or One-Pointedness of Mind, and leading
to *Dhyāna* and *Samādhi*.

[2] Here the figure used is of an arrow-shaft of bamboo, which is commonly
straightened and made even by heat, scraping, and polishing.

[3] Herein, Milarepa justifies the life of ascetical seclusion from the world.
Unknown to the worldly multitude, who regard the *yogī* as a useless member
of society, he is, in fact, the most useful; owing to his thought-force, broadcast
like silent and invisible arrows which fall among all nations, virtue and goodness

Thus are the Enemies, all Evil Passions, overcome ;
And protected are our Kindred.[1]

' " This Horse doth course along the widespread Plain of
    Happiness ;
Its Goal is the attainment of the State of all the Conquerors.[2]
Its Hind-part leaveth, in its rear, attachment to *sangsāric*
    life ;
Its Front-part goeth on to the safe place of Deliverance.

' " By running such a race, I'm carried on to Buddhahood ;
Judge if this be like your own conception of felicity :
Worldly Happiness I covet not."

' On hearing this, they were moved with faith and went away
in that mood.

' I then proceeded towards Chūbar, going through Palkhung ;
and, having arrived at Tingri, was lying on the road to enjoy
a view of the place, when a party of maidens, rather gaily
dressed, happened to pass by on their way to Snag-mo. Seeing
my emaciated body, one of them said, " O see how miserable
this man appeareth ! Grant that I may never be born in such
a shape ! " to which another added, " How piteous ! It maketh
me quite nervous to see such a sight." I thinking them to be
poor ignorant creatures, pitied them, and, getting up, I said,
" O ye girls, do not speak thus. Ye need not be anxious
about that at all ; ye would not be born such as I am even
though ye were to wish and pray earnestly for it. It is praiseworthy to pity, but pity and self-conceit are opposed to each
other, and so inconsistent. Listen to a song of mine." With
that, I sang them this song :

' " At Thy Feet, O Gracious *Guru*, now I pray ;
Grant me Thy Blessings and Thy Grace, O Marpa !

---

are kept alive in the world, and the Pathway leading to the Olympus of the
Gods is guarded and kept open. See, too, our Introduction, pp. 15-24.

[1] These are all sentient beings in all the Six *Lokas* (or Worlds) of the
*Sangsāra*. Thus, not only is the Saint the most essential of all members of
human society, but his field of altruistic service is the whole universe.

[2] Or, Skt. '*Jinas* (the Conquerors, the Buddhas)'.

' " Those creatures, who in evil *karma* are immersed,
    Contemptuously regard all others save themselves;
    Women of evil *karma* think a married life the most desirable
        of things;
    Their self-conceit doth burn as hot as fire:
    Ah, pitiable it is to see these beings thus deluded!

' " In these dark days, of the Kali-Yuga,[1]
    Mischief-making knaves are worshipped as if gods,
    And impostors are prized as if more precious e'en than gold;
    True devotees are cast aside, like stones from off a path:
    Oh, pity these poor ignorant beings!

' " Ye group of maiden sisters, gaily dressed,
    And I, Milarepa of Gungthang,
    Have mutual contempt for each other,
    And mutual pity, too;
    But in the lance-tilt of our mutual pity,
    Let us see who winneth in the end.[2]

' " This truthful sermon is by Milarepa preached,
    In answer to the senseless talk of ignorant beings;
    'Tis exchanging wine for water,
    And returning Good for Evil."

' Upon my finishing the song, the girl who had pitied me
said, " This is the famous Gungthang-Milarepa, and we have
uttered several foolish things in a spirit of self-conceit. Now
let us ask his pardon "; and, with that, they all directed the
girl who had uttered the speech to do so. She, too, was very
sorry; and, producing seven shells, which were used as cur-
rency then, she offered them to me with prostrations, and
prayed that I might be pleased to give them another sermon,
so then I sang to them the following song:

' " I supplicate my Gracious Lord!
    A sermon brief, on Truth, I'm preaching.

---

[1] Or, ' Age of Iron '—the ' Dark Age ', of waning Religion and flourishing
Worldliness, in which the human race now is.

[2] That is, whether worldly enjoyment (Skt. *Pravritti*) or renunciation of the
world (Skt. *Nivritti*) leads to True Wisdom.

' " In the Palaces Celestial of the Gahdan Gods,[1]
Truths Spiritual are prized not, but Truths Scientific are ;
In the Regions Lower, in the Nāga's Palaced City,
Truths Profound and Deep are prized not, but Riches are ; [2]
In this World of Human Beings,
The Wise and Learned are not prized, but Liars are.

' " In the Provinces of U and Tsang and the Four Districts,
Meditation is not prized, but Exposition is ;
In the dreg-like remainder of these evil times [of Darkness],
Good men are not prized, but the wicked are.

' " In the eyes of gay young women,
Not the devotee, but the rake is prized ;
Unto the ears of youthful maidens,
Prosaic sermons on religion sound not sweet, but love-songs
    do.

' " These are the truths in verse,
Sung in payment for the seven shells,
And as a joyful song betokening full pardon."

' On hearing this song they were moved to deep faith, and
proceeded on their way.

' I also went on towards Brin (Drin), where I heard about
both Lapchi-Chūbar (Mt. Everest ?) and Kyit-Phug (Pleasant
Cave), also known as Nyima-Dzong (Sunny Castle), of which I
chose the latter. There I spent some months, and was progress-
ing favourably in my devotion and meditation ; but the people
of Brin visited me, bringing gifts of provisions. Knowing that
this would tend, to some extent, to the deterioration of my
devotional practices, I thought that if I remained in this place
any longer, popularity would only do harm to my meditative
devotions. I had been here long enough, and, thus far, had
gained by my stay. Now I must go to a most solitary region

---

[1] Gods of the Tuṣhita Heavens, who are more intellectual than spiritual.

[2] The Nāgas, or Dragon-demigods, of Hindu mythology, are of four kinds :
(1) celestial, guarding the Heaven-Worlds ; (2) aerial, causing winds and rain,
to benefit human beings ; (3) earthly, demarcating courses of rivers and streams ;
and (4), as in our text here, lovers or guardians of hidden treasures. They are
thus somewhat like the Elementals of Medieval Philosophy, each class of which
inhabited one of the elements.

and seek a cave there. So, according to my *Guru's* command, I resolved to go to Lapchi-Chūbar. While I was about to start on my way thither, my sister Peta came to offer me a piece of blanket-cloth, woven of wool which she had collected from the leavings of others. She had taken it to Dragkar-Taso, and, not finding me there, had come searching for me, inquiring from every one; and hearing, at Gungthang-Tōt, that a hermit resembling a caterpillar which feedeth upon nettles had passed from Palkhung towards La-Tōt-Lho (Upper Hills Facing South), she had come tracking my very footprints. At Tingri, she had seen Lāma Bari-Lotsawa (The Great Bari Translator) seated upon a high seat, with an umbrella over him, dressed in silks of five different colours, and surrounded by his disciples, some of whom blew conchs, cymbals, clarionets, and flutes, with a great crowd round about, all offering him tea and *chang*. Upon seeing this, Peta thought, "Other devotees and religious folk enjoy these things, but my brother's religion is a source of misery and trouble to himself and shame to his relatives. If I now meet my brother, I shall try mine utmost to persuade him to become a disciple of this Lāma." Thinking thus, she asked some among the assembly there whether they had heard or seen aught of me, and, being told that I was at Brin, she had come inquiring after me right up to Kyit-Phug, where I then was. Upon seeing me, she at once said, "O brother, it will never do to go on in this starving, naked condition, which thou sayest is thy mode of living a religious life. Thou art past shame and common decency! Make a lower garment of this blanket, and go to the Lāma Bari-Lotsawa, who is a Lāma indeed, but quite different in style and practice from thyself. He hath a throne under him, and an umbrella over him; he is clad in silken garments, and his lips are always dipped in tea and *chhang*. He is surrounded by his disciples and followers, who walk in front of him, blowing trumpets by pairs. He assembleth a crowd wherever he goeth, and collecteth their offerings in large quantities, thus benefiting his relatives; and is one who can be boasted of as a most eminent Lāma. I would have thee try to enter his service and follow him as his disciple. Even if thou be accepted as his meanest disciple, that would be better than this sort of life. Thy penurious devotion and my luckless life will scarcely do in this world. We cannot thus sustain life." And then she began to weep bitterly, deploring our lot.

' I tried to console her by saying, "Peta, do not speak in that fashion. Thou regardest my naked condition with shame, because I have cast aside clothing and coverings. I am proud that I have obtained the Truth through my being a man; and there is no shame in that. I was born thus; therefore there is no shame in it. But those who knowing certain acts to be sinful commit them, thereby breaking their parents' hearts, and those coveting property dedicated to *Gurus* and the Trinity, committing various acts of deception and meanness to attain their selfish aims, cause pain and suffering to other beings, and hurt themselves in the end. They are objects of loathing and abhorrence to every righteous being among gods and men; and they alone should feel shame. But if thou speak of shame at seeing my body, then thou especially shouldst feel shame because thy breasts, which did not exist at the time of thy birth, have developed so prominently. Moreover, if thou think that I am meditating in this penurious condition just because I cannot earn or obtain food and clothing, thou art quite mistaken. I am frightened at the pains and tribulations of this *Sangsāra*. I feel them as keenly as though I had been cast alive into flames. Worldly acquisitions of wealth and the need of clinging to them, as well as the pursuit of the Eight Worldly Aims,[1] I regard with as much loathing and disgust as a man who is suffering from biliousness regardeth the sight of rich food. Nay, I regard them as if they were the murderers of my father; therefore is it that I am assuming this beggarly and penurious mode of life. Moreover, my *Guru*, Marpa the Translator, bade me to give up all worldly concerns, aims, and objects; to bear the loss of food, clothing, and name; to live in various solitary places [not fixing myself to one place permanently]; and to carry on my devotions most energetically, giving up all prospects in this life. Such being my *Guru's* commandments, I am fulfilling them. By thus obeying my

[1] These are: Comfort, Misery; Wealth, Poverty; Fame, Obscurity; Praise, Blame.

*Guru's* commandments, I shall not only be able to confer temporal ease and comfort on those who are my followers, but I shall earn eternal happiness for every sentient being, including myself. I gave up all thoughts of this life, because I saw that there is no certainty as to when death may come upon me. If I were to think of acquiring wealth and ease, I should be able to acquire as much as Lāma Bari-Lotsawa himself is acquiring; so what need is there to speak of his meanest follower! But I desire Buddhahood in this very lifetime; therefore am I devoting myself to devotion and meditation in such an energetic way. Peta, do thou also give up all worldly aims, and come with thy brother, who is older, to pass thy life in meditation at Lapchi-Kang.[1] If thou can give up worldly thoughts and come to pass thy life in meditative devotions, the sun of thy temporal and eternal happiness will thus shine in full splendour. Give ear to thy brother's song." Then I sang this song:

'"O Lord, Protector of all Sentient Beings, Thou the Eternal
    Buddha!
Since Thou, by worldliness unsullied hath remained,
And blessed Thy *Shishyas* with Thy Grace,
I bow down at Thy Feet, O Marpa the Translator!

'"My sister Peta, listen unto me,
Immersed in worldly wishes as thou art.

'"The pinnacle of gold, placed on an umbrella, at the top,
    for one;
The fringe of Chinese silk, arranged in tasteful folds, below,
    for two;
The ribs outspread, like a peacock's gorgeous feathers, in
    between, for three;
The polished handle of red teak-wood, at the bottom, for
    four:
These four, if needed, thine elder brother could procure.

[A Chorus, the five verses which follow, accompanies this stanza and each of the five following stanzas, as indicated.]

---

[1] Lapchi-Kang is the name by which Mt. Everest is commonly known to the Tibetans (cf. p. 214[n], above).

' " But these are worldly things, and I've eschewed them,
   And, by my thus eschewing worldliness, my Sun of Happiness shineth gloriously.
   Likewise, do thou, O Peta, all worldliness eschew,
   And come to meditate in Lapchi-Kang :
   Let us together go to Lapchi-Kang, to meditate.

' " The white conch-shell's far-sounding note, for one ;
   The practised blower's full and potent breath, for two ;
   The silken ribbons [on the conch], plaited in fine plaits, for three ;
   The vast assembly of celibate priests [summoned thus], for four :
   These four, if needed, thine elder brother could procure.

*[Chorus]*

' " The charming, pretty little temple, just above a village placed, for one ;
   The fluent speech, of youthful novices, for two ;
   The splendid kitchen, well arranged, with goodly stock of Chinese tea, for three ;
   The busy hands, of many youthful novices, for four :
   These four, if needed, thine elder brother could procure.

*[Chorus]*

' " The well-liked trade, in necromantic seership, and in astrology, for one ;
   The correctness and the modesty of a pastor's acts, for two ;
   The performance of the *pūjās*, for enjoying them, for three ;
   The psalms melodious, sung with a view to turn the heads of the laity, for four :
   These four, if needed, thine elder brother could procure.

*[Chorus]*

' " A building, massive, beautiful, and tall, of brick, for one ;
   A field, extensive and fertile, for two ;
   A well-stocked store, of food and wealth, for three ;
   A numerous retinue, and crowd of servitors, for four :
   These four, if needed, thine elder brother could procure.

*[Chorus]*

' " The proud, tall crest of a powerful horse, for one ;
     A saddle, jewel-bedecked and gold-inlaid, for two ;
     An armed escort, splendidly accoutred, for three ;
     And vigilance unceasing, in conquering enemies and protect-
          ing friends, for four :
     These four, if needed, thine elder brother could procure.

### [Chorus]

' " But if thou can not give up worldliness,
     And can not come to Lapchi-Kang,
     No liking have I for thy sentimental, sisterly affection.
     These talks of worldly things disturb my meditation.
     I being born, know I must die ; uncertain of the hour of death,
     No time have I to postpone my devotion ;
     Uninterruptedly will I devote myself to meditation.
     The teachings of my *Guru*-Father are beneficial to the
          mind ;
     Thus, contemplating that which bringeth benefit,
     I'll earn the Great Happiness of Deliverance ;
     Therefore to Lapchi-Kang I'm going.

' " Do thou, my sister, cling to worldliness,
     Acquire sins by the pound and stone,
     Strive to remain, for all the time thou canst, in the *Sangsāra*,
     And strive to win thyself a birth in the Three Lower Worlds.

' " Yet if thou fear the *Sangsāra* in the least,
     Renounce, in this life now, the Eight *Sangsāric* Aims,
     And let us go together, unto Lapchi-Kang,
     Let us, the twain, brother and sister, be high-destined ones,
     And go together to the Ranges of the Lapchi-Kang."

' On my singing thus, Peta said, " I see that thou meanest
ease and comfort by worldliness, my brother. As for that,
both of us have so little to give up. All these fine-sounding
truths and sermons are merely excuses to cloak thine inability
to be as well off as Lāma Bari-Lotsawa ; but, as for me, I will
not go to Lapchi-Kang, where I shall have nothing to eat, nor
anything to wear : it would be unendurable misery, which
I need not go to seek at Lapchi. I do not even know where

it is; and I would entreat thee, my brother, to remain permanently in one place, instead of rushing about and clinging to uninhabited cliffs and rocks, like an animal pursued by dogs. I could find thee more easily then. The people of this place seem disposed to regard thee with veneration, so it would be best if thou remain here permanently. But, in any case, at least stay on for some days more. Please sew thyself an undergarment from this blanket; I will return in a few days." I consented to remain there for a few days, as she requested. Then she went towards Tingri side, on a begging errand.

'Meanwhile, I cut up the blanket which she had brought me, and sewed myself a cape to cover my head entirely; next, I sewed a cover for each of my fingers and a pair of coverings for my feet, as well as a cover for my nakedness; and kept them ready. A few days later, my sister came back; and, upon her asking me whether I had sewn the blanket into a dress, I said that I had; and putting on the coverings, one by one, I showed her what I had done. Upon this, she said, "O brother! thou art no longer a human being! Thou art not only devoid of the sense of shame, but thou hast spoilt the blanket which I prepared with so much trouble. At times, thou appearest to have no time to spare for anything save devotion; and, then, at other times, thou seemest to have ample leisure." I replied, "I am the worthiest of human beings, for I am engaged in turning to the best account the precious boon of a blessed human life. Knowing what is really shameful, I have devoted myself to a religious life, and kept my vows rigidly. But as thou appearest to feel shame at seeing my natural shape, and as I could not afford to cut off the part which thou lookest upon as shameful, I have been at the pains to sew this covering for it, at the cost of my time for devotions, as thou sayest; and, since mine other limbs are also organs of this same body, I thought a covering for each of them would be required similarly, and so I have made these coverings. Thy blanket hath not been wasted, but made to serve the ends for which thou didst intend it, for I have thus prepared a covering for the organ of shame. As thou seemest to be so prudish and more sensitive to the feeling of shame than myself, I must tell thee that if I should feel shame thou shouldst feel more shame. Seeing that it is better to do away with an object of shame than to keep it on, please do away with thine own as quickly as thou canst." When I said this, she kept quiet, and her face was sullen. Then I said, "Worldly folk regard with shame that which involveth no shame. But that which is really shameful is evil deeds and wily deception; and these they do not feel shame in committing. They do not know what really is shameful and what is not. Therefore listen to this song of mine." With that I sang to her the song which showeth clearly what is shameful and what is not:

' "To all the Lineal *Gurus* I bow down!
   Grant me knowledge of what is really shameful.

' "O Peta dear, held fast with prudish shame,
   Give ear awhile unto thy brother's song:

' "Thy shame is born of ignorant conventionalities;
   Shame thou feelest where for shame there is no cause.
   To me, the devotee, who knoweth what shame truly is,
   In showing in its natural shape my threefold personality,[1]
   What shame can be attached thereby?
   When 'tis known that human beings are born, each of a cer-
      tain sex,
   'Tis known, too, that each possesseth certain organs.

' "The most of worldly folk heed not
   Those acts which truly are either mean or shameful:
   The Daughter of Shame is bought with wealth;
   The Child of Shame is dandled on the lap;
   Covetous and harmful thoughts,[2] begot of unbelief,
   Evil deeds, vile frauds, thefts, and robberies,
   Deceiving friends and kindred who confide in one—
   These, indeed, are acts filled full of shame and meanness;
      yet few refrain from them.

---

[1] That is, body, speech, and mind.
[2] Thoughts being things, the thought-waves created by them in the ether are potent to affect for good or ill all beings throughout the universe, as on the Earth.

' " Those hermits who have given up the worldly life
    And taken to the practice of the Spiritual Truths,
    Found in the Sacred Teachings of the Mystic Path,
    They who have vowed to pass their life in meditation,
    See not the need to hold to codes of shame conventional.
    Therefore, do not, O Peta, seek to add unto thy present
        miseries,
    But let thine understanding flow within its natural channels."

' When I had sung this song, she sullenly handed over to me
the provisions, butter, and grease, which she had obtained by
begging, saying, " It is quite clear that thou wilt not do anything such as I wish thee to do, yet I cannot give thee up. So
please use these ; and I will do what I can to obtain more."
Having said this, she was about to go away. I, however,
wishing to turn her heart towards religion, induced her to
remain as long as the provisions might last, so that even though
she did not earn merit by practising devotion, she would for
that much time, at least, be free from committing sin. As long
as she thus lived with me, I talked to her about religious subjects and about the Law of *Karma*. At last, I succeeded in
turning her heart towards the Faith, to some extent.

' At about this time, mine aunt, having lost her brother, mine
uncle, and bitterly, from the very core of her heart, repenting
the wrong they had done me, also came in search of me,
bringing a yak-load of things. She had been first to Brin.
There she deposited the things, and the yak, and came with
whatever she herself could carry, right up to the place where
I was living. Peta having seen her coming from the hillock,
and recognizing her, said, " This cruel aunt who hath caused us
so much harm and misery we must not meet." Suiting her
action to the words, she lifted away the little bridge which
spanned the yawning chasm between the slope on the opposite
side and the front of my cave. Our aunt, coming to the brink
of the slope, on the side opposite to us, said, " Niece, do not
lift up the bridge ; thine aunt is coming over." To this, Peta
answered, " It is for that very reason that I am lifting up the
bridge." " Niece, thou art quite right ; but now I have come,

bitterly repenting of my deeds, to meet both of you; so lower the bridge. Yet, if thou wilt not do this, then, at least, tell thy brother that I have come here," pleaded our aunt.

'Just then, I arrived there, and seated myself on a little knoll on this side of the bridge. Mine aunt bowed down several times from the other side, and pleaded earnestly that she might be allowed to meet me. I thought that it would not become me, as a devotee, to refuse her the interview in the end, but I must first speak plainly to her about her cruelties and persecutions. So I said, "I have given up all attachment to relatives generally, but especially to you, mine aunt and uncle. Ye were not satisfied with greatly persecuting us in our childhood and youth, but even when I had taken to a religious career and happened to come to your door to beg, ye assaulted me so cruelly that I ceased to think of you at all as relatives. I will briefly recall those circumstances in this song, which thou wilt listen to." So saying, I sang to her a song recalling the cruelties and persecutions with which they had pursued me:

' "O Kind and Gracious Father, compassionate to all,
    O Marpa the Translator, I bow down at Thy Feet!
    Be Thou a Kindred unto me, who am bereft of kindred!

' "O aunt, recallest thou all that thou hast done?
    If thou can not, this song of mine will refresh thy memory;
    Attentively give ear to it, and in repentance be sincere.

' "There in the wretched land of Kyanga-Tsa,
    Our noble father dying, left us, the three, a widowed mother
        and two orphans;
    Of all our wealth thou didst defraud us, and brought us unto
        misery.
    And, as peas are by a staff, we were scattered then,
    By thee, O aunt, and by our uncle, too.
    So our attachment unto kith and kin was sundered.

' "Thereafter, when in distant lands I wandered long,
    Anxious to behold my sister and my mother, I returnèd
        home,
    And found my mother dead, and my sister gone.

With anguish pierced, I sought religion, and finding it my
    sole solace,
The life religious thenceforth chose.
Compelled by lack of food to seek for alms,
Before thy door, O aunt, I came to beg,
And thou, in recognizing me, the helpless devotee,
Didst burst forth in a storm of spiteful anger.
With cries of '*Cho! Cho!*' thou didst set thy dogs upon me;
With thy tent-pole thou didst belabour me most heavily,
As though I were a sheaf of corn for threshing.
I fell face downward in a pool of water,
Wherein I almost lost my precious life.
Amidst thy fury, thou didst call me 'Trafficker in Lives';
And likewise, too, 'Disgrace unto my Clan'.
With these rude words my heart was wounded;
And, with despair and misery overwhelmed,
My breath was stopped and I was speechless.
And then, although I had no need of them,
Thou didst, by various wiles, defraud me of my house and
    field.
A demoness thou art, in the body of an aunt,
That sundered me from all my love for thee, O aunt.

'"Thereafter, when I reached mine uncle's door,
Malicious thoughts, injurious acts, vile words I met.
'The destroying demon of the country cometh,' was his cry;
He called the neighbours forth to help in killing me;
And, words abusive uttering,
He pelted me with showers of stones,
And sought to transfix me with a rain of small keen arrows;
With a malady incurable he filled my heart.
There, too, I almost lost my life.
O butcher's heart in an uncle's form!
All my respect for an uncle I lost then.

'"When I was poor and helpless, my kinsfolk were more cruel
    to me than enemies,
Thereafter, to the hill, where I was meditating,
My constant Zesay came to see me, out of love;

And she, with pleasant words, consoled me ;
She comforted my sorrow-stricken heart ;
She brought me nourishing and tasty food ;
And from starvation saved me then.
Kind, indeed, is she, more kind than I can say ;
Yet since e'en she is not devoted to religion,
Little need I see to meet her when she cometh ;
And as for thee, mine aunt, far less I need to meet thee.
Return e'en now, in the manner thou hast come ;
'Tis better to go early, while there is still the time."

' When I had sung thus, mine aunt shed many tears, and,
bowing down several times, said, " Thou art right, O my
nephew ; thus far thou art right ; but be patient, I pray thee."
Then she began to entreat me. I saw that she was really
sincere in her repentance, and had come to ask my forgiveness.
She said, " Not being able to overcome the desire to see thee,
I have come here.  Please grant me the interview which I
seek, or I shall surely commit suicide."  Being unable to harden
my heart any further, I was about to lower the bridge when
my sister whispered many reasons to withhold me from doing
so.  I lowered it nevertheless.  It is said to be undesirable to
live in the same country or to drink of the same fountain [or
well of water] with a person with whom a breach of faith hath
taken place ; and that, if we do so, some obscuration and
defilement will occur ; but the present case was not, however,
a breach of faith in a spiritual matter.  Besides, I myself being
of the Religious Order, was bound to be forgiving ; so I laid
the bridge across, granted the desired interview, and preached
several sermons on the Law of *Karma*.  Mine aunt was thoroughly
converted by the sermons ; and, devoting herself to penance
and meditation, eventually obtained Emancipation.'
Then Shiwa-wöd-Repa addressed Jetsün in these words :
' O Jetsün, it is beyond our comprehension when we hear how
constant in thy faith and purpose thou wert in obtaining the
Truths from thy *Guru* ; how meek and faithful throughout
thy terrible ordeals ; and how persevering and energetic in
carrying on devotion and meditation in lonely hilly solitudes.

When we think of those deeds, our devotion seemeth to be mere sport—done at leisure, by fits and starts; and such devotion [we fear], will not emancipate us from the *Sangsāra*. What, then, are we to do?' Having uttered these words, he wept bitterly.

Jetsün answered, 'When we think of the pains and troubles endured in the *Sangsāra* and in the Hell-Worlds, my faith and zeal do not really appear to have been so very great either. Thoughtful persons, once having heard about the Doctrine of *Karma*, and believing in it, will be able to put forth similar zeal and energy. But those who understand only the wordings of the Doctrine, not having realized the truth of it, are unable to renounce the Eight Worldly Aims and Objects. Therefore, it is of the highest importance to believe in the Doctrine of *Karma*. These [latter folk] always appear not to believe even in the simplest and most generally accepted [or self-evident] of *karmic* laws. Thus, although they devote themselves to various expositions of the Voidness (*Shūnyatā*), as found in the Scriptures and Gospels, the Voidness, being more subtle and intricate, is far more difficult to comprehend, and believe in. But when once one believeth in the Voidness, its very self becometh manifest in the intricate workings of the Law of *Karma*; and a man who realizeth the nature of Voidness necessarily becometh more subtle, and distinguisheth the qualities of actions both good and bad with a much finer power of perception. In short, he becometh more strictly conscientious. All piety consisteth in observing and believing in the Law of *Karma*; therefore it is of the utmost importance to be very persevering in adopting pious acts and rejecting impious acts. I, at first, did not understand the nature of the Voidness, but I believed firmly in the Law of *Karma*; and, being conscious of having committed deep and heinous sins, I believed that I richly deserved to go to the three miserable states of Hell. So I entertained the deepest reverence for, and faith in, my *Guru*, and exerted the utmost energy and zeal during my meditation, as, indeed, I could not help doing. I exhort you all to pass your lives in strict asceticism, in deep solitudes, meditating upon the Sacred Mystic Truths, and carrying into practice the teachings of the Doctrine. If ye do so, I, the old man, assure you of emancipation from the *Sangsāra.*'

Then Ngan-Dzong-Tönpa Budhi-Rāja addressed Jetsün in this eulogistic style: 'O Jetsün Rinpoch'e,[1] thou must be the great Buddha Dorje-Chang Himself, come in human shape, to show those acts for the benefit of the sentient beings of this world. And if not that, then, at least, thou must have acquired much merit in countless Kalpas, and obtained the state of such a Great Being—one who will not return again to the *Sangsāra.* Thou hast been ready to sacrifice life itself for religion, and persisted zealously in the pursuit of devotional meditation. All the signs of an Incarnate Buddha are to be found in thy life. For to beings like us, who live for the individual self, thy meekness and constant and unswerving faith during the time that thou wert under thy *Guru,* and the hardships which thou didst bear, appear quite incomprehensible, even to our hearts. It would be impossible for us to think of undergoing all those hardships for the sake of the Truth; who would be able to do so? And even if any one had the will and hardihood to attempt to do so, the physical frame would not be able to bear it. So it is quite certain that Jetsün must be, or must have been, either a Bodhisattva or a Buddha in the past ; and we are blest in having seen thy face and heard thy voice. Those of us who have thus been favoured are sure of obtaining Deliverance, although we be not able to pursue our devotions so earnestly. Be pleased to reveal to us what Bodhisattva thou wert in the past.'

To this Jetsün replied: ' I myself am not sure whose incarnation I am; but even though I be an incarnation of a being formerly existing in one of the Three States of Misery,[2] yet, if ye regard me as Dorje-Chang, or as any other Deity, ye will obtain the grace and blessing of such Deity, in virtue of your faith. Personal love and regard make ye think that

---

[1] *Rinpoch'e,* meaning 'Precious', is a Tibetan term of great respect. It is commonly applied to Great *Gurus* and *Yogīs.* Padma Sambhava, for example, is popularly called *Guru* Rinpoch'e, 'Precious *Guru*' (cf. p. 5).

[2] Namely, the three miserable planes of existence : the World of Brutes, the World of Unhappy Ghosts (or *Pretas*), and the various Hells.

I must be an Incarnation; but towards the *Dharma* ye commit the great sin of doubt and scepticism. This is because ye have not the power of earnest devotion. For it is by the great power of the Sacred *Dharma* alone that I have been able to attain such spiritual advancement as to be very near Perfect Buddhahood in the latter portion of my years, although I had been guilty of such heinous sins in my youth and early manhood. It was because I firmly believed in the reality of the Law of *Karma* that I applied myself zealously to the Truth, giving up all thoughts of this life and world. And, more especially, was I fortunate in being taken in hand by a perfected *Guru*, who was able to give me those very Truths and Texts which were most adapted to me, and which enabled me to follow the Short Path of the Mystic *Mantrayāna*. He gave me the Truths divested of all superfluous adornments and clothing,[1] conferred on me the necessary Initiations, and empowered me to meditate on these Truths in the right way. If any one else had obtained these, and continued to meditate on them, there is not the least doubt about his obtaining perfect enlightenment within one lifetime. But if one pass a lifetime here doing nothing but committing the ten impious acts and the five unlimited sins, there is not the least doubt that such a one will fall into the most miserable of the Hells. If one do not believe in the Law of *Karma*, one lacketh zeal in the pursuit of his devotional studies; if one believe firmly in the Law of *Karma*, the thought of the miseries in the Three Lower States is sure to fill one with dread and inspire one with the intensest desire to obtain Buddhahood. Then one's faith and meekness towards the *Guru*, zeal and energy in the meditation on the Truth, and, finally, the way in which one beareth the experience of the spiritual growth and knowledge, would altogether equal mine in every point. And when any one obtaineth these spiritual developments, the worldly proudly attribute it to his being an *Avatāra* of some Buddha or Bodhisattva. Actually this is disbelief in the Short Path of the *Mantrayāna*. Therefore, I exhort you all to establish your belief in the Law of *Karma* firmly. Meditate upon, consider, and weigh deeply

---

1 That is, flowery rhetoric and parables.

the serious facts contained in the biographies of previous saintly lives, the Law of *Karma*, the inconveniences and miseries of all *sangsāric* states of existences, the difficulties of obtaining the boon of a well-endowed human life, and the certainty of death and the uncertainty of the exact time of death; and, having weighed these in your minds, devote yourselves to the study and practice of the *Mantrayānic* Doctrines. I have obtained spiritual knowledge through giving up all thought of food, clothing, and name. Inspired with zeal in my heart, I bore every hardship and inured myself to all sorts of privations of the body; I devoted myself to meditation in the most unfrequented and solitary places. Thus did I obtain knowledge and experience; do ye also follow in the path trodden by me, and practise devotion as I have done.'

This is the Sixth Meritorious Act, which telleth how Jetsün, after giving up all thoughts of worldly ease, comfort, name, and fame, obeyed his *Guru's* commands by devoting himself to incessant meditating in the most unfrequented hills and solitudes, and thus passed his whole time in devotion.

## CHAPTER XI

# THE HERMITAGES AND SERVICE RENDERED TO SENTIENT BEINGS

*Telling of Jetsün's Disciples and Places of Meditation; and of the Recorded Writings concerning Jetsün.*

THEN Rechung said, ' Master, thy history could not be excelled for its wonderful humour and interest; and, although there is a vein of humour, which exciteth laughter, running through the whole narrative, yet, on the whole, it is so pathetic, that one cannot help shedding tears. I pray that thou wilt be pleased to tell us now of those incidents which would excite laughter.' And Jetsün said, ' No more true cause for laughter could ye expect than the account of the success attending the zealous devotional efforts which enabled me to save both well-endowed human and non-human beings, and to place them on the Path of Emancipation, and thus to serve the Cause of the Buddhist Faith.'

Again Rechung asked, ' Master, who were thy first disciples; were they human or non-human beings?' To this, Jetsün answered, ' Non-human beings were my first disciples, those that had come with intent to torment me. Afterwards, I gained a few human disciples. Then came the Goddess Tseringma,[1] to test me by displaying various super-normal powers. Subsequently, other human disciples began to gather round me. My teachings, as I now perceive, will be promulgated by Tseringma among non-human beings, and by Upa-Tönpa among human beings.'

Then Seban-Repa asked, ' Master, besides thy chief hermitage in the Cave of Lapchi-Chūbar, and some hermitages in the caves previously mentioned, where else hast thou meditated?' Jetsün replied, ' Another of my hermitages was Yölmo-Kangra, in Nepal. In addition, I had six outer well-known

---

[1] A deity of the Kailāsa Mountain—one of the twelve guardian goddesses of Tibet called *Bsten-mas* (pron. *Ten-mas*). Tseringma (a Tibetan name meaning ' Long-Life ') is probably a form of the Indian Goddess Durgā, the Spouse of Shiva, the God of the Himalayas.

and six inner unknown caves [in high cliffs], and six secret [or hidden] caves—in all, eighteen. Then there were two more caves, making altogether twenty castles. Again, there are four larger well-known caves and four larger unknown caves, which are included among those named before. Besides these, I meditated in various other smaller caves and solitudes wherever necessaries appeared to be plentiful—till, at last, the object of meditation, the act of meditation, and the meditator were so interwoven with each other that now I do not know how to meditate.'[1]

Then Rechung said, 'Lord, by thy having attained the final goal of *Dharma* and exhausted [its Treasures], we, thy humble disciples, enjoy the benefit thereof, for thou impartest the Doctrine to us in such an easy and impressive manner that we can, with very little effort, grasp the true meaning, and attain firmness in our belief without any fear of misconception. This feeling of security in our belief is due to thy kindness and divine grace. But future disciples may wish to acquire merit [by visiting the caves wherein thou didst meditate] ; so, with a view to leaving them some guidance thereto, I pray that thou wilt be pleased to name each of them.'

Then Jetsün replied, as follows : 'The six well-known caves [in high cliffs][2] are : (1) Dragkar-Taso-Ūma-Dzong (Central Castle [or Cave] of Rock White Like Horse Teeth) ; (2) Min-khyüt-Dribma-Dzong (Castle Lying in Shadows to the Eyebrows) ; (3) Lingwa-Dragmar-Dzong (Block Castle of Red Rock) ; (4) Ragma-Changchup-Dzong (Perfect Castle of Ragma) ; (5) Kyang-Phan-Namkha-Dzong (Castle of the Banner-Adorned Sky) ; (6) Dragkya-Dorje-Dzong (Indestructible Castle of Grey Rock). The six inner unknown caves [in high cliffs] are : (1) Chonglūng-Khyungi-Dzong (Castle of Chonglūng-Khyung) ; (2) Khyipa-Nyima-Dzong (Joyful Sun Castle) ; (3) Khujuk-Enpa-Dzong (Castle of the Solitary Cuckoo) ; (4) Shelphug-Chushing-Dzong (Plantain Castle of the Crystal

[1] That is to say, meditation had become so second nature to Milarepa that he, no longer needing to think how to meditate, had forgotten the process.

[2] Jetsün seems to apply the name of *Dzong* (Castle or Stronghold) to those caves which were situated in high cliffs, that is, to caves in the face of cliffs and rocks at a dizzy height.

Grotto); (5) Bektse-Döyön-Dzong (Castle of the Savoury Cabbages); and (6) Tsigpa-Kangthil-Dzong (Castle of the Rock-Foot's Sole). And the six very secret caves [in high cliffs] are: Gyadrak-Namkha-Dzong (Sky Castle Filled with Awesome Symbols); (2) Tagphug-Sengé-Dzong (Lion Castle of the Tiger's Cave); (3) Bayphug-Mamo-Dzong (Castle of the Hidden Cave); (4) Laphug-Pema-Dzong (Lotus Castle of the Grotto); (5) Langno-Ludüt-Dzong (Nāga Castle of the Elephant-Door); and (6) Trogyal-Dorje-Dzong (Castle of the Victorious Bronze *Vajra*). The other two are: Kyiphug-Nyima-Dzong (Sun Castle of the Happy Grotto), and Potho-Namkha-Dzong (Castle of the Sky of Peaks).[1]

' Then, the four well-known larger caves are: (1) Nyanam-Tröpa-Phug (Stomach-like Cave of Nyanam); (2) Lapchi-Dütdül-Phug (Cave wherein Demons were Defeated, in Lapchi); (3) Brin-Briche-Phug (Yak-Cow Tongue Cave, in Brin); and (4) Tisé-Dzu-Trül-Phug (Miracle Cave, in Mt. Kailāsa). The four unknown larger caves are: (1) Tsayi-Kangtsu-Phug, or Kangtsu-Phug of Kyanga-Tsa (Cave wherein he [Milarepa] was set upon his feet in devotion, in Kyanga-Tsa);[2] (2) Ödsal-Phug (Cave of the Clear Light)[3] of Rön; (3) Zawog-Phug (Cave of Silk) of Rala; and (4) Phurön-Phug (Pigeon Cave) of Kuthang. One meditating in these caves will find in plenty the necessities of life [i.e. fuel, water, roots, and herbs] and will be inspired by the grace of the previous Masters of the Apostolic Succession. Therefore go there to meditate.'

On Jetsün's saying this, the whole assembly of disciples—celestial and human, male and female—who had come to hear the *Dharma* preached, were profoundly moved. The narrative excited them to deep and fervent faith, and so touched their hearts that they renounced the Eight Worldly Pursuits, of ambition and affluence. All of them found such complete satisfaction in the religious life, after arriving at the true appreciation of the Sacred *Dharma*, that they became inseparably

---

[1] M. Bacot's renderings of the place-names in this paragraph have, in part, been followed. There is probably an esoteric significance attached to each name; cf. p. 212[1].

[2] This was the cave behind Milarepa's own house.

[3] As to the Clear Light, see p. 145[n].

attached to it. The more highly advanced among the human disciples resolved to devote their body, heart, and speech, to the service of all sentient beings, and to the Faith; and they vowed to pass their whole life in undisturbed and immovable meditation and penance, in caves and solitudes. The non-human disciples promised and vowed to maintain and protect the Faith. And many of the most spiritually developed among the human lay-disciples, both male and female, forsook the worldly life and, following Jetsün wherever he went, spent their time in meditation, and came to realize the True State. Thus several became *Yogīs* and *Yoginīs*.[1] Those of lesser spiritual insight took vows to devote a certain number of years and months to devotion. The least among the lay-followers vowed to give up some particular impious act for the remainder of their life, and to practise some particular pious act. Thus was the entire congregation successfully saved.

The whole of the above history, recorded herein, is what Jetsün himself narrated—an autobiographical narrative taken down in writing. When these historical facts which form the chief subject-matter of his life-history are set forth in more expanded form, they are commonly divided into three principal parts. The first part treateth of the malevolent attacks by the non-human beings, who were eventually defeated and converted. The second part treateth of the human disciples, of whom many of the most fortunate were led to perfect [spiritual] development and Emancipation. The third part treateth of various other disciples, both lay and initiated, to whom Jetsün preached the *Dharma*.

If further expanded, the life-history goeth on to narrate the manner in which the first non-human beings were conquered and converted. Thus, at Dragmar-Chonglung Cave, the King of Sprites, Vināyaka, was conquered by the singing of the song called '*Lāma-Dren-Drug*' ('The Six Ways in which he [Milarepa] yearned for a sight of his *Guru*'). Then Jetsün went to Lapchi-Kang, in obedience to his *Guru's* injunction. There he converted the great deity, Gaṇapati, whence originated the

---

[1] *Yoginī* is the feminine, *Yogī* the masculine, term applied to devotees who practise or, as here, are proficient in *Yoga*.

Chapter on Lapchi-Chūzang. The next year, Jetsün penetrated into the interior of Lapchi, and this resulted in the production of the well-known Song about the great snow-fall [and Jetsün's triumph over the snow], which he sang on his emerging from the snow. Then, again, intending to go to Mount Palbar, in Mangyül, and to Yölmo-Kangra,[1] in Nepal, he returned to Gungthang, where he felt attracted by the Rock Cave of Lingwa, and spent some time there. The Chapter on the malignant demoness of the Lingwa-Cave was the result of this sojourn. Then, in the vicinity of Mount Palbar, where lieth the Perfect Castle of Ragma, Jetsün defeated and converted a fairy goddess and the local deities of Ragma [by chanting a hymn to them]. This is described in the Chapter concerning their conversion. Then, while Jetsün was staying at the Castle of the Banner-Adorned Sky, he did good to a number of both human and non-human beings. Jetsün next visited Yölmo-Kangra, and lived for some time in the Singala Forest, in the depths of which lay the Lion Castle of the Tiger's Cave. There, too, he did good to a great many human and non-human beings. While at this place, Jetsün received a Divine Admonition telling him to go to Tibet and to meditate there for the good of all sentient beings. So Jetsün went to Tibet, and dwelt in the [Pigeon] Cave of Kuthang. It was there that he chanted the Hymn to the Pigeons.

Secondly, there is the account of how Jetsün first met his disciples. Thus, when Jetsün was at the Indestructible Castle of Grey Rock, and doing good to a great many sentient beings, the Divine Mother (Vajra-Yoginī)[2] told Jetsün that many disciples would come to him, and particularly one [Rechung-Dorje-Tagpa] who would bring to Tibet from India the *Ḍākinī Tantra*.[3] The very place where he would be found was made known to Jetsün. Accordingly, Jetsün went to Gungthang and sat meditating in the Silk Cave of Rala, where he met Rechung. Thereafter, Rechung went to India to be cured of a malady [i. e. leprosy]. After his coming back cured, he dwelt with

---

[1] This is a place about two days' journey north of Khatmandu.

[2] Tib. *Rdo-rje-rnal-hbyor-ma* (pron. *Do-rje-Nal jor-ma*) : Skt. *Vajra-Yoginī*.

[3] Or *Karṇa Tantra*, one of the esoteric treatises on Tantric *Yoga*. (See p. 148[2].)

Jetsün in the Clear-Light Cave of Rön, where Tsa-Phu-Repa
joined them. Then, at the Perfect Castle of Ragma, he met
Sangyay-Kyap-Repa. Having gone on to the Stomach-like
Cave of Nyanam, he preached the *Dharma*, and initiated Tönpa-
Shākya-Guna, who had been a lay believer for some time
previously, and set him on the Path of Perfection and Emancipation. Then, while going to Chang-Tago, he met the female
lay disciple, Paldar-Būm, at Chungi-Ketpa-Le-sum. On his
return thence, he met Seban-Repa, at a public rest-house of
Yeru-Chang. From there, he went to meditate in a mountain
called Gyalgyi-Shrī-La, in Latöt, and met Bri-Gom-Repa. While
begging alms, during the autumn, he met Shiwa-Wöd-Repa,
at Chūmig-Ngülbūm. At Chim-lūng, he delivered the sermon
called the 'Bamboo Staff' to Ngan-Dzong-Repa. From Lapchi,
Jetsün. being reminded of his *Guru's* injunction by the *Ḍākinīs*,
set out for Mount Tisé,[1] and met Dampa-Gya-Phūpa. While
approaching [the Mount] he met Khar-Chūng-Repa at the
Lowo-Kara Pass. Then, when in winter retreat, in the vicinity
of the Dritse Peak, near the Purang Hills, he encountered
Tarma-Wangchuk-Repa. During the ensuing Spring, Jetsün
went to [Mount] Tisé, and triumphed over [the magician]
Naro-Bön-chūng, by the display of his magical powers. The
account of this constituteth the Chapter on Tisé [or Mount
Kailāsa].

Next, coming back to the Indestructible Castle of Grey
Rock, he met Rong-Chūng-Repa. Proceeding thence, as
directed by the *Ḍākinīs*, he came across the Castle of the
Hidden Cave, and lived in it for a few days. While there, he
encountered a shepherd, who followed him and became a very
prominent *Yogī*, known as Lugdzi-Repa (Shepherd Repa).
Then he met Shan-Gom-Repa, at the Lotus Castle of the
Grotto. This disciple supplied Jetsün with excellent food and
other necessaries as long as Jetsün thereafter dwelt in the
Nāga Castle of the Elephant-Door and the Castle of the
Hidden Cave. Then, when he was going to Choro-Dri-Tsam,
he met Rechungma, [a female disciple]. At Nyishang-Gurta-

---

[1] Mount Tisé is the Tibetan name for Mount Kailāsa, the Holy Mount of both
Buddhism and Hinduism, and the goal of the famous Kailāsa Pilgrimage.

La, he met Khyira-Repa (Hunter Repa). This led to the fame of Jetsün spreading far and wide towards Nepal, and the Rāja of Khokhom[1] was directed by the Goddess Tārā[2] to send some religious offerings to Jetsün. Then Rechung and Shan-Gom-Repa entreated Jetsün to return to Lapchi; and Jetsün dwelt in the Nyen-yön Cave, at the foot of Lapchi. The next year, Jetsün lived in the rock-cave at Chong-lūng. Coming thence to Chūbar, he preached the three sermons regarding Tseringma.

Coming down thence to the interior of Brin, he came across Dorje-Wangchuk-Repa. Then when Jetsün and his disciples were living in the Stomach-like Cave of Nyanam, the great Indian *Yogī*, Dharma-Bodhi, visited Jetsün and bowed down to him. This circumstance, having added to the respect and veneration felt for Jetsün, excited the envy of a Lāma well versed in metaphysical discourses, and he proposed some metaphysical questions to Jetsün, which Jetsün easily answered by a display of *siddhi* [or occult power]. There is one Chapter which treateth of this contest. The *Yogī's* visit led to Rechung's visiting India again; record is made of this in the Chapter on Rechung and Tiphoo [another Great Indian *Yogī*]. During this time, Me-Gom-Repa joined Jetsün, as a follower, at the Cave of Dröt [in Nyanam]. Again, at Nagtra, in Nyanam, Jetsün met Salewöd-Repa. Then Jetsün, having gone into retreat on the summit of the Red Rock, saw Rechung returning [from India], and went to receive him. This produced the Chapter concerning the Yak's Horn, and the Song about the Wild Asses. At Chūbar he met Tagpo-Lan-Gom-Repa.

It was at Trode-Trashi-Gang, in Brin, that he met with the *Mahā-Puruṣha* (Great Saint), who has been mentioned by the Buddha in His apocryphal sayings.[3] He became the most favoured and eminent among the disciples of Jetsün. He was a fully ordained priest, and a *Guru* of the Vajra-Dhara

---

[1] Khokhom is the modern Bhatgaon, near Khatmandu, Nepal. (Cp. p. 16.)

[2] The National Goddess-Protectress of Tibet, who is imaged in numerous forms and colours.

[3] To judge from this, the Great Saint was one of those who are reputed to have lived on for centuries, and who, so Indians and Tibetans believe, still exist on Earth as the Guardians of the Human Race.

School,[1] a Great Bodhisattva, by name Dawöd-Shyönü (Youthful Lunar Light), but better known as the Peerless Doctor of Tagpo, who has taken birth as a human being in order to benefit all sentient creatures.

At Chūbar-Wom-Chūng, Jetsün made a proselyte of Lotön-Gedün, who, although antagonistic to Jetsün formerly, now became his disciple. At the Sun Castle of the Happy Grotto, Dretön-Trashibar, of Brin, became Jetsün's disciple. On Jetsün's manifesting certain super-normal powers, Likor-Charūwa was moved to discipleship.

The *Ḍākinīs* had foretold that Jetsün would have twenty-five Saints among his human disciples ; and these are : The eight most favoured sons, [born of the heart], the thirteen spiritual sons, and their four sisters in the Faith. There is a Chapter recording how Jetsün met each of them.

Thirdly, with regard to various other meetings and incidents, which occurred while Jetsün dwelt in the secret caves, during the intervals of his encounterings with the spiritual sons, records have been made, but without any accuracy as to the time of their occurrence. Again, there are some [records in the form of] answers to [disciples'] questions. Then, there is the Chapter recording the Songs of the Mountains of Bönpo, dating from the time when Gampopa was with Jetsün. There are also the narratives of how Jetsün preached the *Dharma* and granted initiation to the people at Nyanam ; the Songs about Shendormo and Lesay-Būm, at Tsarma ; and the Song containing Jetsün's exquisite expressions of delight at the prospect of death ; then the Songs about Jetsün's being accompanied by Rechung to Lapchi and their sojourn in the Cave of the Demons' Defeat, and of a pleasure trip, and of Ramding-Namphug, whence Jetsün was invited by the people of Nyanam to the Stomach-like Cave of Nyanam, where he narrated his own life-history. Then come the Songs about Rechung's departure to the Province of Ü, and about Jetsün's meeting afterward with Dampa-Sangyay, at Thong-La, by the special arrangement of the Lion-faced Goddess.

---

[1] That is, the School of which Vajra-Dhara is the Celestial *Guru* ; otherwise known as the *Vajra-Yāna* ('Immutable [*Vajra*] Path') School.

There are still other records : of a funeral ceremony performed by Jetsün, out of compassion for a dead person, at Lay-Shing; his discharge of filial duties to his deceased mother; the final testament to the lay-disciples, at Tsarma; a narrative of Jetsün's performance of a Bönpo-rite,[1] at Tingri, when on his way to Chūbar; the Chapter on the second departure of Rechung to Ü; the Chapter on the lay-donor, Tashi-Tseg, of Ḍin-Lhaḍo; the Chapter on Zesay-Būm, and Khujug, and other female disciples, at Ḍin-Ḍag-Khạr; the Chapter on his triumph over the four Māras [or Evil Spirits], on the summit of the Red Rock; the Dialogue with the Magician; and the display of his super-normal powers for the benefit of his disciples and lay-followers. There is, in addition, quite a large collection of other religious discourses, some well known, some little known.

In this way did Jetsün emancipate a countless number of fortunate beings. The most highly developed of them attained perfect [spiritual] development and Emancipation; those of lesser ability were set firmly upon the Path of Emancipation; the least among them had their hearts thoroughly converted and inclined towards the Noble Path of Righteousness; even those whose *karma* denied them the share of the Most Priceless Boon had an inherent and habitual love of goodness implanted in their hearts, thereby winning the blessing of celestial and human happiness for their immediate future.

Thus, through his infinite love and grace, Jetsün made the Buddhist Faith as luminous as the light of day, saving an innumerable number of beings from Sorrow. All of this is recorded at length in the *Gur-Bum* ('One Hundred Thousand Songs') of Jetsün.

This constituteth the Seventh Meritorious Act of Jetsün, wherein is related how he rendered service to all sentient creatures by the fruits of his devotion.

---

[1] This is interesting, as showing that Jetsün was familiar with the pre-Buddhistic religion of Tibet known as Bön, and sympathetic towards it.

## CHAPTER XII

# THE *NIRVĀNA*

*Telling of how Jetsün came to take Poisoned Curds from Tsaphuwa's Concubine ; of the Last Assembly of Jetsün's Followers and the Attendant Marvels ; of Jetsün's Discourse on Illness and Death ; of His Final Testamentary Teachings ; of the Conversion of Tsaphuwa ; of the Last Will ; of the Passing away in* Samādhi, *and the Resultant Super-normal Phenomena ; of Rechung's Late Arrival and Prayer to Jetsün, and the Answer ; of the Marvellous Events Connected with the Cremation and the Reliques ; of the Execution of Jetsün's Last Will ; and concerning his Disciples.*

AT the time when Jetsün had fulfilled the various duties mentioned above, there lived, in the interior of Brin (Ḍrin), a learned Lāma named Tsaphuwa, very rich and influential, who was accustomed to take the highest seat in the assemblies of the people of Brin. This man feigned great reverence for Jetsün, while at heart he was bursting with envy of him, and desirous of exposing what he took to be Jetsün's ignorance, by putting difficult questions to Jetsün in a public gathering of his own supporters. In this wise he asked Jetsün many and various questions, all the while pretending that it was for the clearing of his own doubts.

Then, in the first month of the autumn of the Wood-Tiger year,[1] there happened to be a grand marriage feast to which Jetsün was invited, and he was placed on the highest seat at the head of the first row of guests, and the *Geshé*[2] Tsaphuwa was seated next to him. The *Geshé* bowed down to Jetsün, expecting that Jetsün would bow down to him in return. Jetsün, however, did not do so ; for never having bowed down to, nor returned the obeisance of, any person save his own *Guru*, he did not depart from his usual custom on this occasion.

Much chagrined, the *Geshé* thought to himself, ' What !

---

[1] This is the forty-eighth year of the sixty-year cycle described on p. 52[1].

[2] The title *Geshé* implies a learned Lāma ; it is equivalent to the Indian term *Paṇḍit*.

shall so learned a *paṇḍit* as I am bow down to an ignoramus like him, and he not condescend to return the salutation! I shall certainly do my best to lower him in the esteem of the public.' And, producing a book on philosophy, he addressed Jetsün thus: 'O Jetsün, please be so good as to dissipate my perplexities by going through this book and explaining it to me word by word.'

Upon this, Jetsün answered, 'As for the mere word-by-word explication of these dialectics, thou thyself art sufficiently expert; but to realize their true import it is necessary to renounce the Eight Worldly Ambitions, lopping off their heads, to subdue the illusion of belief in the personal ego, and, regarding *Nirvāṇa* and *Sangsāra* as inseparable, to conquer the spiritual ego by meditation in mountain solitudes. I have never valued or studied the mere sophistry of word-knowledge, set down in books in conventionalized form of questions and answers to be committed to memory (and fired off at one's opponent); these lead but to mental confusion and not to such practice as bringeth actual realization of Truth. Of such word-knowledge I am ignorant; and if ever I did know it, I have forgotten it long ago. I pray that thou wilt give ear to the song which I am about to sing, to show my reasons for forgetting book-learning.'[1]   And then Jetsün sang this song:

'Obeisance to the honoured Feet of Marpa the Translator!
    May I be far removed from arguing creeds and dogmas.

'E'er since my Lord's Grace entered in my mind,
    My mind hath never strayed seeking various distractions.

'Accustomed long to contemplating Love and Pity,
    I have forgot all difference between myself and others.

'Accustomed long to meditating on my *Guru* as enhaloed
        o'er my head,[2]
    I have forgot all those who rule by power and by prestige.

---

[1] Cf. the teaching of the *Bṛihadāraṇyaka Upaniṣhad* (3. 5. 1): 'Put away scholarship (*pāṇḍitya*) and be like a child'; and also *Luke* (xviii. 17): 'Whosoever shall not receive the Kingdom of God as a little child shall in no wise enter therein.'

[2] See p. 171[1].

'Accustomed long to meditating on my Guardian Gods as
   from myself inseparable,
I have forgot the lowly fleshly form.

'Accustomed long to meditating on the Whispered Chosen
   Truths,
I have forgot all that is said in written and in printed books.

'Accustomed, as I've been, to the study of the Common Science,
Knowledge of erring Ignorance I've lost.

'Accustomed, as I've been, to contemplating the Three
   Bodies [1] as inherent in myself,
I have forgot to think of hope and fear.

'Accustomed, as I've been, to meditating on this life and the
   future life as one,
I have forgot the dread of birth and death.

'Accustomed long to studying, all by myself, mine own experiences,
I have forgot the need of seeking the opinions of friends and
   brethren.

'Accustomed long to application of each new experience to
   mine own growth spiritual,
I have forgot all creeds and dogmas.

'Accustomed long to meditating on the Unborn, the Indestructible, and the Unabiding,[2]
I have forgot all definitions of this or that particular Goal.

'Accustomed long to meditating on all visible phenomena as
   the *Dharma-Kāya*,
I have forgot all mind-made meditations.

'Accustomed long to keep my mind in the Uncreated State
   of Freedom,[3]
I have forgot conventional and artificial usages.

---

[1] The *Tri-Kāya* (or 'Three Bodies'): the *Dharma-Kāya*, the *Sambhoga-
Kāya*, and the *Nirmāṇa-Kāya*. (See p. 167[1].)

[2] Or 'That which hath neither commencement, nor negation, nor place';
that is, *Nirvāṇa*.

[3] That is, the unmodified or natural state of mind, which is the state of mind
of the *Dharma-Kāya*.

' Accustomed long to humbleness, of body and of mind,
  I have forgot the pride and haughty manner of the mighty.

' Accustomed long to regard my fleshly body as my hermitage,
  I have forgot the ease and comfort of retreats in monasteries.

' Accustomed long to know the meaning of the Wordless,
  I have forgot the way to trace the roots of verbs and source
      of words and phrases ;
  May thou, O learned one, trace out these things in standard
      books.'

When Jetsün had sung this song, the *Geshé* said, ' All this
may be very well according to thy *yogī* creed, but, following
our metaphysicians, such religious discourses lead nowhere
[i. e. show no real attainment of understanding]. I bowed
down to thee imagining thee to be a highly advanced person ! '

Upon his saying this, the people (especially his own supporters) showed displeasure, and, as though with one voice,
cried, ' O *Geshé* Tönpa, however learned thou mayst be, and
however many professors like thee the world may hold, the
whole lot of you are not equal to the smallest downy hair on
Jetsün's body, nor able to fill the tiny pore containing it. Thou
hadst better be satisfied with the seat assigned to thee, at the
head of our row, and do what thou canst to add to thy wealth
by usury. As for religion, thou art not in the least permeated
with its perfume.'

The *Geshé* was much angered by this, but as the whole
party were unanimously against him, he could not show fight,
and so he merely sat in sulky silence, thinking to himself,
' This ignoramus, Milarepa, by mere display of eccentric
doings and sayings and telling of lies, which tend to overthrow
the Buddhist Faith, is able to delude the people into making
him numerous alms and gifts, whereas I, though so learned in
book-learning, and the wealthiest and most influential person
in the place, count for less than a dog despite my religious
attainments. Something must be done to put an end to this.'

Acting on this resolve, he induced a concubine of his, by
promising her a valuable turquoise, to go and offer Jetsün
some poisoned curds, which she did, while Jetsün was at Brin-

Dragkar (Rock of Brin). Having fulfilled his duty of setting his *karma*-favoured disciples upon the Path of Emancipation and Perfection, Jetsün knew that his term of life was almost ended, even if he did not take the poison. But foreseeing that unless the woman procured the turquoise now she would not procure it afterward [i. e. after the commission of the crime], he said to her, 'For the present, I will not accept the food thou offerest me. Bring it later on and I will then accept it.'

Thinking that perhaps Jetsün knew her intention, the woman, much embarrassed and distressed, returned to the *Geshé*, and, relating to him the whole incident at length, said that Jetsün, in virtue of clairvoyance, had detected her evil design and refused the poisoned food. But her seducer, trying to embolden her, said, ' If Jetsün possessed this power he would not have asked thee to take the food to him later on, but would have handed it back, telling thee to take it thyself; this is proof that he doth not possess clairvoyance. Thou mayst now have the turquoise, but be sure that he taketh the poisoned food.' Then he gave her the turquoise ; and she said, ' That Jetsün doth possess clairvoyant power is commonly believed, and his refusal of the food the first time proveth it. I am satisfied that he will refuse the food the second time. I do not want thy turquoise ; I am too much afraid to go to him again ; and most certainly I will not go.'

The *Geshé* replied, ' Illiterate folk believe that he possesseth the power, but, not being conversant with the Scriptures, they are duped by his trickery. The Scriptures describe a person possessed of clairvoyance as quite different from a person such as he is ; I am convinced that he doth not possess it. Now, if thou undertake to offer him the food again, and succeed in getting him to eat it, thereupon—seeing that we two have already lived together, and, as the proverb sayeth, " No difference is there in taking a big or a little bite of garlic, since garlic it is "—we will thenceforth live openly as husband and wife. Then not only will the turquoise be thine, but thou wilt be the mistress of all that I own ; and we will share weal and woe together. As we thus have the grudge in common, do thine utmost to bring the attempt to a successful issue.'

Taking the *Geshé* at his word, the woman, tempted to try a second time, again mixed poison and curd together and took the mixture to Jetsün as a food-offering, when he was at Trode-Trashi-Gang. Smilingly, Jetsün took her offering in his hand, and she thought that the *Geshé* was perhaps right in asserting that Jetsün did not possess clairvoyance. Just then, however, Jetsün spoke and said, 'Thou hast procured the turquoise as thy fee for doing this deed.' Overcome with remorse and fear, the woman began to tremble; and, in quavering sob-choked voice, confessed, 'Yes; Lord; I have procured the turquoise'; and, prostrating herself at his feet, she begged him not to partake of the poisoned food, but to give it back to her who was guilty of so heinous an intention [that she might drink it].

Jetsün answered, 'First of all, I cannot, on any account, give it back to thee to drink; my compassion for thee is too great. Were I to do so, I should be transgressing the vows of a Bodhisattva, and thus incur the heaviest of spiritual penalties. Moreover, my life hath almost run its course; my work is finished; the time hath come for me to go to another world.[1] Thy poisoned food would have no effect upon me whatsoever. Nevertheless, I refused it at first, in order to enable thee to gain the turquoise, which was promised to thee as the fee for thy crime. Now that the turquoise is thine, I will take the poisoned food, to satisfy the desire of the *Geshé* and to secure thee in possession of the coveted turquoise. As regardeth the many promises for the future which he hath made to thee on condition that this crime be successfully accomplished, thou needest place no reliance on them; for he will disappoint thee. There is no truth at all in any of the many things which he hath said against me. The time shall come when both thou and he will deeply repent of all these things. When that time cometh, ye will devote yourselves wholly, if possible, to penance and devotion; but if unable to do so much, at least avoid committing such heinous sins, even though your very life be

---

[1] Jetsun is 'to go to another world', whence he will return to this world, to continue his work as a Teacher, in accordance with his Vow not to enter *Nirvāṇa* (the Final Release from *saṅgsāric* existence) until all sentient creatures are led to Salvation.

at stake, and pray to me and my disciples in deep and humble faith.  Left unassisted, ye two would be cut off from happiness for countless ages, and suffering would thus be your lot; so, for this once, I will see if I can absolve your evil *karma*.[1]  But I command thee to keep this affair secret for as long as I am alive; the time will come when it will be known to every one.  Although thou mayst not believe other sayings of mine upon hearing them, yet in this affair thou wilt have an opportunity of believing in me [or of being convinced].  Therefore, bear this well in mind, and await its fulfilment.'  Then Jetsün partook of the poisoned food.

When the woman had reported these things to the *Geshé*, he said, 'Everything that is spoken is not necessarily true.  [According to the proverb], "Not everything that is cooked is fit [for food]."[2]  Enough for me that he hath taken the poison.  Now take heed and keep thy mouth shut.'

Then Jetsün sent word to the people of Tingri and Nyanam, and to all who had known him and had faith in him, to come to see him, each with a small offering.  He sent a like invitation to all who had a wish to meet him, but had never done so.  Also to all his disciples the message was proclaimed; and, greatly impressed by its ominous nature, each of them, male and female, initiated and uninitiated, acquainted and unacquainted with one another, assembled in a great assembly at Lapchi-Chūbar.  Then for many days Jetsün preached to them concerning the Apparent Truth [i.e. the Law of *Karma*] and the Real Truth [i.e. the *Dharma-Kāya*].

During these days, the more spiritually gifted of the hearers beheld the skies filled with gods listening [to the Master].  Many others felt [intuitively] that in the skies and on the earth there was an innumerable congregation of divine as of

---

[1] Evil *karma*, i. e. sin, cannot be absolved.  It can only be neutralized by an equal amount of merit or good *karma*, as in physics two equally balanced opposing forces neutralize one another.  Jetsün's promise to see if he can absolve the evil *karma* is probably intended merely to console the repentant woman.  Cf. Jetsün's teaching concerning the expiation of evil *karma*, pp. 251, 253, and 267 following.

[2] The sense of this seems to be, 'All that is said is not to be believed', in keeping with the context.

human beings, all joyfully listening to the preaching of the *Dharma*; and they felt a joyfulness pervading the whole gathering. And, to every one present, there appeared various phenomenal signs, such as rainbows arching a clear blue sky; [then again] clouds, of different colours, assuming the shapes of [royal] umbrellas, and banners, and different offerings; and showers of variegated blossoms. There was heard by all the most exquisite music from various musical instruments; and the most fragrant odours, such as none had ever before enjoyed, filled the air. Those of moderate spiritual development who experienced these phenomena of good omen, inquired of Jetsün why there was the feeling of wondrous communion between the celestial auditors filling the skies and the human auditors assembled on the earth, and why the various auspicious phenomenal signs, which every person present saw, had occurred.

Jetsün replied, 'Among human beings, the number who are spiritually developed, inclusive of both the initiated and the uninitiated, is not great, whereas those piously inclined among the divine beings, who are ever eager to hear the *Dharma*, fill the very skies and are offering to me in worship the five celestial objects of enjoyment,[1] and radiating, to all alike, joy and cheerfulness of mind. Thus do ye feel thrilled with gladness, and perceive the joyous and favourable signs.'

Thereupon, they asked him, 'Why, then, should the divine beings be invisible to [most of] us?' Jetsün replied, 'Many there are among the gods who have attained the *Anāgāmi State*,[2] and various other degrees of holiness; and, to be able to see them, it is necessary to be endowed with the perfected vision and the highest zeal in the acquirement of the two kinds of merit, and free from the two obscuring impurities born of Ignorance.[3] If the chiefs among the gods be seen, then, too, will their followers be seen. Whosoever desire to see these divine beings, must devote themselves to acquiring merit sufficient for the expiating of all evil *karma*. Thereupon, one may

---

[1] These are such as may be enjoyed by the five senses.

[2] That is, that degree of spiritual development which makes it no longer necessary to be reborn on Earth; *Anāgāmi* meaning 'The Non-Returning One'.

[3] See p. 33[5].

see in oneself the highest and holiest of all gods [which is the Pure Mind].'

Then Jetsün chanted a hymn on the way to see the gods:

'Obeisance at the Feet of Gracious Marpa!
Bless Thy Spiritual Descendants, that they may multiply.[1]

'To me, Milarepa, the Devotee,
Celestial beings, from Tuṣhita Heavens,
And other Holy Regions, come to hear my sermons.
Thy fill all quarters of the skies,
But only those [among my human followers] enjoying the
    five kinds of vision,[2]
Can behold them; the common folk behold them not;
Yet I myself without impediment see each of them.
For the good of all the congregation,
They offer reverence unto me, with heavenly offerings.

'The heavens are filled with radiance of rainbows;
Celestial showers of sweet-smelling blossoms fall;
All beings alike hear harmonies melodious, and fragrance
    of incense enjoy;
Love divine, and happiness, pervade the whole assembly.
Such are the [fruits of] Grace-Waves of the Kargyütpa
    Saints.[3]

'Taking to yourselves the Gracious Refuge of the Faith,
If ye desire to see the Gods and Angels,
Give ear attentively to this, my hymn:

---

[1] And so uphold the Kargyütpa Hierarchy.

[2] According to *lāmaic* teachings, there are, in addition to the normal human eyes of limited vision, five kinds of eyes : (1) Eyes of Instinct (or Eyes of the Flesh), like those of birds and beasts of prey, which, in most cases, possess greater range of vision than normal human eyes; (2) Celestial Eyes, such as the gods possess, capable of seeing the human world as well as their own, and the past and future births of beings in both worlds throughout many lifetimes; (3) Eyes of Truth, like the eyes of Bodhisattvas and Arhants, capable of seeing throughout hundreds of world-periods (or *Kalpas*) backwards and in the future; (4) Divine Eyes, of the most highly advanced Bodhisattvas, capable of seeing throughout millions of world-periods that which has been and that which will be ; and (5) Eyes of Wisdom of Buddhas, capable of seeing, in like manner, throughout eternity.

[3] That is, the Saints broadcast their spiritual influences, and these phenomena result.

'Because of evil *karma*, accumulated by you in past lives,
The moment ye are of your mother born, ye delight in sin-
    ning;
The doing of the good and merit-bringing deeds ye like not;
E'en till ye are grown old, your nature is perverse:
Thus surely must ye garner the results of evil actions.

'If ye wonder whether evil *karma* can be neutralized or not,
Then know that it is neutralized by desire for goodness.

'But they who knowingly do evil deeds,
Exchange a mouthful of food for infamy.[1]

'They who knowing not whither they themselves are bound,
Yet presume to pose as guides for others,
Do injury both to themselves and others.

'If pain and sorrow ye desire sincerely to avoid,
Avoid, then, doing harm to others.

'Repenting and confessing of all previous sins,
At the feet of the *Guru* and the Deities,
And vowing never more in future to commit a wrong,
Are the shortest path to rapid expiation of all evils done.

'The greater part of sinners are sharp-witted;
[Of mind] unstable and unfixed, they delight in various dis-
    tractions;[2]
And unendowed are they with love of the religious life:
This, in itself, doth signify that they are sin-obscured,
And need repentance and confession o'er and o'er.

'Do ye each give yourselves, with zeal,
To expiating sins and winning merit;
If thus ye do, not only shall ye see
The *Dharma*-loving deities celestial,
But the holiest and highest of all gods.

---

[1] This is similar to the saying that for a mess of pottage one selleth his birth-
right.

[2] That is, the worldly, in their attachment to the pleasures of life, are mentally
unstable, one-pointedness of mind, as attained through practice of the science of
mind-control called *Yoga*, being lacking in them; and they continue to be
bound to the Wheel of the *Sangsāra*.

The *Dharma-Kāya* of your own mind ye shall also see ;
And seeing That, ye shall have seen the All,
The Vision Infinite, the *Sangsāra* and *Nirvāna*.[1]
Then shall your *karmic* actions cease.'

Upon Jetsün's chanting this hymn, those of the assembled deities and human beings who were highly developed spiritually, obtained the right view of the *Dharma-Kāya* [or *Nirvānic*] State. Those of moderate development obtained experience of the super-sensuous divine state of Ecstatic Bliss and Voidness[2] such as they had never before known, and were helped thereby to enter upon the Path [of the Realization of *Nirvāna*]. And not one of all the others who were there but was desirous of gaining the Great Emancipation.

Then Jetsün addressed the congregation, saying, ' My disciples, gods, and men, and all who are assembled here to-day, our coming together is the result of good *karma* from past lives ; and in this life we have established a purer and holier relationship by religious communion. Now that I am grown very agèd, no certainty is there of our being able to meet again [in this lifetime]. I exhort you to preserve the religious discourses which I have delivered to you, and not to neglect them, but to carry their teachings into practice, in so far as ye can, in your daily lives. If ye do this, in whatever realm I may arrive at the Perfection of Buddhahood, ye shall be the first body of disciples to receive the Truth that I shall then preach. Therefore rejoice in this.'

When those present from Nyanam heard these words of the Lord Jetsün, they asked of one another whether the Master meant that he was about to leave this world in order to go and benefit some other world ; and said that, if this were his meaning, they should entreat him to ascend to the Paradise Realm from Nyanam, or, if that could not be, at least to bless Nyanam by a final visit. So they went to Jetsün, and, clasping his feet, entreated him with tear-filled eyes and in fervency of

---

[1] Or 'The Vision Infinite, the Round of Birth and Death, and the State of Freedom'.

[2] This is one of the states experienced in the *yogic* trance called *Samādhi*. (Cf. p. 36[5].)

faith and love to grant their prayer. In like manner did the
disciples and lay-followers from Tingri entreat Jetsün to go
to Tingri. To these entreaties Jetsün made reply :

'I am now too far advanced in years to go to Nyanam or
Tingri ; I will await death at Brin and Chūbar. Therefore,
each of ye may give me your parting good-wishes and return
home; I will meet all of you in the Sacred Paradises.'

Then they prayed that, if Jetsün were unable to visit their
countries, he might, at least, utter a blessing upon each of the
places which he had visited, and a special good-wish for those
people who had seen his face, or heard his voice, and listened
to his preaching ; and, in short, that not upon them alone
[should these blessings be], but upon all sentient creatures
throughout the universe.

To this entreaty, Jetsün said: 'Grateful am I for the faith
which ye have manifested in me, and for the necessities of
life with which ye have kept me supplied. I have shown my
thankfulness in having ever wished you well ; and, to do good
to you, I have preached the *Dharma* to you, whereby, through
obligation, a mutual bond hath been established between us.
And, now, seeing that I am a *Yogī* who hath realized the Truth,
it is my duty to utter for you a good-wish for peace and happiness, both temporal and spiritual, for the present time and
for all eternity.'

Then Jetsün sang the following good-wishes in verse :

'O Father and Protector of all Creatures, Thou Who hast
    Thine Own Good-Wishes realized,
Translator Marpa, I bow down at Thy Feet !

'O my disciples, here assembled, hearken unto me.
Kind, indeed, have ye been unto me,
And kind have I been unto you ;
May we, thus bound together by ties of mutual helpfulness,
Meet in the Realm of Happiness.[1]

'Ye donors of alms, who here are seated,
May ye live long, and be e'er prosperous ;

---

[1] Or '*Ngön-gah*' (Skt. *Amarāvatī*); see p. 44[2].

May no perverted thought find entry to your minds ;
May all your thoughts e'er pious be and lead to your success
    religiously.

' May peace harmonious bless this land ;
 May it be ever free from maladies and war ;
 May there be harvests rich, and increased yield of grain ;
 May every one delight in righteousness.

' May all who have beheld my face and heard my voice,
 And all who have my history known, and borne it in their
    heart,
 And all who have but heard my name and story,
 Meet me in the Realm of Happiness.

' May those who make a study of my life
 And emulate it, and dedicate themselves to meditation ;
 And each who shall transcribe, narrate, or listen to my
    history,
 Or whosoe'er shall read and venerate it,
 Or take it as their rule of conduct,
 Meet me in the Realm of Happiness.

' May every being in future time
 Who hath the will to meditate,
 In virtue of mine own austerities
 Be free from all impediment and error.[1]

' To them who for devotion's sake endure hardships,
 There cometh boundless merit ;
 To them who shall lead others to the treading of the Path,
 Boundless gratitude is due ;
 To them who hear the story of my life,
 There cometh boundless grace :
 By the power of this boundless merit, gratitude, and grace,
 May every being, as soon as they shall hear [my history],
    attain Deliverance,
 And [True] Success as soon as they shall contemplate [it].

[1] In *Dhyāna* (or Meditation) there are many subtle dangers ; and, unless
guided by an experienced *Guru*, such as Milarepa herein becomes to all who
follow and venerate him, the beginner is apt to meet with so many impediments
and so much error as to prevent all true spiritual progress on the Path.

' May the places of my sojourn, and the objects whereon I have
    rested,
And every little thing which hath been mine,
Bring peace and gladness wheresoe'er they be.

' The earth, the water, fire, and air,
And the ethereal spaces wheresoever they pervade—
May I be able to embrace them all.

' And may the *Devas*, *Nāgas*, and the Spirits of Eight Orders,
And all the local genii and the sprites,
Do not the least of harm ;
But may they each fulfil these wishes in accordance with the
    *Dharma*.

' May none of living creatures, none e'en of insects,
Be bound unto *sangsāric* life ; nay, not one of them ;
But may I be empowered to save them all.'

At these words, the lay-disciples showed great joy, for they
now doubted whether Jetsün meant to pass away; so that those
of Nyanam and Tingri were all the more eager to seek his
grace and blessings, and to listen to his religious discourses.

As soon as the congregation had dispersed and every one
had gone home, the heavenly rainbows and the other phenomena automatically vanished.

Now the people of Brin earnestly begged Jetsün, through
Shiwa-Wöd-Repa and other advanced disciples, to preach to
them. Accordingly, Jetsün went to dwell in a hermitage which
had been built on the top of a rock known as ' Poisonous-
to-Touch ', for the rock was believed to be the serpent-hood
crowning the malignant Serpent-Spirit of Brin, the hermitage
having been built there in order that the Serpent-Spirit should
be subjugated [in virtue of hermits dwelling therein] ; and
there Jetsün continued his preaching to his lay-disciples of
Brin. When he had completed his sermons, he said to them,
' Those who have points to be elucidated, or perplexities to be
cleared concerning the special teachings which they have
received, should make haste to present them, for I am not
sure of living much longer.'

So the assembled disciples gathered together offerings for

performing a *pūjā*, and having performed the *pūjā*, listened to
the completion of the special teachings [as Jetsün made the
elucidations and cleared the perplexities]. Then Bri-Gom-
Repa and Seban-Repa, addressing Jetsün, asked, 'O Jetsün,
from what thou hast [just] said we have come to fear lest thou
intend to pass away into *Nirvāna*. It cannot be that thy
life hath run its course?' Jetsün replied, 'My life and mine
influence in converting others have reached their completion.
Therefore must I now meet the consequence of having been
born.'

A few days later, Jetsün showed signs of illness, and Ngan-
Dzong-Repa began preparations for making propitiatory offerings in the worship of the *Gurus*, the *Devas*, and the *Ḍākinīs*,
on behalf of the disciples ; and, at the same time, he begged
Jetsün to take medical and other treatment. He was about to
summon all the laymen and disciples to complete the necessary preparations; but Jetsün said, 'It is commonly the rule
that illness befalling a *yogī* is to be looked upon as an exhortation to persevere in devotion, and he ought not to have any
special prayers offered up for his recovery. He should utilize
illness as an aid to progression on the Path, ever ready to
meet suffering, and even death. As for me, Milarepa, I have,
by the grace of my gracious *Guru*, Marpa, completed all
special rites for overcoming illness, according to his particular
method ; and now I need neither forces nor mediators. I have
made mine enemies [1] to be bosom friends ; so I need not the
making of prayers or expiatory offerings. Nor do I need
exorcisms or propitiatory rites to any demons ; for I have transmuted all bad omens and evil presentiments into Guardian
Deities of the Faith,[2] who will perform all the four kinds of
ceremonies. The Maladies born of the Five Poisons, I have
changed into the Bliss of the Five Divine Wisdoms ;[3] therefore do I need not medicines compounded of the six chief
spices.[4] The time hath come when the visible, illusory, phy-

---

[1] These are interruptions and misfortunes whilst following the religious life.

[2] These are the Realizations of Truth, born of the religious life.

[3] See p. 37[1].

[4] Namely, saffron, cardamom, cloves, nutmeg, sandalwood, and dried *ruta* :
cf. p. 155[4].

sical body, the mind-evolved form of the Divine Body [the *Dharma-Kāya*], must be merged into the Realms of Spiritual Light ; and for this no rites of consecration are necessary. Worldly folk who have heaped up evil *karma* during their lifetime, and who anticipate reaping, as the result, the pangs of birth, old age, illness, and death, in this world, vainly seek to evade or ameliorate the intensity and anguish thereof by means of propitiatory ceremonies and medical treatment. Neither through the power or authority of kings, nor the valour of the hero nor the charming form of the belle, nor the wealth of the rich, nor the fleetness of the coward, nor the oratory of an able pleader, can one ward off, or retard for a moment, the Decree of Time. There are no means or methods, be they peaceful, noble, fascinating, or stern,[1] which can buy off or stop the execution of this unalterable decree. If any there be who are truly fearful of those pangs, and sincerely seek to prevent their recurrence, and are really eager to attain a state of eternal bliss, I possess the secret rite for the attainment thereof.'

When Jetsün had thus spoken, some of the disciples prayed him to impart to them this ritual [or science] ; and Jetsün said, ' So be it. All worldly pursuits have but the one unavoidable and inevitable end, which is sorrow : acquisitions end in dispersion ; buildings, in destruction ; meetings, in separation ; births, in death. Knowing this, one should, from the very first, renounce acquisition and heaping-up, and building, and meeting ; and, faithful to the commands of an eminent *guru*, set about realizing the Truth [which hath no birth or death]. That alone is the best ritual [or science]. I have yet my last important testament to impart. This, forget ye not, I will do hereafter.'

Again Shiwa-Wöd-Repa and Ngan-Dzong-Repa addressed Jetsün, saying, ' O Jetsün, were thou to regain health, thou couldst continue to do good to many more sentient creatures. Therefore, even though thou dost not see fit to grant our prayers in full, yet in order that we may not have regrets

---

[1] These are the four divine methods of leading human beings to tread the Path of Emancipation.

hereafter, we again pray that thou wilt be pleased to perform
an efficacious Tantric ceremonial of worship for thy recovery;
and, at the same time, take some medicine.'

Jetsün answered, 'Were it not that my time had come,
I should have done as ye have requested. But, if one were to
condescend to perform a Tantric rite for the prolongation of
one's life without having, as the plea, the altruistic intention
to serve others, it would be as improper behaviour towards the
Divine Deities as it would be towards a king to ask him to
perform the menial service of sweeping and scrubbing one's
floor; and such act carrieth with it its own penalty. Therefore,
I adjure you never to perform sacred Tantric rites with a view
to success in worldly pursuits; though selfish folk [who know
no better] are not to blame in so doing. I have passed my
life in incessant practice of the Highest Tantric Truths, in
order to benefit all sentient beings; this will serve for religious
rites [for warding off evil] now. Because of such devotion, my
mind knoweth not how to move away from the firm Seat of
Truth [in *Samādhi*]; this will suffice for the rites for long life.
Marpa's remedies have eradicated the very roots of the diseases
of the Five Poisons [i.e. lust, hatred, stupidity, egotism,
jealousy]; this will serve for medical treatment. As for yourselves, merely to be devotees, or to have adopted the religious
career, will not suffice; ye must, in addition, use trials and
tribulations as aids on the Path. If one's time have not come,
and some evil interruption threaten one's life, there is no
harm in having recourse to medical treatment and [faith-cure]
rituals for one's recovery, providing such shall assist one on
the Path. Recent evils can be warded off by exercising the
very might of the correlative and interdependent chain of circumstances which result [from them]; and even those evils
themselves can be transmuted into blessings at such times.
Thus it was that in former times the Buddha, too, thinking of
the good of his lesser developed disciples, held out his hand
to have his pulse felt by the physician Jīvaka Kumāra, and
took the medicines prescribed. But when His time had come,
even He, the Lord Buddha, passed away into *Nirvāṇa*.
Likewise, now, my time hath come, and I will not have

recourse to medical treatment or any sort of ceremonies for my cure.'

Thus would Jetsün not allow anything to be done for him. Accordingly, the two advanced disciples entreated him to instruct them as follows : ' If Jetsün is really passing away to some other realm, then, for our good, how should the funeral ceremonies be performed, how should the bones and reliques be honourably preserved, and how should the *stūpas* and *tsha-tshas* be made ? Again, who should be elected as thy successor ; and how are the ceremonies on the anniversary [of thy passing away] to be conducted ? Then, too, which disciple is to follow this or that branch of religious practice, such as listening [to instruction], cogitating, or meditating [in solitude]. In all these matters we solicit thine own verbal directions.'

To this Jetsün answered, ' By the kind favour of Marpa, I have fulfilled all the duties of the *Sangsāra* and attained Deliverance [therefrom]. The three principles of my personality [i. e. body, speech, and mind] having been transmuted into the Body of Truth, there is no certainty that I shall leave a corpse behind me. There is, therefore, no need either of *stūpas* or of clay *tsha-tshas*. As I own no monastery or temple, I need not appoint any one to succeed me. The bleak, sterile hills, and the mountain peaks, and the other solitary retreats or hermitages, all of you may possess and occupy. All the sentient beings of the Six *Lokas* ye may protect as your children and followers. Instead of erecting *stūpas*, cultivate loving fondness towards all parts of the *Dharma*, and set up the Victorious Banner of Devotion ; and, in place of *tsha-tshas*, let there be uninterrupted daily repetitions of the fourfold prayer. For periodical ceremonies [in memory of my passing away], offer me earnest prayer from the innermost recesses of your hearts. As regardeth the method of acquiring practical knowledge, if ye find a certain practice increaseth your evil passions and tendeth to selfishness, abandon it, though it may appear virtuous ; and if any line of action tend to counteract the Five Evil Passions, and to benefit sentient beings, know that to be true and holy *Dharma*, and continue it, even though it should appear to be sinful [to those bound to worldly conventionalities].

' If, after having heard these counsels, one fail to follow them and, instead, infringe and trample upon them in defiance of the [Divine] Law, howsoever well-informed such a one may be, he will merely be earning a place in the lowest Hell. Life is short, and the time of death is uncertain; so apply yourselves to meditation. Avoid doing evil, and acquire merit, to the best of your ability, even at the cost of life itself. In short, the whole purport may be stated thus: Act so that ye have no cause to be ashamed of yourselves; and hold fast to this rule. If ye do thus, ye can be sure of never disobeying the commands of the Supreme Buddhas, notwithstanding any conflicting rules which may be found set down in writing. Herein is contained all guidance concerning listening and deliberating. Satisfied will this old man's heart be if ye act accordingly; for if my heart be satisfied, then will your duties be fulfilled, both towards the *Sangsāra* and *Nirvāṇa*. No other method, howsoever agreeable it may be from a worldly point of view, can in the least satisfy me.' Then, in amplification, Jetsün chanted the hymn concerning things useful:

' I bow down at the Feet of Marpa the Translator!

' Ye, my disciples, here in faith assembled,
Give ear to this, the final testament,
Of me, the agèd Milarepa, the Father [Spiritual]—
I, the *Yogī*, Milarepa,
Who by the Kindness and the Favour of Marpa of Lhobrak,[1]
Have successfully accomplished all my duties.

' If ye, my *shishyas* and my followers,
Will my behests obey, do as I heretofore have bid you;
And thus within this very lifetime ye shall do
A mighty service unto others and yourselves,
Pleasing unto me and to the Supreme Buddhas;
Apart from that, all other acts are profitless
For self and others, and displeasing unto me.

' Unless one's *Guru* be of an unbroken [apostolic] line,
What gain is it to take Initiation?[2]

---

[1] *Lhobrak* means ' Rock of the South '.

[2] That is, Initiation is worthless unless conferred by a teacher to whom the

'Unless the *Dharma* be with one's own nature blended,
What gain is it to know by rote the *Tantras*?[1]

'Without renunciation of all worldly aims,
What gain is it to meditate the Chosen Teachings?

'Without attuning body, speech, and mind unto the Doctrine,
What gain is it to celebrate religious rites?

'If anger be unconquered by its antidote,[2]
What gain is it to meditate on patience?

'Unless all partiality, all likes and dislikes, be abandoned,
What gain is it to offer worship?

'Unless all selfishness be given up, from the very heart's
depths,
What gain is it to offer alms?

'Unless the beings of the *Lokas* Six be known to be one's
parents,[3]
What gain is it to fill a certain seat hierarchical?

'Unless pure love and veneration be innate within one's heart,
What gain is it to build a *stūpa*?

'Unless one have ability to meditate throughout the four
divisions of the day,
What gain is it to mould *tsha-tshas*?

'Unless prayer rises from the heart's recesses,
What gain is it to honour anniversaries?

'Unless the Secret Teachings[4] be retained within one's ear,
What gain is it to suffer sorrow?

Esoteric Lore has been transmitted in such completeness and with such psychic power (or 'waves of grace') as come only through an unbroken apostolic succession of teachers. The Ear-Whispered Teachings are unobtainable from one who has never had them thus conveyed to him.

[1] The sense of this is, without the spirit of the Doctrine, of what profit is the letter of the *Tantras*.

[2] The antidote is Love.                         [3] See p. 203[1].

[4] Or 'Specially-selected Teachings'; that is, the Esoteric, Ear-Whispered Doctrines.

' Unless both faith and love attend the Saint while living,
    What gain is it to contemplate his reliques or his image?

' Unless repentance and remorse are born in one,
    What gain is it to say, " Renounce and make repentance ? "

' Unless one meditate on loving others more than self,
    What gain is it merely from the lips to say, " O pity [sentient
        creatures] " ?

' Unless all evil hankerings be overcome,
    What gain is it to render service now and then ?[1]

' Unless the *Guru's* every word e'er be regarded [and obeyed]
        as being reasonable,
    What gain is it to have a multitude of *shishyas* ?

' All actions which bring naught of benefit,
    Do naught but harm ; so leave them quietly aside.

' To the *Yogī* who hath carried out his mission,
    No need is there to undertake fresh duties.'

The chanting of this left a deep impression upon the hearts of
the disciples.

Then Jetsün began to manifest symptoms of serious illness.
Just about this time the *Geshé* Tsaphuwa came with a small
quantity of meat and *chhang*, ostensibly to present them to
Jetsün, but really to see [for himself] how Jetsün was. He
said to him, ' Such a saintly person as Jetsün should not have
been afflicted with so serious an illness ; but since it hath come,
it ought to be distributed among all thy disciples, if this were
possible ; or, if there be means of transferring it, then it might
be transferred to a person like myself ; but since this, too, is
impossible, what now had best be done ? '

Jetsün smiled and said, ' There really was no reason for this
disease afflicting me, but I had no choice in the matter, as thou
perhaps knowest quite well. Generally speaking, a *yogī's* illness
and that of the ordinary person are not of the same character ;
to the former it may seem to be accidental. But in this particular instance mine illness is to me an adornment.'

---

[1] That is, by fits and starts—between one outburst of worldliness and another.
Service to the world must be unbroken, like the flow of a deep calm river.

Having thus spoken, Jetsün chanted this hymn:

' The Round of Birth and Death and the Deliverance are seen
      [or understood] within the Realm of the Clear Light;
When the hands attain their natural posture,[1]
The Great *Mudrā* upon them placeth its seal.[2]
Thus is there [in me] greatness of indifference,
And courage knowing not impediment.

' Diseases, evil spirits, sins, and obscurations,
But tend to beautify me greatly;
They lie within me, shaped as nerves, as humours, and as seed.
Gifts I use to ornament the signs of my perfection;
May the sins of evil thoughts be expiated.[3]
This illness, which becometh me so well,
I could transfer, but no need is there to do so.'

The *Geshé* thought, ' Jetsün suspecteth me of having been
the means of poisoning him, but is not quite sure about it.
As for transferring the illness, I am quite certain that he could
do no such thing, even had he good reason for so doing. Then
he said, ' O Jetsün, I wish I knew the real cause of thine illness.
If it be caused by malignant spirits, they should be exorcized; if merely constitutional, due to inequality of the bodily
humours, these should be equalized and set right; but I have
no knowledge of this ailment. If, however, thou can transfer
it, please transfer it to me.'

Jetsün made answer, ' A certain sentient being became possessed by one of the most malignant of evil spirits, and that
spirit was the Demon of Egotism. Such was the demon that
caused mine illness, by disturbing the harmony of my constitution. Neither can the demon be exorcized nor the illness cured.
Were I to transfer the illness to thee, not for a moment
wouldst thou be able to endure it, so I will not transfer it.'

[1] This posture, attained through practising *Yoga*, symbolizes, as in Milarepa,
Bodhisattvic renunciation of worldly aims and works, and the dedication of one's
life so as to further the spiritual growth of all sentient creatures.

[2] The Doctrine of the Great *Mudrā* (or Symbol) has in Milarepa produced its
blossom and its fruit, which are the Realization of Truth.

[3] This couplet refers to the *Geshé's* gifts to Milarepa and the *Geshé's* evil
thoughts towards Milarepa.

The *Geshé* thought to himself, ' Ah ; unwilling to admit his inability to transfer the disease, he pretendeth that he doth not wish to transfer it.' So the *Geshé* said, most insistently [to Jetsün], ' Pray, do transfer it ! '

Jetsün replied, ' Very well then, I will not transfer it to thee, but to yonder door ; thou mayst merely observe its force.' So saying, Jetsün transferred it to the door of the meditation-room, whereupon the door began to emit sounds of cracking and splitting ; it throbbed and vibrated, and seemed on the point of crumbling away. At the same time, Jetsün appeared to be free from pain.

The *Geshé* again thought to himself, ' Surely this is magical illusion ' ; and he said, ' Most wonderful ! Pray transfer it to me.'

Jetsün said, ' Accordingly, I will show thee a little of its force, O *Geshé*.' And Jetsün took back the pain from the door and transferred it to Tsaphuwa, telling him that that was only one-half of the pain, and asking him what he thought of its intensity, and whether it were bearable.

The *Geshé* was so overcome with unbearable pain that he was about to faint away. Then, having thus felt the intensity and anguish of the pain to which Jetsün had been subjected, he repented deeply and sincerely of his evil ; and, placing Jetsün's feet upon his head and shedding tears profusely, he wailed forth, ' O Jetsün, Sacred Lord, this illness hath been, as thy Reverend Self hath said, brought upon thee by this creature, obsessed by selfishness and jealousy. Accept, I pray thee, all my worldly goods, movable and immovable ; and pardon me this crime, that the evil *karma* thereof may not overtake me.'

These words being uttered in a spirit of sincere remorse, Jetsün saw that the repentance was really earnest, and gladly granted forgiveness. Taking back the entire pain, he made answer, ' During my whole lifetime, no house or property have I ever owned ; [1] and now, on my death-bed, when I have

---

[1] Milarepa, owing to his renunciation of the world, did not take possession of the ruined house and the land to which by right of inheritance he was entitled after the death of his mother, and so never really owned any worldly estate.

not the least need of possessions, what should I do with worldly goods? Take back thy gifts, and henceforth refrain from transgressing the precepts of the *Dharma*. With respect to thy present transgression, earnestly will I pray that no evil *karma* may overtake thee and that thou mayst not suffer because of it.' Then Jetsün chanted this hymn :

' Obeisance to the Feet of Perfect Marpa !

' Even the Five Heinous Sins, limitless [in evil consequences],
    If speedily repented, may be neutralized.
So may the virtue of my merit and my share of Happiness,
With that of all the Buddhas of the past, the present, and the
        future,
Efface the evil *karma* of all sentient beings :
May all thy share of miseries, too,
Be taken o'er by me and likewise neutralized.[1]

' Pity have I for him who doeth injury
Unto his *Guru*, or preceptor, or his parents ;
And may the evil *karma* born thereof,
Be partaken of by me and thoroughly digested.

' Mayst thou remain apart from vicious comrades,
And in all future states of being
Mayst thou encounter virtuous friends ;
May none do unto thee, by evil intent, aught
Which would exhaust thy store of merit.

' May every sentient creature e'er encounter
Reciprocal goodwill and the nobleness of the Bodhisattvic
    mind.'

On Jetsün's chanting this hymn, the *Geshé* felt greatly comforted. In the fervour of boundless gladness and faith he vowed that henceforth he would shun all impious deeds and give himself entirely to religious devotion till his death ; and he said [to Jetsün], ' The evil deeds which in the past I have been tempted to commit were due to my love of wealth and property. Henceforth, I desire neither houses nor lands nor

---

[1] Or literally : ' Be partaken of by me and withal digested ', as in the fourth verse following.

wealth nor worldly goods. Therefore, even though Jetsün have no need of my possessions, they may serve to assist and maintain the disciples and followers who are engaged in devotional studies. So I entreat thee to accept them.'

Despite the earnestness of this entreaty, Jetsün refused to accept the *Geshé's* possessions; but, subsequently, the disciples took them over and utilized them for defraying the cost of Jetsün's funeral ceremonies, and the periodical festivals instituted thereafter to commemorate Jetsün's passing away, which continue to be celebrated even now. And, eventually, Tsaphuwa himself became a very earnest devotee.

Then Jetsün said, ' As the fruit of my sojourn in this place, a hardened sinner hath been converted through repentance and successfully guided towards Deliverance. My mission here thus having been accomplished, no longer is there need for a *yogī* to remain in a worldly place of abode. For a *yogī* to die in a village is like a king dying in the house of a common rustic. I must go to die at Chūbar.

Seban-Repa replied, ' Owing to thy present illness, it will be too fatiguing for thee to attempt the journey on foot. We will carry thee in a palankeen, Sir.'

To this Jetsün answered, ' To me there is no reality either in illness or in death. I have manifested here the phenomena of illness; I will manifest the phenomena of death at Chūbar. For this I need no palankeen. Some of the younger Repas [i. e. Jetsün's disciples] may go on ahead to Chūbar.'

Thereupon, some of the younger disciples went on ahead, but they found that Jetsün had already reached the Cave of Brilche (Cow-Yak's Tongue). The elder disciples, who followed later, escorted and attended another Jetsün. Another Jetsün was at the ' Poison-to-Touch Rock ', manifesting the phenomena of illness. While the one Jetsün was being escorted and served by the devout followers on the journey to Chūbar, another was preaching to those who had assembled for a final sermon at the Red Rock. And, again, to every one who remained at home and made religious offering in farewell to Jetsün, a Jetsün appeared.

So those who went ahead to Chūbar said that Jetsün had

MILAREPA MANIFESTING OCCULT POWERS

Described on pages xxviii, 269

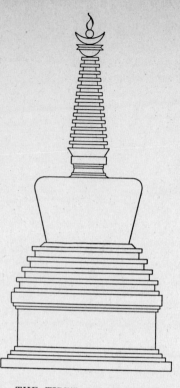

## THE TIBETAN *CH'ORTEN*

*Ch'orten* (*Mch'od-rten*), lit. 'receptacle for offerings' : Skt. *Dhātu-garbha*; corresponding to the *Chaitya* and *Stūpa* (or *Tōpe*) of Indian Buddhism and to the *Dāgaba* of the Sinhalese. Miniature *Ch'ortens*, or *Chaityas*, of metal, stone, wood, or clay, as found adorning *lāmaist* altars, frequently contain reliques; cf. pp. **88, 261, 279, 291-301.** Throughout the lands of Lāmaism small clay funeral *Chaityas* (Skt. *Dharma-sharīra*) are customarily deposited on the ledges or in specially prepared niches of *Ch'ortens*; cf. pp. 175², 178, 261. As to other uses made of *Ch'ortens*, see *The Tibetan Book of the Dead*, p. 163²; also L. A. Waddell, *The Buddhism of Tibet*, pp. 262-4. Exoterically the *Ch'orten* symbolizes the five elements into which man's body is resolved after death. The square base typifies the solidity of the Earth and thus the Element Earth; the globular portion, the water-drop, the Element Water; the spire, triangular like a flame, the Element Fire; the crescent, like the inverted vault of the sky, the Element Air; the acuminated circle tapering in flame into space, the Element Ether: cf. p. 134². Esoterically it symbolizes the Way to Enlightenment, from the Earth (its base) progressively through the Thirteen Bodhisat Heavens (the thirteen step-like segments of its spire) to the Unformed, Uncreated, Beyond-Nature *Nirvāṇa*—beyond the realm of Ether (the last of the *sangsāric* elements), whither the flame (known as the *Jyotih*, or Sacred Light of the Buddha) points and is lost in the Voidness.

preceded them there, while the elder disciples who had gone with Jetsün said that they had escorted him. Each party of those who separately arrived later claimed to have come along with Jetsün. Others asserted that, on that very day, Jetsün had been with them at the Red Rock ; some said that he had been in their house then ; and those who had offered him worship claimed that he had been in each of their houses at the same time. Thus every one claimed Jetsün as having been their honoured guest and recipient of services or veneration, and could come to no agreement. Finally, in one united group, they put the question to Jetsün himself, and he said, 'All of you are right. It was I who was playing with you.'[1]

Thereafter, Jetsün dwelt at the Cave of Brilche, in Chūbar ; and his illness continued. And at this time such phenomena as the feeling of ecstasy and the seeing of rainbows, which had attended his previous sermons, permeated the whole country-side, so that the tops of the mountains were made glorious, and everywhere there commonly prevailed a feeling of auspiciousness. Every one was certain that Jetsün had decided to depart for another world.

Then the foremost disciples, Shiwa-Wöd-Repa, the Master of Ngan-Dzong,[2] and Seban-Repa, together asked Jetsün to which Realm he intended going, and whither they should address their prayers [to him]. They further inquired if he had any last injunctions or commands to impart ; and each prayed for special guidance as to the line of devotion to adopt.

Jetsün replied to them, 'As to the place or direction whither ye should address your prayers, [I command you to] direct them according to your own beliefs and faith. In whatever place ye pray with sincerity and earnestness, there will I be in front of each of you,[3] and I will fulfil your wishes. Therefore, pray earnestly and with firm faith. For the present, I intend

---

[1] The Perfected Yogī possesses the power of reproducing his phenomenal physical body in countless numbers, one such body in one place or world, another in another. The Editor has in his possession one of the yogic treatises concerning the acquirement of this power.

[2] That is, Ngan-Dzong-Repa.

[3] Cf. *Matthew* (xviii. 20) : 'For where two or three are gathered together in my name, there am I in the midst of them.'

going to the Realm of Happiness [i. e. *Ngön-gah*], wherein the
Bhagavān Akshobhya reigneth. And my last injunction, or
will, when I, Milarepa, am dead, is this: To Rechung, who,
as I foresee, will soon arrive, give my bamboo-staff and this
cotton raiment which ye all see with me as my sole possessions; they will serve for him as a sort of success-bringing
talisman in his meditation on the control of the Vital Airs.[1]
Until Rechung arriveth, no one is to touch my body. The hat
of the Master Maitrī and this black staff of *agaru* will carry
with them success in upholding the Faith by means of deep
meditation and high aspiration; see that they are given to
Ūpa-Tönpa. This wooden bowl may be taken by Shiwa-Wöd.
And this skull-cup I give to Ngan-Dzong-Tönpa. To Seban-
Repa, I give this flint and steel. This bone-spoon I give to
Bri-Gom-Repa. To the other disciples I leave this cotton
mantle of mine, which they may divide among themselves in
strips. From a worldly point of view, these things are of little
value, but each beareth with it a spiritual blessing.

' Now hear my principal testament, of which none save my
chief disciples and lay followers, male and female, should be
informed: All the gold that I, Milarepa, have amassed during
my lifetime lieth hidden here beneath this hearth; and with
it there are written instructions as to how it is to be distributed among you all. After my departure, fail not to look
for it, and act according to the instructions found with it.

' As to how ye are to carry the religious teachings into
practice in your everyday life, bear in mind the following:
Some there may be among you who are proud of their apparent sanctity, but who, at heart, are really devoted to acquiring name and fame in this world; they dispense a hundred
necessary and unnecessary things in charity, hoping thereby
to reap a liberal return. This, though displeasing to the
Divinities gifted with divine vision, is persevered in by selfish
beings of obscured vision. The hypocrisy of thus hankering after
the rich juices of this world, while outwardly appearing pious

---

[1] That is, the control of the psycho-physical forces of the human body with
a view to psychic development and success in *Yoga*. (Cf. p. 194.)

and devout, because unable to face the ridicule of the world
[which might otherwise come to know of the hankering], is
like partaking of delicacies and rich food mixed with deadly
aconite.  Therefore, drink not the venom of desire for worldly
fame and name; but casting aside all the fetters of worldly
duties, which but lead to this desire, devote yourselves to
sincere and earnest devotion.'

The disciples then inquired if they could engage in worldly
duties, in a small way, for the benefit of others, and Jetsün
said, ' If there be not the least self-interest attached to such
duties, it is permissible.[1]  But such [detachment] is indeed
rare; and works performed for the good of others seldom
succeed if not wholly freed from self-interest.  Even without
seeking to benefit others, it is with difficulty that works done
even in one's own interest [or selfishly] are successful.  It is as
if a man helplessly drowning were to try to save another man
in the same predicament.  One should not be over-anxious
and hasty in setting out to serve others before one hath oneself realized Truth in its fullness; to be so, would be like the
blind leading the blind.[2]  As long as the sky endureth, so long
will there be no end of sentient beings for one to serve; and
to every one cometh the opportunity for such service.  Till the
opportunity come, I exhort each of you to have but the one
resolve, namely, to attain Buddhahood for the good of all
living things.

' Be lowly and meek.  Clothe yourselves in rags.  Be resigned to hardships with respect to food and dress.  Renounce
all thought of acquiring worldly renown.  Endure bodily
penance and mental burdens.  Thus gain knowledge from experience.  That your study and penance be directed towards
the right path, it is necessary to hold these injunctions in your
hearts.'

[1] This, too, is the supreme teaching of the *Bhagavad Gītā*, that all actions in
the world should be done wholly disinterestedly, and the fruits thereof dedicated
to the good of all beings.

[2] To proclaim as the ignorant do, ' I believe ', leads but to doubt and mental
confusion; the Teacher must be filled with the divine power born of *Knowledge*
of Truth, and his message must be, ' I know '.

Having so spoken, Jetsün sang this hymn :

' Obeisance at the Feet of Lordly Marpa the Translator !

' If ye who would be devotees, and Wisdom win,
Do not procure and serve a *Guru* wise,
Though ye have faith and meekness, small will be the
Grace.

' If ye do not obtain the Initiation deep and mystic,
The words alone, the *Tantras* hold, will merely serve as
fetters.

' If ye keep not the *Tantric* Scriptures as your witness,
All practice of the rites will be but many snares.

' If ye do not the Chosen Teachings meditate,
Mere renunciation of the worldly life will be but vain self-
torture.

' If ye subdue not evil passions by their antidote,
Mere verbal preachings will be but empty sounds.

' If ye know not the Subtle Methods and the Path,
Mere perseverance will bear but little fruit.

' If ye know not the Secret and the Subtle Methods,
Mere exercise of zeal will make the Pathway long.

' If ye do not acquire great merit,
And work for self alone, *sangsāric* being will continue.

' If ye do not devote unto Religion all your worldly goods
amassed,
Much meditation will not gain much Knowledge.

' If ye do not acquire contentment in yourselves,
Heaped-up accumulations will only enrich others.

' If ye do not obtain the Light of Inner Peace,
Mere external ease and pleasure will become a source of
pain.

' If ye do not suppress the Demon of Ambition,
Desire of fame will lead to ruin and to lawsuits.

'The desire to please exciteth the Five Poisonous Passions;
The greed of gain separateth one from dearest friends;
The exaltation of the one is the humiliation of the others.

'Hold your peace and no litigation will arise;
Maintain the State of Undistractedness and distraction will
    fly off;
Dwell alone and ye shall find a friend;
Take the lowest place and ye shall reach the highest;
Hasten slowly and ye shall soon arrive;
Renounce all worldly goals and ye shall reach the highest
    goal.

'If ye tread the Secret Path, ye shall find the shortest way;
If ye realize the Voidness, Compassion will arise within
    your hearts;
If ye lose all differentiation between yourselves and others,
    fit to serve others ye will be;
And when in serving others ye shall win success, then shall
    ye meet with me;
And finding me, ye shall attain to Buddhahood.

'To me, and to the Buddha, and the Brotherhood of my
    disciples
Pray ye earnestly, without distinguishing one from the other.'

Thus did Jetsün sing. And then he said, 'Seeing that I
may not have much longer now to live, observe my teachings
and follow me.

After saying this, Jetsün sank into the quiescent state of
*Samādhi.* Thus did Jetsün pass away at the age of eighty-
four years,[1] on the fourteenth day of the last of the three winter
months of the Wood-Hare Year [A.D. 1135],[2] at dawn.

At his passing, Jetsün exhibited the process of merging the
physical body with the Realm of Eternal Truth,[3] the *Devas*
and *Ḍākinīs* manifested then much greater and more marvellous
phenomena than ever before, and very many of the people

---

[1] 'The Lord Buddha Gautama, too, entered *Pari-Nirvāṇa* in His eighty-fourth
year.'—Sri Nissanka.

[2] This is the forty-ninth year of the sixty-year cycle described on p. 52[1].

[3] The *Dharma-Kāya.*

there assembled beheld the phenomena. The unclouded sky
appeared as if it were palpable with prismatic colours, arranged
in a background of geometrically chequered designs, in the
centre of which were vari-coloured lotuses, some of eight and
some of four petals.  Upon the petals were marvellously
designed *maṇḍalas* [or mystic circular designs] more beautiful
than any that could be made by the most skilful artist [among
men].  The firmament contained many wondrously tinted
clouds, which assumed the form of [royal] umbrellas and banners, curtains, and draperies, and various other objects of
worship.  There were profuse showers of blossoms.  Clouds of
varied colours adorned the mountain peaks and assumed the
form of *stūpas,* each with its head bending towards Chūbar.
Ravishingly melodious music to the accompaniment of heavenly psalms in praise of the departed Saint were heard.  And
a delicious perfume, more fragrant than any earthly essence,
pervaded the air, so that every one perceived it.  Celestial
beings, both *Devas* and *Ḍākinīs*, bearing various offerings, were
seen by many people, as if coming to welcome Jetsün.  More
marvellous yet, the human beings upon seeing the nude forms
of *Devas* felt no sense of shame, nor did the celestial beings
seem to be affected with the unpleasant odour emitted by the
human beings.[1]  Gods and men met and conversed freely with
one another, sometimes exchanging greetings; so that, for
the time being, they were carried back to the Golden Age [or
the Sat-Yuga].[2]

The people of Nyanam, soon hearing that Jetsün had passed
away, went to Chūbar and proposed to the disciples and laymen of Brin that they should have the privilege of cremating
Jetsün's body at Nyanam, but the proposal was rejected.
Thereupon, the people of Nyanam requested that the cremation
be postponed until they could go and bring from Brin all the
faithful, so that these could have a last look at their deceased
*Guru.*  This being granted, they went to Brin and returned

[1] The impure auric emanations of human beings who have not been purged of
worldliness are said to be exceedingly unpleasant to the pure deities.

[2] 'Similar divine manifestations occurred at the passing away of the Lord
Buddha Gautama. Cf. *The Book of the Great Decease* (*Mahā-Parinibbāṇa Suttanta*),
of the Pāli Canon.'—Sri Nissanka.

with a strong body of men, prepared to carry away the remains of their *Guru* forcibly. A conflict seemed imminent, when the chief disciples interposed, and said, 'Ye people of Nyanam and of Brin! All of ye believed in Jetsün, and were his followers equally. Seeing that Jetsün hath passed away in Chūbar, it is not fitting that his body be cremated at Nyanam. Ye who are from Nyanam may remain here until the cremation is over, and will receive a due share of the reliques from the ashes of Jetsün.' But the people of Nyanam, thinking themselves to be the more numerous and powerful, were about to carry off the corpse by force, when a *Deva* appeared from the heavens, and in the voice of Jetsün sang this hymn:

' O ye disciples here assembled!
And ye lay-followers, disputing o'er a corpse!
Give ear unto my judgement:
I am a *deva*-follower of Jetsün,
Come to make peace between you by my counsel.
Milarepa, the best of men,
Hath merged his mind in the unbegotten *Dharma-Kāya*;
And since there is no form that's real except the mind,
Whilst Jetsün's earthly form is [likewise] being merged in
    the *Dharma-Kāya*,
If ye do not obtain the Reliques True,
Foolish is it to quarrel about a corpse.
Only the stupid would dispute o'er Milarepa's body;
Not likely is it that by quarrelling ye'll obtain it.
Pray with meekness, and have faith;
If from the heart's depths ye will pray,
Though the *Dharma-Kāya* hath no birth,
Yet by the grace come of good wishes the Unobstructed [1]
    shineth forth.
And thus shall all of you obtain a portion of the Reliques,
Each according to deserts.'

Having sung this, the *Deva* vanished like a rainbow, and the lay-disciples felt as joyful as if they had once more beheld their beloved *Guru*. They ceased disputing and began to pray.

---

[1] That is, Divine Grace (or Mercy), as vouchsafed by the *Dharma-Kāya*.

Then the foremost disciples and the people of Brin saw that they possessed one corpse of Jetsün, and the people of Nyanam that they possessed another. And the latter took the corpse away and cremated it at the Düt-dül Cave of Lapchi, on the rock called the 'Eagle's Egg'; this cremation, too, being attended with many phenomena. Rainbows arched the skies; there were showers of blossoms; heavenly perfumes filled the air; and celestial melodies everywhere resounded in Lapchi and in Chūbar.

The corpse at Chūbar was attended by the foremost of the disciples and laity. Most fervently they offered up unbroken prayer until, after the sixth day, it was seen that the corpse emitted a halo of radiant glory like that of divine beings, and was no larger than the body of an eight-year-old child.

Then the chief disciples said, 'Rechung seemeth not to be coming; if we postpone the cremation much longer, it is likely that there will be nothing left of the body; and thus losing our share of the reliques we shall have no object to venerate or worship. It would be better to perform the cremation at once.'

To this all agreed; and, after every one had been given the opportunity of taking a last farewell look at the face, a funeral pyre was erected on a boulder from which, as from a pulpit, Jetsün had preached, at the foot of the Brilche Cave. The corpse was carried thither in great state. The *mandala* diagram was outlined in colours.[1] Though the funeral offerings from celestial beings were far more numerous, those brought by the followers on Earth were laid out modestly and to the best of human ability. Then an attempt was made to set fire to the funeral pyre before daybreak, even while it was still night, but the pyre could not be made to burn.[2] At the same moment, five *Dākinīs* appeared from amidst a rainbow-enhaloed cloud, and in chorus sang the following hymn:

[1] This is the funeral *mandala*, outlined on the ground with coloured earth or other substance in such manner that the funeral pyre, like the pericarp of a lotus, occupies the centre. As in Sikkim, it is commonly the *mandala* of the Dhyānī Buddha Amitābha, who as the One of Boundless Light, the Illuminator or Enlightener, symbolizes the Fire which purifies.

[2] 'Similarly, the funeral pyre of the Lord Buddha Gautama could not be made to burn until Kāshyapa arrived seven days late.'—Sri Nissanka.

'*Rom !*[1] the divine fire of the Vital Force
   Having been ever contemplated [by Him],
   What power hath the fire [of this world] over Him?
   For Him Who hath long been engaged in devotion,
   Meditating on His organic body as a shape divine,
   What need is there to leave behind a fleshly corpse?
   For the *Yogī* Who hath the perfect Divine *Maṇḍala*
   Well defined in His own body,
   What need is there of the *Maṇḍala* outlined on the ground?
   For Him Who hath kept the Lamp of Mind
   Ever burning bright, along with Vital Breath,
   What need is there of your petty [worldly] lamps?
   For Him Who ever feedeth on Pure Elixirs,
   What need is there of cakes of cereal?[2]
   For Him Who is clad in the Robe of Chastity,
   Unsullied by the Twofold Defilement,[3]
   What need is there that ye consecrate the Holy Pot?[4]

'The skies are filled with clouds of smoke
   Of incense, and perfumes of heavenly offerings;
   No need is there to-day to offer your burnt incense.

'The Four Orders of the *Ḍākinīs* are chanting,
   And yet higher Orders of the *Ḍākinīs* are offering worship;
   What rites then shall ye celebrate to-day?

'The Lords of Wisdom now surround the pyre,
   And Heroes vie each with the other in offering reverence;
   No need is there for you to touch the sacred form to-day.

'The mortal relique of the Man Who hath realized the
      Thatness
   Hath no need of rituals conventional; let it remain in peace.

'That which is worshipped now by gods and men alike
   Needeth not an owner; therefore worship and make prayer.

---

[1] Or '*Rang*', the *Bīja* (or 'Seed') *Mantra* of the Element Fire.

[2] This refers to the customary food-offerings at the funeral pyre, made to the spirit of the deceased one.

[3] Or 'the Twofold Shadow', which is Illusion and *Karma*, as described on p. 33[3], above.

[4] That is, the Holy Pot filled with lustral holy-water.

'Unto the sacred vows, enjoined by *Devas* and by *Gurus*,
No need is there to add injunctions.

'Before this heap of priceless gems and jewels
Utter not "'Tis mine", but practise meditation.

'With reference to the secret and deep words of *Gurus* and
of Buddhas,
Give not way to prattling speech, but remain in silence.

'The Holy Chosen Teachings, breathing forth the breath of
Angels,
Are polluted by impiety; so seek ye solitude.

'Unto the life which ye have chosen
Many interruptions come; so perform ye rites in secret.

'From the admonitions by your wondrous *Guru* given
There shall come a blessing; so cast all doubts aside.

'The history of your Teacher Jetsün
Hath not need of formal praise.

'From the hymns the *Ḍākinīs* Divine have sung
A certain boon shall come; heed it meekly and with faith.

'Milarepa's spiritual descendants
Shall produce many *yogic* saints, O ye of highest destiny.

'Upon the people and the cattle of this place
No maladies shall come, O ye celestial and terrestrial beings.

'For all the beings here to-day assembled
No birth in the Unhappy Worlds shall come, O ye of human
kind.

'For the *Maṇḍala* of the Thatness,
Appearances external and the mind are one; shatter then
your theory of duality.

'Unto the final words which Jetsün uttered ere He passed
Give greatest heed and His commands obey; of vast import
are they.

'May every one e'er practise the Sacred *Dharma*;
It bringeth Peace and Happiness to all.'

When these words had been sung, Ngan-Dzong-Tönpa said,

'The command that none must touch the Lord's remains until Rechung shall have arrived and the purport of the *Ḍākinīs'* hymn agree. But since there is no certainty that Rechung will come at all, even though we postpone the cremation of the sacred body, it seemeth likely that it will vanish without leaving behind any substantial relique whatsoever.'

Then Shiwa-Wöd-Repa said, 'Jetsün's own command, the *Ḍākinīs'* song, and the fact that the pyre refuseth to take fire all coincide. Rechung is certain to arrive soon. Meanwhile, let us devote ourselves to prayer.' So every one continued praying.

At this time Rechung was staying at the Loro-Döl Monastery; and one night, just after midnight, he had a dream or clairvoyant vision, while in a state of unobscured super-conscious sleep, as followeth. At Chūbar he beheld a radiant *chaitya* (reliquary) of crystal, whose glory filled the skies. It was about to be taken away by a multitude of *Ḍākinīs*, aided by his brethren in the Faith and the lay-disciples of Jetsün, along with numerous other human beings and a host of celestial beings. The skies seemed to be crowded with this multitude, all singing and offering worship. The offerings were unimaginably magnificent and numerous. He, too, was bowing down to the *chaitya*. Then he saw Jetsün leaning out from the *chaitya*, and heard him say, 'My son Rechung, though thou didst not come when I bade thee come, nevertheless it is pleasant to meet thee again; cheering indeed is this encounter of father with son. But, there being no certainty of our meeting soon again, let us seek to appreciate fully this rare pleasure and converse on suitable topics.' He was fondly passing his hand over Rechung's head, stroking it gently and lovingly; and Rechung was thrilled thereby with rare happiness and fond affection and profound faith, such as he had never before felt towards Jetsün. Here, in the dream, he awoke; and recalling all that Jetsün had previously said to him, the thought came to him, 'May it not be that my *Guru* hath passed away?' As this thought flashed through his mind, a feeling of deep faith was aroused in him, so that he prayed; and overcome by an irrepressible yearning he decided to set

out at once to find Jetsün, although this was not at the precise
moment which Jetsün had indicated.  Thereupon, two *Ḍākinīs*
appeared before him in the heavens, and said, 'Rechung, unless
thou now hasten to see thy *Guru* he will soon depart to the
Holy Realms, and thou wilt not see him more in this lifetime.
Go thou without delay.'  As they spake these words, the sky
was flooded with the glory of rainbows.

Much impressed by the vision, and filled with great yearning
to see his *Guru*, Rechung at once arose and started forth on
the journey.  The cocks of Loro-Döl were just crowing.

Exerting his faith in his *Guru* and his knowledge of controlling
the breathing process, in one morning Rechung had traversed a
distance which for travellers mounted on donkeys usually took
two months to traverse.  By the power derived from his suspen-
sion of his respiration, he shot forth at the speed of an arrow ;
and by daybreak reached the top of the Pass between Tingri
and Brin, called Pozele.  While he was resting there for a short
time, the remarkable clearness of the sky and the unusual display of rainbows and other marvellous phenomena which
illuminated the mountain peaks and the entire firmament,
excited in him gladness and sorrow alternately.  He beheld
the summit of Jovō-Rabzang conspicuously lit up with rainbow
radiance.  He also beheld tent-shaped clouds, and issuing
from the midst of them innumerable hosts of celestial beings,
gods and goddesses, all alike bearing countless offerings and
hastening on, nodding and making profound obeisance in the
direction of Lapchi with most fervent prayer.  At this, Rechung
felt great misgiving, and inquired of the Deities the signification
of all the signs and of their own actions.

Some of the goddesses replied, 'Hast thou, O man, been
living with thine eyes and ears closed, and thus askest why
all these things are made manifest?  They are made manifest
because Jetsün Mila-Zhadpa-Dorje,[1] who dwelt on Earth
and is venerated and worshipped by both gods and men,
is now departing to the Holier and Purer Realms.  Therefore
it is that those of the celestial beings who honour the Sacred
*Dharma* [or the White Faith] are offering this obeisance

---

[1] Zhadpa-Dorje is a shortened form of Milarepa's initiatory name.

to Jetsün, while all the human beings assembled at Chūbar are also offering him worship.'

Upon hearing this, Rechung felt as though his heart had been torn from his body, and he hurried on as fast as he could. When approaching Chūbar, upon a boulder shaped like the base of a *chaitya* he beheld Jetsün awaiting him. Jetsün greeted him most cordially, and said, ' Hath my son Rechung come at last ? ' At that, Jetsün passed his hand over Rechung's head, stroking him lovingly, as Rechung had seen Jetsün do in the dream.

Overjoyed with the thought that Jetsün had not passed away, Rechung placed Jetsün's feet on the crown of his head, and prayed most fervently. Having made answer to all of Rechung's inquiries, Jetsün then said, ' My son Rechung, proceed thou leisurely ; I will go on ahead to prepare some reception for thee.' And Jetsün went on ahead, and in a few moments was no longer seen.

On reaching Chūbar, Rechung beheld at the cave where Jetsün was wont to dwell all the disciples and lay-followers assembled round Jetsün's body, mourning and performing various acts of worship. Some of Jetsün's most recently accepted disciples did not know Rechung, and refused to let him go near the body. Greatly grieved at this, Rechung in his agony offered to his *Guru* this hymn, of the Seven Branches of Offering :

' O Lord, Embodiment of the Eternal Buddhas,
   Thou Refuge of all Sentient Creatures,
   Out of the depths of Thy Great Love and Wisdom
   Hearest Thou the lamentation of Thy Suppliant Unfortunate,
   Rechung-Dorje-Tagpa ?

' Unto Thee, in misery and woe, I cry ;
   If Thou wilt not Thy Love and Wisdom now exert
   To shield Thy Son, for whom else shouldst Thou, Lord ?

' Yearning to behold my Father, to Thy Feet I fled :
   Thy Son Unfortunate was fated not to see Thy Face ;
   Exert Thy Kindness, grant Thy Grace, O Father.

' Omniscient and with Love endowed,
To Thee, O Lord, Thou Buddha of the past, the present, and
the future,
I, the mendicant, most humbly pray.

' To Thy Commands obedient, I worship Thee ;
Forgive, I beg, my sins of impious doubts, and my heresy.

' Filled am I with joyous admiration of Thy Great and Noble
Deeds,
And pray that Thou continue e'er to turn the Wheel,
Of the Deep and Mystic *Dharma*.

' All virtue which I've won, by meditation and devotion,
I dedicate, O Jetsün, to Thy Happiness ;
May this, my dedication, be acceptable,
And may I see Thy Countenance.

' I was, O *Guru*, formerly Thy Favoured One,
And now, alas ! not even have I power to behold Thy Body.
Though I may not have power to see Thine Actual Form,
Yet may I be blessed by seeing e'en Thy Countenance.

' And seeing thus Thy Countenance,
In actuality or clairvoyant vision,
May I obtain the Teachings Rare and Precious,
Essential for o'ercoming doubts and criticisms while studying
the Twofold Teachings.[1]

' If thou, O Lord Omniscient, be not merciful
In answer to Thy Son's appeal, to whose else's shouldst
Thou be ?

' O Father, withdraw Thou not Thy Hook of Grace,[2]
But graciously regard me from the Unseen Realms.

---

[1] That is, the teachings concerning the *Sangsāra* and those concerning
*Nirvāna*.

[2] As among Christians, who believe in the saving grace of God, so among
Tibetan Buddhists it is believed that grace-waves are emanated from a Buddha,
Bodhisattva, or Celestial *Guru* in a heaven-world, and from a Great *Yogī* still
in the fleshly form, directly to the worshipper or disciple on Earth. These
grace-waves are figuratively a ' hook of grace ' to catch hold of and thus save
the devotee from falling into the illusion of Ignorance (or *sangsāric* existence)
and set him on the Highway to Emancipation.

On me, Rechung, Thy Witless Suppliant,
Do Thou, O Knower of the Three Times, have mercy.

' O'er me, Rechung, drunk with the poison of the Passions
    Five,
Do Thou keep watch, O Father, endowed with the Five
    Attributes of Divine Wisdom.

' In general, compassion have on every sentient being,
In particular, compassion have on me, Rechung.'

As soon as Rechung began to give vent to this earnest and mournful prayer, and his clear voice reached the corpse, the colour of the corpse, which had faded, became once more bright, and the funeral pyre immediately took fire and blazed up.   At the same time Shiwa-Wöd Repa, Ngan-Dzong-Tönpa, Seban-Repa, and other brethren in the Faith, as well as female lay-disciples, came to welcome him.   But he felt so deeply hurt at having been prevented from approaching Jetsün's body by those disciples who did not know him that he would not move until he had finished his hymn of prayer. So great was the force and earnestness of Rechung's faith that Jetsün, who had already sunk into the state of the Clear Light, reanimated his corpse[1] and addressed these words to the most recently accepted disciples: ' O ye younger disciples, act not thus ; one lion is far more to be preferred than a hundred tigers.   Such [a lion] is my son Rechung.   Permit him to approach me.'   Then to Rechung he said, ' And thou, my son Rechung, take it not so much to heart, but come near to thy Father.'

At first every one present was startled and filled with wonder ;  then this feeling gave way to one of gladness. Rechung himself caught hold of Jetsün, and burst forth in a flood of tears ; and so overcome was he with excess of alternate joy and sorrow that for a while he swooned.

---

[1] ' Jetsün had not expired in the lay sense of the word, but had been in the *Nirodha-Samāpatti* trance and could reanimate his body.   Likewise, when it seemed that the Lord Buddha Gautama was dead, only the Venerable Anuruddha, the greatest of the disciples and possessed of the Celestial Eye, followed the Master's *Nirvānic* Consciousness to the Heavens and back to Earth until it was finally lost in *Nirvāna*.'—Sri Nissanka.

When Rechung had regained consciousness, he found all the disciples and followers seated round about the front of the cremation-house.[1] Meanwhile, Jetsün had risen in the Indestructible Body,[2] into which are merged both the spiritual body and the phenomenal body. The flames of the funeral pyre assumed the shape of an eight-petalled lotus, and from the midst of this, like the stamens of the blossom, Jetsün sat up, one of his knees half raised and his right hand extended in the preaching attitude pressing down the flames. 'Listen', he said, 'unto this old man's last testament.' Then, both as a reply to Rechung's prayer and as his final teachings to his disciples, with his left hand placed against his cheek, he sang this final hymn concerning the Six Essential Commandments from the midst of the funeral pyre, in a divine voice issuing from the Indestructible Body:

'O Rechung, my son, as dear to me as mine own heart,
Hear thou this hymn, my final testament of precepts:

'In the *Sangsāric* Ocean, of the *Lokas* Three,
The great culprit is the impermanent physical body;
Busy in its craving search for food and dress,
From worldly works it findeth ne'er relief:
Renounce, O Rechung, every worldly thing.

'Amid the City of Impermanent Physical Forms,
The great culprit is the unreal mind;
Submissive to the form of flesh and blood,
It findeth ne'er the time to realize the nature of Reality:[3]
Discern, O Rechung, the true nature of the Mind.

'Upon the frontier of the Intellect and Matter,
The great culprit is the self-born [or created] knowledge;
E'er on its guard 'gainst accidental [or destructive] mishaps
    [to itself],[4]

---

[1] Here we learn that the funeral pyre is contained within a cremation-house, perhaps specially erected for the occasion.

[2] Or, 'the *Vajra-Kāya*' ('Immutable or Indestructible Body').

[3] Literally, 'the *Dharma-Dhātu*' ('the Seed or Potentiality of Truth').

[4] Knowledge born of experience of a sensuous universe is (like the personal ego), when devoid of Right Knowledge, ever fearful of some untoward accident which might entail its destruction.

It findeth ne'er the time to realize the true nature of the
    Unborn Knowledge [or Truth]:
Keep, O Rechung, within the safe stronghold of the Unborn
    [or Uncreated].[1]

' Upon the frontier of this and of the future life,
The great culprit is the [self-born or created] consciousness ;
It seeketh e'er a form it hath not,
And findeth ne'er the time to realize the Truth :
Find, O Rechung, the nature of the Truth Eternal.

' Amid the City of Illusoriness of the *Lokas* Six,
The chief factor is the sin and obscuration born of evil
    *karma* ;
Therein the being followeth dictates of likes and dislikes,
And findeth ne'er the time to know Equality:[2]
Avoid, O Rechung, likes and dislikes.

' Within a certain unseen region of the Heavens,
The Perfect Buddha, expert in subtle argument,
Hath propounded' many subtle and profound Apparent
    Truths ;
And there one findeth ne'er the time to know the Real
    Truths :[3]
Avoid, O Rechung, subtle argument.

[1] Mundane or *sangsāric* knowledge (like the personal ego) being compounded
of sense impressions is, like the phenomena whence it arose, transitory and
illusory, and being created (or self-born) is unreal.  True Knowledge (or Truth)
is of the Beyond-Nature, beyond the *Sangsāra* (the Round of Birth and Death),
beyond the realm of phenomena, of appearances, of things, beyond the transitory and illusory, and having had no beginning (or creation) is the Unborn or
Uncreated.

[2] Or 'the Non-Duality'—the Truth that, in the last analysis, all opposites
are at bottom one.

[3] Scientific Truths dealing wholly with Nature, or the *Sangsāra*, are, for
example, apparent Truths, because that upon which they are based, namely
knowledge of Phenomena, is itself unreal, because Phenomena are unreal.  The
Real Truths are those concerning the Voidness, the *Dharma-Kāya, Nirvāṇa*.
As suggested in this stanza, Northern Buddhists believe that the Buddha
taught—according to the need or capacity of His hearers—various kinds of
doctrines, none of which, however, are in conflict with one another.  In like
manner, Tantric Buddhists maintain that the Buddha taught Tantricism as
a doctrine best suited to one kind of human beings, and the better-known
*Dharma* as being more suitable to another kind.

' *Gurus, Devas, Ḍākinīs—*
Combine these in a single whole, and worship that ;
The goal of aspiration, the meditation, and the practice—
Combine these in a single whole, and gain Experimental
    Knowledge ;
This life, the next life, and the life between [in *Bar-do*] [1]—
Regard these all as one, and make thyself accustomed to
    them [thus as one].[2]

' This is the last of my Selected Precepts,
And of my Testament the end ;
Than that, no more of Truth is there, O Rechung ;
Acquire from it Practical Knowledge, O my son.'

Having uttered these words, Jetsün again sank in a trance
into the Clear Light.   Thereupon, the funeral pyre assumed
the shape of a spacious *Vihāra* (Mansion), square in shape,
having four entrances, with pedestals for dismounting and
other embellishments, and was enhaloed by a glorious rainbow
having gleaming and waving curtains of coloured light.   Roofs
and domes appeared, surmounted by banners and flags,
[royal] umbrellas and streamers, and various adornments.
The flames themselves, at the base, assumed the shapes of
eight-petalled lotus blossoms, curling and unfolding into
various designs, such as the eight auspicious emblems,[3] and
at the top [they formed] into the seven royal insignia.[4]   Even
the sparks assumed the shapes of goddesses bearing various
objects of offering and worship.   The very cracklings of the
burning flames sounded like the melodious tunings of various
musical instruments, such as violins, flutes, and timbrels.   The

---

[1] The *Bar-do* (' Between-Two ') is the Intermediate State which intervenes
between death and rebirth, treated of in *The Tibetan Book of the Dead.*

[2] Existence is to be regarded as an unbroken flux of life, subject to incessant
transition and change.  Life in a fleshly form on Earth, life in the subtle after-
death body in Heaven-Worlds, in Hells, or in the Intermediate State, and the
life which seems to take birth through the womb-doors is in reality one.

[3] These are named on p. 33[4], above.

[4] These are : (1) The Precious House, or Palace ; (2) The Precious Royal
Robes ; (3) The Precious [Embroidered] Boots ; (4) The Precious Elephant's
Tusk ; (5) The Precious Queen's Earring ; (6) The Precious King's Earring ;
and (7) The Precious Jewel.

very smoke emitted the sweet odour of different kinds of incense, its eddies assuming various rainbow colours and the shapes of [royal] umbrellas and banners. The sky directly above the funeral pyre was full of angelic beings bearing vessels of nectar, which they poured down in showers. Others bore celestial food and drink, unguents and perfumes, and objects of delight for the five senses, with which every human being assembled there was regaled.

Although the disciples assembled there beheld the same funeral pyre, the corpse itself appeared to one as Gaypa-Dorje, to another as Dēmchog, to a third as Sang-dü, and to a fourth as Dorje-Pa-mo.[1] And all of them heard the *Ḍākinīs* chanting the following hymn :

' Because of the departure of that Wish-Fulfilling Gem, the
   Lord,
Some weep, and some have swooned, through their excessive
   grief.
At such a time of mourning as is this,
Of themselves [unaided] the flames burst out,
Assuming shapes of lotus blossoms of eight petals,
And of the Eight Auspicious Emblems and the Seven
   Precious Insignia,
And various other beauteous objects of religious offering.
The sounds emitted by the flames
Give forth melodious music as of conch-shells, cymbals,
Harps and flutes and miniature cymbals,
Small drums and double-drums and timbrels.
And from the meteoric sparks, emitted by the flames,
Spring forth various goddesses of the outer, inner, and most
   esoteric conclaves,
Who offer offerings most tastefully arranged.
The smoke itself assumeth varied rainbow-colours,
And ornamental shapes of banners and [royal] umbrellas,
The Eight Auspicious Emblems, the *Svastika*, and the
   Good-Luck Diagram.

---

[1] The Sanskrit names of these four Tantric tutelary deities of the Kargyütpas (and of other sects of Northern Buddhism) are, respectively: Hé-Vajra, Sham-vara, Guhya-Kāla, and Vajra-Vārāhī.

' Various goddesses, of charming shapes,
Have borne away from the funeral pyre the charred bones
    and the ashes
Of Him who now hath rendered up his earthly body to the
    element ethereal ;
Your cremation of his form is finished.

' The *Guru*, being the *Dharma-Kāya*, is like the expanse of
    the heavens
Upon the face of which the Cloud of Good Wishes of the
    *Sambhoga-Kāya* gathereth ;
Whence descend the flowery showers of the *Nirmāna-Kāya*.[1]
These, falling on the Earth unceasingly,
Nourish and ripen the Harvest of Saved Beings.[2]

' That which is of the nature of the Uncreated,
The *Dharma-Dhātu*, the Unborn, the Voidness,
The *Shūnyatā*, hath no beginning, nor doth it ever cease
    [to be] ;
E'en birth and death are of the Nature of the Voidness :[3]
Such being the Real Truth, avoid doubts and misgivings
    [about It].'

When the chanting of this hymn was finished, evening had
set in ; and the funeral fire had burnt itself out, so that the
cremation-house was empty again. The multitude could see
through it from end to end ; but when the disciples looked
into it some saw a great *chaitya* of light, others saw Gaypa-
Dorje, Dēmchog, Sang-dü, and Dorje-Pa-mo. Others, again,
saw various religious regalia, such as a *dorje* and a bell,

---

[1] These three verses very concisely state the Doctrine of the Three Bodies
(Skt. *Tri-Kāya*) ; see p. 38[2], above.

[2] As the emanations of the planetary sun sustain all physical manifestation of
life on Earth, so the spiritual forces, disseminated among the human race by the
Compassionate Ones, from the State Beyond Nature, alone make possible the
Higher Evolution and the Ultimate Deliverance from Nature (the *Sangsāra*).
Enlightenment brings with it realization of this.

[3] The Voidness, the *Shūnyatā*, being the Primordial, the Uncreated, to which
no concept of the limited human understanding can be applied, is the Ultimate
Source of the *Sangsāra*, of Nature ; and since death and birth are themselves
merely a pair of natural illusory opposites, mere phenomenal appearances cast
upon the Screen of Time, they, too, in the last analysis of the Illuminated
Supra-mundane Mind, are of the Thatness, the Beyond-Nature.

a holy-water pot, and so on, while yet others saw different letters formed into *bīja-mantras*.[1] Some also saw the cremation-house filled with radiance, like a mass of blazing gold ; [in it], some saw a pool of water, others fire burning, and yet others saw nothing.

The disciples then opened the door of the cremation-house [that the ashes might cool quickly] ; and, being in high expectation of precious reliques of wonderful shapes and virtue, all slept [that night] with their heads pointed towards the cremation-house.   Early in the morning, Rechung dreamt that five *Ḍākinīs*, dressed like celestial *Yoginīs*, in robes of silk and adorned with bone and precious ornaments, surrounded by many attendants of various colours, fair, yellow, red, green, and blue, were worshipping at the funeral pyre and making various offerings.   The five chief *Ḍākinīs* were taking out a sphere of Light from within the cremation-house.   For a while he was fascinated with the sight.   Then it suddenly occurred to him that the *Ḍākinīs* might actually be removing the reliques and ashes.   So he went to see ; and the *Ḍākinīs* all flew away.   Calling his brethren in the Faith, he went inside the cremation-house ; and then it was seen that the ashes and bones had been completely swept away.   They saw not even a particle of dust or ash.   Rechung became very sad ; and, addressing the *Ḍākinīs*, he demanded of them a portion of the reliques, for the benefit of human beings.   The *Ḍākinīs*, in reply, said, ' As for you, the chief disciples, ye have obtained the best of all reliques ; for ye have obtained the Truths, by which ye have found the *Dharma-Kāya* in your own minds. If that be insufficient, and ye must have something more, ye had better pray earnestly to Jetsün, and he may possibly grant you something.   As regardeth the rest of mankind, why, they have not valued Jetsün as much as a fire-fly, although he was like the Sun and the Moon.   They do not deserve any of his reliques at all ; these are our own special property.'   After saying this, the *Ḍākinīs* remained stationary in the sky above.   And the disciples, recognizing the truth of what the *Ḍākinīs* had said, began to pray thus :

[1] That is *seed* (*bīja*) *mantras*, or fundamental *mantras*.

'O Lord, when Thou wert at Thy *Guru's* Feet,
All his commands Thou didst fulfil most faithfully and
    dutifully,
And thus obtained the entire Chosen Teachings, full of
    Subtle Truths;
Graciously be pleased to grant to us [a portion of] Thy
    Sacred Reliques,
To benefit and serve as objects for the faith of Destined
    Ones,
And help all sentient beings in their [psychic] growth.

'O Lord, when Thou wert all alone on solitary hill,
With greatest zeal and resolution Thou didst meditate
And thus obtain miraculous accomplishment [or *siddhi*],
And this hath made Thee famous in all kingdoms of the
    Earth;
Graciously be pleased to grant to us [a portion of] Thy
    Sacred Reliques,
To serve as objects of veneration and of faith
Unto all who have beheld Thee or have heard Thy Name.

'O Lord, when Thou didst dwell with Thy Disciples,
Gracious and kind wert Thou to all alike,
From Thee beamed forth Wisdom and Fore-Knowledge;
Thy Disciples helped Thee, in Thy Kindness and Com-
    passion, to assist all creatures;
Graciously be pleased to grant to us [a portion of] Thy
    Sacred Reliques,
To serve as objects of veneration and of faith
Unto all Thy *Karma*-Favoured Followers.

'O Lord, when Thou midst many didst preside,
Thou wert o'erflowing with the milk of sympathy and love,
And didst save all and set them on the Path,
While those most filled with sorrow Thou didst pity specially;
Graciously be pleased to grant to us [a portion of] Thy
    Sacred Reliques,
To serve as objects of veneration and of faith
Unto them who have not zeal and energy [like Thine].

' O Lord, when the Illusory Body Thou didst cast aside,
Thou didst prove that Thou hadst gained the State Divine of
     Perfected Saints ;
Into the Body of the Truth thou hast transmuted all the
     Universe,[1]
And become the Lord of all the Holiest *Ḍākinīs* ;
O Lord, grant, with Thy Grace, [a portion of] Thy Sacred
     Reliques,
To serve as objects of veneration and of faith
Unto all thy *Shishyas* here assembled.'

When they had sung this mournful prayer, there descended
from the Sphere of Light, which was in the hands of the
*Ḍākinīs*, a lustrous relique like an orb as large as an egg. In
a streak of light it came down directly upon the funeral pyre.
All the disciples stretched out their hands eagerly, each
claiming it for himself. But the relique went back again to
the firmament, and was absorbed in the Sphere of Light which
the *Ḍākinīs* still held in their hands. Then the Sphere of
Light divided itself, one part becoming a lotus throne,
supported by lions, on the surface of which lay a solar and
lunar disk,[2] and the other part resolved itself into a *Chaitya* of
crystal, clear and transparent, about a cubit in height. The
*Chaitya* emitted brilliant five-coloured rays.[3] The end of each
ray was adorned with an image of a Buddha of the Series
of the Thousand and Two Buddhas ;[4] and rays with all these
Buddhas surrounded the *Chaitya*. The four tiers at the base
[of the *Chaitya*] were occupied [by images of] the Tutelary
Deities of the Four Classes of the Tantric Pantheon,[5] in their

---

[1] That is, the *Sangsāra* and *Nīrvāṇa* have in Jetsün blended in the at-one-
ment of *Dharma-Kāya* Mind.

[2] The lotus throne, lion, sun, and moon, symbolize the Glorification or En-
thronement of a Buddha.

[3] These five-coloured rays, which correspond to the five colours of the halo
of the Buddha and of the Buddhist flag, are blue, white, red, yellow, and purple.

[4] This is the well-known Series, as published in Tibetan books, of the
Thousand and Two Buddhas. It may possibly have taken shape as a result of
influences of such Hindu ritual treatises as that containing the Thousand Names
of Vishnu.

[5] These are the Tutelary Deities associated with the four divisions of the

due order.  The inside of the *Chaitya* was occupied by an
image of Jetsün, about a span in height, surrounded by images
of *Ḍākinīs*, bowing down in worship.  Two *Ḍākinīs*, who
guarded the *Chaitya* and offered worship to it, sang the following hymn:

' O Sons, Deva-Kyong, and Shiwa-Wöd,
  Ngan-Dzong-Tönpa, and others,
  Disciples of high destiny, in white cotton robed,
  Out of true faith and great religious fervour,
  Ye called upon your spiritual Father's Name,
  Praying for a relique as an object both of veneration and of
      faith.

' By power of the faith and zeal shown by that prayer,
  An Object that embodieth in itself all virtues of the
      *Tri-Kāya*,
  Which, if merely seen, saveth beings from the Round of
      Birth and Death,
  And which, if believed in, bringeth Buddhahood,
  The *Dharma-Kāya*—a single sphere its symbol—
  Brought forth, to be that relique, which is egg-shaped;
  An object of veneration for all sentient beings it was meant
      to be.
  It could not be of any one the private property, yet ye all
      clutched at it;
  Possessed by vulgar beings, where might it remain?
  But, if ye pray most earnestly again,
  Its Grace and Blessing shall not be diminished:
  This is the Sacred Promise of all Buddhas.

' The Father-Mother Tutelary Deities, Dēmchog in union,
  Sepulchral ornaments of [human] bone adorning them,

---

*Vajra-Yāna* ('Thunderbolt Path') as represented by the four classes of *Tantras*:
(1) *Kriyā-Tantra*, (2) *Caryā-Tantra*, (3) *Yoga-Tantra*, and (4) *Anuttara-Tantra*,
the first two being the Lower *Tantras*, and the last two the Higher *Tantras*
    The first of the four classes of *Tantras* contains injunctions as to ritual; the
second, injunctions relating to the *sādhaka's* conduct in life; the third relates to
*Yoga*; and the fourth describes the excellent or esoteric significance of all
things, being the door to *Ādiyoga*.

By hosts of Heroes and of *Yoginīs*[1] surrounded,
Fill all the skies with their perfect conclaves ;
These Deities Divine, *Sambhoga-Kāya* Wisdom personifying,
Their powers and their [spiritual] gifts grant quickly ;
And if to them ye pray most earnestly,
Their Grace and Blessing shall not be diminished :
This is the Sacred Promise of all *Ḍākinīs*.

' In virtue of the Goodness of the Buddha, the *Dharma-Kāya's*
    Self,
Various phenomena have been vouchsafed—
A crystal *Chaitya*, a cubit long,
A thousand [and two] Buddha images of stone adorning it,
And the Four Orders of the Tantric Deities,
Have been produced miraculously ;
If ye one-pointedly make earnest prayer,
The virtue of that Goodness shall not be diminished :
This is the Sacred Promise of all *Dharmapālas*.[2]

' The *Guru*, Who inseparably is the Embodiment of the *Tri-*
    *Kāya*,
Doth manifest Himself in every form by super-normal power ;
That He should manifest Himself
Within this small and wondrous work of art is marvellous ;
If towards it ye exert your fullest faith and earnest prayer,
Praying from your hearts' depths,
Its boon of gracious blessings shall not be diminished :
This Sacred promise of all the Greatest *Yogīs* ye may trust.

' If Sacred Faith ye keep in all these firmly,
The virtue of such Faith will bring its boon.

' If ye can cling to Solitudes,
The *Mātṛikās*[3] and *Ḍākinīs* are sure to gather round you.

---

[1] 'These *Yoginīs* are in a material sense the *Shaktis* of the *Vīra-sādhakas*. In a subtle sense they are the Goddess Kuṇḍalinī. In a still more subtle sense they are the Forces which work in Nature and upwards to the transcendent Supreme *Shakti*.'—Sj. Atal Bihari Ghosh.

[2] The *Dharmapālas* are the Spiritual Protectors of the *Dharma* or Faith.

[3] The *Mātṛikās* are the Mother-Goddesses.

' If ye in your religious practice be sincere,
    A sign of quick success in *Yoga* it will be.

' If in yourselves ye see no wish for ease,
    A sign 'twill be that in you evil passions are uprooted.

' If ye cling not to self and worldly goods,
    'Twill show that evil sprites and *Mārā* are controlled.

' If difference of caste and creed do not exist among you,
    'Twill show your Views [or Aims][1] are wholly right.

' If ye can see both the *Sangsāra* and *Nirvāna* as the
        Voidness,
    A sign 'twill be that your Meditation, too, is right.

' If zeal and energy flow from your hearts [spontaneously],
    A sign 'twill be that your Acts are right.

' If from your *Guru* ye obtain prophetic utterance,
    A sign 'twill be that the Good Faith is right.

' If ye have power to serve all sentient beings,
    A sign 'twill be that the Result is right.

' If the *Guru* and the *Shishya* in their hearts agree,
    'Twill show that their Relationship is right.

' If ye receive good omens of success and boons divine,
    A sign 'twill be that your Thoughts are right.

' The Good and Mutual Faith, the Experience and the
        Satisfaction,—
    Let these serve as your portion of the Reliques.'

Having chanted this hymn, the *Ḍākinīs* still held the
*Chaitya* aloft in the skies, that the chief disciples might obtain
a good view of it. Then they placed it on a throne made
of precious metals and gems, in order to transport it elsewhere. When they were about to depart, Shiwa-Wöd-Repa
entreated the *Ḍākinīs* to leave the *Chaitya* in the care of the

---

[1] Here, as in the couplets following, the reference is to the Noble Eightfold.
Path ; see p. 140[2].

disciples, as an object of veneration for all human beings, with
the following hymn:

'O Father, Thou Who hast assumed the human form, in
    order to serve others,
  *Yogī* Divine, One of the Order of *Sambhoga-Kāyas*,
Thou dost pervade all Realms Invisible whence Truth is
    born;[1]
To Thee, O Lord, Reality Itself,[2] we pray,
That to us, Thy *Shishyas*, Thou mayst grant
The *Chaitya*, which in their hands the *Ḍākinīs* now hold.

'O Lord, when other Perfect *Yogīs* Thou didst meet,
Like a casket filled with gold Thou wert;
A *Yogī* priceless and peerless Thou wert then, O Lord;
O Master of the Life Ascetic, prayer to Thee we make:
Grant to us the *Chaitya* which the *Ḍākinīs* now hold,
To us, Thy *Shishyas* and Thy Followers on Earth.

'O Lord, when Thou didst serve Thy *Guru*,
Like fleece upon a docile sheep Thou wert,
A *Yogī* prepared to serve, and helpful unto all;
O Lord Compassionate, to Thee we pray:
Grant to us the *Chaitya* which the *Ḍākinīs* now hold,
To us, Thy *Shishyas* and Thy Followers on Earth.

'O Lord, when worldly aims Thou didst renounce,
Like the King of *Rishis* Wise Thou wert,
A *Yogī* immutable in resolution;
O Lord of Mighty Courage, To Thee we pray:
Grant to us the *Chaitya* which the *Ḍākinīs* now hold,
To us, Thy *Shishyas* and Thy Followers on Earth.

'O Lord, when meditating on Thy *Guru's* teachings,
Like a tigress feeding on the flesh of man Thou wert,
A *Yogī* from every doubt set free;
O Thou of Mighty Perseverance, to Thee we pray:
Grant to us the *Chaitya* which the *Ḍākinīs* now hold,
To us, Thy *Shishyas* and Thy Followers on Earth.

[1] Literally, 'Realms Invisible of the *Dharma-Dhātu*'.
[2] Literally, 'the *Dharma-Kāya*'.

' O Lord, when Thou wert passing through the wilderness,
Like a flawless block of iron Thou wert,
A *Yogī* evermore unchanging;
To Thee, Who hast renounced all vain pretence, we pray:
Grant to us the *Chaitya* which the *Ḍākinīs* now hold,
To us, Thy *Shishyas* and Thy Followers on Earth.

' O Lord, when signs of Thy miraculous *siddhi* Thou didst show,
Like a lion or an elephant Thou wert,
A *Yogī* fearless and strong of spirit;
To Thee, Thou One Devoid of Fear, we pray:
Grant to us the *Chaitya* which the *Ḍākinīs* now hold,
To us, Thy *Shishyas* and Thy Followers on Earth.

' O Lord, when Psychic Warmth and [true] Experience [1] Thou
        didst acquire,
Like the full-grown lunar disk Thou wert,
And sheddest Thy Beams o'er all the world;
To Thee, Who hast cast off all hankerings, we pray:
Grant to us the *Chaitya* which the *Ḍākinīs* now hold,
To us, Thy *Shishyas* and Thy followers on Earth.

' O Lord, when Thou Thy Destined *Shishyas* didst protect,
'Twas like the meeting of the fire-glass and the sun.
Thou didst create, O *Yogī*, Masters of *Siddhi*;
To Thee, O Thou Benignant One, we pray:
Grant to us the *Chaitya* which the *Ḍākinīs* now hold,
To us, Thy *Shishyas* and Thy Followers on Earth.

' O Lord, when worldly goods fell to Thy lot,
Like drops of mercury upon the earth Thou wert,
Unsullied by all vulgar greed, O *Yogī*;
To Thee, O Faultless One, we pray:
Grant to us the *Chaitya* which the *Ḍākinīs* now hold,
To us, Thy *Shishyas* and Thy Followers on Earth.

' O Lord, when over congregations vast Thou didst preside,
Like the sun uprising o'er the world Thou wert;
Thou didst enlighten all, O *Yogī*;

---

[1] That is, Realization of Truth born of *Yoga*.

To Thee, Thou Wise and Loving One, we pray:
Grant to us the *Chaitya* which the *Ḍākinīs* now hold,
To us, Thy *Shishyas* and Thy Followers on Earth.

' O Lord, when by the people of the World Thou wert beheld,
Like the meeting of a mother and her son it was ;
O *Yogī*, all things for their good Thou didst ;
To Thee, Affectionate One, we pray:
Grant to us the *Chaitya* which the *Ḍākinīs* now hold,
To us, Thy *Shishyas* and Thy Followers on Earth.

' O Lord, when for the Realms Divine Thou art departing,
Like a treasure-urn of boons Thou art ;
O *Yogī*, Thou Who grantest every wish,
To Thee, Thou Excellent One, we pray:
Grant to us the *Chaitya* which the *Ḍākinīs* now hold,
To us, Thy *Shishyas* and Thy Followers on Earth.

' O Lord, when Thou didst prophesy,
Like bringing to the mouth the hand [in faultless song] it was ;
O *Yogī*, ne'er at fault Thou wert ;
To Thee, thou Knower of the Three Times, we pray:
Grant to us the *Chaitya* which the *Ḍākinīs* now hold,
To us, Thy *Shishyas* and Thy Followers on Earth.

' O Lord, when Thou didst grant a boon,
Like a father endowing a son Thou wert ;
O *Yogī*, Thou didst not spare or hold back anything ;
To Thee, Thou Gracious One, we pray:
Grant to us the *Chaitya* which the *Ḍākinīs* now hold,
To us, Thy *Shishyas* and Thy Followers on Earth.'

When this prayer had been sung, the form of Jetsün that
was within the *Chaitya* gave Shiwa-Wöd Repa an answer in
a psalm, which pointed out the differences between apparently
similar things, as follows :

' O thou, of mighty destiny and faith,
Who prayest unto me with profound earnestness,
Listen unto me, my excellent disciple in white cotton robed.

'Of the all-pervading *Dharma-Kāya* realized by me—
Its true nature being Voidness—
None may say, " I possess It ", or " I've lost It ":
When into Space the fleshly body was absorbed,
An egg-shaped and substantial relique yet remained ;
And this became a *Chaitya*, emitting glorious radiance—
A field wherein all sentient beings might for merits labour.
In a Realm Divine it will now fore'er remain,
Attended by the *Ḍākinīs* of the Five Orders ;
By celestial beings and the *Ḍākinīs* will it be worshipped ;
If in the human world it should be left, it would slowly vanish.

'And ye, my spiritual sons and followers, have had your share
    of reliques—
The Knowledge that hath made you realize the *Dharma-Kāya*
    in your own minds ;
Of reliques and of ashes this is holiest.
When ye shall seek of This the Realization,
These Similarities which lead to Error ye shall know ;
Forget them not, but keep them in your hearts,
And thus hold to the Right, abandoning the Wrong :—

'The serving of a perfect *Guru*,
And the serving of a person of good fortune,
Appear to be alike, but beware, and confuse them not.

'The true dawning of the Voidness in one's mind,
And illusory obsessions of the consciousness,
Appear to be alike, but beware, and confuse them not.

'The knowing of the Pure, the Unalloyed State, by meditation,
And the fondness for the Tranquil State born of the trance
    ecstatic of Quiescence,
Appear to be alike, but beware, and confuse them not.

'The Flood-tide of the Deep of Intuition,
And other deep convictions that " This seemeth right ", " That
    seemeth true ",
Appear to be alike, but beware, and confuse them not.

' The clear perception of the Mind Unmodified,[1]
And the noble impulse to serve others,
Appear to be alike, but beware, and confuse them not.

' The spiritual boon which shineth on one as resultant of
Connected Causes,
And merit temporal, which bringeth much of worldly goods,
Appear alike, but beware, and confuse them not.

' Guidance spiritual and commands prophetic of one's guardian
Mātṛikās and Ḍākinīs,
And temptations from misleading sprites and elementals,
Appear alike, but beware, and confuse them not.

' Good works enjoined by guardian Ḍākinīs,
And interruptions and temptations wrought by Mārā,
Appear alike, but beware, and confuse them not.

' The Orb of Dharma-Kāya, [blemishless],
And a relique-orb formed of earthly matter,
Appear alike, but beware, and confuse them not.

' The Incarnated Blossom of the Realm Nirmāṇa-Kāya,
And the Heavenly Blossom of a Sensual Paradise,
Appear alike, but beware, and confuse them not.

' A Chaitya such as gods miraculously produce,
And a Chaitya such as demons may make manifest,
Appear alike, but beware, and confuse them not.

' The Glorious Halo, symbolizing the phenomenal universe,
And the rainbow born of [common] natural causes,
Appear alike, but beware, and confuse them not.

' The faith resulting from Connexions Karmic of the past,[2]
And faith produced by artificial methods,
Appear alike, but beware, and confuse them not.

' The true faith, thrilling forth from the heart's recesses,
And faith conventional, born of a sense of shame and
obligation,
Appear alike, but beware, and confuse them not.

---

[1] That is, the yogic state of mind, the mind in its natural condition, unmodified
by mundane activity.
[2] That is, in past lives.

' The sincere devotion to religious studies,
    And feigned devotion, for the pleasing of one's *Guru*,
    Appear alike, but beware, and confuse them not.

' The real success, which one hath realized,
    And nominal success, of which rumour speaketh,
    Appear alike, but beware, and confuse them not.

' This *Chaitya*, which belongeth to the *Mātṛikās* Divine and
        *Ḍākinīs*,
    Doth symbolize the Realm of Buddhas of the Past, the
        Present, and the Future ;
    A congregational-hall for Heroes and for *Yoginīs* it is ;
    And, for thy *Guru* Jetsün, is a place of meditation.
    It now is being borne to Ngön-gah [the Eastern Paradise],
    Wherein all *Ḍākinīs* assemble,
    To the Realm of Happiness,
    Wherein the Bhagavān Shamvara,
    Lokeshvara, and the Goddess Tārā meet.
    There, in that blest and happy Realm,
    Hosts of *Ḍākinīs* Divine a welcoming procession form.

' If to the *Chaitya* thou whole-heartedly wilt pray,
    With welling tears, devotion, and sincerity,
    And offerings true, in worship and in veneration,
    Strewing blossoms of keen intellect,
    Sprinkling on it holy-water of a heart made pure,
    Thyself protected and entrenched within a faith immutable,
    And dost wish bestowed on thee the power of the Individual
        Wisdom,
    Beneath the *Chaitya* bow thy head.'

While this hymn was being sung, the *Ḍākinīs* conveyed
the *Chaitya* through the skies and held it directly above the
chief disciples, so that it sent down its rays of light on
the head of each of them, thus conferring upon them its
power. Most of the assembly saw the form of Jetsün projecting from the *Chaitya*. And in the sky there appeared
[the Tantric Deities] Gaypa-Dorje, Dēmchog, Sang-dü, and

Dorje-Pa-mo, surrounded by innumerable hosts, who, after circumambulating the Chief Deity, merged in him.

Finally, the whole conclave resolved itself into an orb of light, and this then sped away towards the East. The *Chaitya* was wrapped in various folds of silk by the *Ḍākinīs*, and put carefully into a casket of precious metals; and then it was transported eastward, amid a peal of celestial music from various instruments. Some saw Jetsün in the garb of a *Sambhoga-Kāya* Buddha, mounted on a Lion, each of whose feet was supported by a *Ḍākinī* of one colour and order, [white, yellow, red, and green]. The halter was held by Dorje-Pa-mo herself. Many Heroes, *Yoginīs*, and *Ḍākinīs* held over him banners, [royal] umbrellas, and other ornaments and objects of worship, while many celestial beings bore in their hands various musical instruments. Some, again, saw a white *Ḍākinī* bearing the *Chaitya* eastward, under an awning of white silk. Thus, different spectators saw different phenomena.

The disciples and all the followers were filled with deep despondency at not receiving a portion of the reliques; and wept loudly, still praying for it. In reply, a voice from the heavens, resembling that of Jetsün, though no body was visible, said, 'O sons, do not take it so to heart. As a substantial relique, for your portion ye will find on the Amolika Boulder four letters [miraculously] produced. Ye may look upon them reverently, and with faith. Go ye and look for them underneath the boulder.'

Having searched all round the boulder upon which the cremation had been performed, they found the place whereon the letters were visible. Thereby was their grief at having lost their portion of the reliques lessened. Even until now this marvellous relique-stone is to be seen—an object of veneration and wonder for all at the Lapchi-Chūbar Monastery.

The most prominent of Jetsün's disciples, although mourning the unavoidable separation from their *Guru*, took comfort in the hope and belief that in whatever realm Jetsün obtained Buddhahood they would be sure to be the first amongst his followers. They felt sure, too, that Jetsün's life and example

had instilled a new spirit and impulse into the religious world
and all sentient beings in general. Moreover, they all realized
that the special teaching and *mantra* received, and to be perfected by each of them, was capable of serving both themselves
and others.

It was then agreed that they should look beneath the hearth,
as Jetsün had requested in his will. Judging from Jetsün's
manner of living, none of them expected that he had accumulated any gold, but, since he had made a special mention
of gold, they resolved to do as he had directed them.

On digging up the hearth, they found a square piece of fine
cotton-cloth, which Jetsün had worn. Wrapped in it there was
a knife, the point of the knife-handle being an awl, the back of
the knife arranged as a steel for striking fire, and the blade
very good for cutting. And with the knife there was a lump
of brown sugar, and a small manuscript which read as follows:
'The cloth and the sugar, if cut with this knife, will never
become exhausted. Cut as many strips from the cloth and bits
from the sugar as possible and distribute them among the
people. All who taste of this sugar and touch this cloth will
be saved from the lower states of existence. These were the
food and clothing of Milarepa when he was in *Samādhi*, and
have been blessed by all previous Buddhas and Saints. Any
sentient being who heareth the name of Milarepa, even though
it be but once, will not take rebirth in a lower state of existence
during seven lifetimes, and for seven lifetimes will remember
past lives. These things have been prophesied by the Saints
and Buddhas of the past. Whosoever shall say that Milarepa
possessed hidden gold, let pollution be placed in his mouth.'

This last passage excited merriment in all the disciples,
despite the sorrow-stricken state of their mind. At the bottom
of the manuscript, they read the following verses:

'The food which I, the *Yogī*, ate,
While in *Samādhi* I remained,
A gracious boon of twofold virtue doth possess;
And they that have the luck to taste it,
Close tight the door of rebirth in the *Preta-Loka*.

' A bit of this white cotton-cloth,[1]
Worn on the body or the neck
While one be meditating on the Vital Warmth,
Will close the doors of Hells both hot and cold.

' And they who eat this food of grace
Are saved from the Three Lower Worlds.

' Those who have formed with me religious bonds,
Henceforth in lower states shall not be born,
But, step by step, shall gain the goal upon the *Bodhi* Path.

' Those who have only heard my name,
And have been moved to faith thereby,
During seven lifetimes will recall their previous names and
    castes.

' For me, Milarepa, the Energetic One,
The entire universe hath been transmuted into gold ;
No need have I to tie gold up in packets or in pouches.

' I bid my spiritual sons and followers to follow my commands ;
And thus to them the same accomplishment shall come,
And further evermore their good and aim.'

Accordingly, they then cut the sugar into countless pieces,
and each piece was as big as the original piece ; yet the original
piece was not exhausted. Likewise, the cloth was cut into many
square pieces, and [with the sugar] distributed to as many
people as were there assembled. And those of the multitude
who were suffering from disease, and from other miseries, were
cured by the eating of the piece of sugar and the wearing of
the piece of cloth as a talisman. Those of evil disposition, or
enslaved to evil passions, were converted into faithful, earnest,
intelligent, and compassionate followers ; so that they escaped
falling into the lower states of existence. And the sugar and
the cloth lasted a lifetime for each of the recipients, without
being exhausted.

On the day of the funeral ceremony, a shower of blossoms,
varying in colour, some blossoms having four or five colours,

---

[1] The white cotton-cloth, in which the Kargyütpa *yogīs* clothe themselves, is
emblematic of Spiritual Intellect.

fell in great profusion. Most of the blossoms descended until
they were just beyond a man's reach, and thence ascended and
disappeared. Those that fell to the ground were seen to be
extremely beautiful, but melted away when touched by human
hands. Some, which were of three colours, and others, of two
colours, were as tiny and as delicately formed as the wings of
bees. In the Chūbar Valley the celestial blossoms lay ankle-
deep on the ground, and in other places were sufficiently
numerous to give a new hue to the earth. Then, as soon as
the funeral ceremonies terminated, the various phenomena
ceased, and the rainbow colours in the heavens gradually faded
away.

On every anniversary of the funeral, the sky was gloriously
clear and there were rainbows and showers of blossoms,
heavenly perfume filled the air and celestial melodies resounded
everywhere, as on the day of Jetsün's passing away.

The marvellous benefits which flowed therefrom, over all the
Earth, are too numerous to be described at length. Thus, for
example, flowers bloomed even in winter; the world enjoyed
abundant harvests; and no wars or epidemics ravaged the
Earth.

When the Great Lord of *Yogīs* passed away to the Purer
Realms, those who are hereinafter mentioned [in the Appendix]
remained to substantiate this written history of his life.

By the virtue of his mighty grace and good wishes he left
behind him saintly disciples as numerous as the stars in the sky.
The number of those who were never to return to *Sangsāric*
existence [1] was like the grains of sand on the Earth. Of male
and female who had entered the Path [to Arhantship],[2] there
were countless numbers.

Thus was the Buddhist Faith rendered bright like the sun,
and all sentient beings were saved from sorrow, and rendered
happy for ever and ever.

This is the Twelfth [and last] Chapter of Jetsün's Biography.

[1] Or 'those who were non-returners' (or *Anāgāmis*).
[2] The first step on the Path to Arhantship is called, in Sanskrit, *Srotāpatti*,
or 'Entering the Stream'; the one who takes this step is called a *Sotāpanno*,
or 'One Who Hath Entered the Stream' (or 'Path').

## THE APPENDIX
### Concerning Jetsün's Disciples

OF Jetsün's *shiṣhyas* [or disciples], indicated by the spiritual directing of the *Ḍākinīs*, through dreams, at the time when Jetsün met Shiwa-Wöd-Repa, the disciple who, like unto a sun, would outshine all others, was the Peerless Dvagpo-Rinpoch'e; [1] and the disciple destined to be of lesser glory, like the moon, was Rechung-Dorje-Tagpa, of Gungthang; and those, like unto the constellations, were Ngan-Dzong-Tönpa-Byang-Chub-Gyalpo, of Chim-Lung (otherwise known as Ngan-Dzong-Tönpa), Shiwa-Wöd-Repa, of Gyal-Tom-mad, Seban-Repa, of Do-ta, Khyira-Repa, of Nyi-shang, Bri-Gom-Repa, of Müs, and Sangyay-Kyap-Repa, of Ragma.   These were the eight chief disciples. [2]   Then there were thirteen lesser disciples: [3]  Shan-Gom, Lan-Gom, Me-Gom, Tsa-Phu, Khar-Chūng, Rong-Chūng, and Stag-Gom-Repa-Dorje-Wang-chuk; and these, who [also] were all *Repas*: [4] Jo-Gom-Repa-Dharma-Wangchuk,  Dampa-Gya-Phūpa,  Likor-Charūwa, Lotön-Gedün, Kyo-Tön-Shākya-Guna, and Dretön-Trashibar.

Of these [twenty-one disciples], Dvagpo-Rinpoch'e and the five last lesser disciples were *yogīs* and *bhikṣhus*. [5]

Among the female disciples there were Cho-nga Rechungma, Sale-Wöd, of Nyanam, Paldar-Būm, of Chūng, and Peta-Gön-Kyit, who was Jetsün's own sister. [6]

There were also twenty-five *yogīs* and *yoginīs* who had made considerable progress on the Path.

---

[1] Another form of this name is Dvagpo-Lharje, otherwise known as Je-Gampopa.  (See p. 8.)

[2] Literally, 'sons of the heart'.          [3] Literally, 'related sons'.

[4] That is, they were all so inured to cold that they wore only a thin cotton robe.  (See p. 41[4].)          [5] That is, they had received full priestly ordination.

[6] It is one of the outstanding glories of Buddhism that the Fathers and Saints of the Buddhist Church have ever extended to woman the solace of religious equality with man.   At first the Buddha hesitated about permitting women to enter the *Saṅgha*, not because He regarded them as morally inferior to man, but because He feared the sex-danger universal among human beings. Eventually, however, if perhaps somewhat reluctantly, He allowed the establishment of the Order of Buddhist Nuns (*Bhikṣhuṇī-Saṅgha*); and, as the recorded *Hymns of the Sisters* suggest, woman shared with man the glory of upholding and propagating the Teachings of the Enlightened One.

Then there were one hundred *Anāgāmis*, including Dziwo-Repa (the Cow-herd Disciple), who had realized the Truth, and one hundred and eight Great Ones who had obtained excellent experience and knowledge from meditation.

Again, there were a thousand *sādhus* and *sādhunīs* and *yogīs* and *yoginīs* who had renounced the worldly life and lived exemplary lives of piety.

Besides these, there were innumerable lay-disciples of both sexes, who, having heard and seen Jetsün, had established a religious relationship with him, and thus closed for ever the gate on the pathway to the lower states of existence.

So much for the human disciples.

Among the non-human disciples, of orders higher and of orders lower than mankind, there were the Five Sister Goddesses [or Fairies] known as the Five Sisters of Durgā, and the Rock-Ogress of Lingwa. Countless other spiritual beings there were who had dedicated themselves to the protection of the Buddhist Faith.[1]

All the human disciples who attended the funeral ceremonies of their Lord Jetsün retired immediately afterward, each to his or her particular cave or retreat, and passed their life in meditation and devotion, as Jetsün had commanded.

Rechung set out to take the articles [or reliques which Jetsün had bequeathed on his death-bed] to Dvagpo-Rinpoch'e [the chief of all the disciples]; and, as he was proceeding with them towards the Province of Ü, he met Dvagpo-Rinpoch'e at Yarlung-Phushar. The latter, although late, had remembered Jetsün's command; and there Rechung handed over to him Maitrī's hat and the *Agaru*-staff, and narrated to him all the latest news, on hearing which Gampopa [or Dvagpo-Rinpoch'e] fell into a swoon for a while.

On reviving, Gampopa addressed many mournful prayers to the *Guru* [Jetsün]; and these are to be found recorded in Gampopa's own biographical history [of Jetsün].[2] Then he

---

[1] Literally, 'the White Side', in opposition to the Black Side (or Black Magic) of non-emancipating religions.

[2] Our version is by Rechung, the second of the disciples.

invited Rechung to his own place of abode, and received from him the complete *Karṇa Tantra*[1] of Dēmchog.

When Rechung had transmitted to Gampopa that portion of the reliques to which Gampopa was entitled, and had imparted to him all the religious teachings which it was necessary to impart, he departed, and went on towards the Loro-Döl Monastery; and therein he sat in deep meditation for the remainder of his life. And Rechung was translated bodily to the Divine Realm, [his physical body being rendered ethereal, so that he left no corpse behind him on earth].

In like manner did Shiwa-Wöd-Repa, Khyira-Repa, and the four female disciples who were sisters, and Paldar-Būm, and Sale-Wöd, transmute their physical body into the ethereal body, and entered the Higher Realms.

The other disciples all passed away in the normal manner, leaving their corpses behind for the benefit of the world and of all sentient creatures.

Thus did the saintly Jetsün Milarepa perform three worldly acts and nine acts of religious devotion, making in all twelve acts, each replete with marvellous events. And with the last act came the greatest of all great successes that can ever fall to the lot of mortal man, namely, the attaining in one lifetime of the Fourfold Body and the Fivefold Wisdom of the All-pervading Holder of the Sceptre of Spiritual Power (Vajra-Dhara); and, with it, the power to traverse all the Holy Buddha Realms, and to develop, and thus save, all sentient beings, countless in number and inhabiting worlds as infinite as heavenly space.[2]

Thus endeth the history of the Great *Yogī* named Mila-Zhadpa-Dorje, the Guide to Deliverance and Omniscience, and the Bestower of the Bliss of *Nirvāṇa* upon all *sangsāric* beings alike, for ever and ever, in the blissful feast of the auspicious gift of eternally increasing blessings.

---

[1] That is, the esoteric teachings which are always transmitted orally, called 'the Ear-whispered Truths'. It is prohibited by the *Gurus*, who are the custodians of these secret doctrines, to set them down in writing, lest the uninitiated and the unworthy gain access to them.

[2] The conception of a plurality of inhabited worlds has been held by Oriental peoples for thousands of years; yet, even when this passage was written— a little more than eight centuries ago—the theory that the Earth is the centre of the universe and the only world, or at least the only inhabited world, was still believed in by the learned of Europe, as by the Christian Church.

# THE COLOPHON

THE beneficent effulgence of the Gem of History,
Of that Lord among men, Jetsün-Mila,
Hath made the Faith of the Buddha like the sun,
And hath fulfilled the hopes and expectations of all sentient
    beings;
May it thus be the best of offerings in veneration of all
    Buddhas and Saints.

This *History* [or *Biography*] hath been made beautiful at the
    beginning and end with ornate language;
May it thus be a feast of delight to all scholars and lovers of
    literature.

Its words stir the very hairs of the body, in faith and
    humility;
May it thus be a feast of delight to all devotees who are
    sincerely attached to religion.

The mere hearing of this *History* moveth to faith despite
    one's self;
May it thus be a feast of delight to all who are of high
    destiny and endowed with good *karma*.

The mere thinking of this *History* cutteth off one's attach-
    ment to the world;
May it thus be a feast of delight to those striving to obtain
    omniscience in one lifetime.

By the mere touching of this *History*, the twofold aims [1] are
    fulfilled;
May it thus be a feast of delight to them who uphold the
    Faith and serve others.

---

[1] That is, one's own aims and the aims of others seeking freedom from
*sangsāric* existence, or from the interminable round of death and birth in worlds
of suffering.

Through one's study and practice of this *History*, the
Dynasty of *Gurus* will be fully satisfied;

May it thus be a feast of delight to them who uphold the
glory of the Dynasty of *Gurus* by living according to
their commandments.

In virtue of the Grace of this *History*, every sentient creature
shall find relief from all sorrow;

May it thus be a feast of delight to all sentient creatures of
the Three Planes [or universe].

[Signed and dated]: Durṭöd-ñyul-vai-naljor-rüpahi-gyen-
chan [or 'The *Yogī* having ornaments of bone who frequenteth
cemeteries'].[1]

The year of Phurbu, the middle autumn month, and the
eighth day, at the sacred Pilgrimage of Lapchi-Kang.[2]

---

[1] This designation is that of a devotee (or *yogī*) who has renounced the world.
The frequenting of cemeteries is a part of the *yogic* practice, and intended to
impress upon the devotee the transient nature of *sangsāric* existence. The ornaments, too, being of the bones of the dead, serve the same end, besides being
symbolic; cf p. xvii. The author's real name is that of the second of Jetsun's
disciples, namely, Rechung-Dorje-Tagpa.

[2] From this place-name it appears that the *History* was either written or
completed while Rechung was on Pilgrimage to Lapchi-Kang (Mt. Everest),
the place sanctified by Jetsün's meditation, or else while he was in hermitage
there.

# INDEX

Black-type figures indicate the chief references, most of which may be
used as a Glossary.